HABITAT, HUMAN, AND HOLY

The Earth Bible Commentary Series, 6

Series Editor
Norman C. Habel

Editorial Board
Vicky Balabanski, Hilary Marlow, Barbara Rossing, Peter Trudinger,
Elaine Wainwright, Joh Wurst

Habitat, Human, and Holy

An Eco-Rhetorical Reading of the Gospel of Matthew

Elaine M. Wainwright

Sheffield Phoenix Press

2017

Copyright © Sheffield Phoenix Press, 2016, 2017

First published in hardback, 2016
First published in paperback, 2017

Published by Sheffield Phoenix Press
Department of Biblical Studies, University of Sheffield
45 Victoria Street
Sheffield S3 7QB

www.sheffieldphoenix.com

All rights reserved.
No part of this publication may be reproduced or transmitted in any form or by any means, electronic or mechanical, including photocopying, recording or any information storage or retrieval system, without the publisher's permission in writing.

A CIP catalogue record for this book
is available from the British Library

Typeset by CA Typesetting Ltd
Printed by Lightning Source

ISBN 978-1-910928-01-1 (hardback)
ISBN 978-1-910928-22-6 (paperback)

Dedication

I dedicate this book to all who share planet Earth as Habitat and Home and to my parents, Kath and Tom, who have returned to the earth they loved.

Contents

Preface	ix
List of Abbreviations	xiv
Glossary of Terms	xv

INTRODUCTION:
INTRODUCING THE EARTH BIBLE COMMENTARY SERIES — 1

Chapter 1
READING THE GOSPEL OF MATTHEW ECOLOGICALLY — 17

Chapter 2
MATTHEW 1–2:
PLACE, POWER, POTENTIALITY—GENEALOGY
AND BIRTH OF EARTH AND OF THE CHILD — 29

Chapter 3
MATTHEW 3–4:
FROM WILDERNESS TO WATERFRONT—
INTERFACING PLACE AND PROCLAMATION — 54

Chapter 4
MATTHEW 5–7:
MOUNTAIN PROCLAMATION—IN-FORMED WITH EARTH — 72

Chapter 5
MATTHEW 8–9:
THE MATERIALITY OF BODIES—TOUCHED AND HEALED — 92

Chapter 6
MATTHEW 10–12:
DOES CO-MISSIONING OBSCURE EARTH
AND WALKING REVEAL EARTH? — 116

Chapter 7
MATTHEW 13:
HABITAT/HUMAN/HOLY IN-FORM PROCLAMATION IN PARABLES — 130

Chapter 8
 MATTHEW 14–17:
 BREAD AND BOATS, MOUNTAINS AND
 MISSION ENGAGED AND OPPOSED   148

Chapter 9
 MATTHEW 18:
 A COMMUNITY OF RECONCILIATION—CAN IT INCLUDE EARTH?   167

Chapter 10
 MATTHEW 19–23:
 HUMAN CONFLICT IMPACTING EARTH   171

Chapter 11
 MATTHEW 24–25:
 PARABLE, PROCLAMATION AND END
 TIME IMAGERY—AND WHAT OF EARTH?   187

Chapter 12
 MATTHEW 26–28:
 LIFE AND DEATH AND LIFE INTERTWINED—AN EARTH PROCESS   200

Bibliography   219
Index of References   239
Index of Authors   248

Preface

This book has been a long time in the making and during that time I have been able to develop and to deepen my facility with the reading of the biblical text from an ecological perspective. As it goes to press, I'm aware, on the one hand, that the urgency of such an approach has escalated as Earth speaks to the human community in violent storms that are becoming almost a common feature in numerous places around the Earth; as political leaders move toward the United Nations Climate Change Conference (COP 21) in December 2015, with the goal of reaching a legally binding and universal agreement on climate particularly in relation to greenhouse gas emissions; and as deep-sea drilling highlights the human community's reliance on oil and other fossil fuels to the detriment of Earth itself. On the other hand, as this book moved from my computer to that of the publisher, the human community had just witnessed two spectacular new images of the universe: of Pluto and its largest moon Charon captured by NASA's New Horizons space probe, and of an exoplanet or extrasolar planet that is Earth's 'closest twin' released from the Kepler space telescope data. These are but glimpses of Earth's agony and ecstacy that inform this ecological reader and these ecological readings of the Matthean gospel.

The project is grounded firmly in/on planet Earth and it is engagement with Earth, with the habitat/human/holy interrelationships, that in-form both my life and my reading of the biblical text. A number of different approaches have developed over recent decades as biblical scholars have sought ways of reading their scriptures anew in light of and engagement with the current ecological crisis. The Earth Bible project directed by Professor Norman Habel has shaped one such approach and it has been my relationship with this project together with the Ecological Hermeneutics Unit of the Society of Biblical Literature that has been foundational in providing a scholarly arena in which my own particular ecological hermeneutic could take shape—in dialogue with the Earth Bible approach and yet developing its own unique interplay between hermeneutic and methodology. This is laid out in Chapter 1 of this book and then is played out in different ways across the following chapters as I seek to read the Gospel of Matthew ecologically. One particular feature of my reading is engagement with contemporary intertexts that give richness and variety to my foundational approach. Also, it has not been possible to address every verse or every section of the gospel and hence readers are invited into their own ecological interpretation of texts not addressed in this work as I believe that we need to learn to read all texts ecologically, caught up in the spiral of *reading ecologically/thinking ecologically*. Having undertaken this ecological reading of the Gospel of Matthew, it is a privilege to have it included in The Earth Bible Commentary Series and I am most grateful to Professor Habel, editor of series, for this.

The commencement of this project was made possible as a result of twelve months' Research and Study Leave from the University of Auckland in 2009 for which I am most grateful. During this time, I was offered the hospitality of Trinity College Dublin's Library through the auspices of the School of Religion and Theology and of the Andover-Harvard Theological Library of Harvard Divinity School for the last three months of that year. This was augmented by one month's research in the Library of the Ecole Biblique de Jerusalem in January 2011 and two months in the Paul Bechtold Library at Catholic Theological Union, Chicago, in late 2013 and I thank both schools for their academic hospitality. These two periods of research were supported by a special Research grant and a further Research and Study Leave grant from the University of Auckland both of which I was able to utilize well to keep my research advancing while carrying administrative and teaching responsibilities. I am also grateful to the Library of the University of Chicago where I was given borrowing rights during my two months in that city. The bulk of the research was undertaken in Auckland with access to the University of Auckland Library and to the John Kinder Theological Library of St. John's Theological College. I am grateful to both libraries and to Mark Hangartner, theological librarian at the University of Auckland Library, the staff of the John Kinder Library and the staff of other libraries listed for their support of this research.

The testing of one's approach and insights among colleagues and, at times, a wider public, is essential and I am most grateful to all those who provided such a service in the bringing of this work to fruition. There are too many scholarly organizatons and invitations to list all here in detail but some specific thanks are in order. First, I thank Professor Donald Senior for the invitation to present at the Colloquium Biblicum Louvaniense 2009 in Leuven where I was able to test out my early engagement with an ecological reading of the Gospel of Matthew among colleagues in the field. Second, since context is foundational to an ecological reading, the opportunity to present an early reading of Matthew 3 at the inaugural meeting of OBSA (Oceania Biblical Studies Association) was most welcome and I am very grateful to my colleagues in OBSA for this invitation. Such reading in context was augmented by a keynote address (2012) and, two years later, a presidential address to the biennial meetings of the Society of Asian Biblical Scholars (SABS). The second address was entitled *Blessed Are the*

Peacemakers: Can Beatitude Address the Ecological/Economic Nexus of Violence? It represents one of a number of avenues in which I have been able to explore an ecological reading of the beatitudes and to contextualize such readings.

It is with a certain trepidation that a Matthean scholar returns to their home town suggesting a new way of reading the gospel as the words of Jesus in Mt. 13.57 echo predictions regarding acceptance in one's own country and one's own house. This notwithstanding, I was honoured and very grateful, to receive the invitation to give the 2012 Concannon Lecture at the University of Southern Queensland in Toowoomba and was encouraged to continue the ecological reading on which I had embraked by the positive responses from a wide range of participants in the event.

The gatherings of colleagues at the annual meetings of our academic associations provide an invaluable opportunity to test ideas and trajectories of research. In this I am most grateful to the Society of Biblical Literature for its excellent international and annual meetings which I attend regularly and at which I have been able to present my ecological readings of the Gospel of Matthew and the development of my hermeneutic and methodology for scholarly critique, especially in the Ecological Hermeneutics section. I am also grateful to the methodological critique given at one such meeting by Professor Vernon Robbins whose socio-rhetorical methodology I have used in a revised form. More regionally, colleagues in the Aotearoa New Zealand Association of Biblical Studies, the Bible and Critical Theory Seminar and the Australian Federation of Biblical Scholars have offered significant scholarly critique that has enhanced the development of this project.

As well as this broad group of academic colleagues, there are those who engage with one's work more explicitly and more critically and to this group I want to express a sincere gratitude. One of the first of such colleagues to read my initial foray into an ecological reading focussed on the parables was my mentor and friend, Professor Sean Freyne. As always his critique was substantial and constructive. Sadly, Sean's death in 2013 means that he will not see the work that has come to fruition but my hope is that this work honours his memory and expresses my gratitude for his collegiality and friendship. Similar gratitude goes to another such colleague and friend, Professor Jerome Murphy-O'Connor, who also died in 2013 before this work was completed. Jerry too gave his usual incisive response to work that he read in the earlier part of the year in which he died. Both of these scholars/friends are honoured in my memory with gratitude for their mentoring they gave me as a new emerging scholar and their ongoing friendships that grew from those early encounters.

Another two long-term colleagues and friends, Dr Anne Elvey and Dr Veronica Lawson, have supported this work from its inception and have offered consistent critiques of papers and articles that have finally been incorporated into a completed Earth Bible Commentary on the Gospel of Matthew as well as encouragement to persevere to the end of the work. It is impossible to express the depths of my gratitude to each of them. Anne's own ecological readings in the Gospel of Luke have provided me with many points of dialogue for the undertaking of my own readings as well as the development of my unique ecological hermeneutic. I gain insights from the scope of her engagement with contemporary intertexts, especially that of critical theorists, as well as the interface she develops with literary works. She has heard and/or read a number of my papers across the span of this project and has critiqued chapters both early in the project and, more recently, the penultimate draft. For all these contributions I am most grateful.

Veronica must know this manuscript almost as well as I do. She has been my most constant critic of papers given at conferences, of drafts of chapters from their early inception to their final incorporation into the manuscript, and of the final manuscript itself. Just a few weeks before the completion of the manuscript, we sat together at my dining room table across a whole week doing the initial critical reading of the manuscript in its entirety. Her critiques extended from the constant removal of 'however' used incorrectly to significant discussions around some of the key aspects of the way of reading and the readings themselves. Our shared engagement with ecological readings of biblical texts is not confined to this project or manuscript but flows over into much of our work around which we constructively support and critique one another's papers/lectures and ideas. I want to acknowledge this collegiality together with our friendship that supports and sustains me. Thank you.

Together with these specific contributors to this work, there are many others sometimes too numerous to mention who have contributed in a range of ways. First my recent colleagues in theology at the University of Auckland, particularly Caroline Blyth, Nick Thompson, Stephen Garner, Helen Bergin, John Dunn, Nasili Vaka'uta and Derek Tovey for their collegiality and their commitment to excellence in research which has provided a context in which this project could be completed, albeit slowly. Second, my research has been supported and challenged by my engagement with all the postgraduate research students whom I have supervised, but in particular and most recently the three new Matthean scholars: Robert Myles, Carlos Olivares and Vaitusi Nofoaiga; and the ecological scholar of the Hebrew Bible: Emily Colgan. The work of each has informed and challenged my own. With these, I thank all my research students whose work has stretched my thinking and developed further my critical facilities.

The context for this collegiality has been the University of Auckland. I am most grateful for the University's support of academic research in the variety of ways that I have already acknowledged and to those individuals who have explicitly supported my academic career at the University.

My family, friends, and my Mercy community constantly remind me that life is more than academic research. I am grateful to each of them for the myriads of ways in which they call me forth to celebrate life and love and to cherish the Earth as gift. I hope they too can enjoy this book, albeit if only for an occasional foray for some.

During the course of this research, I have published material that has contributed significantly to this completed Earth Bible Commentary. I wish to acknowledge these contributions and the permissions granted by publishers for the inclusion of this material in a new and revised context. These works are also acknowledged at appropriate points in the commentary.

2010   'Place, Power and Potentiality: Reading Matthew 2:1-12 Ecologically', *ExpTim* 121.4: 159-67.
2011   'Beyond the Crossroads: Reading Matthew 13,52 Ecologically into the Twenty-First Century', in *The Gospel of Matthew at the Crossroads of Early Christianity* (BETL, 243; Leuven: Peeters) 375-88.
2012a 'Images, Words and Stories: Exploring their Transformative Power in Reading Biblical Texts Ecologically', *BibInt* 20: 280-304.
2012b '"Hear then the Parable of the Seed": Reading the Agrarian Parables of Matthew 13 Ecologically', in *The One Who Reads May Run: Essays in Honour of Edgar W. Conrad* (ed. Roland Boer, Michael Carden and Julie Kelso; New York: T. & T. Clark) 125-41.
2013a 'Reading the Gospel of Matthew Ecologically in Oceania: Matthew 4:1-11 as Focal Text', in *Matthew: Texts @ Contexts* (ed. Nicole Wilkinson Duran and James Grimshaw: Minneapolis: Fortress Press) 255-70.
2013b 'Of Borders, Bread, Dogs and Demons: Reading Matthew 15.21-28 Ecologically', in *Where the Wild Ox Roams: Biblical Essays in Honour of Norman C. Habel* (ed. Alan H. Cadwallader with Peter L. Trudinger; Hebrew Bible Monographs, 59; Sheffield: Sheffield Phoenix Press) 114-28.
2014   '"Save Us! We are Perishing!": Reading Matthew 8:23-27 in the Face of Devastating Floods', in *Bible, Borders, Belonging(s): Engaging Readings from Oceania* (ed. Jione Havea, David J. Neville and Elaine M. Wainwrigh; *SemeiaSt*, 75; Atlanta: Society of Biblical Literature): 21-38.

With Robert J. Myles and Carlos Olivares
2014   *The Gospel according to Matthew: The Basileia of the Heavens is Near At Hand* (Phoenix Guides to the New Testament, 1; Sheffield: Sheffield Phoenix Press).

ABBREVIATIONS

ABD	David Noel Freedman (ed.), *The Anchor Bible Dictionary* (New York: Doubleday, 1992). Accessed *Accordance* 11.0.6bl. Oaktree Software.
Ant.	*Jewish Antiquities* (Josephus)
ABRL	Anchor Bible Reference Library
BDAG	Danker, Frederick W., Walter Bauer, Wiliam F. Arndt, F. Wilbur Gingrich. *Greek-English Lexicon of the New Testament and other Early Chrisian Literature*. 3rd ed. Chicago: University of Chicago Press, 1979. Accessed *Accordance* 11.0.6bl. Oaktree Software.
BAR	*Biblical Archaeology Review*
BETL	Bibliotheca Ephemeridum Theologicarum Lovaniensium
BibInt	*Biblical Interpretation: A Journal of Contemporary Approaches*
BRev	*Bible Review*
BTB	*Biblical Theology Bulletin*
BZNW	Beihefte zur Zeitschrift für die neutestamentliche Wissenschaft
CBQ	*Catholic Biblical Quarterly*
Div	*On Divination* (Cicero)
ExpTim	*Expository Times*
Geogr.	*Geography* (Strabo)
JBL	*Journal of Biblical Literature*
JSNT	*Journal for the Study of the New Testament*
JSNTSup	*Journal for the Study of the New Testament*, Supplement Series
JSRNC	*Journal for the Study of Religion, Nature, and Culture*
J.W.	*Jewish War* (Josephus)
LXX	Septuagint
Mos.	*On the Life of Moses* (Philo)
Nat.	*Natural History* (Pliny)
NIGTC	New International Greek Testament Commentary
NIV	New International Version
NRSV	New Revised Standard Version
RB	*Revue Biblique*
RSV	Revised Standard Version
SemeiaSt	Semeia Studies
SNTSMS	Society for New Testament Studies Monograph Series
WUNT	Wissenshaftliche Untersuchungen zum Neuen Testament

GLOSSARY OF TERMS

Other-than-human	all participants in the Earth community (Earth designating the planet which is alive with interconnecting webs of life) other than the 'human' a category with which we are familiar.
More-than-human	will refer to all that constitutes the Earth community, the human and the 'other-than-human'.
Materiality	the vitality of matter that belongs to both the other-than-human and the human.
Sociality	a more comprehensive term than 'social' which designates the interconnections in/among the more-than-human (which by way of its definition includes the human but within a much broader web of interconnections).
Inter-con/textuality	refers to the processes that hold together attentiveness to the materiality of the more-than-human in interrelationship with place and time and other features of the ecological texture with/in habitat and as encoded in the ecological texture of the text.
Earth/earth	I use 'Earth' to refer to the planet with all its complex interrelationships of biotic and abiotic materiality and sociality; and 'earth' to refer to the ground.

Introduction:
Introducing The Earth Bible Commentary Series

Norman C. Habel

The five volumes of *The Earth Bible* (2000–2002) represent a landmark in the development of an ecological approach to reading and interpreting the biblical text. The Earth Bible team situated in Adelaide, South Australia, and led by Norman Habel, formulated a set of principles in consultation with ecologists and representatives of other disciplines. The opening chapter in each volume of this series examines key issues that emerged in response to this approach.

The aims of the Earth Bible project were:

1. to acknowledge, before reading the biblical text, that as Western interpreters we are heirs of a long anthropocentric, patriarchal and androcentric approach to reading the text that has devalued Earth and that continues to influence the way we read the text;
2. to declare, before reading the text, that we are members of a human community that has exploited, oppressed and endangered the existence of the Earth community;
3. to become progressively more conscious that we are also members of the endangered Earth community in dialogue with ancient texts;
4. to recognize Earth as a subject in the text with which we seek to relate empathetically rather than as a topic to be analysed rationally;
5. to take up the cause of justice for Earth and to ascertain whether Earth and the Earth community are oppressed, silenced or liberated in the text;
6. to develop techniques of reading the text to discern and retrieve alternative traditions where the voice of Earth and Earth community has been suppressed.

To guide writers in achieving these aims, a set of ecojustice principles were articulated (Habel 2000b). These principles were developed over a number of years in dialogue with ecologists such as Charles Birch (1990). The principles articulated below were refined in consultations and workshops concerned with ecology in general, and ecological concerns linked to theology and the Bible more specifically.

The principle of intrinsic worth
The universe, Earth and all its components have intrinsic worth/value.

The principle of interconnectedness
Earth is a community of interconnected living things that are mutually dependent on each other for life and survival.

The principle of voice
Earth is a subject capable of raising its voice in celebration and against injustice.

The principle of purpose
The universe, Earth and all its components are part of a dynamic cosmic design within which each piece has a place in the overall goal of that design.

The principle of mutual custodianship
Earth is a balanced and diverse domain where responsible custodians can function as partners with, rather than rulers over, Earth to sustain its balance and a diverse Earth community.

The principle of resistance
Earth and its components not only suffer from human injustices but actively resist them in the struggle for justice.

The various writers in the series focused on one or more of the six principles enunciated in volume one of *The Earth Bible* series and explored the way in which those principles were either supported or suppressed in a given biblical text. The overall aim of the writers was to read the text 'from the perspective of Earth and/or the Earth community'.

Our approach in this new *Earth Bible Commentary* series attempts to move beyond a focus on ecological themes to a process of listening to, and identifying with, Earth as a presence or voice in the text. Our task is to take up the cause of Earth and the non-human members of the Earth community by sensing their presence in the text—whether their presence is suppressed, oppressed or celebrated. We seek to move beyond identifying ecological themes in creation theology to identifying with the Earth in its ecojustice struggle.

After consideration of the various critiques of the Earth Bible principles, dialogue within the Earth Bible team and an analysis of so-called second level hermeneutical approaches—such as feminism and post-colonial hermeneutics—a more precise set of steps was developed for exploration as part of a Consultation for Ecological Hermeneutics at the annual meetings of the SBL (Society of Biblical Literature). These meetings were held in the USA between 2004 and 2008, again under the leadership of Norman Habel. Since that date ecological hermeneutics has been included as a regular session of the SBL meetings.

This led to the reformulation of the principles enunciated in *The Earth Bible* as a hermeneutic of suspicion, identification and retrieval. The approach was developed through the papers and research of that consultation. Selected papers from that consultation were then published in a SBL symposium volume entitled *Exploring Ecological Hermeneutics* in 2008 (a summary of the fundamental hermeneutical steps outlined below are also found in the introduction to this volume; Habel 2008).

In a subsequent volume entitled, *An Inconvenient Text: Is a Green Reading of the Bible Possible?*, the assumptions and technique of ecological hermeneutics were developed further in relation to a series of key biblical texts where God is associated with nature (Habel 2009). A major feature in this study is the classification of biblical texts as 'green' or 'grey'. Green texts are those texts where nature, creation or the Earth community is affirmed, valued and recognised as having a role and a voice. Grey texts are those texts where nature, creation or the Earth community is devalued, oppressed, deprived of a voice or made subject to various forms of injustice at the hands of humans or God.

It is important to recognise that the identification of texts as green or grey is grounded in an ecological hermeneutic and not to be confused with the identification of texts as green in *The Green Bible* (2008). This volume prints in green any text that relates to creation, nature or living beings without any apparent critical awareness of ecological hermeneutics.

A revised ecological hermeneutic requires a radical re-orientation to the biblical text. The task before us is not an exploration of what a given text may say *about* creation, *about* nature, or *about* Earth. In this context, Earth is not a *topos* or theme for analysis. We are not focusing on ecology *and* creation, or ecology *and* theology (Habel 2000a). An ecological hermeneutic demands a radical change of posture both in relation to Earth as a subject in the text and also our relation to Earth as readers. Here the term 'Earth' refers to the total ecosystem, the web of life, the domains of nature with which we are familiar, of which we are an integral part and in which we face the future.

1. *Context—The Environmental Crisis*

No biblical interpreter reads the text in a vacuum. One or more living contexts are likely to influence both our conscious choice of a specific approach when reading the text and our associated worldview, orientation or cosmology as contemporary readers. Two dimensions of our current context are explicit: our environmental crisis and our ecological orientation. The degree to which readers in this commentary series interact with either of these contexts will no doubt vary, depending on their particular text and context.

We read the text today in the midst of a global environmental crisis. The disastrous effects of climate change surround us as readers. If we dare to stand, for example, on the shore near Puri in Orissa and look out into the

Bay of Bengal, we can see sand bars shining golden in the sun. The local fishermen may remind us that only a few years ago a village covered those sandbars. In the past 15 years the sea has encroached five kilometres and destroyed several such villages. Islands in the Pacific are waiting for the day when the seas will engulf them. For the villages on the shores of Orissa that day has come. The reader may then wonder about the words of Wisdom in Proverbs:

> God assigned the sea its limit, so that the waters might not transgress his command (Prov. 8.29).

Paleoclimatologists may be able to demonstrate that our planet has undergone a range of climate cycles in its history. Climate change has been a feature of this planet's history from its beginnings (Jenson 2006: 201). The current change in climate, however, is a frightening fact and the current evidence indicates that the cause is not necessarily volcano eruptions, variations in Earth's orbit around the sun or some meteorological phenomenon. The problem is the greedy way humans have exploited our fossil fuels and pumped greenhouse gases into the atmosphere at random.

Climate change has produced hot spots, intense weather experiences that differ radically from past weather patterns. In the State of Victoria in Australia, for example, the bushfires of Black Saturday in February 2009 are evidence of one such hot spot. On that Black Saturday, all the known patterns of a typical Australian bushfire were transcended.

Instead of plumes of swirling smoke and burning leaves flying into the sky, imagine a tornado with massive balls of fire leaping over an entire valley and landing on houses on the opposite hillside. The height and force of the typical bushfire had changed.

Instead of ferocious flames fanned by a hot North wind, imagine a hurricane like Katrina, with temperatures of 110 degrees Fahrenheit, blasts of over 100 miles an hour and fierce fires—like open mouths, consuming all in their path. The heat and energy of the typical bushfire had changed. According to one analyst, the inferno generated enough 'energy to fuel 1500 atomic bombs the size of Hiroshima' (*Adelaide Advertiser*, Friday May 22, 2009).

It seems we are entering a new age, a Greenhouse Age in which the ecosystems of Earth will necessarily have to adapt to the new gases in her lungs. Lovelock reminds us that the

> few things we do know about the response of the Earth to our presence are deeply disturbing. Even if we stopped immediately all seizing of Gaia's land and water for food and fuel production and stopped poisoning the air, it would take Earth more than a thousand years to recover from the damage we have done (2006: 6).

As we read the biblical text we are surrounded by a range of serious environmental crises which are liable to impact on the way we interpret the text. We are reading in a climate changing context that is threatening to affect the future of our planet.

2. Context—An Ecological Worldview

In his general audience address in January 2001, Pope John Paul II introduced the need for an *ecological conversion*. Catholic theologians such as Denis Edwards have promoted this concept as integral to the development of ecotheology (2006: 2-4). The context of this concept is the growing ecological crisis and our emerging awareness of its implications. The dilemma before us is the way we understand this laudable idea. In the words of Edwards,

> [c]ommitment to ecology has not yet taken its central place in Christian self-understanding. It is far from central in terms of its structure, personnel and the struggle of justice and to the side of women in their struggle for full equality, so the church itself is called to conversion to the side of suffering creation (2006: 3).

If this conversion means taking a stand at the side of suffering creation, joining the struggle for ecojustice and seeking to heal the wounds of our planet, the process is indeed worthy and vital. In this context, the question at hand is how ecology contributes to our worldview or cosmology, and how, in turn, this new ecological awareness influences our interpretation of that biblical tradition.

Another way of addressing this challenge is to speak of 'greening' our world and our way of thinking. In the past, 'greening' has been viewed as a rather trite popular term for eccentrics in the ecological movement. The term 'green', however, has come of age and is now employed to identify the orientation of those seeking to integrate ecology with a range of fields of thought and action. To be 'green' is to empathise with nature.

We are faced, it seems, with a new view of the natural world, a new understanding of the universe, a new cosmology that has little in common with the biblical, the geocentric or the heliocentric cosmologies of the past. We are becoming aware of an eco-cosmology, a worldview where ecology conditions our thinking.

Many writers still view ecology as but one scientific discipline among many. In reality, ecology has now become an integral part of our social, political and personal worlds. And if we are to face the challenge of ecology in biblical studies we need to articulate what ecology really means as part of our emerging worldview. How might we describe the essence of ecology that informs this emerging worldview? One option is the formulation of Thomas Berry.

> In reality there is a single integral community of the Earth that includes all its component members whether human or other than human. In this community every being has its own role to fulfil, its own dignity, its inner spontaneity. Every being has its own voice. Every being declares itself to the entire universe. Every being enters into communion with other beings. This capacity for relatedness, for presence to other beings, for spontaneity in action, is a capacity possessed by every mode of being throughout the entire universe. So too every being has rights to be recognised and revered (Berry 1999: 4).

Writers like Lorraine Code speak of ecology as

> a study of habitats both physical and social where people endeavour to live well together; of ways of knowing that foster or thwart such living; and thus of the ethos and habitus enacted in the knowledge and actions, customs, social structures and creative-regulative principles by which people strive or fail to achieve this multiply realizable end (Code 2006: 25).

In our current cosmology or ecology informed view of life in the natural world—and more particularly of Earth—I would suggest many have become conscious of the following understandings.

1. Earth is a planet that originated in cosmic space and evolved into a living habitat that influences how we act and think; in this habitat humans are living expressions of the cosmos.
2. Earth is a fragile web of interconnected and interdependent forces and domains of existence that not only interact with but create complex identities in diverse worlds; in this web humans are intelligent carbon creatures.
3. Earth is a living community in which humans and all other organisms are kin who live and move and influence each other's destinies and perceptions of those destinies; in this community humans are conscious Earth beings.

Earth is a living planet. All of its components—from the mountains to the forests, from the oceans to the Antarctic—are part of a complex living entity called Earth. And human beings, along with all other living beings, are privileged to be an integral part of this living planet. Not only is Earth a unique living planet in our galaxy, Earth provides the habitat in which we live and nurtures all consciousness as we know it. We no longer dwell 'on Earth' we live 'in Earth'. Earth is our habitat, our home and our mentor. Earth is a complex world that influences how we live, move and think about our being. In this world we are an expression of the cosmos; we are beings informed by the evolution of all galaxies and planets.

Earth is a fragile web of interconnectedness. As human beings we are not separate or disconnected from the various forces and domains of nature. We are totally dependent on the various ecosystems of Earth for survival;

Earth's ecosystems have existed for millennia. The movement of oxygen in the atmosphere is necessary for us to breathe. The movement of moisture in the clouds and the seas is essential for us to enjoy a drink. The movement of worms in the soil is vital for us to receive our daily bread. Ultimately, we are carbon creatures totally interconnected with all other animate and inanimate carbon domains.

The reality that we are Earth is expressed well in the following statement:

> Matter is made from rock and soil. It, too, is pulled by the moon as the magma circulates through the planet heart and roots such molecules into biology. Earth pours through us, replacing each cell in the body every seven years. Ashes to ashes, dust to dust, we ingest, incorporate and excrete the earth, are made from earth. I am that. You are that (Macy and Seed 1996: 501).

Earth is also a community of kin. Recent research in biology, genetics and evolutionary science has reminded us that we are kin with all other living things on Earth. As human beings we are related to all living things; some creatures are close relatives and other are distant kin. Some seem friendly and others fierce. But we are related to all—whether they are ants or elephants, sea horses or hidden organisms. Deep within, the genetic coding of humans is little different from that of most other animals. We belong to the same family, a community of kin.

Beyond the strictly biological and geological interdependency we experience, this habitat called Earth is composed of a complex world of presences that impinge upon us from birth to death, forming and transforming us as Earth beings, human beings and thinking beings. From towering mountains and threatening storms to delicate wings of butterflies and so-called weeds that invade our gardens, we are enveloped by environmental influences that mould our minds.

Berry (1999: 4) maintains that there is a capacity in all beings to enter into communion with other beings. Living beings are not only biologically related; they also possess an inner impulse to commune with the other beings and to relate to the rest of the universe. The research of scholars such as Ursula Goodenough illustrates that there are numerous modes of communication, awareness and communion that characterise living beings in Earth's diverse family (Goodenough 1998).

As we read the text we are now acutely conscious that we are Earth beings; that Earth is our habitat in the cosmos; that we part of a kinship called Earth community.

3. Suspicion—Anthropocentric Bias

A radical ecological approach to the text involves a basic hermeneutic of suspicion, identification and retrieval. This progression bears obvious similarities with several approaches of well-known feminist hermeneutics. The difference, of course, is that we are not reading from within the worldview of women, but first and foremost from within the orientation of an ecosystem called Earth. We are not identifying with women in the text on the basis of our experiences, but with non-human characters and habitats within the plot of the narrative. We are reading as Earth beings, members of the Earth community, in solidarity with Earth.

First, we begin reading with the suspicion that the text is likely to be inherently anthropocentric and/or has traditionally been read from an anthropocentric perspective. At the outset, anthropocentric needs to be distinguished from two related terms: anthropogenic—a text originating from humans; anthropotopic— a text in which humans are a central *topos* or theme.

The anthropocentric bias that we are likely to find both in ourselves as readers and in the text we are reading has at least two faces. First, the assumption or condition we have inherited as human beings, especially in the Western world: that we are beings of a totally different order than all other creatures in nature; in other words, in the hierarchy of things there is God, human beings and the rest. Even where scholars have insisted that texts are theocentric rather than anthropocentric in character, the writer may ultimately be more concerned about God's relation to humanity or a group within humanity than about God's relation to Earth or the Earth community as a whole.

The Bible has long been understood as God's book for humans. And for those of us who have been reading biblical texts that way for years, this understanding has come to be self-evident. Should we not then, with a new ecological consciousness, legitimately suspect that the text and its interpreters have been understandably anthropocentric?

A second face of this anthropocentric bias relates to nature as 'object', never subject. We have for so long viewed nature and all its parts—both animate and inanimate—as the object of many forms of human investigation, of which scientific analysis is but one. This process has not only reinforced a sense of human superiority over nature; it has also contributed to a sense of distance, separation and otherness. The rest of nature, especially the inanimate world, has been viewed as separate, other and a force to be harnessed and subjected.

This phase of the hermeneutical process is related especially to the principle of intrinsic worth articulated in *The Earth Bible* (see Habel 2003). When viewed through a traditional anthropocentric bias, other parts of nature are considered of less value. Often they are viewed merely as the stage, scenery or background for God's relationship with humanity. They are seldom regarded as valued subjects in their own right.

One of the reasons for this anthropocentric blind spot in our interpretative work as readers of an ancient text, is that we are still influenced by traditional dualisms about reality. This view of reality has only developed since biblical days but because these dualisms are so much part of our Western view of reality, we may assume they are an inherent aspect of the biblical text. The key elements of the dualistic structure of Western thought are outlined by Plumwood (1993: 43). These include, among others, the following sets of contrasting pairs:

culture	/	nature
reason	/	nature
male	/	female
mind, spirit	/	body (nature)
reason	/	matter
reason	/	emotion (nature)
rationality	/	animality (nature)
human	/	nature (non-human)
civilised	/	primitive (nature)
production	/	reproduction (nature)
freedom	/	necessity (nature)
subject	/	object

To this listing, in the context of our project, I would add the following closely related pairs:

animate	/	inanimate
spiritual	/	material
heavenly	/	earthly
heaven	/	earth
sacred	/	profane

It is immediately apparent from these pairings that the realities associated with the human pole of the pairing are understood to be superior in some way to the nature pole of the pairing. These dualisms necessarily devalue Earth as inferior. Perhaps the most destructive form of this dualism developed as a result of the mechanistic approach of Descartes and his successors. According to Ponting, Cartesian dualism was

> reinforced by a mechanistic approach to natural phenomena, which can again be traced back to Descartes who wrote, 'I do not recognise any difference between the machines made by craftsmen and the various bodies that nature alone composes...'. His mechanistic view of the world seemed to be vindicated by the spectacular success of Newton in the late seventeenth century in applying physical laws, such as that governing the force of gravity, to explain the workings of the universe (1991: 147).

Ecofeminists have also recognised a social and symbolic connection between the oppression of women and the domination of nature. When Earth has been viewed as female—Mother Earth or Mother Nature—Earth has often been abused and denied its rights. Eaton contends that as

European societies developed, the combined influences of the rise of science, the dualisms of the Christian worldview, the philosophy of modernity and the industrialisation of the economy became the cultural forces that entrenched the feminising of nature... The influence of hierarchical dualisms, a core piece of patriarchal ideology and described by Habel in this volume, is central to feminist critiques (Eaton 2000: 55).

We also read, therefore, with the suspicion that, in Western culture, the text has traditionally been interpreted from a dualistic perspective, regardless of the basic cosmology or sociology of the text. An ecological hermeneutic begins with the suspicion that text and interpreter may reflect an anthropocentric bias which is part of a wider dualistic orientation to the universe.

4. *Identification—Empathy with Earth*

The second element of a contemporary ecological hermeneutic is the task of empathy or identification.

In the light of my experience as an editor and writer in the *Earth Bible* project, it has become clear that the activity of identification now deserves to be highlighted as a distinct step in the hermeneutical process. As human beings we identify, often unconsciously, with the various human characters in the biblical story, whether that be an empathetic or antipathetic identification. We can identify with the experiences of these characters—even when we do not necessarily admire or would not seek to emulate the individuals.

Even before reading the narrative or poetry of the text, readers using this approach must—at least to some extent—come to terms with their deep ecological connections. Before we begin reading and seeking to identify with Earth in the text we need to face the prior ecological reality of our kinship with Earth: that we are born of Earth, and we are living expressions of the ecosystem that has emerged on this planet. Our identities are influenced by the various environmental influences we experience in a given habitat. This step relates to the fundamental principle of interconnectedness explored in *The Earth Bible*.

Identification with Earth and members of the Earth community raises our consciousness to the injustices against Earth reflected in the text—and portrayed as consequences of the actions of humans and God. Exegetes who pursue a radical ecological approach ultimately take up the cause of the natural world, seeking to expose the wrongs that Earth has suffered, largely in silence, and to discern, where possible, the way Earth has resisted these wrongs. Our aim is to read in solidarity with Earth. We are Earth beings reading in empathy with Earth.

Our approach is to move beyond a focus on ecological themes to a process of listening to, and identifying with, the Earth as a presence, character or voice in the text. Our task is to take up the cause of the Earth and the non-human members of the Earth community by sensing their presence in the text—whether their presence is suppressed, oppressed or celebrated. We seek to move beyond identifying ecological themes in creation theology to identifying with the Earth and the Earth community in their struggle for ecojustice.

The most obvious dimension of this step is to identify with non-human figures in the narrative, empathising with their roles, character and treatment and discerning their voices. Another dimension of this process is to locate ourselves in the habitat of all the participants in the narrative, and discerning any forces, whether positive or negative, interacting with the characters in the text and determining their identities. These interactions may reveal how entities have been isolated, suppressed or devalued by the dominant figures and forces in their habitat.

The wisdom school in texts, such as Job and Proverbs, provide an interesting parallel to this approach of discerning both the character and habitat of every entity. In this school of thought, the essential character of any part of nature is its *derek* (way) and each entity in nature has its intended *maqom* (place or habitat) in the universe. An important task of the wise in this school was to discern the *derek* and *maqom* of each domain, entity or being in nature. That is precisely the challenge God presents Job in the speech from the whirlwind (Job 38-39). And in Job 28, even God seeks to discern both the 'way' and the 'place' of wisdom, searching everywhere on Earth beneath the heavens in the process (Habel 2003).

In this step, when we read the text as Earth beings, we seek to identify with one or more of the non-human characters in the text and to locate ourselves in their respective habitats to ascertain what forces or factors we might legitimately claim these characters experience.

5. *Retrieval—The Voice of Earth*

The third facet of this radical ecological hermeneutic is that of retrieval. Retrieval is closely related to the prior steps of suspicion and identification.

As the interpreter exposes the various anthropocentric dimensions of the text—the ways in which the human agenda and bias are sustained either by the reader or the implied author—the text may reveal a number of surprises about the non-human characters in the story. Earth or members of the Earth community may be revealed as playing a key role or be highly valued in the text, but because of the Western interpretative tradition we have inherited, that dimension of the text has been ignored or suppressed.

Where we meet non-human figures communicating in some way—mourning, praising or singing—we have tended in the past to dismiss these expressions as poetic license or symbolic language. Our anthropocentric bias leads to classifying these elements as mere anthropomorphisms.

Discerning Earth and members of the Earth community as subjects with voices is a key part of the retrieval process. In some contexts their voice is evident but have been traditionally ignored by exegetes. In other contexts their voices are not explicit, but nevertheless present and powerful though silent. These non-human subjects play roles in the text that are more than mere scenery or secondary images. Their voices need to be heard, their voices may not correspond to the languages and words we commonly associate with the human voices.

To illustrate this point, we might turn to the prophets. In a number of passages in Jeremiah we are told the land is mourning (4.28; 12.11). A close reading reveals that the text includes a double entendre and could be rendered 'dries up.' The physical act of 'drying up' is a way of expressing Earth mourning. The parallel to Earth 'drying up/mourning' in Jer. 4.18 is the sky becoming dark. Physical acts such as drying up, becoming dark, and quaking are ways in which parts of the Earth community communicate, in this case, their grief. This form of communication even reaches Yhwn in Jer. 12.11.

Discerning this voice may even take the form of reconstructing the narrative—as a dimension of the interpretation process—in such a way as to hear Earth as the narrator of the story. In the process, Earth becomes an interpreter. Such a reconstruction is, of course, not the original text, but a reading as valid, I would argue, as the numerous efforts of biblical scholars over the centuries to reconstruct the history, literary sources, social world or theology behind a text.

The essence of this approach is expressed quite clearly by Hilary Marlow in an article on Amos. Marlow asks how:

> can I have read the book of Amos so many times and not noticed the part the natural world plays within it? Why have I allowed my anthropocentric bias to muffle the voices of the rest of creation?
>
> The questions raised by the Earth Bible project include asking whether Earth is an active voice in the text or a passive lifeless entity, and if Earth is treated unjustly, and if so, to what extent that is acknowledged in the text. These concerns have promoted my re-examination of the text of Amos and a discovery that the natural world is an active participant in the Earth's story in this book (2008: 75).

The task before us is to re-read the text to discern where the Earth or members of the Earth community may have suffered, resisted or been excluded by attitudes within the text or in the history of its interpretation.

Retrieval demands a strategy for reclaiming the sufferings and struggles of Earth, a task that involves regarding the wider Earth community as our kin. The aim is to read as Earth beings in tune with Earth, the very source of our being.

There is a strong possibility that biblical texts may be more sympathetic to the plight and potential of the Earth than our previous interpretations have allowed, even if the ecological questions we are posing arise out of a contemporary Earth consciousness. We also need to consider the possibility that there are suppressed Earth traditions that resist the dominant patriarchal anthropocentric orientation of the text. By counter-reading the text it may be possible to identify alternative voices that challenge or subvert the normative voice of the dominant tradition. Whether these sub-texts point to the continuing voice of ancient traditions still in touch with Earth, or whether these alterative perspectives arose as a mode of resisting the patriarchal orientation of monotheistic Yahwism, is a task for interpreters in this series to explore.

Especially significant in this context is the contribution of feminists and ecofeminists. Not only have they focused on identifying the patriarchal orientation and bias of both text and interpreter, they have also developed techniques of 'reading against the grain' and discerning traces of anti-patriarchal resistance in the text. Clues are sought within the text that point to traditions where the suppressed voices of women resisting a patriarchal society can be detected and the tradition itself retrieved. Ultimately, writes Schüssler Fiorenza,

> [r]ather than abandon the memory of our foresisters' sufferings, visions and hopes in our patriarchal biblical past, such a hermeneutics reclaims their sufferings, struggles, and victories through the subversive power of the 're-membered' past (1985: 133).

This technique of retrieval has been developed in a more 'revolutionary' way by feminists such as Pardes who discerns counter-traditions, sub-texts that read against the grain of the dominant rhetoric of the main text. The patriarchy of the Bible is 'continuously challenged by antithetical trends' that need to be uncovered (Pardes 1992: 51). Pardes' goal is 'to reconstruct, in the light of surviving remains, antithetical undercurrents which call into question the monotheistic repression of femininity' (1992: 2).

Similarly, interpreters employing an ecological hermeneutic may pursue counter-readings that seek to retrieve elements of resistance, hidden undercurrents and suppressed voices that reflect the perspective of Earth or the Earth community and challenge the dominant anthropocentric voices of the biblical text. These suppressed elements provide the basis for reconstructing the voices of Earth and the domains of Earth that have been silenced by traditional readings.

6. *Contexts—Literary and Cultural*

Fundamental to any close reading of the text is a detailed analysis of the literary dimensions of the materials being examined. A priori is a consideration of the literary forms of the text. Is it a hymn, a myth, a legend, an oracle or some other literary genre that is being employed to present the materials? How has the narrator incorporated this literary unit in the wider literary context? And in so doing, has a literary design been created that highlights the specific orientation of the narrator?

In the light of the preceding hermeneutics of suspicion, identification and retrieval, we may ask whether the narrator or compiler designs the material in such a way as to highlight the human characters rather than the non-human dimensions of the text. Or is there a subtle way in which the narrator has emphathized with Earth or members of the Earth community by using a particular genre that we, as anthropocentric and Western interpreters, have not discerned? Is the narrator conscious of being an Earth being as well as a human being?

Moreover, as we review the history of interpretation of a given biblical text we will discover numerous connections that have been made between components in the text and the intertextual context. Past readings may have also contributed to a widely accepted understanding of the terminology, symbols and concepts of the text. A radical ecological reading dares to test these understandings, taking into account both the hermeneutics and the ecological context enunciated above.

Intertextual connections between a given text and related texts have played a significant role in biblical interpretation in recent years. A text is no longer viewed as a text in isolation, but connected with a wider context of passages where the same topic, terminology or symbol system is present. The interpreter can no longer ignore, for example, the possible connections between the *imago dei* text in Gen. 1.26 and references to the image of God in Gen. 5.1 and 9.1-6. Do the latter passages provide evidence for a particular nuance of meaning in Gen. 1.26? Do they indicate the inclusion of a myth that might be designated the *Tselem* (image) myth?

Cultural connections are also important in seeking to discern the symbolic or metaphorical dimensions of the text. In an ancient Near Eastern world where the images of deities were common and where Aaron constructed an image for the people of Israel at Sinai, the particular connotation of the image of a deity in Gen. 1.26 cannot be ignored.

Nor can we ignore the widely accepted connection between the image of God in Gen. 1.26-28 and the practice of certain ancient Near Eastern kings who erected images of themselves throughout their empires to proclaim their jurisdiction over a given domain. This connection has been cited to justify the royal imagery of the text and the ruling of humans as God's representatives.

A review of the traditional readings of the *imago dei* in Gen. 1.26, for example, leads us to suspect that these intertextual and cultural connections have been read in the light of a dualistic understanding of reality. The image of God in humans has been widely understood as a non-physical dimension of human beings, such as reason, consciousness, or capacity to worship. And this dualistic anthropocentric mindset has influenced the interpretation of the nature and function of the *imago dei* in the text of Gen. 1.26-28. We are led, therefore, through an intertextual 'green' reading to ask what the *imago Dei* might mean if we dare to identify not with the humans of the text, but with those domains over which humans are given dominion. Our aim is to read as Earth beings from within the habitat of Earth.

Various writers in this series may well identify connections with other contexts and approaches that are relevant in discerning the meaning of the text from the perspective of Earth and the Earth community. Crucial in the assessment of these connections is the ecological hermeneutic of suspicion, identification and retrieval outlined above.

7. Application

This basic hermeneutic of suspicion, identification and retrieval will be employed by the writers in this series, not in a pedantic way, but in a manner that facilitates a genuine ecological interpretation of the text or book involved. Nor will interpreters necessarily follow a traditional pattern of examining all the textual and exegetical debates associated with a given text or textual unit. Writers are free to focus on those texts which uncover insights and issues that this approach highlights and to note the obvious anthropocentric biases of past interpreters that have blinded us to ecological or 'green' dimensions of the text.

It is also expected that each interpreter will re-examine the literary dimensions of the text to ascertain whether past examinations of the plot or structure of the unit under investigation have tended to be governed predominantly by an interest in the human subjects involved. Earth or members of the Earth community may well be characters in the narrative rather than mere scenery.

This hermeneutical approach needs to be distinguished from the reader-centred approach represented by Tim Meadowcroft in the new series published by Sheffield Phoenix Press. Meadowcroft, in his reading of Haggai, quite legitimately seeks to discern the relevance of a text for the reader in a given contemporary context by exploring how the intention of the text/ author might speak to the modern reader. In connection with the current environmental crisis he writes that

> the church has an important role to play in calling people in this direction, not least because the call to rebuild the temple and the call for a sustainable approach to the environment are closely related concepts (2006: 240).

We are Earth beings, not merely human beings. As such we are invited to read from the perspective of Earth, and from within this habitat called Earth. This is the invitation extended to the several authors in *The Earth Bible Commentary* and to you as readers of this commentary series.

Chapter 1

READING THE GOSPEL OF MATTHEW ECOLOGICALLY

Habitat, Human, and Holy as the title of this Earth Bible commentary or ecological reading of the Gospel of Matthew arises both from the gospel story itself as well as from my own journey in shaping an ecological way of reading. A key thematic of the Matthean gospel story is *Emmanu-el, the with-us G*d*[1]—'us' being the entire Earth community. The Holy is intimately bound up with habitat, and the human is but one participant in a rich and complex interrelationship of beings and actants in both the Matthean narrative and the unfolding universe.

Thomas Berry exclaimed, in his groundbreaking challenge to the story of humanity, divinity and the universe encoded in the scriptures and the theology of western Christianity, '[i]t's all a question of story' (1988: 123). His exclamation echoes through the Earth Bible project and this current commentary series in which this volume finds its place. It is indeed a question of 'story' and how each biblical story, and in this instance, the Gospel of Matthew, can be 're-told' in the face of not only a new story of the universe but also the daily challenges of both ecological crisis and ecological opportunity facing planet Earth. Gloria Anzaldua recognizes the need for 'a new story to explain the world and our participation in it…that connect(s) us to each other and to the planet' (1999: 81). She goes on to say that 'for images, words, stories to have this transformative power, they must arise from the human body—flesh and bone—and from the Earth's body—stone, sky, liquid, soil' (97). For the ecological interpreter of a gospel narrative, there is not only the human body and Earth's body and their stories but there is also a gospel story, there is a text that will require, in the words of Adrienne Rich, an 'entering [of] an old text from a new critical direction' (1972: 18).

---

1. I use the designation G*d throughout this commentary when I write the divine. I do so in order to recognize the mystery of divinity, of the Holy, which can never be named adequately and, in particular, to break the hold of much of the naming that has rendered that mystery in human terms that are masculine and imperial, to note just two problematic characteristics. It is hoped that this designation will intrude into our religious imaginary and invite us to think the divine anew in the context of emerging ecological thinking. I am indebted to Elisabeth Schüssler Fiorenza (1994: 191 n. 3) for this practice and a shared recognition of the inadequacy of language.

This ecological commentary on the Gospel of Matthew will arise from the flesh and bone of this human interpreter who is participant with/in Earth's body with all its constituents which I name the 'more-than-human'.[2] These constituents are animate and inanimate, biotic and abiotic, forming and co-forming in-habitant and habitat. The commentary, therefore, also arises from Earth's body with all its manifold material, social, cultural and other elements, processes and ecosystems both small and large. Such a new attending to images, words and stories and their transformative power within biblical interpretation requires not only new ways of engaging the biblical text but also new ways of thinking that inform our being and living as well as our work of interpretation. Such an approach is outlined in the Introduction: *Introducing the Earth Bible Commentary Series*. It provides a background to the approach taken here. I do not intend to repeat the foundational tenets of this commentary series that are laid out there but rather to assume on them or to discuss them when relevant in the context of my own particular approach. In this chapter, therefore, I develop the perspective/s and process/es that I employ in this volume to read the Gospel of Matthew ecologically.

1. *Thinking Ecologically*[3]

Ecological reading/reading ecologically belongs within a significant shift in human consciousness that Lorraine Code calls *ecological thinking*. She recognizes it as a new social imaginary (Code 2006).[4] She describes 'social imaginary' as a 'loosely integrated system of images, metaphors, tacit assumptions, (and) ways of thinking' giving rise to concepts, values and practices that circulate in the 'social-material-intellectual-affective atmosphere(s), like the air we breathe' (28-29). Such a shift in the human social imaginary calls on human thinkers, knowers and actors to examine

---

2. I use the following two terms throughout this commentary: 'other-than-human' to refer to all participants in the Earth community (Earth designating the planet which is alive with interconnecting webs of life) other than the 'human', a category with which we are familiar. The term 'more-than-human' refers to all that constitutes the Earth community, the human and the 'other-than-human'. I avoid the term 'non-human' except in quotations because it functions as a negative identifier. I am aware, however, that these terms continue to classify in relation to the 'human' but as yet I have no viable alternative. I use the term 'universe' to refer to that living and expanding 'world' in which Earth has a place. I am grateful to Anne Elvey for conversations and writings (2005: 3-4 by way of example) that have assisted me in refining a terminology to use in ecological reading.

3. Material in this section draws on a more extensive article (see Wainwright 2012). I acknowledge the permission given by Brill Publishers to use this material.

4. Note also Timothy Morton's title, *The Ecological Thought* (2010).

much more intimately the complex interrelationships between and among all Earth-beings or Earth-constituents of all life-forms. For those whose social imaginary includes the sacred or divine or the '*more* than nature' for which John Haught uses the term 'mystery' (2006: 22), the shift to ecological thinking requires that we extend the intimate re-examination of the complex web of interrelationships addressed above so that it includes the divine/mystery within that web.

Such a re-examination of perspective or hermeneutic characterizes many of the aims of the Earth Bible project as these are articulated in Norman Habel's introduction to this commentary series. They point to the profound anthropocentrism or human-centredness that has developed in at least most western but also many other human and cultural understandings of Earth and its more-than-human constituents. This anthropocentrism is characterized by mastery, as Val Plumwood has demonstrated (1993). Ecological thinking recognizes that, into this 'instituted imaginary' of mastery, many perspectives are interwoven with the anthropocentric: androcentric, colonial, racist, classist, sexist and others. This emerging new epistemology needs, therefore, to be multi-faceted and critical, engaging with many of the recent shifts in perspective that have sought to counter mastery in its multiple forms and that have informed biblical interpretation over recent decades: feminist, postcolonial, indigenous and other ideological hermeneutics. The uniqueness of this project will be its significant focus on the profound shift that a turning toward Earth entails and the ways that other such perspectives as identified above not only can but must co-constitute an ecological perspective.

I do not wish to articulate a full-blown ecological hermeneutic here. Aspects of this are included in the Introduction and I have addressed my own particular approach in more detail elsewhere (Wainwright 2012 in particular). They will become more evident as the commentary unfolds. One key aspect of my approach is a dialogue that I set up with a number of ecological thinkers who assist in shaping my interpretation of the Matthean text. Key insights from these appear in an indented section entitled 'Ecological Intertexts' at strategic points in each chapter. Cumulatively, then, we might exit this commentary with more highly developed ecological thinking together with a reading practice that opens up the gospel anew in a way that can speak to issues and concerns of the twenty-first century. It is within the context of thinking ecologically that I locate such a practice.

2. *Reading Ecologically*

Reading ecologically is a *process* that engages selected biblical methodologies with ecological thinking. It participates in the multidimensionality of our emerging understanding of ecology within a growing knowledge of an expanding universe (Edwards 2010: 1-14; Primavesi 2000). It is a critical conversation engaging the principle of *suspicion* in the face of pervasive anthropocentrism and a domination and/or erasure of women, the colonized and the other-than-human that has characterized the ideology of/ in author, text and reader from the genesis of the biblical text through its long history of interpretation to the present (although manifestations of this will differ in different ages and contexts). Such a process will be attentive to the interlocking processes of erasure and mastery that characterize every phase of the ecological reading process. It will be undertaken as conversation, since critical engagement in an ecological reading must always be intimately inter-connected with *reconfiguration* or *re-reading* which I use to name 'retrieval' as outlined in the Introduction. From this dance between interpretative stances of suspicion and reconfiguration, a new interpretation will emerge that is attentive to Earth and all its more-than-human constituents as these function in the narrative and as we recognize them from within a newly formed attentiveness. It is these aspects of the text that are foregrounded in a reconfigured reading.

Closely allied to the hermeneutical moves of suspicion and reconfiguration is that of *identification*. In an ecological reading, the human gaze and human concern shift to include other-than-human ones as key actants in the narrative and not simply as 'context'. They are engaged as characters with agency and as key contributors to the gospel story. Particular attention is paid to the ways in which they are oppressed by systems of domination. A new reading will emerge, a reading with Earth and all its participants. The foregrounding of Earth and Earth's constituents is, therefore, the way that this commentary engages the principle of identification.

Where one of these three constituent processes within an ecological reading begins and the other ends will not be sequential. Rather, they will be interwoven within an interpretative process that is attentive to animals, plants and all the more-than-human others as well as to climate, location, and the many other material as well as social and cultural processes that constitute the Matthean story. These will be given attention, not just as background to or context for a divine/human narrative, but as constitutive elements in the narrative in which human and divine are intimately interconnected with Earth and all its constituents in the telling of the good news/ *euangelion*.

A reading process attentive to Earth and critical of the negation of any of its constituents will need to be informed by a range of new dialogue partners. Scientists such as cosmologists, evolutionary biologists, climatologists and others provide biblical scholars seeking to read ecologically with new insights into Earth processes and the story of an emerging and expanding universe (see Russell 2008; and Butkus & Kolmes 2011 by way of example). Critical theorists introduce new ways of thinking about space, time, geography, and other aspects of Earth woven into the biblical narrative (Soja 1996; Massey 1999; Knappett and Malafouris 2008). In this search for new images and metaphors that can enable new ecological readings of the gospel to emerge from Earth's body, Joel Primack and Nancy Abrams note that '[p]oets, artists, prophets, and other thinkers through history have…shaped cosmologies with words and images' (2006: 8). Thus, poets, nature writers and others who are reading/storying Earth anew at this time will also be dialogue partners in an ecological reading process.

3. *Turning toward Text in Reading Ecologically*

At the heart of an ecological reading process is *text* whose materiality and history of materiality stretch from the original author and hearers to today. Anne Elvey (2011a: 182-83; 2011b: 14-21) explores this materiality of text and text production from its inception using papyri, velum/animal skin, and paper to today's computer chips. She demonstrates that it was not an innocent process but entailed the giving up of both plant and animal life. Traces of this history remain in the text and connect the biblical author/s and centuries of readers so that the text functions in its very materiality and sociality to make meaning. It is a place or site in/from which meaning is made, when initial attention is given to the marks on paper in the context of shared socio-cultural codes of grammar, of semantics, of language and of meaning-making narrative. It evokes habitat as both materially and socially constituting the text such that 'habitat' can function as a key category in turning toward the text in an ecological reading process.[5]

Habitat within ecological thinking is the dynamic context and contextualizing of interrelationship/s between the material, temporal, spatial and social (Wainwright 2012: 292-94). It shifts the nature/culture divide and as Code would say, it is a 'place to know' such that 'social-political, cultural, and psychological elements figure alongside physical (and I would add material) and (other) environmental contributors to the "nature" of a habitat and its inhabitants at any historical moment' (Code 2006: 37). For an ecological reader attentive to the complex web of author/text/reader in context, habitat will be significant when considering each of these and their interrelationship in order to re-turn the reading process toward Earth (the process of retrieval and identification as discussed in the Introduction). Habitat is not just place in its materiality but place in which materiality is inextricably linked to sociality[6]. In the words of Lorraine Code, habitat includes:

---

5. The term 'materiality' is used to draw attention to the vitality of matter in relation to the other-than-human and the human.
6. I define 'sociality' as a more comprehensive term than 'social' which designates

ethologies, genealogies, commitments, and power relations that shape the knowledge and subjectivities enacted there; the intractable locational specificities that resist homogenization or suggest novel connections; the positionings available or closed to would-be knowers; the amenability or resistance of both human and nonhuman entitites to being known (2006: 100).

Attention to habitat as analytic category together with a recognition of the materiality and sociality that constitute it as it is encoded in the text is foundational for this ecological reading. It is not only the materiality of the text that requires attention but the materiality of the more-than-human that is encoded into the text and its narrative (Rigby 2004: 436-37). In terms of the sociality that constitutes habitat, Elvey (2011a: 182-83) highlights a significant distinction which will inform my ecological reading, namely the use of 'the social' to refer to interconnections in the human community and 'sociality' as a more comprehensive term which references such interconnections in/among the more-than-human (which by way of its definition includes the human although within a much broader web of interconnections). Rasmussen recognizes something of this web of interrelationship when he says that 'what we call society and culture are dramatic episodes of what earth does through us as part of earth itself' (1996: 32). Interconnectivity and interrelationship between the other-than human and the human (in other words within the more-than-human) and the material agency of each constitute habitat and are central within ecological reading processes.

We turn now not only toward the text but also to the biblical methodology that will best enable ecological reading/s that contribute to the shaping of a new imaginary as explored above. The methodology that I have been developing over recent decades is a nuancing of the *socio-rhetorical* approach developed by Vernon Robbins (Robbins 1996a). It is a text-focussed approach constituted by an analysis of what Robbins calls different *textures* of the text, an apt term for an ecological reading. Robbins says of these textures that they are 'a result of webs or networks of meanings and meaning effects that humans (and I would add "Earth") create' (18). They are encoded in the text that is now accessible to us as twenty-first century interpreters but these textures also carry traces of the social, cultural and the material world/s from/in which the text originated. Hence it will be necessary to explore those social, cultural and material elements encoded in the first century text of the gospel of Matthew, not in order to recreate that world but to read the gospel text through an understanding of its encodings of that world.

---

the interconnections in/among the more-than-human (which, by way of its definition, includes the human but within a much broader web of interconnections).

Robbins focusses a first-stage engagement with the text on what he calls its *Inner Texture*, aptly sub-titling the process as 'Getting inside a Text'. He highlights six key narrational and rhetorical features of the text that he considers will facilitate such 'getting inside a text' (1996b: 7-39). Given that he has not attended to his own anthropocentric perspective, his analysis of the six aspects of the text's inner texture attends almost predominantly to the human element in the text. Within an ecological reading, an analysis of what have generally been identified as narrative characteristics (character, plot, setting) and rhetorical effects in the text will also include attention to the material and social actants constituting *habitat* within the inner texture of the text. And so, all more-than-human *characters*, that is, all Earth constituents, will be considered within the complex web of relationships woven by the text. In such a reading, what has so often been called *setting* as 'the background against which the narrative action takes place' (Resseguie 2005: 87) will function as constituent/s of habitat, and will be attended to in the analysis of the inner texture of the text within an ecological reading.

The second texture that Robbins highlights is *Intertexture*. This is founded on the recognition, familiar to biblical scholars and theorized by Julia Kristeva, that there is, in any text, a range of other texts which may be cited, evoked, reconfigured or alluded to in different ways in the text and which now function evocatively for the reader. Robbins does not limit intertexture to texts. He recognizes that the language of the text, in this instance the gospel, encodes social, cultural and historical traces constituting the *intertexture* (Robbins 1996b: 40-70). The ecological reader would want to extend those encodings to include all elements of habitat, focussing, therefore, on the more-than-human materiality and sociality and its history, not just on human socio-cultural features. In this reading, these features will tend to be considered within a third texture of the text as discussed below, namely the *ecological texture*.

Anne Elvey theorizes another aspect of intertextuality that will constitute this ecological reading. Along this axis one finds 'a mode of reading performance between later texts…and biblical ones'. Elvey identifies, by way of example, 'literary works, visual arts and film' (Elvey 2011a: 186). I would add contemporary theories of time, space, materialities and geographies together with poetry and nature writing, to name but a few. These fold back into the text's intertexture, as it were, to contribute to ecological readings and as noted above, will be highlighted in this commentary at strategic points in each new chapter.

The third texture that Robbins identifies is the *Social and Cultural Texture* (Robbins 1996b: 71-94). Here one finds characteristics of the socio-cultural life of the human community that are encoded within the text to shape meaning. As an ecological reader, I want to expand this focus on the human community by using the central analytic category of *habitat*. It is not just a new name for what biblical scholars call 'context' in inner text and its intertexts. Habitat is constituted by the materiality and sociality of the more-than-human (that is human and other-than-human) as these are embedded within the text. It is intimately connected with, intimately shaped by and shaping of Earth constituents and their story or history as well as their interrelationships.[7] It is marked by the embodiment and materiality of the more-than-human, by the physicality of space as it is shaped by and shapes relationships within the Earth community, and by the socio-cultural interdependence of these within their historical unfolding.

These aspects of habitat cannot be fully explored within the *social and cultural texture* of the text as laid out by Robbins. Both these categories are inadequate because of their focus on the human community socially and culturally. His more recent attention to rhetography ('the graphic picturing in rhetorical reasoning') and rhetology ('the logic of rhetorical reasoning') within first century Christian rhetoric has turned his analysis to include 'bodies and geophysical location' (Robbins 2009: 16). This is a significant move for the ecological interpreter seeking to engage with Robbins' methodology. His focus, however, is still not broad enough to include all the aspects of habitat that evoke attention and inclusion within an ecological imaginary. As a result, I name the third texture in my reading the *ecological texture* of the text. This will allow for consideration of the human social and cultural texture in the context of more-than-human materiality and sociality in integral relationship with/in *habitat*.

I employ the term *inter-con/textuality* for the processes that hold together attentiveness to the materiality of the more-than-human, to Earth and Earth elements in interrelationship with place and time and other features of the ecological texture with/in habitat encoded in the ecological texture of the text. I use this term in order to highlight the complex reciprocity of author-text-reader in habitat as place to know and place from which to know (textual and physical/material) in an ecological reading attentive to the ecological texture of the text. This constitutes a shifting of the overall designation of the reading approach from *socio-rhetorical* to *eco-rhetorical*.

As a result of such a shift, what Robbins identifies as the *ideological texture* of text and reading process (1996b: 95-119) is ecompassed by the three previously identified textures of the text, especially when informed by an Earth-focussed hermeneutics of suspicion. I do not, therefore, isolate

---

7. Hughes (1994: 3) says in this regard that '[h]umans are a species within an ecosystem, so that the condition of the ecosystem as it changes through time influences the direction and development of human affairs. Ecological analysis is, therefore, a crucial means of gaining understanding of human history.'

it specifically as does Robbins. I take a similar position in relation to his notion of *sacred* texture. I noted earlier that ecological thinking was characterized by a repositioning of humans in relation to all Earth-constituents of a wide range of life-forms and with the sacred or mystery. In reading biblical texts ecologically through attention to inner texture, intertexture and ecological texture, attention will be given to habitat, human and the holy in their intimate interconnectedness. The one/s named divine, holy or spirit-infused (whether that spirit be good or evil) are woven into the text, as is the human, in relation to habitat, whether that be backgrounded or foregrounded, noticed or unnoticed. It is these interrelationships that will be given attention in the process/es of reading the inner, inter- and ecological textures of the biblical text.

Below, I modify Robbins' diagram of his socio-rhetorical reading process (1996b: 21) to demonstrate the key features of the eco-rhetorical approach I am proposing. I share his recognition that the text, its world and the interpreter are separate and the focus of a socio-rhetorical reading is on the text. There is, however, a permeability of their boundaries indicated by the broken lines. The contemporary interpreter also belongs within a world and is shaped by a social imaginary that in its turn shapes the reading of both world and text. It is the text and its textures that is the primary focus of an ecological reading.

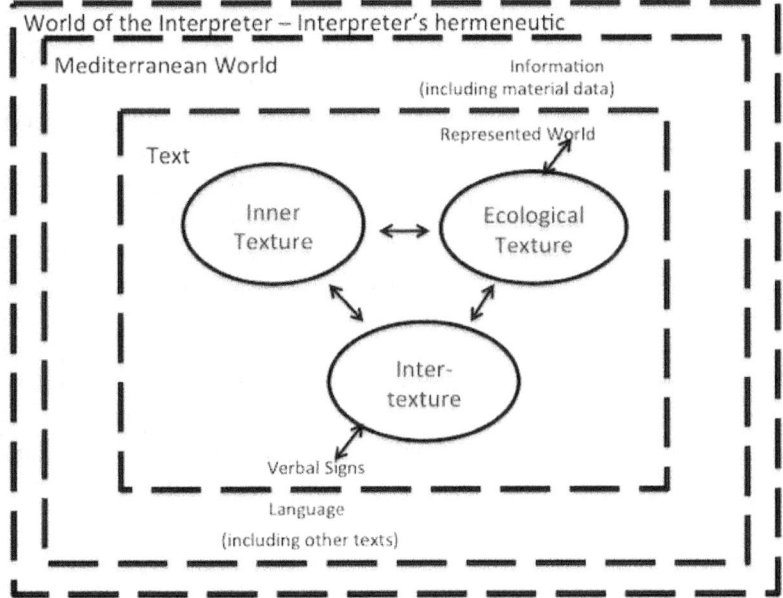

(This diagram is modified from that of Robbins [1996a: 21])

4. *Taking up the Text*

The very act of engaging the Gospel of Matthew from an ecological perspective has itself an ecological texture. I take into my hands the printed text comprised of paper and ink and all the other Earth products that have been brought together at various stages in the making of two books, *The Bible* and the *Greek New Testament*, which I hold and read. My hands touch the text while my eyes engage in the social process of reading in my own language as well as the Greek language in which the narrative was originally composed, linking me across centuries of texts and readers. Alternatively, I read the text on a computer screen, another material medium in the long tradition of transmission of text. In this mode, I do not touch the text but rather the keyboard which intervenes between myself and the text in another form (see Elvey 2010 and 2011b).[8]

The opening phrase of the gospel, *biblos geneseōs*—the account or the book of the genealogy or the family tree of Jesus *Christos*—recalls another *biblos geneseōs*, that of the 'heaven(s)/sky and earth' or the universe and all its constituents in Gen. 2.4a. This is the climactic verse of Gen. 1.1–2.4a, Earth's family tree as Habel calls it (2011). The gospel closes with another reference to 'heaven(s)/sky and earth' in 28.18 thus placing the Jesus story within the frame of Earth and its story both at the beginning and end.

Within this frame, the Matthean gospel is predominantly a narrative focussed on the Jesus story, a story of the human Jesus from birth through death to life beyond death. The primary focus of Matthean scholarship has been on Jesus' relationship with divinity and humanity. An ecological reading, as I have developed it above, takes account of such emphases both in the story and in the history of scholarship. In this reading our purview expands to include habitat as constitutive of the interrelationship between physical place/time and other processes and all Earth beings as well as relationships with the sacred. Aspects of habitat are foregrounded and backgrounded within the movement of the narrative. They will be explicitly foregrounded in this reading that seeks to be attentive to Earth in order to re-read and understand anew a well-known gospel story.

In turning attention to Earth in the Matthean gospel, I have used the alternating narrative/discourse structure within the frame of the Infancy and Passion Narratives. Attention to Earth and to habitat as reading categories has provided a different focus for these narratives and discourses as laid out below.

---

8. Understandings of the materiality of text and of the reading process have been developed by Anne Elvey in her recent works, as noted above, and they have significantly informed my own ecological thinking. I am most grateful to Elvey for her creative insights and for conversations shared.

The ecological reading that I am proposing is one that can be used for interpreting any text. It is a way of reading the entire biblical narrative and not just selected text/s that refer explicitly to 'nature'. I make no attempt to discuss each verse as is the custom in traditional commentaries. Rather, attentive to the narrative texture of the text, this commentary unfolds in sectional rather than verse-by-verse readings.

Since the gospel has a provenance or habitat of origin, traces of which are encoded in the text and will be engaged in my ecological reading, it is important to identify my position in relation to this. I share the argument of Alan Segal who proposes that the early inception and reception of the Matthean gospel took place in 'a rather loosely confederated group of congregations, united by missionaries' across 'an arc of settlement that included both the Galilee…and Pella…arched into Syria through Antioch and Edessa', with Galilee and Antioch being two fixed points (Segal 1991: 3-37). Within the Galilean context, I include Sepphoris as a potentially participating city in the circulation of traditions shaping the Matthean narrative (Gale 2005). This ecological reading will attend to the ecological texture of the Matthean text that encodes the materiality as well as the sociality of its provenance. The reader is invited to be attentive to traces or encodings of the socio-political, cultural and ecological features of early first century Galilee and Judea in the text, the context of the life of Jesus which is storied.

Finally, I wish to acknowledge that this ecological reading has been shaped by my own provenance as it shapes me. My context is that of Oceania—an Australian citizen of Anglo-Celtic origin and traditions now living and working in Aotearoa New Zealand, and influenced by the multiple cultures of this region called Oceania and their histories together with its complex ecologies and habitats. As just one of Earth's constituents within this complex web, I undertake an ecological reading of the Matthean text that will follow the structure suggested below. I invite you, the reader, to engage with the Gospel of Matthew, with this commentary, and with your own context or provenance to undertake your own ecological reading of the text.

A Guide to an Ecological Reading of the Gospel according to Matthew

The *biblos geneseōs* of the Heavens/Sky and Earth and of Jesus *Christos*

  Matthew 1–2 Place, Power, Potentiality—Genealogy and Birth of Earth and the Child

    Matthew 3–4 From Wilderness to Waterfront—Interfacing Place and Proclamation

      Matthew 5–7 Mountain Proclamation–In-formed by Earth

        Matthew 8–9 The Materiality of Bodies: Touched and Healed

          Matthew 10 Co-missioning: does it obscure Earth?

            Matthew 11–12 Walking: does it reveal Earth?

            Matthew 13 Habitat/ Humanity/Holy In-form Parables

          Matthew 14–17 Bread and Boats, Mountains and Mission—Engaged and Opposed

        Matthew 18 A Community of Reconciliation—Can it include Earth?

      Matthew 19–23 Human Conflict Impacting Earth

    Matthew 24–25 Parable, Proclamation and End Times Imagery—and What of Earth?

  Matthew 26–28 Life and Death and Life Intertwined: an Earth Process

All authority in heaven/sky and on earth has been given…to the end of the age

Chapter 2

MATTHEW 1–2:
PLACE, POWER, POTENTIALITY—GENEALOGY
AND BIRTH OF EARTH AND OF THE CHILD[1]

1. Matthew 1.1: A New Birth within Earth's Unfolding

Biblos geneseōs, the book of the genealogy (RSV), the account of the genealogy (NRSV) or a record of the genealogy (NIV) are the first words the reader's eyes encounter as s/he begins to read the Gospel of Matthew. *Biblos geneseōs* is a phrase rich in intertexture that contributes significantly to the inner texture of the text. It is woven into that inner texture and it points forward to a very specific genealogy, namely that of Jesus *Christos*. It also points back to David and to Abraham (1.1b). This opening phrase also functions intertextually with Gen. 2.4 and 5.1. It evokes the *geneseōs* of the heavens/sky and the earth[2] together with all Earth's constituents as Gen. 2.4 echoes through the first words of the Matthean gospel. The intertexture with Gen. 5.1-2 and the *geneseōs* of the human community, of the *anthrōpōn* (the human), male and female, functions to place the human story within the story of Earth, and the heavens/sky.

The evocation of the 'genealogy of the heavens/sky and the earth' functions inter-con/textually in an ecological reading. It draws the human genealogy into the cosmology of its readers. It would have done this for its

---

1. Some of the material in this chapter has appeared in the following articles: Wainwright 2009a, 2009b, 2010.

2. The Greek word *ouranos* has many layers of meaning that can play within an ecological reading. In the phrase 'heaven and earth', it can indicate those realms of the universe that, distinct from earth, form the canopy above the earth within a first century Jewish consciousness. It can also designate the 'sky' or the firmament over the earth. See BDAG 737-39 for a wide range of meanings. Since 'heaven' has taken on connotations of the transcendent as separate from earth, I use both heavens and sky to keep before us the interrelationship of 'heaven and earth' and their materiality within the universe as well as the traces of the divine that the designation 'heavens' (in the plural) leaves in the text. See Pennington (2007) for a very thorough study of 'heaven/s' and 'earth' in the Gospel of Matthew and its intertexts in the LXX and the Hebrew Bible (39-66, 99-124, 163-92).

first-century readers/hearers calling to mind, as Carter suggests, 'the larger narrative of God's creation of the world and of humans' in an imperial world, contending with the sovereign power of Rome and its gods' (Carter 2005: 154). In *A View from the Center of the Universe*, a contemporary intertext for the Genesis and Matthean texts, Primack and Abrams suggest that genealogy cannot be limited to the human community or to a particular sector of that community. Genealogy, from a cosmic viewpoint, includes, they say, 'our distant ancestors [who] are what everyone on Earth shares... [the] billions upon billions of creatures [that] have struggled so that their children would survive, and those children have led to us' (Primack and Abrams 2006: 291-92). What is important, they say, is 'to develop imagery that will bridge the incomprehensible gap between us and our 14-billion-year-old source' (293). Similarly Heather Eaton notes that for many contemporary ecotheologians 'the primary religious story is that of the emergence of life: immanent, transcendent and panentheistic' (Eaton 2005: 101). Genealogy can take the reader back to the beginning, back through the unfolding of Earth's story (and of the universe), the story of every fossil, every evolving creature and species, their emerging habitat, their interrelationships, their ecosystems. These are encoded into the ecological texture of the Matthean text through its opening phrase.

This story of Earth and of the universe functions intertextually not only at the very beginning but also the very end of the Gospel of Matthew when Jesus locates his authorization to commission disciples in the heavens/sky and on the earth (28.18). This repetition of the heavens/sky and Earth form a frame for the Matthean narrative, for this *biblos geneseōs*. Tsumura suggests that the author of Genesis 1, who tells of the creation of the heavens/sky and the earth, 'uses experiential language...to explain the initial situation of the earth as "not yet"' (1994: 327). The ecological reader must search for language to point to the 'not yet' nature of our understanding of the expanding universe drawn into this text.

The opening phrase of the Matthean gospel also evokes, as noted above, the *anthrōpōn*, male and female that, in the Genesis narrative, is placed within the frame of the genealogy of the heavens/sky and the earth. Genesis 5.1-2 echoes the language of Gen. 1.27: humanity created in the image of divinity and created male and female in the context of the emergence of other Earth constituents—the sun, moon and stars, water, and land, habitat for the flora and fauna in their multiple kinds which will reproduce in order to guarantee their continuation. This earlier text (Gen. 1.27) is, however, intimately connected with and followed by Gen. 1.28 with its command not only to fertility but also to dominion. The intertextual allusion to Gen. 5.1-2 in the opening phrase of the Matthean gospel echoes the story of the human ones within the story of Earth and the universe but carries the hint of domination, not only of human over the other-than-human (Gen. 1.28) but also that of male over female (Gen. 3.16). While Genesis proclaims the species as created male and female (Gen. 1.27; 5.2), the genderizing of the narrative is predominantly male (Bird 1994: 357).

For the contemporary ecological interpreter, there is a tension drawn into the opening phrase of Mt. 1.1. On the one hand, the human, male and female, is located poetically within Earth's unfolding and linked intimately with divine creativity. On the other hand, mastery is conferred upon the human identified predominantly as male. Reproduction that is linked to this mastery and as a blessing has become a problem for the current constituents of planet Earth,[3] as has human mastery and the gendering of that mastery. It functions as the dominant paradigm, at least in the West, and it has been recognized by Val Plumwood and Lorraine Code as shaping what Code calls the 'instituted imaginary' (Plumwood 1993 and Code 2006: 28-33).

Inter-con/textuality in the opening phrase of Mt. 1.1 also invites readers to draw into the text's ecological texture a range of indigenous cosmologies that interweave genealogy and land. For New Zealand Maori, by way of example, *whakapapa* or genealogy is a key to identity conceived not narrowly but cosmically. The poet Apirana Taylor captures this:

> Whakapapa whakapapa ties you to the land…
> this is your inheritance
> the sky and earth and all that lies between (Taylor 1996: 10-11).

This can remind readers that for each generation of the Matthean genealogy, there is a habitat, there is the land to which they are 'tied' while belonging to the genealogy of the heavens/sky and earth or 'sky, earth and all that lies between' in Taylor's words.

Warren Carter has drawn attention to further inter-con/textuality in Gen. 2.4 and 5.1-2. He notes that intertextually Mt. 1.1a makes clear the claim that the genealogy of the heavens/sky and the earth and the human community is intimately linked with divinity in contrast to the claims of first century Romans for whom their emperors were 'lords of the world' (Virgil, *Aeneid* 1.282) and 'master[s] of sea and land' in Philostratus, *Life*

---

3. Countless works address this issue. See for instance Ehrlich, Ehrlich and Daily (1995) who study the intersection between population and food supply, issues with which the authors of Genesis also seemed to be concerned. They note that '[i]n human beings, as for all other sexually reproducing animals, issues related to reproducing and eating pervade virtually ever aspect of human existence. This means that keeping the plow ahead of the stork cannot be viewed simply as a face-off between agricultural and contraceptive technologies. People's relationships with each other—social, economic, and political—strongly influence their patterns of reproduction. Those relationships along with the size of the population in turn shape the all-important biophysical, social, economic, and political environments in which the agricultural system must function.' Habitat and humanity are intimately linked within the network of all Earth constituents.

of Apollonius 7.3 (Carter 2004a: 261-63). Contemporary ecological readers are therefore attentive to those imperial political and socio-economic powers that claim and act out of the claim that they now are 'master(s) of sea and land'.

The *biblos geneseōs* becomes very specific in the second half of the verse and provides the focus of this particular human genealogy—it is of the one who is designated *Iēsou Christou*. This same name frames the genealogy (1.1 and 1.17) and provides a textual link between 1.16 and 1.18. In v. 16, the name Jesus is followed by the phrase 'who is called the Messiah (the anointed, the *Christos*)', whereas in v. 17 *Christos* stands alone in designating Jesus. Verse 18 parallels v. 1 in that *Christos* follows immediately upon the name Jesus. It seems that by the time of the compilation of the Gospel of Matthew, *Christos* or anointed one had become synonymous with the name Jesus.

Reading inter-con/textually in relation to the name *Christos* can turn attention to Ps. 72, the psalm of the ideal king (Ps. 72.1). The psalm does not use the term *Christos* or 'anointed one' but in the religious imagination of Israel, the king was the anointed one and the anticipated anointed one was imaged as ideal king among some first century Jewish communities. Psalm 72 is replete with language that readers of the Matthean narrative will encounter as the story unfolds, especially that of 'righteousness' or *dikaiosynē* (Mt. 3.15; 5.6, 10, 21; 6.1, 33; 21.32). The psalmist's ideal vision is one of right relationships within the Earth community. The prayer is that there will be peace and justice especially for the poor and the needy as the mountains and hills yield in righteousness (Ps. 72.1-7, 12-14, 16). The images of this psalm combine kingship and liberation or justice in a way that can inform the meaning-making of contemporary ecological readers. A note of caution should be sounded, however, in that the psalmist also prayed for the king to have dominion, dominion over land and over nations with all their resources. Reading critically against the grain or with a suspicion of this aspect of the image of the ideal king, as was necessary earlier in relation to human dominion, will be important in relation to the alternative vision of *basileia* which will be introduced into the gospel as Jesus takes up his *basileia* ministry.

Rhetorically, Mt. 1.1 and its rich inter-con/textuality prepare readers for the possibility of a new narrative, a new story of the heavens/sky and the earth, a new story of Earth held together within the woven tapestry of text, the *biblos*. *Biblos*, like *genesis* or genealogy, functions multivalently in an ecological reading of Matthew's gospel. Prior to its designation of book or narrative, *biblos* named the bark, the inner bark of the papyrus plant from which the sheets of papyrus were made to be used as the carrier of writing, of narrative, of story (the original gospel texts were most likely written on papyrus). This designation carries the reader back to the papyrus plant. Theophrastus, *Enquiry into Plants* 4.8.3, situates the familiar use of the *biblos* or inner rind of the papyrus as material for the making of rolls on which writing was done among other uses such as for clothing as well as for food (see also Pliny, *Nat.* 13.12, 71-72). *Biblos* functions within the web of life of the Earth community. Theophrastus also specifies its habitat, in the shallow waters of the Nile and around a lake in Syria. There is a genealogy here also from the *biblos* as rind of the papyrus to the sheet on which the Matthean gospel was written and from which it would have been read over generations and perhaps centuries. This involved reciprocally the papyrus, the human labour (perhaps of slaves) which transformed it, the culture that surrounded its making and perhaps a lake in Syria from which it was harvested together with all those places where it would have been housed and the hands which would have carried and unrolled it or turned its pages (see Elvey 2011b: 2-21).

Pliny links the papyrus with the human 'employment of paper' reminding readers of the giving up of a life, that of the papyrus, to constitute this *biblos*. Such a gift invites respect and attentiveness to gift and gift giving as well as to the possibility of exploitation of the gift as the human community devours old-growth forests to serve its needs or wants. Gift and reciprocity function as key themes of the Matthean gospel narrative that follows and require careful and ethical attention in ecological thinking and reading today (see Manolopoulos 2009). It will be particularly manifest in the giving up of the life of Jesus, the central human character in the narrative.

2. *Matthew 1.2-17: Genealogy Unfolding*

Mt. 1.2—Abraham was the father of Isaac, and Isaac the father of Jacob, and Jacob the father of Judah and his brothers.

This is the first of the thirty-nine times repeated 'male was the father of male' formula. It is the human genealogy of Jesus *Christos* with the emphasis on the representative male as in Gen. 5.1-32. Others have explored the biblical intertextuality operative in the Matthean genealogy, most notably Marshall Johnson (1988: 146-228). Reading ecologically, it would seem that all that was evoked by the *biblos geneseōs* has been erased, directing the reader exclusively to the human story. Attention to inter-con/textuality, however, alerts readers not just to successive generations of human kin giving identity to Jesus *Christos* as subject of the genealogy, but also to their habitats. Verse 2—'Abraham was the father of Isaac, and Isaac the father of Jacob, and Jacob the father of Judah and his brothers'—as exemplary of each of the remaining 38 parallel phrases, draws initial attention to the socio-cultural matrix of family (albeit with female members erased) in the text of Genesis 12–50 and to the history of this family that is drawn into the Matthean text intertextually.[4] But Mt. 1.2 also evokes inter-con/textually, the land of Canaan through which Abraham journeyed and in which other peoples dwelt, a land which is characterized by a number of different eco-zones and Earth's constituents (Hillel 2006). It is land in its specificity. At the beginning of the Abraham story stands the divine demand that he leave his country or his land and go to another land that will be shown to him. Just as it is not possible to trace the intricacies of kinship through Genesis 12–50—they are merely evoked by the short verse of Mt. 1.2—so too is it impossible to trace through all the ways in which family and land are interconnected in those same stories. Some brief critical comments will have to suffice.

Norman Habel draws attention to the intimate connection between the immigrant Abrahamic family and the land. The family is not threatened by eviction nor do its members dominate the land. Instead the land offers them hospitality so that Habel can claim that '[t]he ancient trails of the ancestors and the sacred sites they establish turn the territory into a storied landscape in which the history of Israel's beginnings is tangibly recorded' (1995: 119). What is silenced by this story is that of the inhabitants of the land (Canaanites among others—Gen. 10.18; 12.6; 13.7; 15.21) and the way that they storied that land and related to it– a way that likewise belongs to the genealogy of the heavens and the earth, the unfolding of Earth's story. What is also silenced in the Genesis story is the voice of Earth's multiple constituents telling their story or their genealogy. Only land is storied and that in and through the voice/s of a small human group who are designated as 'chosen'.

Gene McAfee, who brings a specific ecological perspective to the reading of Israel's origins, recognizes some of the problematics in the Abrahamic narrative that is drawn into the Matthean gospel intertextually. Indeed, he sees the Abrahamic narrative at odds with ecojustice principles, saying that '[n]one of that narrative's central concerns are focused on the natural environment as an active participant in Abraham's story' (McAfee 2000: 159). Examining the link between land and the fertility of a chosen group, McAfee draws the radical conclusion that

> [t]he desideratum of the chosen people in a chosen land emphasizes separation, distinctiveness, hierarchical relationships and exclusiveness—a worldview that is deeply at odds with a sensibility that views interconnectedness as the fundamental fact of ecological existence (174).

Matthean inter-con/textuality carries a warning, therefore, as well as a potential. It draws land with all its contours—its well-watered plains (Gen. 13.10), its wilderness (14.6; 16.7, 21, 14. 20, 21), its springs (16.7) and its

---

4. Reference to 'Judah' not only evokes the tribe but could also encode within the ecological texture of the text, the land that would later be given that name.

valleys (14.3, 8, 10, 17; 26.17, 19) into the remembering of Abraham, Isaac and Jacob together with Sarah, Rebecca, Rachel and Leah as the ancestors of Jesus. The contemporary ecological reader will want to read against the grain of the Abrahamic evocation and make a space for the silenced story of the land of Canaan and its constituents of the Abrahamic period to find their voices, as well as to allow the reproduction connected with privilege and chosen-ness to sound its warning. Similar critiques could be brought to each of the generations of the genealogy.

For the Matthean reader, Mt. 1.3 (*and Judah the father of Perez and Zerah by Tamar, and Perez the father of Hezron, and Hezron the father of* Aram) together with vv. 5 and 6 form a pattern that breaks the overall pattern of the genealogy already established in 1.2 (see Wainwright 1991: 60-69, 160-70). This opens up a space for an ecological reading. In vv. 3 and 5, the phrase *ek tēs* is followed by the name of a female, Tamar, Rahab and Ruth, and in v. 6, it is followed by the phrase 'the wife of Uriah'. Thus only four of the women of the thirty-nine generations are explicitly named. Their naming, however, alerts readers to the erasure of other women from the verses of the genealogy: Sarah, Rebecca, Rachel, and the many other mothers whose names have been lost to us. Their birthing processes need, therefore, to be re-membered. In that remembering, Tamar, Rahab, Ruth, and Bathsheba, named as the 'wife of Uriah', echo through women's search for new ways of both re-imagining and enacting the interconnection between gender, nature and culture, an important aspect of ecological thinking (see Ortner 1974: 67-87).

Inter-con/textuality alerts readers to the mosaic not only of texts but of habitats in Genesis 38 which are woven into Mt. 1.3. Bath-Shua carries in her womb/conceives and gives birth to Judah's first three sons—Er, Onan and Chezib. The materiality of the pregnant female body of Bath-Shua, three-times pregnant, alerts readers to the gestation and birth process over time, nine months of time, together with the material changes in the body of the woman, that is obscured not only by the brief *Judah the father of Perez and Zerah* but in each of the entries in the genealogy.[5] Bodily processes are woven into culture by way of Judah's evocation of the Levirate law following the death of his first-born son, Er. Tamar, Er's wife, is given to Onan (his spilling of his seed on the ground alerts readers to the materiality of male generation also) but when he too dies, Judah does not give Tamar to Chezib in accordance with the cultural custom or law but returns her to her father's house. Tamar, therefore, stands ambiguously in relation to the profound intersection of nature and culture.

She inserts herself into a designated place, Enaim 'on the road to Timnah' (Gen. 38.14) where Judah was going up 'to shear his sheep' (Gen. 38.13).

---

5. See Elvey 2005: 31-110 for a general discussion of the pregnant bodies and Earth informing an ecological reading of biblical texts.

Habitat is evoked as both Tamar and Judah are in relationship with place and animals. Tamar does not accept the offer of a kid from Judah's herd in payment for his having intercourse with her, an offer which would keep her, in the world of male power and generation, linked only to the materiality of the other-than-human, a link perpetuated by patriarchy.[6] Rather she takes hold of the symbols of culture, male culture: your signet and your cord, and the staff that is in your hand (Gen. 38.18). In an ecological reading, Judah's proclamation that Tamar is more righteous, more in the right than he (Gen. 38.26) can be heard as a challenge to the gender–nature–culture divides that Tamar has crossed. This text is rich in materiality: the male seed, the pregnant female body, animals, place and the symbols of culture (the ring, the cord and the staff). Materiality and gendered socio-cultural mores intersect profoundly with-in the human drama and call for attention.

The analysis above has pointed beyond suspicion and reconfiguration. Attentiveness to the subtle intersection of nature and culture in the text and the gender infusion encoding this intersection can facilitate an ecological reading that participates in the unravelling of the long-standing distinctions between nature and culture and their gendering. The emerging new way/s of reading contribute to the new social imaginary that is ecological thinking.

In Mt. 1.5—Rahab and Ruth: *and Salmon the father of Boaz by Rahab, and Boaz the father of Obed by Ruth, and Obed the father of Jesse*—two more women are named. Matthean storytelling seems to collapse history so that the Rahab of Josh. 2.1-21; 6.16-17 and 20-22 is named as the mother of Boaz who with Ruth gave life to Obed. In this way, the stories of Rahab and Ruth are closely connected. Theirs are the stories of the 'outsider' in relation to the authoritative narrative voice and perspective. Rahab belongs among the inhabitants of Canaan, a resident of the city of Jericho before its destruction. Ruth is a Moabite of the 'scandalous country of Lot's daughters', as Laura Donaldson notes (2006: 161). Women, land and city are closely identified as objects for mastery in the narratives of these two women, highlighted by way of their inclusion in the Matthean genealogy. Having explored in the previous section ways of reading that might undo the gender/nature/culture nexus viewed hierarchically, I turn here to the potential for an ecological reading that attention to Rahab and Ruth makes possible through their unpredictable inclusion in the Matthean text. Musa Dube draws attention to 'the ideology of employing gender in narratives that legitimate the domination of one nation by another'. She goes on to say:

---

6. There is a danger, however, in such a critique of the patriarchal linking of the female with the material (not the cultural) that we obscure or background the material integrity of the 'other', in this instance, the kid. An ecological reading needs to foreground this more-than-human actant while maintaining the patriarchal critique.

> I note how Jericho itself has been portrayed as the body of a sex worker, which easily changes hands from one master to another. The story tells us that Jericho must be entered and taken and indeed Jericho is entered and taken (Dube 2005: 179).

Such a reading intervenes in the colonial and sexual/heterosexual dominations that Rahab is intended to serve. Dube invites a reading of Rahab as one who intervenes in the destructive politics of domination, being prepared to intercede for at least one family to be saved, 'to look through a small window of hope', to 'hang a red ribbon' (180). Attentiveness to such colonial and sexual intersections in the ecological texture of a text is an important constituent of an ecological reading.

What Dube does is to map power in the Rahab narrative in a different way—neither as the 'sovereign model' of hierarchical power nor necessarily on the postmodern 'globalized, flattened but mobile, gridlike terrain'. Rather she maps power as a 'site of multidimensionality' (Sandoval 2000: 72-78). It is a mapping and recognition of the performance of power.

An ecological reading turns attention to how power is mapped in relation to Earth. The reader recognizes a very different construction of land from that in the Abrahamic narrative. Land is to be 'viewed' by the Israelite spies (Josh. 2.1), to be the object of their gaze indicating a power over the land or desire for power over. Its city, Jericho, the place of abode of many households and families like that of Rahab, together with 'oxen, sheep and donkeys', is to be entered, conquered and 'devoted to destruction' (Josh. 6.21). War and ideologies of war impact not only on the human community but also on the entire ecosystem/s where they are perpetrated (see Ruether 1992: 102-111). They are acts of power often expressed sexually as rape, as entering the house of Rahab (Josh. 2.1) and the entering of the body of Rahab implied in the text, as Dube suggests.

Before leaving the Rahab narrative as evoked in the Matthean genealogy, with its theme of destructive mastery, I want to return to the narrative's placing of Rahab in the borderland. She is placed in the physical space of the house built into the wall, one of the casemate rooms within ancient walled cities. She did, indeed, reside within the wall itself (Josh. 2.15). She represents the human in relation to habitat, in this context built habitat, and such built habitat can remind readers of the multidimensional relationality that location entails. There is also a brief but very explicit reference to Rahab's relationship with the other-than-human in her context. The text tells us that she hid the spies 'with the stalks of flax that she had laid out on the roof' (Josh. 2.6). There is a sense in this text of temporality—the event intrudes into the seasons of Rahab's life and the seasons of Earth. That she had laid the stalks of flax out on the roof indicates that she was engaged in a life-supporting industry with Earth elements, namely flax which was, as Oded Borowski says, 'a raw material in weaving...and making clothes... It was used for belts...

ropes, …and wicks for oil lamps' (Borowski 2002: 98-99). This brief reference places Rahab on another border, that between city as built environment and land as agricultural space. It places her not only in relationship with those men who would use her body for their pleasure but also in relation to the multidimensionality of participating in Earth's unfolding.

Ruth too draws a complex web of relationships into the Matthean genealogy. She is ethnic outsider to the storyteller of Israel's narrative, hated outsider. She, like Rahab, forsakes her own people, her culture, and her land to become incorporated into Israel's narrative. She too is a borderland woman: a book in Israel's sacred narratives bears her name but she, like so many other women in Israel's story is erased from genealogy even within that book (see Ruth 4.18-22). Also, the child she bears in her body is claimed by the women of Bethlehem as the son who is born to Naomi (Ruth 4.17).

Laura Donaldson draws attention to the social imaginary that informs the Ruth narrative, namely what she calls 'social absorption' of the outsider or the 'other' (2006: 164). The counter-sign that the narrative evokes for her, however, is that of Orpah who returns not just to her own land but also to her 'mother's house' (Ruth 1.8). Donaldson says of the contrast between the two Moabite women:

> [f]or 'Ruth the Moabite', the translation from savagery to civilization (or from Asherah to Yahweh) similarly involves the relinquishing of her ethnic and cultural identity. For Orpah, it necessitates a courageous act of self and communal affirmation: the choosing of the indigenous mother's house over that of the alien Israelite Father (168).

An ecological reading that is shaped by and is shaping a new social imaginary will not only read against the grain of the insider/outsider construct of the Book of Ruth, it will also read Ruth anew as Dube did with Rahab. Ruth's commitment to Naomi can be read beyond the patriarchal, Israelite and dominant religion constructs. A young woman commits herself to an older woman in the intimacy of relationship beyond the socio-religious and even familial constructs. Just as she and her kinship group opened their land, their space, their dwelling and their burial places to Naomi, Elimelech and their two sons, Mahlon and Chilion as a result of variations in ecosystems, Ruth trusts that she will receive the same hospitality even to the point of the hospitality of burial (Ruth 1.16-17) as a result of her faithful relationship with Naomi. Both women can live in new ways in Beth-lehem, the house of bread. In a world in which entire communities are being forced to become refugees (as were Naomi, Elimelech, Mahlon and Chilion) because of climate change and rising sea levels, hospitality beyond cultural and religious domination and mastery will be essential. The story of Ruth read from the perspective of Earth can inform such a hospitality.[7]

---

7. See by way of example Emma Brindal, 'Climate Change Refugees the Forgotten

Matthew 1.6—*Jesse the father of King David. And David was the father of Solomon by the wife of Uriah*—brings readers to the end of the first section of the genealogy that is framed by Abraham and David, the two ancestors with whom Jesus is associated in Mt. 1.1. The reference to David as king draws the narratives of David's kingship into the Matthean text intertextually with evocations that we will explore later in the gospel. The reference to the mother of Solomon as 'wife of Uriah' draws into this verse echoes of 2 Samuel 11–12 but especially the narrative of 2 Samuel 11 and the reference in 2 Sam. 12.24 to Bathsheba bearing a son named Solomon.

Liliam Klein provides one way of reading Bathsheba as her story is narrated in 2 Samuel 11–12. She notes that Bathsheba's body acts and speaks before she is given actual words (2 Sam. 11.5) intimating that 'motherhood' may have been her desire in bathing in a public place, relating her closely to Tamar and Ruth (Klein 2000: 54-55). The naming of the *anthropos*, predominantly male but four times female in the genealogy, can obscure the material process of conception, pregnancy and birth, all of which are evoked in the inter-con/textuality of 2 Samuel 11–12. And there is also the stages of life as the one born grows to the maturity necessary to engender the next generation. This is a process not only confined to the human species but belonging to fauna and flora also.

Culture, however, shapes this process in the human community and often obscures it as the story of David's violation of Uriah and Bathsheba's marriage relationship and his authorization of Uriah's murder demonstrate. 2 Samuel provides the critique of such power residing in culture. Nathan concludes the parable of the ewe lamb that a rich man takes from one who is poor with a pointing of his finger at David: 'You are the man!' (2 Sam. 12.7). The story of David and his use and abuse of power especially in relation to generation requires further significant critique which must be undertaken elsewhere. Suffice here to note the inter-con/textuality of human generation as it is drawn into the Matthean genealogy highlighted by the naming of the wife of Uriah/Bathsheba.

The genealogy will go on for several generations (Mt. 1.6-16) and with each, the ecological reader will need to read against the grain of isolated human generation and read with other Earth constituents who participate in the many habitats in which the named humans function. These Earth constituents and the more-than-human sociality encoded into this genealogy indeed constitute it—it is a genealogy or a book of the genealogy of heavens/sky and Earth. I now turn to the final generation.

People', *The Age*, 18 March, 2008. http://www.theage.com.au/opinion/climate-change-refugees-the-forgotten-people-20080617-2s5b.ht?page=-1 (accessed 7 March 2009).

3. *Matthew 1.16-25: Birth in an Ecological Context*

...and Jacob the father of Joseph the husband of Mary, of whom Jesus was born, who is called the Messiah...
Now the birth of Jesus the Messiah took place in this way. When his mother Mary had been engaged to Joseph, but before they lived together, she was found to be with child from the Holy Spirit...

We have noted earlier that male engendering in the context of genealogy tended to obscure the materiality of the birth process as well as the unfolding of the heavens/sky and the Earth and all their constituents. Both vv. 16 and 18 appear as if they will return the readers' attention at least to the process of pregnancy and birthing in their materiality. The second half of Mt. 1.16 that should provide the culmination of the genealogy, in fact completely undermines its careful patterning. Mary, of whom Joseph is husband, is the one of whom the child called the *Christos* was born, the *ek hēs egennēthē* of this verse linking this birth explicitly with those of vv. 3, 5 and 6 in which the mother was named: Tamar, Rahab, Ruth and 'the wife of Uriah'. Here rupture and displacement, characteristics that Foucault recognized as constituting genealogy (Foucault 1977: 149),[8] open up the textual potential for an ecological reading that displaces readings characterized by mastery, whether human or divine, and make possible new ways of reading and theologizing. The birth of Jesus, the *Christos*, is located within a genealogy, namely of Earth, in and through which traces of the divine may be heard. The text does not explicate this but intertextually and inter-con/textually, G*d, the divine mystery, is revealing G*dself in this *biblos geneseōs* that belongs within the broader canvas: that of the heavens/sky and Earth in which the *genesis* of the *anthropōn*, male and female, takes its place as does this particular birth of Jesus Christos.

Pregnancy in 1.18 is hedged around with cultural mores. The betrothal period of Jewish law is the temporal setting of 1.18-25 and it draws into the narrative the future potential of a shared physical space for Joseph and Mary: 'before they lived together'. Elements of habitat seem shadowy or almost absent from this narrative. What is not shadowy or absent is the materiality of pregnancy: Mary has a child in her womb (*en gastri echousa*). Almost before readers can appreciate the materiality of this pregnancy and the birth of Mary as mother (see Elvey 2005: 111-42), the Matthean narrator inserts the phrase *ek pneumatos hagiou* (1.18, 20—from, out of, or by a spirit that is holy), to describe the *genesis* of Jesus. Denis Edwards in *Breath of Life: A Theology of the Creator Spirit* envisions the spirit that is holy as

---

8. Foucault's own words in relation to genealogy are significant here: '(it) is not the erecting of foundations: on the contrary, it disturbs what was previously considered immobile; it fragments what was thought unified; it shows the heterogeneity of what was imagined consistent in itself' (1977: 149).

'breathing life into the universe in all its stages: into its laws and initial conditions, its origin and its evolution' (Edwards 2004: 43). It is this spirit that links the birth of the human Jesus to all other births of the more-than-human or Earth constituents, in the ongoing becoming of what is new:

> [t]he Creator Spirit is not to be thought of as simply sustaining the universe, but must be thought of as enabling and empowering the genuinely new to occur. The Spirit can be understood as the immanent divine power that enables evolutionary emergence, continually giving to creation itself the capacity to transcend itself and become more than it is (Edwards 2004: 43-45, 48).

The spirit who can be linked, in this view, to the genealogy of the heavens/ sky and the Earth in its unfolding over billions of years and through multiple processes is also intimately connected to the unfolding of genealogy, male and female and in this particular birth which is being storied, namely that of Jesus. Habitat and the holy are intertwined.

The gestating child has a habitat—*en gastri*, in the womb, in the body of the woman Mary, his mother (1.18). Anne Elvey explores in great detail the significance of the pregnant body for an ecological reading of the Gospel of Luke (2005: 31-110). She notes that 'in pregnancy the male is not autonomous' (45) and that the birth of the child from the pregnant woman also represents the birth of the mother (111-17).[9] In the Matthean narrative, *mētēr*/ mother does not occur until 1.18 in relation to the *genesis* of Jesus when both the mother and the child are born in and through their interconnectedness with/in the pregnant body. This pregnancy and birth are bound up with kinship as Joseph struggles with the pregnancy of his betrothed from a source other than his seed. It is the divine voice which assures him that this pregnancy is holy and the narrator confirms this with the fulfillment text: in this child, in this pregnancy, in this birth, G*d is with G*d's people in a new way (1.22-23). The pregnant body, the materiality of this body, its potential to birth the new and hence its intimate relationship with life (and with death) is the site of divine/human encounter in the context of biotic community. John Haught has suggested that the evolution of the cosmos is the most 'fundamental mode of the unfolding of the divine mystery' (Haught 2004: 236). Within that, the birth of this child is a particular manifestation of that unfolding and has its place within it.

In the Matthean narrative, this birth has a purpose: Jesus is to save his people (1.21). This claim is informed by way of its intertextuality with Israel's sacred story (Wainwright 1998: 59; Carter 2001: 75-90; Carter 2005, 156-57).[10] Just as G*d saved the enslaved Hebrews from the imperial power

---

9. Note that so many mothers have not had their birthing as mothers narrated or evoked in the genealogy.

10. In the first reference, Carter explores the intertextuality with Moses in the

of Egypt through Moses whose birth narrative is told in the opening chapters of the Book of Exodus, so too G*d is now going to demonstrate G*d's power to save through Jesus whose birth narrative is unfolding in this opening chapter of the Matthean gospel.

There is also another birth evoked intertextually in Mt. 1.21 and cited explicitly in v. 23, namely that of the child who will be called Emmanuel (Isa. 7.9). Imperial powers loom one behind the other in this intertext as Israel and Syria join forces against Judah with all, in turn, being under the threat of Assyrian invasion. A woman pregnant with child constitutes the symbolic force that stands against these powers of empires. The task of 'saving', the task given to Jesus, has not only religious but political implications. It is important, however, to critique the mapping of power in this text's intertexts, especially the Joshua narrative as evoked by the name *Jesus/Joshua*, in particular their construction of divine power that destroys one people for the sake of saving another attendant on a theology of choice or election. Only after such a critique can this Matthean text and its intertexts be read as a remapping of power: G*d is with G*d's people in the birth of the child of the endangered pregnant mother, Mary.

Power is not operative only within the human community but always functions and is performed within the biotic community and the unfolding cosmos. In the face of the current ecological crisis, the cry—can we 'save the earth'? (Primack and Abrams 2006: 37)—is one which calls for a much more expansive reading of the birth narrative of Jesus who will save.[11] While Carter notes that an interpretation that separates a religious or moral interpretation of Jesus' saving from its political implication is inadequate (Carter 2001: 106), I would argue that failing to extend considerations of power beyond the socio-political to include the ecological and the functioning of power within ecological communities is likewise inadequate. Kate Rigby, drawing on Heidegger, offers one way to understand 'saving' ecologically. It is not so much a rescuing but rather 'freeing something into "its own presencing"', namely, freeing Earth into its own presencing (2004: 431).

Within such a reading, the Matthean gospel is suggesting that G*d is with 'us', Earth and all Earth's constituents (1.23), not just as a particular

---

Exodus narrative and in Isa. 7–9. In the second, he examines the intertext for the name of Jesus—Joshua/Jesus. He points to Joshua's mission to complete the work of saving G*d's people begun in the Exodus by obtaining the land of Canaan. He does not, however, draw attention to the model in the book of Joshua which is conquest of land and destruction of animals, the built environment and human 'others'.

11. I am conscious, in engaging with this text of Primack and Abrams, that it is important not to read the notion of saving from an anthropocentric perspective but rather to listen to Earth, to learn from Earth as well as from the human community within it, how Earth can be engaged in the process of restoration to wholeness/holiness.

geographical, historical, political and economic community but as all who participate in the biotic and abiotic Earth community within the context of a new ecological imaginary. The Matthean depiction of Jesus as 'G*d with us' recognizes a particular moment in the unfolding of the Earth story in and through which traces of the divine revealed in a particular human/earthed being (Jesus) are freed into their own presencing. G*d has been 'with us' from the beginning as indicated in the genealogy's opening and unfolding. G*d is now with us, the contemporary Earth community, in the birth of this particular child in all his materiality and his con-textuality replete with the web of multiple interrelationships that constitute this Jesus.

This story participates then in what Eaton calls the 'primary religious story' which is 'the emergence of life: immanent, transcendent and panentheistic' (2005: 101). Indeed, it is a particular moment within that emergence. Or as James Nash indicates, '[i]n the incarnation, God identified with the Representative of Humanity, and entered thereby into solidarity not only with all humanity but also with the whole biophysical world' (Nash 1996: 8). It is the unfolding of this identification, of this solidarity that will characterize the Matthean gospel narrative until its closing frame of 'heaven and earth' (28.18).

4. *Matthew 2.1-12: Place and Power*[12]

In the time of King Herod, after Jesus was born in Bethlehem of Judea, wise men from the East came to Jerusalem.

The opening phrase of the Greek text of Matthew 2, *tou de Iēsou gennēthentos* (when Jesus was born), links this chapter with the *genesis* or birth theme of Matthew 1. This link together with the physical and temporal location—Bethlehem of Judea and the days of King Herod—encode into the ecological texture of this text the material, social and political characteristics that constitute habitat (Code 2006: 69; Hagner 1993: 23; Davies and Allison 1988: 232-33, 235).[13] An ecological reader will note that reference to the small village or town of Bethlehem, south of the large city of Jerusalem (both built environments) precedes that of reference to the days of Herod, the king—an order that is often reversed in translation (NRSV has '[i]n the time of King Herod, after Jesus was born in Bethlehem of Judea').

The *genesis* of Jesus takes place in Bethlehem of Judea (2.1; cf. 2.5, 6, 8, 16), the very name of the village being evocative. Literally, it means 'house

---

12. Material in this section appeared earlier in Wainwright 2010a: 159-67. It has been re-worked and abbreviated.

13. Code (69) notes that 'temporal, physical, social location and interdependence are integral to the possibility of being, knowing and doing'. I would add 'interpreting ecologically'.

of bread' and so links the place of Jesus' birth with human habitation or house and all its constituent materiality. In this instance, house is linked etymologically with bread, the staple of human sustenance. This bread requires the agricultural activity that takes account of soil and seed (see Mt. 13.3-9) to produce grain and the domestic work with mortar and pestle to produce flour and the other ingredients that go into the production of bread (Mt. 13.33). This naming of place and its symbolism locates the birth of Jesus within the rich and diverse relationships within the Earth community. Just as the pregnant Mary gave of her body and its nutrients to the growing foetus, so too the grains of wheat are given up to the making of flour and bread that feed the human community. There is in these connections the traces of death and life preparing the reading community for the giving over by Jesus of his life for the sake of life later in the narrative.[14]

The explicit naming of Bethlehem of Judea as the birth-place of Jesus draws the reader's attention to habitat as a constituent of both the inner and ecological textures of the Matthean text. Bethlehem of Judea was a small village approximately five miles south/south-west of Jerusalem. Archaeology yields little evidence of this village from the first century CE or thereabouts (Manor 1997: 302), leaving us to assume that at the time of the birth of Jesus, it was a small village servicing the agricultural activity of its environs. Its houses, like that in which Mary and Joseph dwelt (2.11) and presumably in which Jesus was born (2.1), would have been typical of the area, a simple house possibly with courtyard and second-storey (Hirschfield 1995: 24-44). The village does not seem to have major social, political or cultural importance at the time of Jesus' birth but would have participated like many other villages of the region of Judea in the rhythms and seasons of agricultural and human life. Its importance in this narrative is that it is the birth-place of Jesus. It locates this birth in which G*d is with us, the Earth-community, in a very specific place, one rich in inter-con/textualities too numerous to develop further (see Wainwright 2010a: 161-62). What is evident, however, is that habitat, the human and the holy are inextricably intertwined.

The *genesis* of Jesus as well as being associated with a specific place also takes place at an explicit time, in the days of Herod who is named *basileus* (2.1). These days can be charted chronologically as many have done, locating the death of Herod referred to in Mt. 2.19 'just before Passover 4 BCE' and hence calculating approximately 7 BCE for the birth of Jesus

---

14. Mt. 20.28 speaks of the giving of life as a 'ransom' for many. While an ecological reading would question the scapegoat aspect of this reference and its link to atonement theologies, it is possible to explore the potential meaning of this verse within the context of gift and exchange, an aspect that will receive further attention later in this commentary and to which I simply draw attention here. Note also G.C. Spivak (1993: 151), who discusses how '[g]estation is thus inscribed into this larger economy of death'.

(Richardson 1996: 296), emphasizing the locating of Jesus within the construct of time. The reference, however, is not just to chronological time (Lucas 2005: 1-31). Herod's designation, *basileus* (J *Ant* 14.381-389 in context of 14.158–17.191), encodes in the ecological texture of the Matthean text the political, social and cultural resonances of the time of Herod's reign. Herod's 'days' as king were marked by the materiality of his extraordinary building programmes (Richardson 1996: 174-202) as well as socioculturally the familial nepotism and its attendant brutality to the people, even the assassinations of a number of his own children.

Into this complex web of elements constituting the ecological texture of Mt. 2.1 is drawn a reference to *magoi* from the East appearing in Jerusalem at the time of the birth of Jesus. The narrator explicitly draws readers'/hearers' attention to this part of the verse by the use of *idou* which has that very function.[15] The simple designation *magoi* with its accompanying geographical locator 'from the East' is tantalizing for scholars (Davies and Allison 1988: 228-37; Carter 2000: 74-75; Brown 1993: 166-70; Powell 2000a: 459-80, 2000b: 1-20). It may have functioned intertextually for Matthean readers/hearers to designate those who were advisors to an Eastern ruler, carrying out such tasks as the interpretation of dreams (Josephus *Ant.* 10.195-218 and LXX Dan. 1.20; 2.2, 10, 27; 4.7; 5.7, 11, 15),[16] or the undertaking of rituals on behalf of the ruler or nation (Strabo, *Geography* 15.3.15; Pliny, *Nat.* 30.6.16-17; Dio Chrysostom, *Discourses* 49.7). Dio Chrysostom says explicitly of the Persian *magoi* that 'they were acquainted with Nature' and indirectly associates wisdom (*sophian*) with them. There is, however, an ambivalence toward the knowledge and skill of the *magoi* in Pliny for example (*Nat.* 30.6.17–8.21) and in Philo *On the Life of Moses* (1.90-95 and 276-277).[17] All of this and more may be functioning in the text's intertexture but the simple designator *magoi* does not give the reader significant guidance except perhaps to point to the *magoi* as accessing particular ways of knowing associated with dreams, ritual, and nature. This is significant for an ecological reading seeking to construct a new social imaginary. Alternate ways of thinking and knowing are essential and it is

---

15. Mark uses this word seven times and Matthew 62 times and Luke, 57 times.

16. In Josephus, the *magoi* are associated with Chaldaeans and soothsayers and in Daniel, groups designated as magicians, Chaldeans, and wise ones. In the English translation of Josephus, *magoi* is not translated whereas in the NRSV of Daniel, it is rendered as 'enchanter'. Those who belong to the court of Nebuchadnezzar are not successful in their task of interpreting the king's dream while Daniel who associates himself with this group is successful.

17. Philo calls the attendants of Pharoah who contend with Moses wizards and magicians (*sophistai* and *magoi*) and Balaam (cf. Num. 22–24) a *magos* but the biblical texts do not use this terminology. Some scholars see Num. 22–24 and especially 24.17-19 as a possible intertext for Mt. 2.2, but this is very tenuous.

to these that the *magoi* point. Also, they do not emerge as having political power. Indeed, they often find themselves at risk in relation to tyrannical rulers, Herod being one such example (Powell 2000a: 470-73).

The *magoi* are said to come from the East (Mt. 2.1). Like the reference to *magoi* themselves, their association with place is also tantalizing. *Magoi* are associated with the East: with Persia (Cicero, *Div* 1.23.46, and Dio Chrysostom, *Discourses* 49.7) and with Chaldeans (Josephus, *Ant.* 10.195-203; and the Book of Daniel). The East is also the place of the garden (Gen. 2.8) where the human couple lived harmoniously with the animals and with the land and its vegetation. The biblical narrative moves inexorably from the East as the first couple is driven from the Garden (Gen. 3.23-24) and Abraham and his family migrate from the East (Gen. 11.2). It becomes the place from which Israel's oppressors come (Isa. 41.2; Ezek. 25.4, 10) but in Isaiah's vision of restoration, people will be drawn from the East as well as the West. *Magoi*, who come from the East with alternative sources of knowledge, point to an expectation of something new, a restoration. The *magoi*, as outsiders to the genealogy of Israel but with a place in the cosmic genealogy it evoked, come to Jerusalem.

The naming of Jerusalem carries first and foremost connotations of political power. At the end of the second half of 2.1, it parallels the reference to Herod the king at the end of the first half of the verse and links the city with him. One of the key legacies Herod left at the end of his reign was the built or material environment of Jerusalem resulting from his programme of construction. This included the Antonia fortress, the rebuilt Hasmonean palace, his royal palace, and the three towers of Phasael, Mariamne and Hippicus (Richardson 1996: 174-96, 197-98). Jerusalem was a royal city and hence the place where one would expect the servants of foreign rulers to come. Jerusalem was, however, also the place where the G*d of Israel was considered present in the temple, an alternative source of knowing to that of the political power of Herod and of Rome behind him. In the first century CE, the temple was an ambivalent symbol in that it had been rebuilt by Herod as part of his reconstruction of the city. An ecological reading recognizes the hybrid nature of this geographical reference and warns against a dualistic construction of village over against city/built environment and other dualisms that will emerge around the symbol of Jerusalem as this segment of the gospel narrative unfolds.

The scene having been set by the rich and dense opening verse of this chapter, the Matthean ecological reader begins to be drawn into the tension in this text. The *magoi* ask, of whom we are not told, where they will find the one born 'king of the Jews', a phrase which is never used in the Jewish scriptures to refer to Israel's king or desired messianic king but is used by Josephus to refer to Herod (Josephus, *Ant.* 14.9; 15.409; 16.291, 311) and in Matthew on the lips of those who are not Jewish (27.11, 29, 37). The source of the *magoi's* knowledge is a planetary body, a star in the sky, that they have seen in its rising and which they have interpreted as pointing to the rise of a new leader among the Jewish people. This is an alternate source of knowledge to the political manoeuvring that brought Herod to kingship of the Jews.

Many explanations have been given for the star, perhaps most expansively by Mark Kidger who explores a number of theories such as a conjunction of planets, a comet, a meteor or shooting star (1999 and see also Brown 1993: 170-73). Finally, however, Kidger concludes that '[u]nfortunately, we will probably never know for certain what exactly did happen' (287). First-century Matthean readers may well have been familiar with movements of heavenly bodies in the sky and with heavenly phenomena being associated with significant events in their own lives as well as in the lives of those with political power and these are encoded in the ecological texture of the Matthean text. Pliny the Elder ponders human relationship with the stars and 'whether our souls are a part of heaven' (*Nat.* 2.24.95) and goes on to link a range of celestial and astral phenomena with human events especially the rise and fall of the politically powerful (*Nat.* 2.25.95–2.37.101). Philostratus tells of the thunderbolt that 'seemed about to fall to earth and then rose up into the air and disappeared aloft' as indicating 'the great distinction to which the sage (Apollonius) was to attain' (Philostratus, *Life of Apollonius* 1.5). As a result of the hybrid network of actants (Whatmore 1999: 27) encoded in the Matthean text, contemporary ecological readers are alerted to be attentive to Earth and cosmos in all its interactive manifestations or its more-than-human constituents and to the wisdom that can be learnt from such attentiveness.[18]

> **Ecological Intertexts.** Sarah Whatmore is one among many geographers who are contributing to the new social imaginary named ecological especially by way of a rethinking of nature not as object but as subject. She engages the 'concept of hybridity to implode the object-subject binary that underlies the modern antinomy between nature and society and to recognize the agency of non-human actants, acknowledging their presence in the social fabric and exploring ways of making it register in the vocabularies of social analysis.' She goes on to recognize that '[a]n actant network is thus simultaneously an assemblage of actants, whose activities are constituted in and through their connectivities with heterogeneous others, and a network that performs as a more or less durable (extensive in time) and more or less long (extensive in space) mode of ordering amongst its constituent parts' (Whatmore 1999: 27-28). She uses the term 'actant' to give agency to all more-than-human constituents.

18. Berry 1999: 31-32, speaks of a new attentiveness when he says that '[t]o appreciate the numinous aspect of the universe…we need to understand that we ourselves activate one of the deepest dimensions of the universe…the human is neither an addendum nor an intrusion into the universe. We are quintessentially integral with the universe.'

Space/place, time and human characters play within the inner texture of Mt. 2.1-12. References to Herod and to kingship (v. 2) alert readers to the function of power encoded within the text's ecological texture. Jesus, who is named in this chapter's opening verse, is born a peasant with no political power but he has already been characterized in the inner texture of the text with cultural or religious power. Similarly Bethlehem the village of Jesus' birth has no political status but the intertext encoded in the narrative in vv. 5-6 evokes a different power.

> And you, Bethlehem, in the land of Judah,
>   are by no means least among the rulers of Judah;
> for from you shall come a ruler
>   who is to shepherd my people Israel (Mt. 2.5-6).

This text cited in Mt. 2.6 differs from its potential intertexts, Mic. 5.2 (LXX 5.1) and 2 Sam. 5.2, subtly shifting focus to a political power that is named as 'shepherding'. Readers might, therefore, imagine the chief priests and scribes of whom Herod has made inquiries regarding the expected messiah constructing the text they offer to Herod, subtly reading their scriptures in a way that is subversive of his hegemonic power. If this were so, their activity of re-textualizing would be an instance of a colonized people who know the language of their scriptures as well as the language of the colonizer, Herod, who represented Rome.

Within the reshaped text as it appears in 2.5-6, Bethlehem is located in the *gē*, the land, of Judah, bringing place and the materiality of geographic location to the fore. Into this, references to power are subtly woven as Micah's recognition of the smallness of Bethlehem among the clans of Judah, like David as the last son of Jesse, is changed to render the village 'by no means least' and among the 'rulers' rather than the clans of Judah.[19] The final phrase of the Matthean intertext reflects the language of 2 Sam. 5.2. The promised ruler will shepherd Israel, named as *ton laon mou* (my people)' reminding readers that Jesus has already been characterized as the one who will save his people (*ton laon autou*). The shepherd image also draws into the text the interrelationship between the human shepherd and the sheep. It is a relationship that requires geographic location and hence the agricultural association, already noted in relation to Bethlehem, is further emphasized.

Two prophecies, one through a star and another through a papyrus scroll, interpreted in turn by the *magoi* from the East and the chief priests and scribes, surround the birth of Jesus with language of power. The Matthean inner and inter-texts have the *magoi* and the prophet attributing to Jesus

---

19. The reader is conscious here of the ambivalence surrounding David and power, remembering his 'taking' of Bathsheba as evoked in the genealogy.

what readers recognize as political power—kingship of the Jews and 'ruler'—tasks that he will not take up in their political dimension even as the story unfolds. Prophecy is not, therefore, working here in terms of literal or historical fulfilment. The star as medium of prophecy for the *magoi* and the texts of the prophets as scriptures of Israel have cultural power and they incite conflict because they give authority to sources of power other than the political associated with Herod. One can only wonder at this point whether in the interpretation of the scriptures given by the chief priests and scribes (vv. 5-6) there is not the hope that once again a reversal of power might be associated with Bethlehem. Read in this way, the Jewish interpreters are not set over against the prophesied saviour. Such an interpretation also nuances the fear of 'all Jerusalem' who, like the leaders, were colonized people with their fear perhaps mimicking that of Herod. Such a reading recognizes that power is neither monolithic nor dualistic but multi-dimensional when the text is read with a new lens.

The *magoi* travel with assurance to Jerusalem seeking the one whose birth the star predicted and they come to pay homage (v. 2), to recognize power. While they mistake that power as political ('king of the Jews'), the reader can recognize another power that could be described as religious or cultural or that which leaves traces of divinity. That power permeates Jesus' humanity and his habitat, material place and human time, through the language and imagery of the narrative. Herod, on the other hand who is named *basileus*, having significant political power, is frightened (even terrified) by what he perceives as a threat to his political power and Jerusalem, the centre of that power is characterized likewise. But already we have seen that easy dualisms in relation to place and power are significantly nuanced in the text. Such nuancing of place and power within human socio-political and cultural relations and played out in physical and material locations will continue to constitute the textures of the text as it unfolds.

In v. 7, the two key players in the drama of power and place meet. Herod is clearly in command. He obtains from the *magoi* information about the time of the star's rising, continuing the narrative's explicit time location. He also orders the *magoi* to go to Bethlehem, the place he had learnt from his consultation with the religio-political leaders (chief priests) and the religio-cultural experts (the scribes). He mocks the language of the *magoi* who ask about the one to whom they have come to pay homage, suggesting that he too wishes to recognize and honour the newborn 'king'. The play between places, Bethlehem and Jerusalem, continues to be backgrounded as does that between the days of Herod and the time of the rising star. Hostility and hospitality, the two options open to Herod and to the city of Jerusalem are also at play in the narrative.

The sacred text interpreted by the colonized Jewish leaders in Jerusalem and conveyed through Herod's orders pointed the *magoi* toward Bethlehem.

The star, the cosmic element, leads them to the place 'where the child was'. Both modes of communication advance the Jesus story. We have also seen that the cosmos and its signs could be evoked as good omens for the rise of imperial powers. This too plays within the ecological texture of this text. It is not just the presence of sacred texts or cosmic signs that emerge in this narrative but their function within the hybrid web of associations of political and cultural power. This may remind contemporary readers of the function of the cosmos and its myriads of galaxies, stars and planetary bodies which are often rendered of no account in the race for control of space. The 'heavenly bodies' can function to stir the human imagination and consciousness in a way that can lead to discovery of the new in the Earth/ heaven(s)/divinity relationships and to transformative praxis for the sake of the entire Earth community.

But this is to run ahead without noting the final verses of this section. The reader is drawn into that element of habitat with which we began our exploration of 2.1, namely 'the house'. In v. 11, it is the material space in which there is exchange of gifts between the wise ones and the mother and child. It also carries significant social, religious and economic implications that will emerge as the narrative unfolds, especially given Crosby's recognition that 'house' is a primary Matthean metaphor (Crosby 1988: 11-12). Traces of the materiality of the pregnant body of the child's 'mother' still linger through her naming in the text, drawing attention to the materiality of other bodies—of the child and of the wise ones. There is also reversal in the performance of power imaged and described in this text as the *magoi* fall down and pay homage to the child.[20] And other Earth materials are drawn into this reversal. To this child are offered the gifts that Isaiah predicted the nations would bring to the G*d of Israel (Isa. 60.6—gold and frankincense) and the homage paid to the child (*prosekynēsan* in v. 11) echoes that of the kings of the nations (*hoi basileis*) who fall down (*proskynēsousin*) before the king's son in Ps. 72.11. The gifts which play in this scene are material: frankincense and myrrh are gum resin of native trees known both for their perfume and their healing qualities; and gold, a naturally occurring metal is found amid the rocks of Earth. They invite reflection on gift and exchange (Primavesi 2003), thematics that have already emerged from the ecological reading of this Matthean text. The child is honoured in the gifting and the gifts.

Another alternative form of knowledge and wisdom, and hence of cultural power, functions within the closing verse of this narrative (v. 12), namely

---

20. The verb *proskyneō* can carry the sense of 'worship' but in this context it seems more appropriate to use the term 'pay homage' since the narrative portrays the *magoi* seeking a political ruler or king. Later in the narrative, *proskyneō* may point toward the notion of 'worship'. The Matthaean text's designation of Jesus as 'the child' is repeated many times through Matthew 2 contrasting the lack of political power that rests with him in contrast to Herod (see Mt. 2.8, 9, 11, 13 (twice), 14, 20, 21).

that of the dream. This is a form which readers have already encountered in Mt. 1.20 when Joseph was given, in a dream, knowledge that the readers already possessed, namely that Jesus was conceived by the power of a spirit that is holy. In this instance, the dream and the *magoi's* compliance with its message thwart the political power of Herod and the scene closes with their returning by an alternate route to their own country. This scene, that opened with an explicit geographic reference, Bethlehem, likewise closes with a focus on place, the unknown country of the *magoi*. Herod and his political power likewise frame the section although that power is thwarted by another power, namely cultural and religious.

5. *Matthew 2.13-23: Displacement and Death*

Anachōrēsantōn (having gone away), the opening word of the second half of Matthew 2, provides a link back to the two-fold use of the same verb in 2.12. It reminds readers of the movement between places that has characterized the narrative of Mt. 2.1-12. Just as *idou* drew attention to the *magoi* in 2.1b and their journeying from the East, so too in 2.13, the use of *idou* draws attention to the two-fold source of alternate knowledge and power: an angelic appearance and dream. Matthew 2.13-14 and 2.19-20 mirror image one another in the reporting of a dream and Joseph's compliance with it; the first to go to Egypt and the second to return. In fact, the appearance of an angel to Joseph in vv. 13 and 19; the command to 'rise', 'take' and 'go/flee' (vv. 13 and 20) and his obedience mirroring the angel's command (vv. 14 and 21) act as a frame around the central section of this narrative, namely vv. 16-18. Hence for an ecological reader, alternate knowledge, place, power and pain thread their way through this narrative.

The ecological reader has already been alerted to sources of knowledge and wisdom alternate to the foregrounded world of Herodian power, namely the star and the scriptures. In the inner texture of the Matthean narrative these alternate wisdoms point to what has until now been backgrounded, namely traces of the divine who even in this section still remains in the shadows. Angelic appearances and messages as well as dreams, which I am describing as alternate forms of knowledge/wisdom and which characterize the Christian Old Testament,[21] could be described in the words of John Haught as 'encounter(s) with unseen agents, powers and personalities... experienced as emerging out of the background of a more fundamental

---

21. Such occurrences are too numerous to list here with 'angel' occurring 131 times across 121 verses and 'dream' 68 times in 58 verses. I wish to acknowledge here also that much of what I am calling the 'Christian Old Testament' both was and is the scriptures of the Jewish faith. Adequate terminology which avoids Christian supersessionism is difficult in this regard.

transcendent mystery' (Haught 2006: 22). They draw this transcendent mystery into the foreground of the Matthean narrative by way of the 're-mark', a process whereby what is backgrounded can be brought to the forefront. Human and habitat and their interconnectedness that Haught would call 'nature' are brought into relationship with a 'mysterious presence' that 'simultaneously penetrates, encircles, grounds and enlivens nature without being reducible to nature' (22). This presence of transcendent mystery will become more explicit as the Matthean narrative unfolds.

> **Ecological Intertexts.** Timothy Morton says of 'ecological writing' what could also be said of 'ecological reading', namely that 'it wants to undo habitual distinctions between nature and ourselves'. Human storytelling, of which the biblical narrative is a part, tends to foreground 'the human' and background the 'other-than-human'. To undo this process in ecological reading, Morton suggests that we attend to the 're-mark' which he recognizes as a kind of echo in the text that makes readers aware that there is but a 'hair's breadth' between foreground and background in a way that leads to 'questioning the genuine existence of these categories' (Morton 2007: 47-63).

Place and power intersect as the message Joseph receives in each encounter is that he must take 'the child and his mother' and move, first to Egypt and then back to 'the land of Israel' and finally to Galilee. Intertextually, the first journey is that of Jesus' ancestors and hence functions symbolically as well as materially in the narrative. Egypt is a place of refuge for a family displaced as a result of Herod's destructive political power (2.13) just as it was a place of refuge for the father and brothers of Joseph displaced by famine and the power of 'nature' (Gen. 41.57–46.7). This reminds readers of the millions of political, economic and ecological refugees currently in the foreground of the unfolding Earth story. Being called 'out of Egypt' evokes the exodus traditions and situates Jesus within the sacred narrative of his people as did the genealogy and hence within the greater Earth story. The chapter concludes with a new geographical or place referent, the district of Galilee and the town called Nazareth (2.22-23). It concludes therefore as it began, with Jesus and his family in place, albeit a new place.

What remains for consideration is the intersection of power and pain in the middle section of 2.16-18. It makes explicit what is backgrounded in the section's two frames, namely the pain associated with displacement. We have already considered above how transcendent mystery was narrated as permeating the habitat/human interconnectivity in Joseph's taking of 'the child and his mother'[22] to Egypt, back to Israel and then to Galilee/Nazareth. As a result they escape the destructive power of Herod. But this power

---

22. This phrase 'the child and his mother' continues to remind readers/listeners of the birth of Jesus from the body of Mary. He is also the one in whom G*d, the transcendent

that saved Jesus from the rampage of a tricked Herod (Mt. 2.13-15) does not do the same for the children of Bethlehem. The cries of these children are erased, as are the cries of their mothers, who like Mary would have been 'with' their children (see Mt. 2.11, 13, 14, 20, 21). Only the intertexture, the voice of Rachel weeping for her children with loud lamentation intervenes. Her voice challenges the divine compassion that is absent from the narrative (see Wainwright 1998: 64-65). In an ecological reading of these verses, the loud lamentations of the mothers and sons of Bethlehem must be allowed to rise up. Attention to these voices in pain may turn readers to the erased voice of Earth, the erased pain and cry of Earth destroyed by the rampages of human power, erased by hierarchal and dualistic consciousness, and annihilated from memory.

Lament characterizes the voices of many who mourn the destruction of habitat for the benefit of the human in a way that not only wounds and annihilates the more-than-human other in its hosts of manifestations but also breaks down the hybrid interconnectivity of human and habitat. Lament accompanies the destruction of habitat and human as a result of climate change. And so the lament of Rachel echoes with that of Jordi Albiston in our day as she grieves in the face of the horrific fire that destroyed the town of Kinglake, Victoria/Australia on 7 February 2009 along with more than twenty of its residents:

> Kinglake and the ways to Kinglake do mourn: all her gates are desolate: her hilltops
> sigh, her soil is afflicted, and she is *in* bitterness black.
> Look! all her beauty is departed: her trees are become like hearts without pasture,
> and they are gone without strength in the moment of the day.[23]

Together they rise up with many other voices in a 'public processing of pain' (Brueggemann 1987: 16-20). These voices remind us of the potential in the human heart for destruction that finds a mirror in the heart of Herod, destruction in the present time of not only human life but many of Earth's other-than-human constituents. The saving of the one from destruction gives a sign of hope but also cries out against the erasure of the many. It is the story of the one, Jesus who shall be called a Nazarene, one named according to place or location, Nazareth of Galilee, which will continue as the gospel story unfolds.

---

mystery that Haught highlights, will be with G*d's people, the community of Israel (Mt. 1.23).

23. For a brief discussion of the link between the Victorian fires of February 2009 and climate change, see Elvey 2009: 33-34. She drew my attention to Albiston's lament which can be accessed in full online at http://www.eurekastreet.com.au/article.aspx?aeid=26864#.Vab4h2DzmS0 (volume 21, No. 12, 20 June, 2011).

Chapter 3

MATTHEW 3–4:
FROM WILDERNESS TO WATERFRONT—
INTERFACING PLACE AND PROCLAMATION[1]

An explicit time referent opens Matthew 3–4: in those days/*en de tais hēmerais ekeivais*, the days in which John the Baptist came preaching in the wilderness (3.1). The opening verse with its interplay of place, time and proclamation characterizes this section of the narrative in which the habitat/human nexus guides an ecological reading.

Turning an inter-con/textual lens onto Matthew 3–4, the eco-rhetorical reader notes the interweaving, in hybrid ways, of time, place/space, and a range of actants (see 'Ecological Intertexts' above for Sarah Watmore's discussion of attentiveness to hybridity in order to break what has been constructed as a nature/society binary). An ecological reading of these two chapters will, therefore, be attentive to this hybrid interweaving of time, place/space and the human and 'other-than-human' actants in the inner texture of the narrative. The intertexts will not only be those explicitly and implicitly echoing through the text but also contemporary theories of TimeSpace, highlighted in the 'Ecological Intertexts' below. A focus on the sociality of the hybrid actants encoded in the ecological texture of the text will contribute further to an ecological reading of Matthew 3–4 beyond attention to inner texture and intertext.

Ecological Intertexts. In relation to time and space, the geographers May and Thrift have employed the term 'TimeSpace' to bring to awareness that 'time is irrecoverably bound up with the spatial constitution of society (and vice versa)' (May and Thrift 2001: 3-4). Earlier, Thrift had spoken of 'an imbroglio of heterogeneous and more or less expansive hybrids performing "not one but many worlds" and weaving all manner of spaces and times' as they do so (Thrift 1999: 317). Their insights can be engaged together with the theory of Soja (1999) in relation to space. Soja proposes a framework for understanding space which functions well with the notion of hybridity that Whatmore and Thrift address. For him, 'Perceived Space' or 'First-space' is that

---

1. Some of the material in this chapter has appeared in Wainwright 2013a.

> which is experienced and mappable, such as the physical wilderness of Judea. 'Conceived Space' or 'Second-space' is concerned with the conceptual and symbolic ways in which space is understood in human perception—wilderness as place of trial or temptation. His 'Third-space' as 'Lived Space' opens up the potential for the radically different in relation to spatiality in human life beyond the binary of First/physical and Second/symbolic space (Soja 1999: 260-69). It will function as a tool in ecological readings of the Matthean text. These theories will inform this ecological reading as intertexts.

The opening referent 'in those days' (*en de tais hēmerais ekeivais*) traverses the mappable time since Joseph took the child Jesus and his mother (see Mt. 2.21) to Nazareth in Galilee (Mt. 2.22-23). While there are many references to time across the gospel, the *en de tais hēmerais ekeivais* of 3.1 is the first of only four very explicit time referents (13.1; 17.1; 22.23). This reference in 3.1 is more general than the other three and leaves open meaning potential which the unfolding narrative will activate.

1. *Matthew 3.1-12: Wilderness Embraced*

'[T]hose days' are characterized by the appearing of John the Baptiser, or the Immerser (Taylor 1997: 49-50), his very title linking him intimately with water. Ironically, however, in the third segment of the opening verse, the reader learns that this Immerser, a new character in a new time frame in the narrative, is found in the wilderness (*erēmos*).[2] TimeSpace frames the appearing of the Immerser and highlights the hybridity of habitat woven into the text in which wilderness and water are never far one from the other.

Inter-con/textually, the wilderness of Judea can be understood in terms of its geographic location ('First-space'), the area extending west of the lower Jordan and Dead Sea into the central plateau or hill country. It evokes the extraordinary habitat of the Sea of Salt, of desert flowers and animals, of particular soil types, and a geography and climate which result in wadis whose torrents rush to the sea when occasional rains occur on the plateau (Zohary 1952; Aschbel 1939). While for Soja this 'First-space' layer of meaning may be considered insignificant, for an eco-rhetorical reader it is an important reminder of the rich materiality of place that is encoded in the text.

---

2. Joan Taylor explores some of the possible understandings of John's immersion process; namely ritual purity and a call to return to observance of the purity code; proselyte baptism which seems unlikely given that those coming for baptism are Jerusalemites and Judaeans; symbolic initiation which she rejects on the grounds of the influence of later Christian baptism on this; immersion at Qumran; repentance baptism; or an immersion of repentance for remission of sins.

At the level of 'Second-space', the wilderness referent has rich intertextual connotations. Wilderness is the place of escape from oppression and danger leading to encounter with the divine liberator for Hagar (Gen. 16.7; 21.14-19) and for Moses and Israel (Exod. 1.1–3.15; 13.17–20.26). It is a place of divine encounter in which discipline, purification and/or transformation take place, as articulated by Robert Leal (2004: 135-71) and as instanced, for example, in Deut. 8.1-10 and Deuteronomy 30. It also carried connotations in Graeco-Roman Israel of those regions that were considered 'uninhabited or uninhabitable' by human Earth-beings who did not cultivate it or live there, as Eric Stewart has demonstrated (2009: 149).

Such claims in relation to First and Second-space as made above need to be nuanced as they are impacted by the varying interrelationships between physical location and its symbolic naming across histories and geographies. One instance is that of indigenous Australians who have lived on their continent for 40,000 years or more, and for some in what the white settlers of just over 200 years call 'wilderness' or 'desert'. This report by Deborah Bird Rose, a long-standing anthropologist working in the 'top end' of Australia, of a conversation with Daly Pulkara as they observed the erosion, the desertification of the land by white settlers in a way that renders 'wilderness' multivalent is poignant.

> The concept of wild country was brought home to me in a conversation with Daly Pulkara. We had stopped to look at some of the extreme erosion on Humbert River Station, and I asked Daly what he called this country. He looked at it long and heavily before he said: 'It's the wild. Just the wild'. Daly went on to speak of quiet country—the country in which all the care of generations of people is evident to those who know how to see it. Quiet country stands in contrast to the wild: we were looking at a wilderness, man-made and cattle-made. This 'wild' was a place where the life of the country was falling down into the gullies and washing away with the rains.
>
> ...Wild people (colonisers) make wild country (degrading, failing). Colonisation and the wild form a matrix: settler societies and their violence (Rose 2004: 4).

An eco-rhetorical reading will also interface intertextually with 'Second-space' or symbolic understandings of wilderness that idealize it. This is particularly evident in some of the slogans within modern tourism that construe wilderness as a place of escape where pristine ecological habitats can be encountered (often, however, only available to the wealthy and with little attention to the ecological crisis facing Earth or the colonization of those spaces as noted above).[3] In a world challenged by widespread degradation, such understandings need to be engaged with a hermeneutics of suspicion.

---

3. One such disturbing example is the claim that '*[u]nderwater is unspoiled wildernesss*', http://www.whalestonga.com/ (accessed 14 April 2010).

Leal draws attention to the perspective of Roderick Nash who claims that 'our relationship to wilderness...has extraordinarily ancient roots ...[and that] our kind has lived in wilderness at least one hundred times longer than it has lived in civilization', an insight not foreign to indigenous Australians as noted above. Leal goes on to suggest that '[f]or Nash, as for many other environmentalists, the wilderness, from which humanity emerged only relatively recently, is essential to humanity's self-understanding' (2004: 15), or as Casey notes '[p]aradoxically, only with the recognition of the primacy of wilderness will a deeper commonality of the human and natural worlds become evident' (1993: 187).

Wilderness can, therefore, be seen to participate in the genealogy of Mt. 1.1 evoked by the opening phrase 'the book of the genealogy' catching up readers into the long process of evolution of the wilderness as part of the cosmos as discussed earlier. An inter-con/textual engagement with the location of John in the wilderness in Mt. 3.1 demonstrates the hybridity among the network of actants encoded in the text and in the reader's engagement with the text.

This takes us then to a 'Third-space' approach to Mt. 3.1 which recognizes that John the Baptist is characterized in the inner texture of the text as an active human agent who enters the space of the desert. Desert/wilderness is, as we have seen, a place of multiple meanings. It is encoded in the text in all its materiality and with all its unique agencies. It can be perceived to be at the edge of where most of the human community lives and undertakes its life processes: a marginal, boundary or liminal space in human reckoning.

It is from this marginal yet very material space, his chosen *lived space/ habitat*, that John calls for *metanoia*. This *metanoia* means a change of mind and of heart that is open to new possibilities. John calls for such a change with the message: the *basileia* of the heavens/sky is near. This Matthean phraseology, *hē basileia tōn ouranōn*, is unique in the New Testament and also intertextually. It brings together the material and spatial term, the *ouranōn*/the heavens or sky with *hē basileia*–the socio-political designator evoking power or empire. The heavens/sky connotes first and foremost that aspect of the universe that, together with Earth and yet distinguishable from it (Pennington 2008: 29), makes up the universe—a perceived 'First-space' perspective (BDAG 737). In ancient Israelite cosmology, the heavens were considered a vault or vaults over the earth with the outer- or uttermost of these being the abode of the god/s, a 'Second-space' signification.[4]

---

4. Pennington (2007: 135-40) seeks to distinguish the singular and plural usage of *ouranos* in the Gospel of Matthew, with the singular generally indicating the sky or what he calls 'the created order' and the plural the 'abode of God'. In this eco-rhetorical reading, I do not want to make this distinction but to allow the two possibilities to play throughout the Gospel so that the divine and the material or earthly are not separate/d.

Hellenistic cosmology envisioned 'the earth surrounded by concentric planetary spheres' with the 'terrestrial, sublunar realm…sharply separated from the celestial' (Martin 1987: 7). The marginal preacher, John the Immerser, links the material and metaphorical designation with the *basileia* that would immediately connote in the ecological texture of the text the power of Rome or the reign of the emperor. Intertextually, however, the *basileia* of the heavens could evoke the reign or power of G*d in Jewish thought even though the explicit Matthean phraseology is not present (Wis. 10.10; Isa. 52.7). The phrase also carries a material aspect, namely the territory or geographical space ruled by the emperor. This alternative of a *basileia* of 'the heaven/heavens or sky' could function as a critique of the empire of Rome in first century emerging Christian Judaism. There is a danger, however, which has been borne out in history, that when Christianity becomes the empire then the language of empire/*basileia* no longer functions prophetically but supports Christian imperialism (Carter 2001: 172-79).[5]

This phrase becomes the kernel of John's preaching of a Third/lived space that resists the *basileia* of the emperor and all empires as well as the dichotomizing of the material and the metaphorical, Earth and the heavens. The divine, the one named as G*d, is associated with material space and with human structures of power in and through the language of the *basileia* in the phrase, the '*basileia* of the heavens'. The proclamation of the Immerser can be seen to function in a way similar to the designation of Jesus in 1.23—Emmanuel or the divine with us, with the Earth community. This thematic characterizes the Matthean story and hence will characterize an eco-rhetorical reading of it. It is further emphasized by the fact that what is preached by John (Mt. 3.2) is also preached by Jesus (4.17).

Returning to John's location in the marginal space between wilderness and waterfront, the text characterizes him as bearing in/on his person the material and the social. In v. 4, John is 'in place'. His clothes are of camel's hair, the belt around his waist is of hide or skin and his food is locusts and wild honey. He is in place in the complexity of relationships within Earth and its constituents. Verse 4 evokes the gift exchange, the giving up of life within the Earth cycles that constitute habitats that there might also be gift. The processes of gift exchange must be attended to respectfully, in all their hybridity and complexity, within the call to ecological *metanoia* (Manolopoulos 2009; Primavesi 2003). This is no easy conversion. It requires attentiveness to the complexity, the hybridity that constitutes

---

Indeed Mt. 1.23, the claim for the divine being with the Earth community in the birth of the child, has already ruptured any such distinctions.

5. Carter raises the question: '*how can Christian readers bring the Gospel's critique of imperialism into play against the Gospel's and against our own, imperialist hopes for God's triumph?*' (italics that of the author).

3. Matthew 3–4

'Third-space', the place where repentance, turning, change is possible, and is not separate from the materiality of 'First-space'. Intertextually, John is constituted prophet through association with Elijah (2 Kgs 1.8; see also Yamasaki 1998: 84). He is, however, marginal as is the space he occupies. Thus, in his person, in relation to TimeSpace, he points to a change of ways of being and living in the Earth community as does the message he preaches. Wilderness holds potential for what is neither idealization nor exploitation.

As the narrative continues in 3.5-6, those who are characterized in the inner texture of the text as coming out to the wilderness/waterfront space that John occupies are also designated in spatial terms. First they are equated with the built environment of Jerusalem that has already been characterized at the 'Second-space' or symbolic level in Mt. 2.1 and 3 as hostile to Jesus. Second, they are called 'all Judea'/*pasa hē Ioudaia*, Judea having been contrasted with Jerusalem in Mt. 2.2 and 5. The third group is also named in terms of location: all the region along the Jordan/*pasa hē perichōpos tou Ioudanou*, the waterfront which has not yet appeared in the gospel. It is here that John is immersing or baptizing, taking people who have come out from their habitable spaces into the wilderness—and there is waterfront in this wilderness. Their entry into the marginality that characterizes John is augmented by their immersion in the waters of the Jordan and their confessing of their sins, an indication that they have heard the message of John to repent (see 3.2) or to change their mind, their perspective, their behaviour.

Wilderness is alive with potential, demonstrated through the network of multiple actants within the opening verses of Matthew 3. This is not, however, an idealized potential as the preaching of John in 3.7-12 indicates. Wilderness preaching calls for a change of mind and heart, a change of lifestyle. The ecological texture of this preaching is visible in the verses directed to the many Pharisees and Sadducees who likewise come to the wilderness/waterfront to be baptized (3.7). Metaphorically, John characterizes them as a 'brood of vipers', using an animal group to characterize negatively an unrepentant human group. Already in Gen. 3.1, the snake (*ophis*) is designated as *phronimōtato*, an adjective meaning wise and prudent but also used more negatively as shrewd or crafty (BDAG 1066). The Matthean characterization of the Pharisees and Sadducees coming for baptism as a 'brood of vipers'/snakes/*ekidnōn* seems to pick up on a similar negative characterisation given that the *ekidna* generally designates a poisonous snake. Approaching the text from an ecological perspective, the reader brings a hermeneutic of suspicion to such a negative characterization of an animal to serve human story-telling. On the other hand, if the characterisation of the serpent of Genesis is read as wise and prudent, then the *ekidnōn* might be characterized as such, making for a much more positive characterization of the Pharisees and Sadducees who are wisely fleeing the end-time divine wrath. The ecological reader will still be wary of using an animal group metaphorically, especially when it is a negative characterization contributing to the anthropocentric perspective that views animals as of less significance than and only useful to the human actors in the narrative.

Matthew 3.8 characterizes the repentance associated with the coming of the *basileia* being preached by John as 'bearing fruit', a metaphor that draws readers' attention to the life-producing features of the plant world. In this it is reminiscent of the ideal world of Gen. 1.11-12 with the divine word bringing forth 'plants yielding seed, and fruit trees of every kind on earth that bear fruit with the seed in it'. The metaphor of 'bearing fruit' will weave through the Matthean narrative as challenge to live the ethic of the *basileia of the heavens/sky* which both John and Jesus preach (see 3.10; 7.16-20; 12.33; 21.19, 34, 41, 43). Earth and Earth's processes are valued. In the narrative they serve its human recipients by demonstrating the right ordering or righteousness of the *basileia* and *basileia* living. The attentive ecological reader will value Earth's processes such as plants bearing fruit in their own right. The repentance preached by John entails attentiveness to these processes, with v. 10 drawing attention to the cutting down of the tree that does not produce fruit. The language of the text recognizes the violence of this process which has the axe laid to the root of the tree that does not bear fruit and its being cut down and thrown into the fire as will happen to the chaff that is winnowed out from the wheat (v. 12). These evocative agricultural images point to the significance of attentiveness to Earth's processes in understanding the *metanoia* associated with the *basileia* that John is preaching.

All of this takes place in those days, the time designator with which this section of the narrative opened and in the material space of desert/waterfront where human bodies are located and where a 'Third-space' is created that opens up to the change that will render the *basileia* of the sky/heavens near at hand. Through such change the divine mystery shall be with the Earth-community in the unfolding of the central gospel message.

2. *Matthew 3.13-17: A Waterfront Encounter*

In Mt. 3.13, the reader encounters another time designator (*tote*), with the same verb that introduced John in 3.1 (*paraginetai*). This time, however, it is Jesus who is introduced, not in the desert as was John, but coming from Galilee, making his way to the Jordan waterfront in order to be baptized by John. Intertextually and at the level of 'Second-space', the Jordan represents the place of transition for the people of Israel from their desert wanderings into a land that was promised to be flowing with milk and honey (Exod. 3.8, 17; 13.5 and Deut. 27.3). The reader can expect, therefore, that

Jesus' coming to the Jordan (the waterfront between the desert and the waters of the river) likewise opens up the possibility of transition. Place points to potential. The river Jordan that is encoded into the ecological texture of the text is water in the wilderness, flowing as it does along the edge of the wilderness of Judea. The contrasts in the material referents are the context for the contrast between Jesus who presents himself for baptism and the one whom John depicted in the previous verses as baptizing with a spirit of holiness and with fire and coming as an eschatological judge in the imagery of the winnower on the threshing floor (3.11-12).

The 'actant network' that is operating in Mt. 3.13-17, the scene at the Jordan, is rich with relationships. John and Jesus negotiate the power relationship between them as John seeks to demur to Jesus as eschatological judge even while Jesus refuses such a stance, claiming that his baptism by John is a fulfilling of all righteousness (*plērōsai pasan dikaiosynēn*). Righteousness is a complex Matthean theme that has already been given a little attention and will be explored further in the next chapter. Here, however, we can designate it as that right ordering that is of G*d and that is in keeping with the divine dream with and for the Earth community.

It is right that Jesus go down into the water although it is not this action that is encoded in the narrative's inner texture. Rather, with the right ordering of human relationships between John and Jesus established, the attention shifts to Jesus coming up out of the water as Earth itself emerged from water. The ecological reader will be attentive to the centrality of water in Earth's genealogy and its ongoing maintenance,[6] as well as to the survival of so many species including the human.[7] Water is a complex and powerful material element as well as a symbolic one. In relation to Jesus' baptism, the waters of the Jordan are not the water of *metanoia* or repentance. Rather, they are the waters of heavenly authorizing. Attention is drawn by the signifier *idou* to the heavens or the sky being opened. This imagery evokes intertextually the ancient Hebrews' understanding of the cosmos in which the heavenly vault or the skies separated the waters above the firmament from the earthly waters below (Gen. 1.6-8; Ps. 148.4). The heavens were then the storehouse for rain and snow, hail and thunder (Exod. 9.22-35; Isa. 55.10; Josh. 10.11; Rev. 11.19) and the opening of the heavens allowed the rain and snow to fall to earth (Reddish 1992: 253).

The opening of the heavens in Mt. 3.16 is not, however, meteorological. Rather, the heavens are opened or unlocked ('to Jesus' if one takes account

---

6. This story is available now not only in print but also in a series of DVDs such as Cox, *Our Planet: The Past, Present and Future of Earth*; *Wonders of the Solar System*; *Human Planet*; and *Planet Earth*.

7. See also the collection of articles on Water from a biblical perspective (Habel and Trudinger 2011).

of the variant *autō* in the dative). Both waters and sky open up to make way for the divine affirmation of Jesus who sees 'the spirit of God descending like a dove and alighting on him' (3.16). The material sensory experience of Jesus *seeing* and the metaphorical play within the imagination of the eco-rhetorical reader contribute to the hybridity of meanings that intersect in this text.

Scholars have struggled to understand the image of the dove in the narrating of the baptism of Jesus. Engaging eco-critically with the work of Silvia Schroer who has examined this in much greater detail than is possible here (Schroer 2000: 132-63), one can see the material, the metaphoric and the mythical functioning together in a 'reflective mythology' (Schroer: 142). Here, Schroer draws on the work of Elisabeth Schüssler Fiorenza who emphasizes that '[r]eflective mthyology is not a living myth but is rather a form of theology appropriating mythical language, material, and patterns from different myths' (Schroer: 142). As the Matthean community together with other early Christian communities sharing similar sources theologized Jesus, his birth, ministry and death/resurrection, they drew on images, language and patterns belonging to the myths of their ancestors and those with and among whom their ancestors were engaged. We have seen above that these elements function intertextually in reading the Matthean narrative.

Readers have already encountered a spirit that is named as 'holy' being associated with the birth of Jesus/Emmanuel (1.18, 20). Also, John contrasts his baptism by means of water with the baptism that Jesus will perform which will be by means of a spirit that is holy (3.11—it should be noted, however, that Jesus does not perform any baptisms in the Matthean gospel whereby readers might see and know the difference described here). In 3.16, the spirit that descends from the opened heavens/sky onto Jesus is named as 'spirit of God'. The divine mystery, G*d, who is said to be with the Earth community in the earlier naming of Jesus (Mt. 1.23) is now, through a spirit named to be of G*d, very explicitly descending on Jesus. How does one name divine mystery 'with' the Earth community? The evangelist demonstrates that it is necessary to draw on mythical images and language—the spirit of G*d is 'like a dove'.

Among the religions of the Ancient Near East, the dove was associated with the love goddesses and, as Schroer claims, it was the 'representative symbol or companion animal' signalling 'the presence and sphere of the goddess' (Schroer: 136-37). It was also messenger of the divine. In the reflective theologizing of Second Temple Judaism, imagery from the goddess traditions was appropriated to Sophia/Wisdom, the dove in particular, through the work of Philo of Alexandria. The spirit of G*d descending on Jesus 'like a dove' can evoke, through this material symbol, divine Wisdom/Sophia's message of love and affirmation of the adult Jesus which is confirmed intertextually through the heavenly voice that speaks not to Jesus (see Ps. 2.7—'you are my son') but to whoever is listening—'[t]his is my son'. It is perhaps in the evocation of Isa. 42.1 in which the divine speaker is said to delight in 'the chosen one' that elements of the eroticism of divine love have been retained although obscured through centuries of patriarchal theologizing (Schroer: 138-40).

Through a consideration of the ecological texture of this Matthean text (3.13-17), reflective mythologizing within an early Christian community has modelled ways in which Jewish myths informed early Christian theologizing. This opens the way for reflective mythologizing on myths familiar to today's readers: myths of indigenous communities of Oceania for instance, including Australia as already noted above.

Thus, just as attention to habitat and 'TimeSpace' functioned to open up a way of reading the baptism of Jesus ecologically so too has reflective mythologizing. The desert functioned as lived space in which the marginal character, John, could proclaim something new for Earth and all its constituents. TimeSpace functioned in the Matthean narrative to render Jesus a 'Third-space' marginal character. The one named in 1.23 as Emmanuel, the one in whom divinity is with Earth and all its constituents, is also the one affirmed from the heavens or sky. Wilderness and waterfront are marginal spaces that function materially and metaphorically to open up new meaning possibilities for the Matthean text read in the context of the ecological challenges of the twenty-first century.

From the Jordan waterfront, that space between wilderness and the water of the Jordan that symbolizes a crossing to newness, a 'Third-space', Jesus is led by the divine spirit into the wilderness (Mt. 4.1). Following the narrative of Jesus' temptations in the wilderness (4.1-11), he will journey from wilderness to the waterfront at Capernaum (4.12-13). This reading of Matthew 3 has demonstrated the potential for reading newness in and through the marginal or 'Third-space' associated with John. The same will be true in relation to Jesus in Matthew 4. This newness is, however, undermined by the gendering that permeates this section of the gospel: the new is gendered male and the female is obscured, almost erased from these two chapters. At the same time, Earth elements function significantly in the text as we have seen. For the ecological reader conscious of the layers of erasure of different human and other-than-human groups and species, the call for *metanoia* of Mt. 3.2 is urgent and must be specific. The new vision, the *basileia* of the sky/heavens is near but not quite yet. Wilderness and waterfront are not in opposition. They function within the heterogeneity of this section of the text in a way that challenges readers to be attentive to the hybridity of materiality, sociality, of power and of erasure in order to hear what is new when one reads from the marginal lived space.

3. *Matthew 4.1-11: Wilderness Challenges*[8]

In the process of reading Matthew 3, it has become evident that both John and Jesus move almost imperceptibly between wilderness and waterfront. Given that the Jordan River flows through the wilderness of Judea, the boundaries between the two are somewhat porous. Inter-con/textually, therefore, both wilderness and waterfront characterize Matthew 3 and 4: its inner, inter- and ecological textures.

From the very outset the narrative of Matthew 4 continues the TimeSpace relationship that has characterized Matthew 3. The now familiar time designation '*tote*'/'then' opens the chapter. It is followed by the account of Jesus being led into the *erēmos*/desert. The text does not, however, give readers any glimpse of Jesus' interaction with the space that is the wilderness/desert as it did in relation to John (3.4). Rather, it points to the fact that Jesus did not eat of the sustenance that the desert can provide, as he was fasting (Hirschfeld 1990). Reading through the lens of the re-mark, one recognizes the 'hair's breadth' between background and foreground in the text and the possibility of bringing the 'First-space' appropriation of wilderness/desert to the foreground. This opens up at least imaginative exploration of the wilderness in interaction with Jesus. It also allows for a reading of wilderness that is not idealized by the human community but which is the place with all its diversity of habitat/s and Earth constituents in which Jesus fasts.

The fast of Jesus in the desert is in contrast with John's being sustained by the fruit of the desert, by his habitat (Mt. 3.4). The ecological reader will, therefore, be attentive to the encoding in the ecological texture of the text of the relationship of first century inhabitants of the region of the Jordan with their desert/wilderness environment through the characterization of John. Contemporary readers may also be attentive to the challenge of 'desert' and draw into this ecological texture of the text the processes of desertification that are common across much of the land mass of Australia (as noted earlier) but that are also now being visited on the once exceedingly fertile islands of the Pacific with land degradation (Nunn 1997).

Robert Leal summarizes the intertextuality that seems most appropriate to the 'Second-space' understanding of Mt. 4.1, conceiving wilderness as the place of divine encounter in which discipline, purification and/or transformation take place, often as a result of the harshness of the environment in relation to human habitation (2005: 135-71). Stegner also links wilderness with the theme of testing (1967: 18-27). Thus the reference to wilderness can function geographically and metaphorically. It is a space that has its own particular eco-systems but a place that can be harsh for those of the

---

8. This section draws on Wainwright 2013a.

human community who have not learnt to live there.[9] It tests such human persons to determine their ability to relate with such an environment. Given such liminality, it is conceived of as a place of encounter with the divine and with the *diabolos*. The spirit who has been characterized earlier as 'holy' (1.18, 20; 3.11) and 'of G*d' (3.16) leads Jesus into the wilderness where he is tested by the *diabolos* as were his ancestors, tested to determine his nature and character (BDAG 793).

Reading the *erēmos*/wilderness or desert through the lens of Soja's 'Third-space', it can be seen as a site of marginality but not a marginality that is 'imposed by oppressive structures'. It is rather a site that 'one chooses as a site of resistance' (1999: 271). It is a place where Jesus fasts for forty days and forty nights. In this way he is characterized intertextually through the lens of the prophet and mediator of a covenant with the divine, particularized in Moses and Elijah (Exod. 34.27-28 and 1 Kgs 19.8). Moses fasted for forty days and forty nights and Exod. 34.28 goes on to say 'he neither ate bread nor drank water'. Drink is given by Earth for the sustenance of the human community in the case of water and from the Earth into human hands that process it, in the case of bread. Elijah journeyed for forty days and nights on the strength of the food and drink that he was given in the wilderness. Thus fasting can be read intertextually as a symbol not only of human reliance on divinity but also on Earth and the gifts that it gives into human hands. The abstaining from food brings an awareness of this— Jesus is hungry (4.2). The one with/in whom G*d is with G*d's people (Mt. 1.23) or the beloved in whom G*d is well pleased (3.17) must know this reliance, the hunger that comes from the choice neither to eat nor to drink for a period of time.[10] Jesus has been lead into this marginal or liminal space not as a location imposed on him but a space that he clearly embraces and from which prophetic resistance will be possible.

This resistance becomes manifest as one reads the account of the three tests or temptations that Jesus faces (4.3-10) through the lens of Soja's First-, Second- and Third-space. The 'First-space' location of the three tests differs. The wilderness or desert remains the perceived space for the first test and in it Jesus experiences hunger as a result of his fast. The test offered to Jesus is to manipulate the fine balance between Earth and human processes that transform grain and water into bread. Rather he is challenged

---

9. It has been noted earlier that the Australian indigenous peoples have lived in its interior desert/s for 40,000 or more years prior to European invasion.

10. McVann 1993: 14-20, reads the fasting and the testing of Jesus through the lens of the ritual process constituting Jesus as a prophet. One critique that I would bring to McVann's article from an ecological perspective is that he sets up a contrast: Jesus' 'submission' to the devil in 'nature' so that he can overcome him 'in *culture*' (17). It is just such a divide that has shaped much of the oppression of both women and Earth and which was critiqued earlier in this work.

to change stones into bread, to intervene in Earth/human processes and the delicate interrelationship between the human and other-than-human Earth elements. Jesus resists the challenge. Reading his response from a 'Third-space' or place of resistance represented by an ecological perspective, one can hear him affirming Earth/human interrelationships and their interconnectedness with the divine. The *alla* or 'but' in the phrase 'the human one/the *anthrōpos* shall not live by bread alone, *but* by every word that proceeds from the mouth of God' (v. 4) could be interpreted as opposing the sustenance of human food with the sustenance of G*d's word.[11] BDAG (45) offer another way of understanding the connective, precisely as an alternative. It could mean both 'by bread alone' and 'by every word…'. The human one must be in right relationship with both Earth elements and with G*d.[12] In his response, Jesus also resists the diabolic proposal to manipulate Earth's elements for his own satisfaction or gratification, providing a challenge to contemporary readers in a world where such manipulation is contributing to ecological degradation in multiple ways.[13]

The 'First-space' location of the second test is the pinnacle of the temple in the city of Jerusalem. Already in Matthew's gospel, Jerusalem has been portrayed as the centre of political power with Herod's building programme providing it with the built environment of a royal city. It was also the religious centre, given the location of the temple within the city. This temple had been reconstructed by Herod using the massive stones that can still be seen on the site. But the temple also bears all the ambiguity of this reconstruction by Herod whose use of power and the material was in opposition to claims of divine presence. Some of this ambiguity is already woven into Mt. 2.1-12, where Jerusalem was contrasted with Bethlehem, the place of Jesus birth. The devil's taking of Jesus to the 'holy city' and placing him on the 'pinnacle of the temple' evokes these First- and Second-space connotations inter-con/textually as Jesus is represented in the inner texture of the text as having the entire city within his extraordinary purview. Place and power with all their material, political, social, cultural and religious connotations play within the ecological texture of this text.

---

11. McVann, p. 17, represents such a reading when he claims in relation to 4.4 that 'fidelity to God's word supersedes even basic necessities such as food'.

12. Mt. 3.15 associates the unfolding of Jesus' story in terms of 'fulfilling all righteousness' and such righteousness or right ordering or justice will characterize Jesus' own preaching (see 5.6, 10, 20; 6.1, 33). Reading from an ecological perspective, such right ordering will not be seen solely as right relationships within the human community and between the human community and G*d but all Earth's constituents will be included in the interconnected web/s of right or just ordering.

13. The text does not speak against such manipulation but puts it into the complex of right relationships that Jesus constructs. It challenges the human community to careful ecological evaluation of the scientific and industrial processes it puts in place.

Jesus' claim on power is being tested in the second temptation by the *diabolos* or tempter in the context of the intersecting web of power functioning in this text. The tempter places Jesus in a position of oversight of all the visual symbols of Herod's political and economic power, the result of the transformation of material resources into the reconstructed city. He then challenges Jesus within the framework of the challenge/riposte functioning between them. In the first such contest, Jesus bests the tempter/tester with his citation of Deut. 8.3. The tempter then throws out the challenge of a different text to Jesus: Ps. 91.11a, 12. This is a psalm that uses multiple layers of imagery in order to evoke G*d's assurance of protection. It is interpreted literally by the tempter, challenging Jesus to throw himself down and to expect extraordinary divine intervention to counteract his human action. Jesus interprets divine power very differently from the tempter. He cites Deut. 6.16 and its prohibition against testing G*d and in doing so evokes the intertext Exod. 17.1-7 and the people's 'testing' of G*d at Massah and Meribah.[14] There the people trust neither G*d nor Earth to provide them with water to drink along their wilderness journey and yet it is the intersection of the power of both that will sustain them. This is the reliance that must not be tested.

Power emerges even more explicitly in the third temptation whose location is the top of a very high mountain from which 'all the kingdoms/*basileias* of the world' are visible. Intertextually, the tops of high mountains are the abode of divine power: of the gods of those whom Israel contested (Deut. 12.2), and of Israel's G*d (Ezek. 20.40). Also, Moses and Elijah encounter G*d on the mountain height of Sinai or Horeb—Exod. 34; 1 Kgs 19). It is also the locale of the gods of Rome who 'were thought to reside on Mt. Olympus' (Carter 2000: 110). From this place of divine power, the tempter shows Jesus 'all the kingdoms/*basileias* of the world' as noted above. These '*basileias* of the world' are the political, economic, social and religious centres which are being offered to Jesus with all the 'honor…, fame, recognition, renown… (and) prestige' (BDAG 257) that accompanies them. In particular, they are the realms and powers of Rome (Carter 2004a: 266-67). Already in the narrative John the Immerser has proclaimed that the *basileia* of the heavens is at hand (3.2) and that there is one coming after him who will carry on the task of eschatological prophet (3.11-12). Jesus has been intimately linked with John by way of John's baptizing of him to fulfil all righteousness or right ordering. According to McVann's interpretation, Jesus is thereby initiated as such a prophet by way of the ritual process that he, McVann, identifies in Matthew 3–4 (1993: 14-20).

The price offered to Jesus for these kingdoms with all their political, social, economic and religious power is worship of Satan. Jesus once again speaks from the 'Third-space' of the mountain top, a third word of

---

14. The LXX of Exod. 17.2 uses the verb *peirazein* that is similarly used in Mt. 4.1-12.

resistance—only G*d shall be worshipped, only G*d will be given the homage of one's life. But we have already seen that this G*d is with the Earth community in and through Jesus. The *basileias* that the tempter shows Jesus embrace the entire more-than-human community/ies. They are not just constituted by the human community and its political, social, economic and religious inter-relationships. Indeed, the reader knows that the gospel narrative has already been placed within the scope of the genealogy of the heavens/sky and earth (Mt. 1.1) and that G*d is with this Earth community in and through Jesus (1.23). These *basileias* in their fullness of habitat and humanity are not for the *diabolos* to give.

While the first two tests of the beloved one point to the web of right relationships that connect the divine, human and the other-than-human, the third test, which purportedly challenges the power that characterizes the *basileias* of the cosmos, in fact breaks the web. At first reading, it seems to focus only on divine power or the divine/human interrelationship presented as cultic service.[15] Earth appears to be excluded at this climactic point in the pericope as are divine-human relationships imaged in ways other than power. I have noted above that it is possible to read against the grain of this aspect of the narrative in a way that alerts the attentive ecological reader to the exclusion of the female from this entire narrative. Jesus, the tempter (4.3) and G*d (explicitly in 4.10 but implicitly throughout by way of pronouns) are all gendered male. The ecological reader will, therefore, need to take up the space of resistance given to Jesus in the text and to read against the grain of this gendering, bringing into the imaging of G*d at least echoes of Sophia or of the female divine imaged as dove from 3.16-17. It will also be necessary to carry the web of relationships which function in Jesus' successful negotiation of the first two tests into that of the third, reading against the grain of the text, as demonstrated above. Recognition of the *basileias* of the world must include the material, must include habitat as well as humanity with its socio-political and cultural inter-relationships, its sociality.

4. *Matthew 4.12-25: A New Waterfront*

As the ecological reader moves to the next segment of the unfolding Matthean story, time, place, proclamation, people/humanity and habitat are inextricably intertwined to provide meaning. Political tension encountered in the infancy of Jesus (2.13-25) now extends to his adult life and that of his associates. John has been arrested, by whom the reader is not told but could presume by those Judaean authorities disturbed by his attracting of large crowds from Jerusalem, Judea and all along the Jordan. Only later does the

---

15. BDAG, 587, give the meaning of *latreuein* which occurs in the text of Deut. 6.13 cited in Mt. 4.10 as servitude or cultic service.

reader learn that it is Herod Antipas who has had John arrested (14.3). As a result of hearing of John's arrest, Jesus withdraws (*anachōrēsein*) from the wilderness to Galilee just as he had been withdrawn from conflict earlier by Joseph in response to the commissioning of the angel (2.14, 22). Without explanation, Jesus makes his home in Capernaum 'by the sea', a new waterfront, a new habitat (4.13) characterized by all the complexity involved in such an explicit location.

The phrase 'by the sea' draws into the narrative the abundance of life associated with the sea/the waterfront, the place where sea and land meet, both first century Galilee and twenty-first century shorelines.[16] The naming of Capernaum evokes the human community of this thriving town/village on the edge of the Sea of Galilee in the first century, its built environment of regional basalt, and the complex relationships between the human and other-than-human participants in this habitat, especially its fishing and agricultural industries (Edwards 2007: 366, 373-74). Jesus becomes an inhabitant (*katōkēsen*) of this town, opening up the potential for the development of the complex web of relationships that in-habiting such a material and cultural location can involve (Strange and Shanks 1982; Tzaferis 1989; Hoppe 2005).

Such potential is captured intertextually in the evoking of Isa. 9.1-2 (LXX 8.23–9.1) with the named regions of Naphtali and Zebulun providing the connection with the entire poem of Isa. 9.1-7. The contrast between light and darkness at the opening of the poem makes way for the hope for the child who will bring deliverance, articulated in the imagery of his *basileia* which is to be characterized by justice and righteousness (Isa. 9.1-7).[17] Place and political potential provide the context for proclamation, for a new dream, a new envisaging of the divine dream. The phrase 'Galilee of the nations' functions intertextually, however, to remind readers, especially in Syria or Galilee after the Jewish war of 70 CE, of the world of materiality and mastery in which the dream is envisioned. Carter (2004a: 266) describes this well when he says that 'Rome's control of Galilee and Judea had been freshly asserted post-70 not only by military conquests, but also by redistributing seized land to loyal elites and through taxation' (Josephus, *J.W.* 7.216-217).[18] The problematic of imperial power and the potential of a promised liberator meet, opening the way for the proclamation of Jesus.

Jesus now begins to preach the same message as that of John (3.2): repent for the *basileia* of the heavens/sky, G*d's being with the Earth community, is

16. As an example of the richness of such life, see Rosenfeld and Paine.
17. Note the intimate link between Isa. 7.14 cited in Mt. 1.23 and Isa. 9.1-7 evoked in Mt. 4.15-16. For further elaboration, see Carter 2004: 264-66.
18. Note also Chancey (2002) who critiques the 'myth' of a Gentile Galilee in the first century CE that has characterized biblical scholarship.

near at hand (4.17).[19] It is this message that will characterize and will shape the subsequent unfolding of the Matthean narrative. Jesus, the beloved of the heavenly one (3.17), the one in whom G*d is with the Earth community in all its materiality and sociality, begins his mission to 'save/liberate', liberate both earth and heaven (1.21). Catherine Keller calls this '"metanomic" consciousness' and she sees it as our way of participating, 'in our finite, interconnected creatureliness', in the central gospel imperative of Mt. 4.17 (Keller 1994: 343). It is a con-version to and towards Earth, to habitat as well as to the human and the holy.

Extraordinarily, before Jesus is presented as explicitly undertaking his proclamation in any specific way, he invites others to share in this mission, this proclamation. He calls four Capernaum fishermen to join him as he walks the waterfront, presumably of this village (4.18-22). The narrative is replete with the rich inter-con/textuality of the material, socio-economic and cultural imagery associated with fishing, perhaps the most significant industry of first-century Capernaum (Nun 1993; Hanson 1997: 99-111).[20] Jesus sees (*eiden* which draws attention to the materiality of the human and other-than-human actants in this hybrid network) two sets of two brothers (vv. 18 and 21) engaged in the fishing industry that characterized this north/north-western section of the Sea of Galilee. Indeed Peter and Andrew are explicitly named as fishermen (*halieis*) and are observed as casting their nets into the sea, the most characteristic activity of this occupation (Nun 1993). James and John are in the boat with their father, Zebedee, mending their nets (v. 21).

At the invitation (*legei autois* of v. 19) or call (*ekalesen autois* of v. 21) of Jesus[21] the four leave (*aphentes*) their nets (*diktua*—v. 20), the boat (*to ploion*) and their father (*ton patera autōn*—v. 22), all that represents the material, socio-economic and kinship aspects of their lives and they follow (*ēkolouthēsan*) Jesus into a new fictive kinship. It would be easy to read the response to Jesus' invitation to join him in his proclamation of the *basileia* vision of G*d as simply causing a rift from the material and social aspects of the fishermen's lives. Indeed it does threaten 'kinship and household' on which 'the traditional village economy' is based (Moxnes 2010: 405, 413) as well as the honor and shame system operative in this agrarian society (Neyrey 1998: 164-98). As the story unfolds, however, their following of

---

19. See earlier for a more extensive exploration of this proclamation that characterizes the preaching of John the Baptist and Jesus in the Matthaean Gospel.

20. Hanson, p. 100, notes that 'scholars of the Jesus traditions have seriously underplayed the role and significance of the physical and social geography of Galilean fishing on Jesus' development of his network.'

21. See 1 Kgs 19.19-21 as model for the type of 'call story' that Matthew employs here and in 8.14-15 and 9.9—Davies and Allison (1988: 393) and Wainwright (1991: 178-82).

Jesus and their association with and learning within and from his ministry will reveal new kinship possibilities (12.46-50) grounded in the material, the socio-economic, political and religious aspects of not only the districts around the Sea of Galilee and beyond but also in the proclamation of the *basileia* vision. An ecological reading will be attentive to these features first presented in the summary verses that follow (4.23-25) and which, with 9.35, form a frame around the 'Sermon on the Mount' that will be examined in the following section and the healing narratives of Matthew 8–9.

Chapter 4

MATTHEW 5–7:
MOUNTAIN PROCLAMATION—IN-FORMED WITH EARTH[1]

This section of Matthew' gospel, the first discourse or detailed proclamation (Mt. 5–7), and the next section which is comprised of a number of healings (Mt. 8–9), are together framed by parallel summary passages, making them a narrative unity (see 4.23 and 9.35). Not only are place and proclamation intimately linked as in the previous section but proclamation (articulated now as teaching in their synagogues and proclaiming the good news of the *basileia*) is extended to include the healing of 'every disease and every sickness' (4.23//9.35). The summary passages direct the reader's attention to the named region of Galilee with all its physical/geographic, socio-political and cultural features (see by way of example Freyne 1980, 1988, 2004; Chancey 2005; Horsley 1995, 1996). This suggests to the reader that proclamation always occurs within the rich inter-con/textuality of habitat. And while 4.23 evokes all of this under the rubric of 'Galilee', 9.35 makes more specific reference to the built environment of 'cities and villages' while both verses identify the 'synagogues' as the location in which teaching takes place. Jesus' reputation also spreads beyond his ministry context. It extends 'throughout all Syria', and great crowds 'follow', as do the four who are called (4.20, 22), but now not only from Galilee but from 'the Decapolis, Jerusalem, Judea, and from beyond the Jordan'.

Already in the narrative, Jerusalem and Judea have been places of resistance to the infant Jesus' birth and also the object of John's challenge in his proclamation of the *basileia* of the heavens/sky. The attentive reader will, therefore, be wary of hearing these extensive geographic claims of the narrator as acceptance of Jesus' proclamation and healing. They focus the reader's attention on con-text, on built environment, on the materiality of bodies tormented by 'every disease and every sickness' (4.23//9.35) and afflicted by 'various diseases and pains' (with 4.24 listing demoniacs, epileptics, and paralytics) in a way that alerts readers to the very specificity of these bodily afflictions, and to bodies speaking and listening.

---

1. Some of the material in this chapter has appeared in Wainwright, Myles and Olivares 2014: 61-74.

These summary passages also reiterate that the ministry of Jesus, whether his words or his healing actions, take readers into the realm of power. The waters of the Jordan and the words of the heavenly voice authorised Jesus (3.16-17) and it is as authorised teacher and preacher in the synagogues of Galilee that he proclaims the good news (*euangelion*) of the *basileia* (see 3.2 and 4.17). This proclamation takes place in a context of Galilee/Syria, a region that belongs within the political realm of the empire of Rome. Power and contesting/contested power, functioning vertically and horizontally, are never far from the unfolding story of this new *basileia* that is at hand. This will be evident in the ethic of this new *basileia* that Jesus preaches from the mountaintop in Matthew 5–7.

At the outset, it is clear that in this section of the Matthean gospel, framed and informed by 4.23 and 9.35, there is an integration of 'the cultural with the natural' (Curtin 2005: 195). To read the proclamation of Jesus in Matthew 5–7 in a way that recognizes such integration or 'reintegration' to use Curtin's word, calls for a significant shift to an ecological hermeneutic. This is in response to the nature/culture divide which constitutes one of the dualisms within the instituted imaginary of mastery which both Val Plumwood (1993) and Lorraine Code (2006) critique as do many other feminists since the famous article of Sherry Ortner (1974: 67-87) together with a growing number of ecological thinkers, writers and ethicists. It is only as a result of such a shift that humans recognize themselves as members of the 'ecological community'. Indeed Curtin demonstrates that '[a]n environmental ethic should see environmental justice, social justice, and economic justice as parts of the same whole, not as dissonant competitors' (2005: 7; see also Eaton 2005, 105; Nash 1996: 10). This is not simply adding ecology to already existing reading paradigms but significantly shifting one's way of thinking. It returns us, therefore, to the ecological hermeneutic outlined at the beginning of this volume. Inherent in this is the recognition that reading ecologically is reading an ancient text with new eyes. This new reading will be shaped and formed by the rich inner, inter- and ecological textures of the text. Along one axis of intertexture will be the work of ecological ethicists, scientists and theologians which folds back into the text's intertexture. Along the other axis will be the encoding of ancient texts together with social, cultural and ecological traces of the text's con-texts.

It will not be possible in this work to read the proclamation of Jesus in Matthew 5–7 in the same detail as I have read texts up to this point. This is a task that opens up in front of this commentary, given that it is important to be able to read all texts ecologically. I will focus on selected texts either because of their significance in the Christian tradition or their strategic placement in the Matthean community's structuring of this proclamation or the ecological attention that has already been given to them: Mt. 5.1-12; 6.9-15, 25-34; and 7.21-29.[2]

1. *Matthew 5.1-12: The (Ecological) Ethic of the Basileia*

Matthew 5.1 opens very explicitly with Jesus 'seeing' the crowds and going up the mountain. He is in an other-than-human context, described in relation to his own sensory activity of 'seeing' the crowds (5.1 and 4.25) and his going up the material location of 'the mountain'. There he sits down, presumably on the ground or on a rock or stone and a group called 'disciples', a group not previously named in this way in the gospel, come to him and he relates to them bodily and socially: opening his mouth and teaching them.

The sensory activity of seeing (5.1) links Jesus by way of awareness to the crowds who are following him (4.25). The narrator does not explicitly locate the crowds in 5.1 in relation to the subsequent phrase describing Jesus' going up the mountain. However, the concluding verses of the teaching of Jesus (7.28-29) correct this lacuna, making it clear to the reader that the crowds have been recipients of Jesus' teaching. Also, the narrative does not identify the 'mountain' nor does it give details of what would have been a difficult process of getting not only Jesus but disciples and crowds up a 'very high' mountain such as that identified in 4.8 and 17.1. BDAG (724) recognize the locational relativity of what is called a 'mountain'. Hence Jesus may be characterized as going up an incline that provided him with a place from which to preach/teach. In such a way, we might imagine the materiality or 'First-space' meaning of this reference (see the many other occurrences of 'mountain' in the gospel: 4.8; 5.1, 14; 8.1; 14.23; 15.29; 17.1, 9, 20; 18.12; 21.1, 21; 24.3, 16; 26.30; 28.16).

Mountain, however, also functions symbolically, or with 'Second-space' significance within the Matthean gospel. Intertextually, mountains are places of encounter with G*d for Abraham (Gen. 22.2-19), for Elijah (1 Kgs 19.8-18), and for Moses (Exod. 19.1-6). The mountain is also the place from which Israel receives G*d's covenantal law (Exod. 19.17-20; 24.12-18; 32.15-19; 34.1-9). The placing of Jesus 'on the mountain' authorizes him for teaching, a teaching that comes from his experience of encounter with the divine or the holy, the one with the Earth community. Jesus' bodily placement, namely sitting, further emphasizes his symbolic association with Moses and also with the rabbinic teachers in his religious tradition (see Allison 1993: 175-79; cf. Mt. 23.2). The phrase that follows, 'he opened his mouth' is not common in Matthew's gospel (5.2; 13.35). The strongest intertextuality is with the wisdom tradition where it is linked with the justice or righteousness

---

2. For exploration of animals used as ciphers to think with ethically in the Matthaean sermon, see Wainwright 2015.

of the sage who 'opens the mouth' for the 'rights of the destitute' (Prov. 31.8) or defends the 'rights of the poor and needy' (Prov. 31.9). The material, the social and the symbolic intersect in this opening verse to characterize Jesus the teacher/preacher. The introduction to Jesus' teaching (5.1-2), concludes with the words 'and he taught them' further identifying him with both the sages and Sophia/Wisdom (Deutsch 1996: 81-83) and enabling male and female metaphors to play inclusively in this intertextual characterization of Jesus who begins to preach/teach.

The first word that the listeners hear from the opened mouth of Jesus is *makarioi*/fortunate, happy, privileged, blessed (BDAG 610). Indeed, this same word is repeated eight more times as Jesus begins his first explicit preaching of the *basileia* of the heavens/sky (4.17). The first eight repetitions are followed by the third person plural article *hoi* (blessed/happy/privileged *the*...) while the ninth or last repetition is followed by the second person plural verb *este* (blessed/happy/privileged are you), distinguishing the last from the set of eight. Carter says of these proclamations that open Jesus' teaching that they 'do not offer "entrance requirements to God's reign" for humans to meet' but rather they describe God's *basileia* already present (Carter 1997: 25), a presence which an ecological reader would locate in the Earth community as G*d's very self is with that community in Jesus (1.23). This is evident in the inner texture of the text in that the phrase 'theirs is the *basileia* of the heavens' frames the first eight proclamations (5.3b and 10b).

Intertextually, *makarioi* evokes the repeated affirmation by the psalmists of those who are in right relationship with G*d (Pss. 1.1; 32.1-2; 34.8; 40.4; 41.1; 65.4; 84.4-5, 12; 89.15; 94.12; 128.1; 146.5) and who do what is right and just (Pss. 106.3; 119.1, 2). It also echoes the proclamation of the sages in relation to those who are wise and who live the wisdom of Sophia (Prov. 3.13; 8.34; Sir. 14.1, 2; 14.20; 31.8; 34.17; 50.28). Such intertextuality confirms the claims of Hans Dieter Betz that the *makarioi* proclamations are 'declarative statements' and they are 'connected with ethics and morality' (1995: 93; see also Neyrey 1998: 164-67, for discussion of this terminology within the honour/shame culture of the first century). For the ecological reader, there is a strong awareness of what seem to be the profoundly anthropocentric aspects of these *makarioi* statements or makarisms, focussed as they seem to be on divine gifting and human virtues. Indeed, they could be said to demonstrate James A. Nash's powerful critique that '[t]he Bible is ... ecologically unconscious' (Nash 2009: 214). For the contemporary ecological reader, exploration of the ecological texture and the intertextuality emerging from Israel's scriptures as well as dialogue with contemporary ecological ethics, science and theology, render it possible to take up Nash's challenge to undertake 'an ecotheological revisioning of the central affirmations of faith', the makarisms of Mt. 5.3-12 being one set of such central affirmations.

Those first proclaimed *makarioi* are the 'poor in spirit'. This particular phrase evokes little intertextually in that it occurs nowhere in the Jewish scriptures in this way nor indeed, Betz claims, in the Greek language (1995: 113). Betz goes on to point to potential intertexts which capture the 'blessed condition' of being 'poor in spirit' such as Sir. 40.1-11 which recognizes that all living beings return to the earth or Isa. 40.6-8 that likens humans to grass as both wither and fade. Each intertext emphasizes the 'materiality' that all Earth's constituents share. Betz recognizes humility, 'a virtue highly praised in antiquity' (116), as corresponding to being poor in spirit. But such humility, such recognition of what the human person shares with all Earth constituents, is not only an ancient virtue to be named as blessed or favoured. Nash recognizes it among the contemporary ecological virtues (2009: 235; 1991: 66-67, 156-57). Bringing his exploration of this ecological virtue of humility into dialogue, in the intertexture of Mt. 5.3, with Sirach and Isaiah's recognition of the life potential and life fragility that all beings share in the more-than-human community, leads to a recognition that 'the poor in spirit' know who they are in the simplicity of their being, which is gift, and how they are in relation to all Earth's others.

Anne Elvey explores such humility, describing it as a 'kind of kenosis' (Elvey 2009: 39) that echoes Nash's linking of humility with the self-emptying of G*d who enters and identifies with humanity (1991: 156). I would extend this divine identification beyond humanity to all Earth beings with whom the self-emptying one shares life.[3] Lisa Gerber (2002: 42) makes more explicit the shift of focus from oneself as self- or human-centred that is necessary for the humility that I am associating with Jesus' affirmation of the 'poor in spirit' from an ecological perspective. She suggests it entails a recognition of other-ness which calls forth awe, an awe which a reader might imagine that Jesus the preacher recognized as he engaged with the habitat in which his mountain-side preaching platform was located and an awe that his human listeners may have shared while also recognizing in him the one in whom G*d was with the Earth community, one who had *exousia*/authority (7.29). Indeed, being poor in spirit as an ecological virtue enables relationship or identification within the more-than-human Earth community, an identification that expands the self and enables meaningful action on account of a vision which in the Matthean gospel is named the *basileia* of the heavens.

---

3. Anne Primavesi (2011) likewise speaks of the ecological virtue of humility saying that 'scientific revelations make it theoretically and physically impossible for us to claim pole position in the evolution of life or to be an exception to evolutionary rules. Accepting the implications of this truth and acting accordingly is what I call *ecological humility*' (emphasis mine).

In the second half of v. 3, Jesus gives the reason why the 'poor in spirit', those who recognize their kenotic participation with all other beings in the more-than-human community, are proclaimed blessed/honoured/happy: theirs *is* the *basileia* of the heavens/sky. The proclamation of John the Baptizer (3.2) and of Jesus (4.17, 23), the *basileia* of the heavens/sky, is present to/in those who live in the right ordering of the Earth community. The metaphor carries in it the materiality of the *ouranoi*, the heavens or sky, together with the galaxies, stars and heavenly entities that constitute the universe. The metaphor is not limited to one place given the plural *ouranoi* but it gives place to Jesus new social imaginary that he calls the *basileia* of the heavens (see Moxnes 2003: 108-113). This *basileia* is among those of the disciples of Jesus gathered around him who are named as 'poor in spirit', who recognize their inter-connectedness with all Earth's constituents now and not just in some future time. It is in contrast to the *basileia* of Rome in which political and military power-over facilitated and constituted their vision of the *pax Romana* with little attention given to the relationship/s between the humans and other-than-humans who inhabited this *basileia*.[4]

The second proclamation of honour is directed to those who mourn (5.4). Intertextually, the verb designates those who have lost someone or something that they hold dear (Gen. 23.2; 37.34; 50.3; 1 Sam. 15.35). The sage mourns his ignorance of Wisdom (Sir. 51.19) and in Hos. 4.3, the land and all beings who live in it mourn as Earth's creatures vanish (cf. Isa. 33.9; Jer. 4.28; 12.4) and people mourn the fate of Earth (Amos 8.8). Mourning accompanies the loss of right relationships in the Earth community and in that community's relationship with the divine. Many scholars consider Isa. 61.2-3 to be the key intertext of Mt. 5.4. Carter comments that 'they mourn or lament the destructive impact of imperial powers such as Babylon (and Rome) which oppress God's people' (2000: 132). Relationships have been out of order at designated points in Israel's unfolding story and mourning has been the response of those members of the Earth community who recognize this, including the land and the living beings it supports. It is all these who mourn that Jesus proclaims as blessed. Such grief and mourning for Earth's broken relationships characterize many today who work for ecological transformation. It also characterizes those Earth creatures who

---

4. Plumwood (1993: 195-96) in the concluding paragraphs of *Feminism and the Mastery of Nature*, articulates a vision for human reason which could inform the revisioning of the 'poor in spirit' beatitude that I am proposing: it is to 'find a form which encourages sensitivity to the conditions under which we exist on earth, one which recognizes and accommodates the denied relationships of dependency and enables us to acknowledge our debt to the sustaining others of the earth. This implies creating a democratic culture beyond dualism, ending colonizing relationships and finding a mutual, ethical basis for enriching coexistence with earth others.'

mourn the loss of companions from a species or habitat or whose kin have been wantonly destroyed by expansive human power. Phyllis Windle recognizes and explores the significance of mourning and rituals of grief as habitats, trees, grasses, animals and many others disappear from our world, often at the hands of a range of 'imperial' human powers in rural and urban places, in nations and globally (Windle 1992: 363-66).[5]

While mourning is recognized and affirmed as a significant moment in Jesus' proclamation of G*d's *basileia* dream, it is not to become a permanent mode of being. Rather, the second half of this second beatitude points to a future beyond mourning, namely, being comforted. In seeking to understand this comforting, I imagined that many of the 65 occurrences of the verb *penthein/to mourn* in the LXX would have been followed by *parakaleein/to comfort*. This is not so. There are only four verses in which the two verbs occur together (Gen. 37.35; 1 Chron. 7.22; Sir. 48.24 and Isa. 61.2). One of these refers to the prophet Isaiah's comforting of the people of Zion while a second is in the prophetic words of Isa. 61.2-3. It is perhaps these verses that offer most to making meaning of Mt. 5.4b. In the *basileia* vision, transformation can and will happen. Those who mourn will be given 'a garland instead of ashes' and the 'oil of gladness instead of mourning' (Isa. 61.3). The rich diversity of life on land, in the sea and in the skies and the very Earth itself, all who have mourned, will be comforted when their diversity is able to flourish and be enhanced. Indeed, Isaiah says of all these metaphorically that they will be called 'oaks of righteousness' (61.3c). They become symbols of a restored right ordering;[6] but more importantly, relationships within the entire more-than-human community are to be characterized by this right ordering. Nash captures a similar vision within the virtue of biodiversity whose goal, he says, is 'a commitment to sustaining viable populations of all species in healthy habitats until the end of their evolutionary time (Nash 1991: 66; see also Milton 2002: 110-28).

Many have noted the close relationship between the first and third beatitude (Davies and Allison 1988: 449; Betz 1995: 126), between the poverty of spirit and meekness that are honoured or proclaimed blessed. Intertextually, the NRSV translation of *praus* in the First Testament is often 'humble' (Num. 12.3; Pss. 25.9; 34.2; 149.4; Zeph. 3.12; Zech. 9.9), the virtue associated above with the 'poor in spirit' and important for an ecological ethic. Extending this intertextuality, it can be demonstrated that

---

5. For a heart-wrenching example of this see Bernie Krause (2013), a TED talk in which he plays the plaintive sound of a badger whose entire family were destroyed by a gelignite blast which destroyed their home, their habitat.

6. Note that the theme of *dikaiosynē* or 'righteousness' weaves its way through the mountain proclamation (5.6, 10, 20; 6.1, 33).

meekness or gentleness was a prized virtue among the Greeks (Hauck and Schultz 1968: 645-46; Davies and Allison 1988: 449; Betz 1995: 124-25), carrying connotations associated with true strength rather than arrogance and roughness. The most significant intertexture is Psalm 37 in which the phrase 'shall inherit the earth' occurs five times and in v. 11 it is followed by the same phrase as occurs in the Matthean beatitude—'they shall inherit the earth'. Attentiveness to the ecological texture of Mt. 5.5 raises the question as to whether, subsequent to the biblical inclusion of the land and Earth's others among those who mourn, the 'meek' might also include the other-than-human. The relationality or sociality inherent in those honoured or blessed in these beatitudes can function beyond the confines of the human community and constituting the sociality encoded in the ecological texture of the text.

I turn now to a brief intertextual analysis of Mt. 5.5 in relation to Psalm 37 in which v. 11, 'but the meek shall inherit the land and delight themselves in abundant prosperity' is embedded. The psalm belongs to an older wisdom tradition than that of Hellenistic wisdom according to Brueggemann (1978: 162). He critiques its 'perception of the world that is skewed by supreme and uncritical confidence in the system' (1988: 115), evident particularly in vv. 25 and 28b-29. The ecological reader will bring a hermeneutic of suspicion to the structures of power inherent in the socio-political texture of this text as well as that of Mt. 5.5 and its echoes of the links between land (*gē*), human power and possession as privilege.

In reconfiguring Jesus' reference to inheriting the land, the ecological reader will be aware that land can be understood in its materiality and sociality. It is not simply dirt or ground. It is rich with diversity and relationality. Within Israel's biblical tradition, land belonged to G*d as the psalmist sings (Ps. 24.1) and it was gifted to Israel as an inheritance (Num. 26.53; Ps. 105.11), their task being to till it and keep it (Gen. 2.15).[7] The ecological reader might here evoke intertextually Sallie McFague's metaphor of Earth as the 'body of God' (1993) and how attentiveness to oneself in one's own body might inform a meek attentiveness to Earth as body of G*d. Israel's history was fraught with abuse of land by those among them who accumulated ownership to enhance power. It was also fraught with loss of the land. First century Galilee was no exception. The Matthean phrase 'inherit the earth' encodes in its ecological texture the loss of land by small landholders to the gradual process of wealthy owners, Jewish or Roman, gaining more and more land at the expense of the small farmers who were often overtaxed (Goodman 2000: 33; Freyne 1994: 105-110 and Fiensy 1991:

---

7. An ecological reader will be conscious of and bring a hermeneutics of suspicion to the alternate tradition of Gen. 1.26 of human dominion over all the other Earth creatures.

75-117). The beatitude, therefore, holds out a hope that the power of imperial acquisition might be reversed and that land might be accessible to all to sustain life.

The wisdom of Psalm 37 also infuses Mt. 5.5 intertextually. It contrasts the wicked or wrongdoers with those who do good. This second group is named in different ways, one of them being 'meek' (v. 11). The others of whom it is said that they shall 'inherit the earth' are those who wait for G*d (v. 9); those who are blessed by G*d (v. 22); the righteous (v. 29); and the one who is exhorted to wait for G*d and keep G*d's ways. Each of these phrases could describe the meek as they function interactively in the psalm and while each of the groups who will inherit the earth are named differently, the group repeatedly identified with 'doing good' in this psalm are 'the righteous'/*dikaioi* (vv. 12, 16, 17, 21, 25, 29, 30, 32, 39). Inheriting the earth in Mt. 5.5 can be understood, therefore, as being righteous, living according to the right ordering of the entire Earth and all its constituents and with divinity. The beatitude honours those who engage in right acting, right living in relation to Earth, not from a position of arrogance but from humble right relationship.

The righteousness that plays within the intertexture of 5.5 becomes explicit in the fourth beatitude (5.6) when those who hunger and thirst for that righteousness are proclaimed blessed. This interweaving and structuring for meaning characterizes the eight beatitudes. Righteousness/ *dikaiosynē* concludes the first four beatitudes (5.6) and is also a characteristic of the eighth beatitude that concludes the second group of four (5.10). Together with the entire framing of the eight beatitudes with the central Matthean theme of the '*basileia* of the heavens' in vv. 3 and 10, these two thematics infuse each of the makarisms as each, in turn, nuances these key Matthean themes. One could say that at the heart of the *basileia* vision that Jesus preached is *dikaiosynē* or righteousness, envisaged in the multifaceted features of the beatitudes.

Righteousness is a key factor within the repetitive texture of Matthew's gospel. We have already seen it on the lips of Jesus assuring John of the right ordering of John's baptism of Jesus (3.15). It occurs five times in Jesus' mountain proclamation (5.6, 10, 20; 6.1, 33) and its final occurrence is in 21.32. It is within Jesus' initial preaching that it has most significance. An exploration of the rich intertextuality infusing the use of *dikaiosynē* in the Matthean text would take us far beyond the scope of this study. Just briefly, I note that in translation it is rendered as righteousness or justice (Isa. 9.7; 11.5 NRSV) and it is often linked with *krima* or justice as in Isa. 9.7. It is G*d's desired ordering of all relationships and so is praised by psalmist and prophet in texts too numerous to mention and it is the desire of the sages. Its centrality overflows in Ps. 85.10-13 where it is linked to other key attributes of G*d's relationship with the Earth community:

Steadfast love and faithfulness will meet;
   righteousness (*dikaiosynē*) and peace will kiss each other.
Faithfulness will spring up from the ground,
   and righteousness (*dikaiosynē*) will look down from the sky.
God will give what is good,
   and our land (*hē gē*) will yield its increase.
Righteousness (*dikaiosynē*) will go before God,
   and will make a path for God's steps.

This righteousness is characteristic of divine, human and Earth interrelationships—habitat, human and holy. The Matthean Jesus calls blessed those who hunger and thirst for such righteousness or justice, who long for it and who strive to enact it. It is here that indeed ecological and social justice meet and embrace or as Curtin envisaged earlier, 'environmental justice, social justice, and economic justice' come together 'as parts of the same whole' (2005: 7). What this right ordering means explicitly will need to be worked out in each unique location and community. It is in this way that those hungering and thirsting will be satisfied and when that goal is reached, the *basileia* of the heavens will have been realized. The vision must be enacted in the now toward a realization in a future that one can only imagine.

Jesus' naming of the honoured ones in the new *basileia* of the heavens does not stop at this climax point of the first four makarisms, but continues into 5.7-10 where the merciful, the pure in heart, the peacemakers and those persecuted on account of Jesus' vision of righteousness are named as blessed. This second group of four makarisms could be seen to be turning different lenses on 'righteousness'. This would be in keeping with Betz's claim that '[e]thically, righteousness is the standard for human conduct and therefore for all ethical thinking and action. Ethical awareness means continual self-examination with regard to the principle of righteousness' (1995: 130). I examine them briefly for any further nuances that they add to this ecological reading of Jesus' opening proclamation from the mountain.

Intertextually, mercy is a manifestation of the divine in the First Testament, rendered in a number of ways. One rendering, significant for this reading, is *rachamim* or womb-compassion (Trible 1978: 38-56). This metaphor is grounded in the corporeal. Like righteousness in Ps. 85.10-13 (see above), it intersects with a number of other divine manifestations that are less corporeal. In Exod. 33.19 and Isa. 30.18, G*d's womb-compassionate mercy is linked with G*d's graciousness and in Isaiah with G*d's justice. In the second citation, it is followed by a makarism: blessed are those who wait for G*d. Isaiah 49.13 identifies the suffering ones as those who call forth G*d's womb-compassion and Isa. 54.10 extends further the web of manifestations of mercy to God's steadfast love and covenant of peace.

   For the mountains may depart
      and the hills be removed,

> but my steadfast love (*hesed/eleos*) shall not depart from you,
> and my covenant of peace shall not be removed,
> says the One/G*d,[8] who has compassion (*rachamim/eleos*) on you.
> (Isa. 54.10)

The merciful whom Jesus proclaims honoured in Mt. 5.8 can be understood intertextually, therefore, as those who are moved corporeally with womb compassion as G*d is said to be so moved for the ones who suffer. This is captured in the repetitive texture of Matthew's gospel when this womb compassionate mercy is contrasted with sacrifice (Mt. 9.13; 12.7). It called for personal and economic engagement not only within but across households as resources needed to be shared for mercy to be enacted in first century Galilee. For today's ecological reader, suffering is not confined to the human community. Earth itself and all its constituents suffer the ravages of industrialization, over-farming, dumping of toxic waste, disregard for animals and other devastations. It calls forth the corporeal womb compassion that can create communities of compassion, Earth communities of compassion in which mercy is given and received. Nash's ecological virtues of frugality and equity (1991: 65) may contribute to the establishment of such communities of compassion.

The honouring of the 'pure in heart', who are promised that they will *see* G*d, continues to emphasize the corporeality of the dispositions or the ethics of the makarisms, contributing to the sensory-aesthetic within the inner texture of the narrative. Within the ecological texture of the text, the heart and the eyes, evoked in the seeing of G*d, function both corporeally and socio-culturally. They belong to the zone of what Bruce Malina calls 'emotion-fused thought' (1993: 74). They point to a human disposition, a way of turning toward one's being as Earth creature in relation to the divine and to Earth and all its constituents. Denis Edwards captures this in a description of Jesus that echoes Mt. 1.23: 'when one of us in the human and creaturely community, Jesus of Nazareth, is so radically open to God, so one with God…we rightly see him as God-with-us' (2010: 158). This beatitude seems to call for such openness: to G*d, to one's own corporeality, and to other Earth beings so that we will see G*d because G*d will be with-us, the Earth community, as a result.

Making peace in first century Galilee draws into the ecological texture of 5.9 Rome's domination of all peoples in its vast empire, gathering into their fold the ruling classes of their occupied territories so resistance could be quickly quelled (Carter 2000: 135). This is the *Pax Romana*. This is not the peace that Jesus honours. Rather, the peacemakers he calls blessed are

---

8. I have chosen here to translate Yhwn/*kyrios* as 'the One' or 'G*d' in order to decentre the term 'Lord' by which it is often translated into English with all the implications of 'power' and 'power over' in that term.

4. Matthew 5–7

members of G*d's household. The ecological reader, will, however, extend a hermeneutics of suspicion to the gendering of the human householders as sons/male as well as to the type of peace proposed in the context of empire.

As we have come to expect, studying 5.9 intertextually can yield further insights. The *shalom* of G*d permeates the First Testament but there is just one use of the term 'peacemaker', in Prov. 10.10, which yields little. Psalm 72 images the ideal king and, as with the *Pax Romana*, the dominion of this ideal king within the context of hierarchical structures needs to be approached with suspicion (Ps. 72.8-11). That critical reading having been undertaken, the psalm praises those dispositions that make for an ideal *oikoumenos* (Ps. 72.8), dispositions which we can extend from the ideal king to the ideal members of the *oikoumenos*/household of G*d. As with the beatitudes, *dikaiosynē* is prominent in the psalm (Ps. 72.1, 2, 3, 7). In vv. 3 and 7, *eirēnē*/peace and *dikaiosynē*/righteousness occur together. The psalmist draws Earth's others into the vision of peace and justice (vv. 6 and 16), where they too flourish in the right relationships of the ideal society.

We have seen how the values, the ethical disposition and the actions honoured in the opening proclamation of Jesus from the mountain are interwoven into an artfully constructed piece through which righteousness/ *dikaiosynē* and the *basileia* of the heavens are threaded. These threads come together in the last of the eight benedictions, Mt. 5.10—'blessed are those persecuted on account of righteousness because theirs is the *basileia* of the heavens'. As we have seen, any one of the features named blessed could be understood in relation to righteousness, the right ordering or justice that is of G*d and is proclaimed in Jesus' vision of the *basileia* of the heavens/ sky. Any one of these or their combination practised or enacted could bring about persecution. This summary beatitude indicates that these virtues or dispositions are not pious hopes but they are to be enacted in the face of the opposition which they will draw as they did in the past for the prophets and the wise ones of old (5.12; Wis. 2.12-20). These final verses (10-12) may well encode experiences of the followers of Jesus and/or of the Matthean community in Galilee or Galilee/Syria of the first century. They also function in similar ways for the contemporary ecological reader who is attentive to the ecological texture of the Matthean text and to the challenge that an ecological reading provides in front of the text.

As the mountaintop proclamation continues, the ecological reader encounters Jesus using imagery of 'salt' and 'light' to characterize the human community in constant interrelationship with the other-than-human, encoding these material actants in the text (5.13-16). The reader is then drawn into the world of Jewish law and Jesus' interpretation of some of those laws (5.17-42). While a hermeneutics of suspicion recognizes their human-centredness, the attentive reader will also note where the other-than-human actants feature and where they are absent. As this section concludes (5.43-48), Jesus places the laws, including the final law of love, within what can be read as a cosmic framework: G*d's sun rises on 'evil' and 'good' and the rain falls on the 'just' and the 'unjust' (5.45). The reading of the beatitudes has demonstrated that the ethic of the *basileia* involves the entire more-than-human community in right relationship. Here, this relationship is named as 'love'.[9] The encoding of the 'sun' and 'rain' into the ecological texture of 5.45 confirms such a reading: the sun and the rain are gifts to the entire Earth community and it is this community, not just the human, that must strive toward the *teleios* or the 'meeting [of] the highest standard', 'being mature', 'being fully developed in a moral sense' (5.48; BDAG 995).

2. *Matthew 6.9-13:*
The (Ecological) Prayer of the Members of the Alternative Basileia

The preaching of Jesus moves from the laws that characterize the 'righteousness'/*dikaiosynē* of the *basileia* of the heavens (5.20 and 21-48) to what the text calls the 'doing of righteousness' (6.1)—*tēn dikaiosynē... poiein*. The deeds specifically identified are giving alms (6.1-4), praying (6.5-15) and fasting (6.19-21). A repeated pattern links the three sections. Here, I focus only on one of these deeds, namely praying and that limited to the explicit prayer itself which Jesus gives. I wish to note, however, that exploration of the texts on giving alms and fasting would each yield rich insights for the ecological reader.

The prayer of Jesus in Mt. 6.9-13 takes the reader into the heart of the relationships captured by the oft-repeated 'heaven/s and earth' phraseology in Matthew (see Pennington 2007). Not only for the contemporary ecological reader but also for first century readers/hearers, the phrase evokes at one level the cosmos and all that constitutes it. The terminology also links Earth beings in their sociality with heavenly beings in their relationality including the divine one who is named as 'father' forty-four times in Matthew (Pennington 2007: 231-36). While Pennington seeks in an extensive study to distinguish different phraseology around 'heaven and earth', an ecological reader will want to hold in creative interrelationship the notions of 'earth', 'sky', 'cosmos' and 'abode of the divine', recognized in the Matthean phraseology. This is in keeping with a Matthean thematic noted earlier, namely that of Mt. 1.23, that G*d, the divine one, is with the Earth

---

9. 'Love' as a key ethical imperative of the gospel and its ecological implications will be explored more fully in relation to Mt. 19.19 and 22.37-39. I simply draw attention here to the ecological ethics of James Nash for whom '[l]ove is the center of the gospel which everything else radiates from or revolves around. It is the metaethical source of Christian ethics—including, therefore, an ecological ethic' (1991: 140).

community (and we might add 'with the cosmos') in all its materiality and sociality, a thematic which infuses the whole gospel.

The one to whom the prayer that Jesus teaches is to be addressed is named 'our father' (6.9). The familiar 'our' links the disciples intimately with one another and with Jesus in this prayer whose opening address echoes intertextually with other Jewish prayers of the time (D'Angelo 1992). The ecological reader can expand the realm of the 'our' to include all the more-than-human constituents of both the heavens and Earth. It can, indeed, be the ecological prayer of the heavens and the earth, of the cosmos.

A hermeneutics of suspicion, however, draws attention to the fact that the term 'father' or *pater* in the first century took its meaning from the patriarchal family in which the 'father' as *pater familias* or *kyrios* had power and control over all the people and all the material resources of the household of which he was the head (Schüssler Fiorenza 1992: 114-20; see also Dube 2000a: 618).[10] Warren Carter has demonstrated that the title was that appropriated to the emperor as 'father of the fatherland,' as in the *Res gestae* of Augustus (Carter 2011), who likewise had power and control over all the human and material resources of the empire. The title or address, 'father', carries with it, therefore, patriarchal and imperial echoes and imagery that are encoded in the text. Ecological readers will need to read against the grain of such kyriarchal and imperial imagery while engaging with the cosmic imagery and vision that the phrase 'in the heavens/sky' evokes.

This is a 'Third-space' reading that, in the words of Carter, functions to create 'a hybrid identity that permits, employs, and restricts imperial (and I would add kyriarchal) engagement'. It should be noted, however, that despite the potential that a Third-space reading renders possible, the eco-feminist reader may wish to evoke the 'moratorium' on masculine language and imagery for the divine, on the journey toward inclusive imagery, that Elizabeth Johnson comes near to proposing (Johnson 1992: 56-57). For such a reader, a similar 'moratorium' may need to be placed on exclusively human imagery and language in relation to the divine. The cosmic evocation contained in the phrase 'in the heavens' and the inclusion of all more-than-human Earth constituents in the 'our' of the initial address open up potential for further 'Third-space' re-imaging of the divine addressed here in prayer. In this way the name of the divine mystery may be rendered or recognized as holy (6.9b).[11]

---

10. Elisabeth Schüssler Fiorenza names this system *Kyriarchy*. Dube reads the prayer in the context of the two-thirds world of contemporary society. Her analysis could be read along with the one undertaken here to engage another significant dimension.

11. Intertextually, engagement with eco-theologians in their rearticulating of the divine can also fold back into the reading of the text. See by way of example Edwards (2010) and Haught (2006) who have already been intertextual dialogue partners.

Readers are already familiar with the paradigmatic proclamation in the gospel, namely, that the *basileia* of the heavens/sky is near at hand. It is not surprising, therefore, that Jesus includes in the prayer the plea that this alternative *basileia* (3.2; 4.17), which he here associates with the divine one (*sou*/ your), might come (6.10). It is a prayer for the right-ordering/*dikaiosynē* that has already been seen as characterizing the preaching of the *basileia* by John and by Jesus, and that is explicitly evident in the beatitudes which are framed by this right-ordering and by reference to the *basileia* (5.3, 6, 10). It is, however, a right ordering that is to characterize Earth, including the sky/ heavens.[12] The second half of v. 10 echoes back into the first half in different words: that the will of the holy one would come to fruition on Earth as in the heavens. Again the ecological reader is drawn into the interrelationship of Earth, sky/heavens, cosmos and divinity and invited to pray for right ordering in these interrelationships. The divine *thelē* or 'will' first evoked here runs as a thread through the gospel (7.21; 12.50; 18.14; 21.31; 26.42) and can be intimately associated with the Matthean central proclamation of the *basileia* of the heavens/sky.

The prayer turns now to a familiar material—daily bread. Intertextually, it evokes the Israelites being fed daily by the manna/bread for that day (Exod. 16). At the same time, however, it encodes into the ecological texture of the text the process of and need for daily sustenance within the entire more-than-human community if the 'us' of the prayer is extended to include all the constituents of this community. Also encoded into the ecological texture of this first-century text are the subsistence issues that not only the poor in the human community but also their livestock faced daily in Galilean villages (Malina and Rohrbaugh 1992: 59). These were accelerated by the incursions of the Roman Empire into their economy and their politico-economic structure (Horsley 1995: 202-21). In similar ways today, wealthy companies and regimes threaten the daily sustenance of peoples and species. The prayer each day for the bread of that day, the product of gift event, rises up with both ancient and contemporary echoes, from all Earth's constituents.[13]

---

12. Primavesi (2003: 87-100) discusses the philosophical and theological problems created by the notion of 'heaven' which sets it over against earth and earthly existence when she says that 'earth is simply not good enough for us: that we are philosophically...or theologically...destined for somewhere better. When we imagine that better place we call it heaven. A theological corollary to this is the assumption that if earth is not good enough for us, it is certainly not good enough for God' (95).

13. Primavesi (2003: 115-22) explores the nature of 'gift exchange' noting (115) that '[i]ts proper practice ultimately requires seeing the vital components of one's life as gifts from other living beings: gifts often given to us through their death. And as they have been freely given, they have to be received and treated as gifts: not as possessions.' She

> **Ecological Intertexts.** Anne Primavesi, in *Sacred Gaia* and *Gaia's Gift* develops the concept of 'gift' in order to understand Earth relationships. In this she supplies a significant intertext for this ecological reading of the Gospel of Matthew. She notes that 'life is... ultimately characterized by dependence. It is continually constituted by prior and present gifts which make our self-making possible: by gifts which presuppose and involve us in relationships with other people and with other organisms; with the air we breathe and the land we walk; with the food we eat and the love, joy and understanding we receive from others. Some of these gifts we hand on in modified energy exchanges. Some remain with us, becoming constitutive of bone and blood, of health or disease... Compounded of independence/dependence in relation to the earth, we act as givers/receivers in relation to it and to other living entities' (2000: 156-57). Dialogue with Primavesi can inform an intertextual reading of the Matthean text at particular strategic points.

The language of the next petition (v. 12) is rich and multivalent. Intertextually, the imperative, *aphes*/forgive, turns the reader's attention to the release associated with the Jubilee year. Indeed the language dominates the LXX Leviticus 25 (see vv. 10, 11, 12, 13, 28, 30, 31, 33, 40, 41, 50, 52 and 54) and appears less often in Deuteronomy 15 (vv. 1, 2, 3 and 9), both of which are concerned with the enactment of Jubilee and sabbatical years. These were periods in which the right-ordering of all the relationships among the Earth community—human and other-than-human (land, animals, material dwellings and many more) were to be restored.

This petition also encodes the socio-cultural context of debt and remission in first-century Palestine. Douglas Oakman says that the presupposition for 'the biblical view of debt' was 'the equality, with various qualifications, of each member of Israel before Yahweh. This meant equality of access to the goods of life as well' (Oakman 2008: 15). He goes on to demonstrate that such equality was significantly threatened by Roman and Herodian rule of Galilee especially in the first century. The petition calls for a reciprocity of release from indebtedness in the cycle of indebtedness that made the vulnerable more vulnerable. Oakman provides a significant insight for the ecological reader, namely 'the *material* link' between the previous petition for daily bread and this petition for forgiveness. He explains the connection in this way: '[i]ndebtedness threatens the availability of daily bread. Conversely, the petition for daily bread is at the same time a petition for a social order that will supply such basic human needs in a regular and consistent manner' (31). This is a prayer for a radical re-ordering of the socio-cultural context or, for the ecological reader, the sociality of the entire more-than-human context.

---

goes on to say that '[t]his fact confronts us most plainly at every meal, where life and death are inextricably intertwined'.

In vv. 14-15, which appear almost as a footnote to the prayer for forgiveness, Jesus extends the forgiveness prayed for in the material and sociopolitical arena to the human-divine relationship. The language of debt is replaced by *paraptōmata* translated as 'trespasses' ('a violation of moral standards'—against humans and against God, BDAG 770). Given the divine desire for right-ordering within all realms of the cosmos, both divine and human forgiveness is to be characterized by reciprocity or right relationship among all Earth and cosmic constituents. This sends us back then to v. 13, the final petition of the prayer ('lead us not into temptation but deliver us from evil'). Echoes of Jesus being tried or tested in the wilderness to determine his fidelity to the right-ordering of material, socio-political and religious relationships permeate v. 13 and could be said to gather together the threads of this ecological prayer. Evil and temptation have a different face in different contexts, in different eras. Today as our exploration of the temptations of Jesus have demonstrated, temptation and evil wear the face of manipulation of the material, of unjust relationships of power in relation to people and resources, and of a substitution of these for the divine. Dube (2000a: 613-16) articulates such an analysis prior to her engagement with the Prayer of Jesus. To be delivered from these evils is to enact the *basileia* of the heavens as preached by John and Jesus. It is likewise to embrace the new social imaginary that Code calls ecological thinking and the ethic that it entails, or in the words of Dube (2000: 629), it 'entails repentance followed by action'.

3. *Matthew 6.25-34: Birds of the Air and Lilies of the Field*

Jesus' preaching of the *basileia* of the heavens/sky or skies continues drawing other-than-human beings and a range of processes that constitute Earth and its more-than-human constituents into that preaching. Ecological readers are invited to be attentive to the Earth materials they store up as 'treasure' and to the work of 'moth' and 'rust' (6.19-21). The human body and its corporeality also provide images that inform the ethics of the *basileia* that Jesus preaches (6.22-23) as does the service of a master which constituted the lives of so many of Jesus' audience (6.24). These vignettes are indicative of Israel's wisdom tradition that Dianne Bergant (1997: 12) describes as being 'awed by the wonders of nature and concerned with human behaviour, human accomplishment and human misfortune'. She goes on to say that

> [o]bservation of nature and reflection on life led the sages of Israel to conclude that there was some kind of order inherent in the world. They believed that if they could discern how this order operated and harmonize their lives with it, they would live peacefully and successfully in attentiveness to all life and the life processes of all that wisdom and ethics can be grasped.

Jesus, the wise sage (Deutsch 1996) invites such 'attentiveness to all life and the life processes of all' in a way that catches up the contemporary ecological reader.

The '*dia*/therefore' of 6.25 acts as a connective between the wisdom reflections of 6.19-24 and the more expansive vignette of 6.25-34 that continues in the same genre and so continues the call to attentiveness to life and life processes. The reader/hearer of this text is left no room for doubt about the import of this text: it is a challenge not to be anxious—six times the verb *merimnaein* is used to warn against worry, three times in the imperative (25, 31, 34), twice interrogative (27, 28) and once descriptive (34b). Apart from Mt. 10.19, these are the only occurrences of this verb in the gospel. Given its repetition in this pericope, anxiety is clearly the focus.

The opening and closing verses (vv. 25 and 34) set the scene. Verse 25 commands the reader not to be anxious about food, drink and clothing and v. 34 reiterates the command not to be anxious but the focus shifts to the temporal designator 'tomorrow' in a way that locates the anxiety very specifically. Richard Baucham (2009: 76-88) has explored this text intertextually and contextually 'in an age of ecological catastrophe'. He has alerted readers to the socio-economic features of first century Galilee encoded in v. 34, namely the situation of the day labourers in particular but also the vulnerable poor who did not know from day to day if they would have food for tomorrow (79-80).

Attentive to life and life's processes, Jesus the wisdom teacher invites his listeners to 'observe' the birds of the air (v. 26) and 'consider' (or 'notice' and 'learn from'—BDAG 522) the lilies of the field/the wildflowers. A creative G*d engaged in the process of life unfolding, evidenced in the intertextuality that Baucham lays out (80-82) and which I won't repeat here, knows and cares for all—in this instance all biotic life (v. 30).[14] There is however a need for a hermeneutics of suspicion in relation to this text as it values the human over the other-than-human (v. 30) which may have lead James Nash (2009: 223) to question the text's contribution to an ecological ethic:

> Jesus' preaching about the beauty of the lilies and feeding the 'birds of the air'… contribute little to the control of anthropocentric inclinations. The point of the story is not to call humans to a love of the flora and fauna in order to reflect divine affections. Rather the point is to reduce human anxieties about the adequacy of food and clothing since G*d values humans far more than otherkind and will take care of them proportionately better.

---

14. See Celia Deane-Drummond (2006) who explores such relationships through the themes of 'wonder' and 'wisdom' in an age of theories of evolutionary biology and psychology and new cosmologies.

In light of this valuing of the human at the expense of other-than-human, the text's challenge to the contemporary ecological reader is to be attentive to what is eaten, what is drunk and how one is clothed (v. 25). These are significant ecological issues in relation to the gift exchange already evoked and as a counter-measure to the extraordinary (even excessive) focus on production and consumption within the human community globally which leaves many poor even destitute. The invitation or the ethic in this text is to 'observe' the birds of the air (v. 26) and 'consider' the lilies of the field/the wildflowers and all that we encounter day by day as the human, other-than-human, and the divine interrelate in the cosmos which is gift.

As the mountain-top preaching of Jesus continues, it could be characterised as using both human and the other-than-human beings and processes to think with ethically. Jesus, the wisdom teacher, evokes human experiences such as the noting of a speck in another's eye (7.1-5), the gift exchange process (7.7-12) and the entering of a city (7.13-14). A range of animals also appear in this continuation of Jesus' ethical teaching: dogs and swine (7.6), fish and serpent (7.10), sheep and wolves (7.15).[15] Material actants and processes, other than human and animal, are also drawn into Jesus' wisdom ethics: pearls (7.6), bread and stone (7.9), the gate (7.13) and fruit/s, thorns, figs, thistles, and tree, all of which contribute to the imagery of bearing fruit (7.15-20).

In seeking to read this text ecologically, beyond using the other-than-human actants as merely something to think with, I find Sarah Whatmore's proposal regarding 'embeddedness' to be helpful (1999: 30). She speaks of 're-embodying' human *being* which she describes as 'recalling our place as organisms and acknowledging our varied and changing *embeddedness* (emphasis mine) in the material properties and presences of diverse others'. I invite the reader to begin to re-read the wisdom ethic in this section of the sermon through the lens of the embeddedness that Whatmore proposes. In this way we can read with all Earth constituents.

4. *Matthew 7.24-29: Of Rock and Sand: Concluding the Mountaintop Preaching*

These verses form the conclusion to the mountaintop preaching of Jesus—they continue in the wisdom tradition, encoding into the ecological texture of the text two foundational and interrelated Earth elements: rock and sand. The Matthean story-teller opens this pericope with a characterization of the listener to the Sermon: the one hearing the words of Jesus and doing them (7.24). This echoes the previous verse (7.21) in which the ideal listener/doer does not just mouth titles but does the ethic of the *basileia*.

---

15. For further analysis of animals in this narrative and beyond, see Wainwright 2015.

The experience into which Jesus draws his listeners is a very significantly Earth-bound one. It is that of rock and sand and human engagement with these as places for building a house. For the contemporary ecological reader, rock and sand are key elements of Earth's unfolding history. Rock was an early element in the formation of the planet during the 14 billion year history of the universe and the 4.6 billion year history of Earth since it emergence in the solar system.[16] Sand had its later origins in rock as this was eroded away in multiple ways across millennia. Much later, the human community emerged and engaged with Earth's elements, one aspect being the building of houses as shelter. There was a wisdom developed by this new ecological community (the human constituents) not only as to how to build their houses but also where. It is these elements that Jesus draws into the conclusion to the mountaintop preaching as sources for foundational human wisdom. In this, he echoes Israel's sages who wove such human experience into their teachings, Wisdom herself building a house and inviting those not yet wise to come into her banquet (Prov. 9.1-6; 14.1; 24.3).

Jesus the sage demonstrates how attentiveness to Earth's processes and to human processes can inform one's ethical thinking—to rock and sand, wind and rain, and to the building of a house. One might suggest that there is a reciprocal process taking place. Attentiveness to ethical decision making, an integral aspect of the preaching of Jesus, beginning with the beatitudes of 5.3-10, can turn one toward Earth and its processes, what makes for life for all Earth constituents and what makes for destruction.

Matthew 7.28 is a formulaic statement that closes off this first discourse just as a similar statement will close off other discourses of Jesus (11.1; 13.53; 19.1; 26.1). The reader learns here that 'the crowds' have also heard Jesus' teachings and hence have been with the disciples on the mountain. We noted at the beginning of this section that it could be said that 'the mountain' authorizes Jesus' teachings. That mountain is, indeed, one constituent in the Earth community within and among whom G*d is present (1.23). We have also seen through our analysis of Matthew 5–7 that the wise preacher has learnt much wisdom through his engagement, not only with the law and the human community, but with the more-than-human Earth constituents. Inter-con/textuality has been woven through the interpretation of Jesus' mountaintop preaching so that engagement with the human and other-than-human community has been threaded into the textures of the text. What has emerged is indeed wisdom, ecological wisdom.

---

16. Resources that recount the unfolding story of the universe are multiple. See by way of example *Our Planet: The Past, Present and Future of Earth*, Disc 1—'How the Earth was Made' (A & E Television Networks, 2011).

Chapter 5

MATTHEW 8–9:
THE MATERIALITY OF BODIES—TOUCHED AND HEALED

> 'Jesus went throughout Galilee…healing every disease and every sickness among the people…and they brought to him all the sick, those who were afflicted with various diseases and pains, demoniacs, epileptics, and paralytics, and he healed them' (Mt. 4.23-24).

The ecological reader has been prepared for Matthew 8–9, which narrates ten healing stories punctuated by two narrative buffer pericopes (see Wainwright 1991: 81), by the summary verses 4.23-24. The language of the text is that of 'disease' and 'sickness' and the naming of various categories of people with illnesses: demoniacs, epileptics/those moon-struck and paralytics. Little recognition has been given by interpreters of Matthew 8–9 to the materiality of bodies touched, bodies healed, bodies embedded in geographic, social and cultural habitats.[1] One of the reasons for this may be, as Jennifer Glancy has pointed out, that '[a]s historians we do not have access to corporal exchanges themselves but only to representations… [W]e lack access to ancient bodies' (2010a: 347). It may also be the result of an anthropocentrism that takes little account of the material. This does not mean, however, that as interpreters we can be inattentive to bodies. On the contrary, Glancy recognizes that it is 'through bodies and embodied exchanges that cultural complexity takes place' (362). The material and the socio-cultural are intimately intertwined especially in the ecological texture of biblical texts. Aware of this pervasive inattention to bodies among biblical interpreters and yet conscious of the representations of embodiment in the narrative, I read selected texts of Matthew 8–9 for the materiality of bodies (bodies broken and bodies healed) as this is encoded in the text and for the sociality and inter-con/textuality that such embodiment makes available to the reader.[2] Particular attention will be given, therefore, to the ecological texture of the text in dialogue with its inner and inter-textures.

---

1. Recent studies of healing in the New Testament have recognized that it functions within a complex web of physical, socio-cultural and symbolic elements of a health care system. See Avalos 1999 and Pilch 2000.
2. Glancy (2010a: 342-23), says of the 'representations' of 'the exchanges of Jesus

> **Ecological Intertexts.** The reading proposed above will be undertaken in dialogue with Jennifer Glancy's corporeal reading strategies (2010a). She says of 'social location', which I would extend to habitat, that '[it] takes place in the body, but it is also negotiated—asserted and reinforced or contested and redefined—in the context of both verbal and nonverbal corporal exchanges… As historians we do not have access to corporal exchanges themselves but only to representations—written or visual—of corporal exchanges…we lack access to ancient bodies…we have no sensuous access to ancient bodies. We cannot see or hear them or touch or smell them' (345, 347). As we have already seen, however, an eco-rhetorical reading is attentive to the way such exchanges are encoded in the ecological texture of the text. Glancy's work will, therefore, function as significant intertexture for a consideration of healing as will Anne Elvey's recognition of the contribution of the senses to an ecological reading of biblical texts (2011b).

Given the significance of habitat in relation to healing, I also take account of the range of constitutive features of health care seen as complex system (Avalos 1999; Pilch 2000) as these contribute to an understanding of healing in/and habitat. Among these features are geographical location, climatic factors and other ecological processes that are intimately connected to health and healing. Indeed, Howard Clark Kee says in this regard, with particular reference to the Hippocratic health care system that '[d]iagnosis involved not only the specifics of the individual's symptoms, but also information about race and sex, location, climate, water supply, and even social and political conditions' (Kee 1986: 29). While we do not have precise evidence of how significant these features were in the emerging Christian health care system represented in the gospel narratives, an ecological reading will draw attention to any such features, foregrounding what may be backgrounded in the text.[3]

Matthew 8–9 opens into embodied social location: Jesus comes down from the mountain of proclamation (5–7) and large crowds are following him (8.1). Glancy says in relation to the crowds that 'bodies are simultaneously conditioned by and expressive of social location and that our gestures and postures constitute a corporal vernacular…[and that] when such markers are present in a text they are not incidental' (2010a: 362). A 'Second-space' or symbolic reading of Jesus' preaching on the mountain in Matthew 5–7 recognizes the authorization that such a location gives to that preaching and to Jesus as his story unfolds in the Matthean narrative. Jesus carries that authorization in his body, into his healing ministry, even though he comes down from

---

of Nazareth with those he encountered' that they 'are already informed by the culturally complex worlds of their creators'.

3. See Hippocrates, *Airs Waters Places* and *Epidemics* I, as evidence of the ecological context of diseases within the Hippocratic system.

the mountain. That large crowds are following him, a corporeal activity that earlier characterized those who are beginning to form a new fictive kinship with him (4.18-22), constructs Jesus' 'growing fame, reputation, and worth' (Neyrey 1998: 34). This narrative segment opens, therefore, in a physical and geographical location: down from the mountain. The itinerant nature of Jesus' healing will become evident (Wainwright 2006: 143)—attention to bodies in place/s will, therefore, characterize the reading throughout this section.

1. *Matthew 8.1-4: Touch Makes Clean*

The now familiar Matthean indicator *kai idou*/behold draws attention to the first of these bodies. It is that of a *lepros* or 'leper'. His location in place is very generic—the bottom of the mountain that Jesus and the crowds have just descended. The leper's very posture in relation to Jesus is to kneel (*prosekynei*) before him. He gives voice, in and through his body, to his recognition (and perhaps acceptance) of the marginalized and stigmatized identity that first century Jewish religiosity constructed for one who bore on his/her body the marks of the disease of leprosy. The leper's bodily gesture of kneeling also constructs Jesus as one who bears the authority and power that calls forth homage, even worship (BDAG 882; see especially Mt. 4.9, 10 and perhaps 14.33 and 28.17).[4] Viewed from this point of view, the verb *proskyneein* constructs the leper as supplicant. What seems very clear is that he is not isolated from the community. As Pilch says, 'he seems to be in a public place, mingling with others, and has rather easy access to Jesus' (Pilch 2000: 51). The stigmatization in the narrative would seem, therefore, to be socio-religious or ideological.[5] This, however, ought not to obscure the physical manifestation of the leprosy on the body of the supplicant even though this is not made explicit in the text.

From his embodied place constructed by way of the inner texture of the text, the leper addresses Jesus directly with the title, *Kyrie*. This intersects with the homage element of his bodily prostration and confirms his embodiment of marginality and stigmatization associated with his being named *lepros*/leper by the narrator.[6] As he continues to speak though, his words 'if

---

4. While it is difficult to determine whether specific Matthaean uses of the verb *proskyneein* should be translated as simply paying homage or as worshipping, Glancy, p. 350, notes that the verb 'does extensive theological work for Matthew', an aspect that will be explored further. See also Nolland (2005: 349), who notes that the gospel 'blurs the distinction between deferential respect and religious worship'.

5. The leper may, however, have been excluded from social functions such as wage-earning according to Avalos (1999: 24).

6. The *Kyrios* title given to Jesus is one to which an ecological reader brings a hermeneutics of suspicion. It is a title associated with imperial power or divine power imaged in imperial mode. In both instances, it images power over the heaven/s and

you wish/will/choose, you can make me clean' throw down a challenge to Jesus in the challenge/riposte society of first century Galilee.[7] His words, however, his bodily speech that accompanies action, further construct his cultural body—it has been named 'unclean' according to the ideological construction of his cultural context.

Weissenrieder has clearly demonstrated that *katharizein*/to cleanse, the verb in the leper's request, 'refers to healing in a purely physiological sense and not in a ritualistic sense' in the Hippocratic literature (2003: 151-54) thus, constructing Jesus as healer. The verb also draws into the text the purity system of first-century Galilee whose mapping of both human bodies and also the other-than-human—places, times and other Earth beings (Neyrey 1991)—renders the supplicant unclean. And while the focus of the text is on uncleanness as borne in/on the human body, it alerts the ecological reader to the ways in which cultural ideological systems can name Earth and its other-than-human constituents as 'unclean', marginalized, not worth/y of human consideration.[8]

Both the action and speech that characterized the leper in v. 2 are predicated of Jesus in the first part of v. 3. Bodies meet in the corporeal exchange as Jesus stretches out his hand and touches the leper (*ekteinas tēn cheira hēpsato autou*). This narrated action stands between the words of the leper (v. 2: 'if you wish/will/choose, you can make me clean': *ean theleis dunasai me katharisai*) and those of Jesus (v. 3b: 'I do wish/will/choose; be made clean': *thelō katharisthēti*). Jesus' words mirror the words of the leper in what Luz calls a chiastic structure (2001: 5). Between the two sets of words is the touch of Jesus.

Recent studies of touch by French philosophers such as Jean-Luc Nancy, Jacques Derrida and Jean-Louis Chrétian provide insight into such a gesture, an aspect that has been explored by Elvey (2011b). She draws the ecological reader's attention to 'touch' as a reciprocal action made clear in Derrida's claim that '[t]o touch…amounts…to letting oneself be touched by what one touches' (Derrida 1993: 136 in Elvey, 2011b: 78-79). Jesus' embodied touch of the leper is at the same time an allowing of himself to be touched. This act of interconnectedness[9] together with the words 'I will/

---

all Earth's more-than-human constituents. It functions tensively with the metaphor of Emmanuel, the divine who is 'with' the Earth community.

7. Neyrey (1998: 45-52) summarizes a discussion of 'Honor Challenges to Jesus' in these words: 'every time Jesus appears in public…people engage him in honor challenges' (45).

8. This is the social imaginary of mastery that Code (2006) and Plumwood (1993) have identified. It is more manifest in Jesus' action of sending demons into a herd of pigs.

9. Elvey, p. 80, links the function of 'touch' with 'interconnectedness' that is one of the Earth Bible principles.

wish/choose; be made clean' construct Jesus as healer, one who draws on the healing power of the G*d who is central to healing in the socio-religious healthcare system of Judaism (Avalos 1999: 22).

The embodied touching and being touched of bodies, particularly the body of Jesus, enact one of the ways in which G*d is with the Earth community. Jesus' touching and being touched can erase the boundaries that naming 'clean' and 'unclean' effect. In the words of the text 'immediately he (the leper) was cleansed of his leprosy' (8.3b). Verse 4 provides a narrative challenge to the Levitical system: a *touched* leper has been cleansed. That system seems to have been more concerned with the socio-religious categorizing of the leper and his/her subsequent isolation and stigmatization (physical at certain times and always religio-cultural and ideological) than with the bringing about of his/her cleansing/healing.[10]

The first of the healing stories in Matthew 8–9 demonstrates, therefore, that healing happens through the intimacy of human bodies constructed as touching/being touched in the context of call and response. It enacts the divine engagement with the corporeality and materiality of the human and by implication in an ecological reading of the entire more-than-human web of interconnectivity. The narrative turns now to bodies speaking and hearing which enact healing in Mt. 8.5-13.

2. *Matthew 8.5-13: Words Heal Embodied Distress*

The opening verse of Mt. 8.5-13 narrates Jesus' coming into Capernaum, the material and spatial setting for a healing narrative that is very explicitly encoded into the ecological texture of the text. Inter-con/textually, excavations show Capernaum to be a small town with simple dwellings, one room basalt houses around an open courtyard (Strange and Shanks 1982: 34). The basalt stone of the area functions interactively with the human community providing shelter/houses in which human-to-human interrelationships take place as well as human-to-'other-than-human' relationships, since the house was the location of much of the town's industry (Meyers 2003: 44-69; Jensen 2006: 170). There is also archaeological evidence that points to the possibility of a first-century basalt synagogue, a place where the Jewish community gathered for socio-political and cultural activities, including religious

---

10. Avalos, p. 71, considers that 'Christianity may, therefore, be described as a Jewish sect that aimed to resolve a social crisis caused by the more stringent health care policies in Leviticus and other more conservative strains of Judaism in the first century… The resolution proposed by Christianity aimed not only to heal but to reinterpret purity laws so that the sick could again be part of the Jewish and human family.' This is not to set Christianity over against Judaism but within the complexity of its first century sects or streams of tradition.

5. Matthew 8–9

gatherings, again showing the interconnections within Capernaum's Earth community (Tzaferis 1989: 203). Together with other species, including all those that belong to the waterfront habitat, Capernaum's human community and its built environment participate in the regions ecosystem/s. Apart from the account of the birth of Jesus (Mt. 2.1-12), this is the first extended narrative in Matthew's gospel that is located in a built environment where the human community interacts with the Earth community to produce that environment (houses, places of worship, and places for industry including food production and supply).

The first character woven into the inner texture of this text is a 'centurion' who approaches Jesus. Generally, the word 'centurion' refers to a Roman soldier who commanded a cohort of around 80-100 soldiers in the Roman army. As both Saddington (2006: 141-42) and Hobbs (2001: 328-48) indicate, however, there were no Roman legions stationed in Galilee prior to the Roman war of 66 CE. Soldiers serving in Galilee in the story-time of this pericope were auxiliaries whose ethnic origins were not known. They were supporting the reign of Antipas on behalf of Rome and hence represented the empire. For Matthean readers in the post-70 era, the character may have been seen as Roman as the presence of Roman soldiers in their midst would have informed their reading of the text. Any soldier in Capernaum may well have been part of a protective force for the collection of taxes and would be encoded into the socio-cultural fabric of the text's ecological texture as belonging to the retainer class with power over the local population.[11]

This commander of soldiers is, therefore, associated with the power of the empire and hence with power over the merchants, artisans and peasants who would have made up the population of Capernaum (Freyne 2002). He also has power over the Earth's resources associated with Capernaum, in particular the fish of the Sea of Galilee and the produce of the rich surrounding countryside, in addition to overseeing the payment of taxes placed on both the produce and its transportation. The extraordinary thing in the story is the embodied gesture of the centurion toward Jesus who belongs among the large peasant population. He approaches Jesus (*prosēlthen*) with an urgent request (*parakalōn*).[12] He thereby places himself culturally in a client relationship to Jesus, constructing Jesus as patron.

While the embodied mode dominating the previous healing was that of touch, in this second story it is that of speaking/hearing. The centurion

---

11. Many New Testament scholars using social scientific models to analyse first century agrarian society draw on a social model proposed by Gerhard Lenski. See by way of example Duling 2012: 67-75.

12. BDAG 764-65, uses the language of 'to urge strongly, appeal to, to exhort, to make a strong request…implore, entreat'.

addresses Jesus (*legōn*) with the honorific title *kyrie* but his words are in the form of a statement as to the bodily condition of his *pais* (not a request or entreaty as the language of v. 5 suggested). And so while the narration of v. 5 evokes a client-patron relationship, the centurion's spoken words in v. 6 seem, in the agonistic or challenge/riposte social structure of the first century, to throw down a challenge to Jesus. His *pais* is cast onto a sickbed (*beblētai*), paralyzed (*paralytikos*) and suffering greatly (*deinōs basanidzomenos*). The description conveys the power relationship encoded in the verbal designation, 'my' *pais*, while also evoking the bodily or embodied aspect in the description. The reader is reminded of the materiality of the human body, its very earthiness that, in its extreme suffering, is presented as a challenge to Jesus, the indigenous healer. Given the ambivalence between narrative and direct discourse in the text's inner texture, power, indeed imperial power seems to play or shift within these two verses.

In v. 6, as in the remainder of this narrative, the *pais* is present and yet absent. He is described in his very materiality and embodiment but given this materiality only in and through the voice of the centurion, the representative of the empire. His corporeality is constructed, as Glancy indicates above. One could suggest, therefore, that the *pais* represents socially and politically all those who are under the control of the 'centurion' who is backed by the empire so that when the centurion/the empire says 'go', 'come', 'do this', it is carried out (v. 9), carried out in/on the bodies of all those whom the *pais* represents, all suffering bodily under oppression.

The *pais* in his suffering body, suffering profoundly as the piled up language suggests, can also represent all the materiality that the empire commands in Capernaum and its hinterland. This comprises the ecosystems of the lake and the rich agricultural land of the Gennesaret plain together with the people of the region under that power. It is to and within this broader context that the human body represented by the *pais* belongs. Indeed, Carter suggests that the paralysis experienced in the body of the *pais* is a manifestation of the paralyzing power of Rome/of the empire as experienced in first-century Galilee. He notes that the verb *bassanidzein* describes the 'intense suffering' of 'resistant Jews' under Antiochus Epiphanes in both 2 and 4 Maccabees (Carter 2000: 200-201 and 584 n. 29).

In relation to the *pais*, Jennings and Liew argue for his being the centurion's 'boy-love' or 'beloved' in a pederastic relationship (2004: 467-94). As such he would be a young man, probably in his late teens in a relationship that Jennings and Liew demonstrate was 'well-attested concerning Greco-Roman military in general and Roman centurions in particular' (473 n. 16; 474). From this reading perspective also, socio-political and ecological power and control are written large on the body of the *pais*, particularly if the *pais* is Galilean, a feature about which we are given no information in the text but which complies with Jennings and Liew's suggestion that

'Roman soldiers are (discursively and/or factually) known for what they do to their captives' (475).[13] They conclude that 'such relations between a Roman soldier and a youth who was *not* a Roman citizen were both legally permissible and socially prevalent' (476). The same could well apply to Herodian mercenaries.

The verbal response of Jesus is enigmatic. It could function in the verbal encounter as question or statement with either one or the other constructing the cultural interaction between himself and the centurion in and through his body. Rather than trying to adjudicate between these two possibilities, both can be allowed to function rhetorically within the text. As a question, the reply of Jesus to the centurion, 'Shall I come to heal him?' can be heard to challenge his power. How is it that the empire which claims the power to heal and to save[14] and which has within it many healing shrines, especially those of Asklepios, even on Galilean soil in nearby Tiberias (McCasland 1939: 223-24),[15] has not been able to bring healing to this *pais*? Jesus' words challenge the power of empire represented in the centurion.

Jesus' question can also be heard as: 'am I to come to heal him?' Am I to come to heal all the paralysis, all that is thrown onto a sickbed in the house of the empire, all that suffer greatly? Near at hand were those who fished on the lake who were subject to the exacting system of taxation (Hanson 1997: 99-111), overseen as it was by the presence of the garrison of Herod Antipas in Capernaum of which the centurion was a part, possibly a leader. Right relationships within the more-than-human community that included human interaction with other Earth constituents had been co-opted by the empire.

Jesus words heard as statement, 'I will come and heal him', seem initially to read like acquiescence. Jesus could be heard as responding to the demand of the empire represented in the centurion and his power simply to state a need that will be attended to by the subjects of the empire or by the Earth that is likewise under subjection to the empire. The statement may, however, be read in another way. It could be heard as Jesus' recognition of the inability of the empire to heal and the inability of its representative,

---

13. Note also their citation of Tacitus, *Hist.* 3.33 describing the sack of Cremona (69 CE), in particular the claim that '[w]henever a young woman or a handsome youth fell into their hands, they were torn to pieces by the violent struggles of those who tried to secure them...'.

14. Josephus, *J.W.* 7.71 in which Vespasian is 'styled' as 'Benefactor and Saviour' and Aristides, *Roman Oration*, p. 97, who says of the civilized world that had been 'sick from the beginning' that it had been 'brought by the right knowledge to a state of health' by way of the healing power of the Empire.

15. McCasland cites Josephus, *J.W.* 2.21.6 and draws attention to a bronze coin dated 99 CE whose reverse depicts Hygeia as evidence for the cult of Asklepios associated with the hot springs at Tiberias. I am grateful to Anne Priestley for alerting me to this reference.

the centurion, even to request healing of the indigenous Galilean healer (he simply makes a statement in relation to the young man's illness). Jesus' statement that he will come to heal the centurion's *pais*, despite all the sexual and power-related ambiguity of the situation, demonstrates a recognition that healing, the healing which characterizes his ministry, can cross the multiple boundaries that play in this scene especially as these relate to empire and to Earth. Indeed, the healing associated with the *basileia* of the heavens/sky must cross those boundaries.

For contemporary readers a similar challenge can function across the human/other-than-human boundaries that constitute empire and its control over Earth resources. Such a reading participates in the mode of decolonizing strategy for biblical interpretation that Elisabeth Schüssler Fiorenza highlights, namely making 'political-religious connections to the struggles, interests, and aspirations of wo/men [and Earth] for survival and justice today, in a global empire that makes life increasingly poorer and more insecure for the majority of people [and for Earth]' (2007: 28).

Whichever challenge the centurion is represented as hearing within the question/statement of Jesus, he responds in a way that shifts the rhetoric of empire. He proclaims himself as *ouk hikanos*, as not fit or appropriate or qualified (BDAG 472) that Jesus would come into the house in which his *pais* is lying ill (v. 6). The centurion uses the phrase 'under my roof' rather than house, evoking the materials of Earth, the branches and clay/earth mixed to make the flat roof of a typical first century Palestinian house, and in particular those in Capernaum (Laughlin 1993: 60). He has associated himself with Earth and disassociated himself from all the qualifications whereby he was *hikanos* within the power and prestige structures of empire. Disassociated from these processes, he is now able to ask Jesus to heal, challenged as he has been by Jesus' question/statement, Will I/ I will come to heal him. His request is extraordinary—it is for Jesus to heal by a word only and from a distance[16] and he uses his own experience within the imperial system and structure of authority to underpin his request that Jesus use his word to heal. His shift in embodied language constructs him as a client seeking the healing power of Jesus, the patron or the broker of divine healing power.

Seen from within a postmodern ecological hermeneutic, power is not necessarily hierarchical. The centurion's description of his power structure and his understanding of Jesus' authority over the 'demonic chain' as

---

16. Avalos (1999: 102-103) in his analysis of geographic accessibility within the early Christian health care system, suggests that 'healing at a distance' may have developed from the Jewish scriptures to emphasize the significance of 'faith', an aspect not yet encountered in the Matthaean healing narratives but which will follow immediately in this story.

Jennings and Liew put it, certainly suggests hierarchy (484-88). We have however seen that, within this encounter between the centurion and Jesus, power has been 'performative' (Sandoval 2000: 76). Jesus belongs to peasant society and is under the authority of the centurion as retainer. The latter throws down the gauntlet to Jesus as to whether he can heal his paralyzed *pais* whom the imperial health care system could not or at least did not heal. Yet the centurion, as client, approaches Jesus as patron/broker, recognizing Jesus' power to heal even at a distance. All the time within the shifting power relationships between Jesus and the centurion is the *pais* (present in his absence) and the ambiguous power that he holds in his body and his illness in order to call for a change in the centurion and in the Galilean healer.

Having recognized the shifts in power functioning in the narrative, the reader will note the shifting performance of power in a way that shocks in vv. 10-12. Jesus praises the *pistis*, the faith or belief of the centurion in his power to heal, claiming that others will come from east and west, evoking all peoples and even Earth itself, all in the entire web of more-than-human connectivity, to take their place in the new *basileia* of the heavens.[17] These will all be participants in the blessings associated with Abraham, Isaac and Jacob (a metaphor for inclusion whose gendering fails to include). They are contrasted with another group called 'heirs of the *basileia*' who are generally understood as the Jewish people who fail to hear the *basileia* message that Jesus preaches (Carter 2000: 204; Hagner 1993: 205-206). Within such a reading, Jesus' words challenge established structures of privilege or 'chosenness' as Leticia Guardiola-Saenz calls it (1988: 70) and so shift the sharing in the divine healing power Jesus represents onto a horizontal rather than vertical frame.[18] A similar shift occurs, also, if one understands the 'heirs of the *basileia*' as referring to those of the empire of Rome who unlike the centurion fail to recognize that healing lies elsewhere than with the empire—privilege or chosenness is likewise challenged.

The concluding verse of the pericope returns the reader's attention to the *pais*, to the one who is thrown on his sick-bed and whose body suffers

---

17. Already in Mt. 2.1, *magoi* have come from the East and been caught up in Jesus story.

18. Jennings and Liew, p. 489, say in this regard that 'Matthean "faith" which is mentioned along with "justice and mercy" in 23.32, hinges more on what one does (orthopraxy) than on what one says or knows (ortho-doxy)'. They likewise note that while the leaders oppose and criticize Jesus' healing, the centurion 'favours…and even begs for it' (491). Sandoval (2000: 74) speaks of a postmodern understanding of power that is interactive (or horizontal) rather than hierarchal and hence can be, in her words, 'figured as a globalized, flattened but mobile, gridlike terrain. This terrain comes complete with power nodules inhabitable by collective subjectivities who are perceived as capable of accessing, with equal facility, their own peculiar quotients of power.' Her theory will be highlighted as an intertext later in the commentary.

incredibly. Consideration shifts to materiality and corporeality that is intimately interconnected with power and negotiated through the speaking body/bodies in this story. The body of the *pais* is healed by the word of Jesus. It is, however, a word spoken to the centurion and not to the *pais* himself, continuing to render him absent as actant in the narrative web, especially speaking actant as this is the key characteristic of this story. And even though he is healed in body, there is no indication that he will find a new place within the grid of power that shifts within this unfolding story. He is left, one assumes, as *pais* to the centurion just as he was before his bodily healing and readers must be careful that claims of a symbolic healing of imperial power do not obscure this. A 'limited' healing happens in this narrative through speaking/answering and hearing bodies. It is negotiated through the shifts and changes in a web of power within the context of empire catching up the *pais*, Jesus and the centurion. *Pistis* or faith becomes a new element in the healing that is brokered through Jesus even at a distance. Given that the terrible suffering of a *pais* could claim the attention of a loyal servant/heir of the empire, a centurion, in a way that turned his heart, suggests that the profound suffering of the wider Earth community might turn the hearts of the human community in order that the claims of Earth might begin to dismantle empire. But if this is to happen, both the *pais* and the other-than-human must be given a new place on the horizontal power grid that removes them from systems of hierarchical domination.

3. *Matthew 8.14-15: Bodies Touching Calls Forth*

Matthew 8.14-15 turns the ecological reader to a very short account of healing, just two verses. It functions with the story of the healing of the leper as a frame around the previous story (8.5-13) especially given that healing in the first and this third story is enacted by/on bodies which touch. Together these two healings frame a story in which bodies speak and hear. The location shifts from the broader context of the waterfront town/Capernaum into 'the house of Peter'. This is a story that I have explored extensively at least in two previous studies (1991: 83-97, 178-91; and 2006: 143-46). I will presume on these studies and simply draw attention to insights emerging from the ecological reading of Matthew 8–9, especially its emphasis on corporeality.

The material and social texture woven into this healing is the house of Peter/*oikia Petrou*. Archaeologically we know that the first century Capernaum houses were basalt but probably with roofing of branches and clay (Strange and Shanks 1982: 34). Attention has already been drawn to the network of materiality and sociality within Capernaum, its houses and its resident human community. Eric Meyers has demonstrated the fluidity of gendered activities carried out in the simple or courtyard houses that characterized towns in Galilee of the first century. Activities associated with food production and other industries are evidenced as being carried out in rooms in the house or in the courtyard with no indications of exclusive gendered space (Meyers 2003: 58-60). This highlights the gendered aspect of this story, one of only three healing stories in this collection of ten that involve female characters.

Attending to the inner texture of the text, the reader notes that Jesus enters one of these typical Capernaum houses, a house that is said to belong to Peter. Woven into the ecological texture is space that was likely characterized by the complex mix of materials such as grains, fruits, fish and other foodstuffs together with wood, flax, stone and the multiple resources associated with the fishing industry (see Meyers, 59 and Hanson 1997: 106). It also evokes the social space in which various extended family members interact. Jesus enters the house alone and uninvited, an action which created a borderland (or 'Third-space') 'on the boundaries of both gender and space constructions' (Wainwright 2006: 144). With his body, Jesus enacts the authority that has characterized the narratives in this section of the gospel.

Attentive to the inner texture, the reader notes that once inside, Jesus *sees* Peter's mother-in-law who is described as being cast down on a sickbed (BDAG 163) as was the centurion's *pais* in the previous story (v. 6). The verb *beblēmenēn*/cast down conveys the violence of illness on the human body while *pyressousan*/feverish connotes a condition associated with a range of illnesses in antiquity (Wainwright 2006: 108). Jesus' seeing of her brings the woman, her body and her illness into focus. It also introduces a new element into the healing narratives, an aspect that is a-typical of such narratives, namely the healer seeing the person with an illness and as a result of such seeing taking the initiative to heal. It is this sensate experience of seeing which begins the healing process. Exploring the use of *eiden* in relation to Jesus within the unfolding narrative to this point provides important insights. In the first usage (3.16), Jesus *sees* the spirit descending on him, a symbol of his being anointed for the *basileia* ministry he will take up in 4.17. In 4.18 and 21, Jesus *sees* two sets of brothers whom he calls into this ministry, to be 'fishers of humans'. And it is the *seeing* of the crowds (5.1) that impels Jesus to go up the mountain to begin his preaching of the *basileia*. Seeing encodes a sensory activity that leads to Jesus advancing his *basileia* ministry. The ecological reader will be attentive to this function of seeing which leads to healing, a seeing which recognizes the dis-ease, the brokenness, the mal-functioning of bodies within socio-cultural and ecological systems, all of which are in need of healing. This recognition can be extended to the dis-ease within any or all of the more-than-human entities in their materiality and their sociality that are likewise in need of healing.

As in the first healing story, Jesus touches the one who is ill or unclean, in this instance, touching her hand, acting in his body toward the body of the other, a woman who is struck down with fever. The dynamic of touching and being touched functions in this narrative as it did in that of the leper. Jesus is touched by this woman, touched by illness, touched by the brokenness of the material body, by the brokenness of all that is material. In this borderland or 'Third-space', resistance to such brokenness becomes possible through the touched one who touches the other. Jesus touches her hand in a gesture that calls forth the fever from her body ('the fever left her') but also which calls her to a response. I have argued elsewhere (1991: 180-82) that this narrative is in the form of a vocation/call story, parallel to Mt. 9.9 (cf also 4.18-22). The woman's body responds to the call of Jesus offered in his touch. It had been cast down with illness and now that same body has been transformed and 'raised up' (from her sickbed) as Jesus' own body is later in the narrative raised up (from the grave—28.6, 7).

She responds further by serving him, not momentarily but in a way that is ongoing, as the imperfect form of the verb indicates (*diēkonei*). Such *diakonia* is to be engaged in the ministry in which Jesus is engaged, not receiving *diakonia* but doing *diakonia* (20.28). It is not appropriate here to explore the understanding of *diakonia* as Collins has done (1990). Suffice to note that the healed woman's taking up of the ongoing task of doing *diakonia* parallels the following of Jesus taken up by the four fishermen who are called (4.18-22) and the later following that will characterize the tax-collector Matthew who is likewise called (9.9)?. The closing words of v. 15 construct the woman as a disciple, her healing being a call into the community forming around Jesus, her task the doing of *diakonia* rather than the fishing for people. Each is caught up into the preaching and enacting of the *basileia* of the heavens/sky. There is a *dikaiosynē*, a justice or a right ordering enacted in the touching/being touched of bodies—Jesus and Peter's mother-in-law—which evokes a re-ordering of gender. Such a re-ordering or right ordering can be extended to embrace all more-than-human interrelationships. This is captured narratively and symbolically in the piling up of healings in v. 16 that opens the buffer pericope (vv. 16-22) that separates the intricately structured and intimately related first group of three healings from the second more diverse group.

4. *Matthew 8.23-27: Healing Earth*[19]

During my first foray into an ecological reading of this small segment of the Matthean narrative, I was ensconsed in the library of the Ecole Biblique in Jerusalem, but all my senses were strained elsewhere, namely to the devastating floods which were wreaking havoc in my home state of Queensland,

---

19. A reading of Mt. 8.23-27 from an ecological perspective is published as Wainwright 2014. This segment draws on this research.

Australia. Walls of water were taking before them crops and trees, roads/ bridges and houses, livestock and other animals small and large, together with human lives—no more-than-human constituent (no-body, no-thing, no ecosystem) was safe before the power of water, wind and storm swamping the state.[20] What does it mean to read Mt. 8.23-27, the story so often called the 'Stilling of the Storm', in the face of what would seem to be yet another example of the wild storms that have threatened and are threatening much smaller islands in Oceania as well as continents like Australia in recent years as a result of what many scientists are naming as global warming and resultant climate change?

In this story, seemingly included in this collection of healing stories by way of a logic which is not easily apparent to the anthropocentric reader, it is not the corporeality of bodies which touch or which speak/hear. Rather it is Earth that speaks in a language that is loud and even abrasive. The story opens in the human/material nexus. Jesus gets into a boat (*ploion*) and his disciples (*hoi mathētēs*), a group whose membership is undefined at this point in the narrative, were following him (*ēkolouthēsan*). The language situates this story firmly within the unfolding Matthean narrative. *Ploion* recalls the fishing boat that James and John left (4.21-22) to follow Jesus (*ēkolouthēsan*), a boat traces of whose very materiality still linger in the Matthean text, accentuated for those readers who have either seen or touched the Galilee boat excavated at Kibbutz Ginosar (Wachsmann 1988: 18-33).

The Matthean 'attention seeker', *kai idou*, turns the readers toward Earth, to Earth which speaks in the *seismos megas* that occurs on the sea and its swamping of the boat by the waves. The human community of disciples and their material context (the boat) are no match for the power of Earth's processes, an insight that provides an important challenge to contemporary readers. The Matthean narrative contains hyperbolic language here. *Seismos* generally indicates an earthquake (see 24.7, 54; 28.2) or a storm of earthquake proportions at sea (perhaps what we have come to know as a tsunami in these days of global warming and violent movements of Earth). *Seismos megas* brings to greater awareness the power of such a movement of Earth. It also draws into the ecological texture of the text the metereological conditions around the lake where, during the summer months at least, Mediterranean breezes coming from the west increase or almost double their speed over the lake due to the 'rift relief' leading to regular and at times violent storms (Volohonsky *et al.* 1982: 149-50; Nun 1989: 3, 20).

In the intertexture of this text, readers hear echoes of prior encounters with the power of the sea from their sacred story. Exodus 14 was a foundational

---

20. These floods occurred during the latter half of December and the early half of January 2010/2011.

memory and also functioned symbolically in Israel's yearnings for return from Exile (Isa. 51.10).[21] Within this tradition, rescue from the power of the waters belongs to G*d and to those who in their wisdom trust in G*d.

For Matthean readers, therefore, this *seismos megas* carries both cosmic and metaphoric ('Second-space') significance. It can also draw readers into the ecological texture of the text that encodes the violent storms on the lake that first century residents of the lake's waterfront and its fishing industry had come to expect and to relate to in their habitat ('First-space' significance).[22] Inter-con/textually and metaphorically the *seismos megas* could also evoke the political, social and economic storms that readers faced in the context of the empire (Carter 2000: 210). In this reading, however, I want to give primary attention to the materiality of the *seismos megas* without neglecting the socio-political.

Later in the gospel, readers will encounter *seismos* with an eschatological import (Mt. 24.7, 54; 28.2). In that context, it characterizes the end times in a future imaginary that belongs to G*d, if Malina's understanding of how time functioned for the gospel writers is correct (1989: 1-31). In the Matthean gospel that future imaginary circles back into the present of Matthean ethics. The response to those eschatological phenomena, which include earthquakes, is to endure to the end so that the good news of the *basileia* will be proclaimed (24.13-14), implying the ongoing activity of disciples to preach that good news. The ecological, ethical and political intersect in this Matthean narrative as they do in contemporary contexts in which the effects of global warming, the result of socio-political and economic nexes, are threatening entire eco-systems. The effects are evoked in the gospel in vivid material terminology: the boat is being covered or swamped by the waves, reminiscent of the wall of water eight metres high that raced through the streets of Toowoomba, my home town, during the 2011 flooding, taking cars, furniture and people, indeed all in its path.

In the face of the seismic storm at sea, the text makes the simple statement about Jesus: he was sleeping (*autos de ekatheuden*), oblivious to the *seismos megas*. This may evoke intertextually Jonah's sleep in the face of a mighty storm (Jon. 1.4-5). In the Book of Jonah, however, it is G*d who casts a great wind on the sea, giving rise to the storm whereas the Matthean text gives no cause. The *seismos megas* simply appears on the sea.

---

21. See Batto (1987b: 18-20), who places Isa. 51.9-11 within the context of G*d's resting after the work of creation, seeing the call to 'awake' in v. 9 as an implication that G*d has continued to sleep until hearing this call.

22. Nun (1989: 3) suggests that the occurrence of sudden storms on the Sea of Galilee lead to the construction of 'protected mooring place[s] for their boats' because of the lack of natural inlets. This demonstrates the complex interrelationships within the materiality and sociality of the more-than-human Earth constituents.

Batto has drawn attention to further intertextuality (1987a: 153-77 and 1987b: 16-23), namely the sleep of the deity in Israel's scriptures. He recognizes in texts such as Ps. 35.22-23 and Isa. 51.9-11 a theme of G*d resting as a divine prerogative after the work of creation. In these same texts there is also a call rising up to the deity from the human community experiencing threat. Such biblical intertexts can be brought into dialogue with the contemporary intertext of Denis Edwards' theologizing. G*d is as Edwards says:

> acting in a way that lovingly respects and accepts the limits of finite processes and entities... God waits upon, empowers, and enables the 3.7 billion-year history of life on Earth with modern human beings appearing only in the last 200,000 years... All of this suggests that the God of creation is a God who loves to create through processes that involve emergence and increasing complexity and who is a God of immense patience (Edwards 2010: 51).

Significant in the emergence and increasing complexity of Earth are the seismic movements of plates and continents that have occurred over millennia down to our own day.

Wendy Cotter draws attention to a different intertextuality that may have functioned for first-century Matthean readers, namely that of the sea-storm stories of the Hellenistic era which find their meaning within a 'new' cosmology that differed from the three-tiered structure of the universe of ancient Israel (Cotter 1997: 118-31). This new cosmology was geocentric with the orbs of the moon and other planets circling earth. The sublunar sphere between the earth and the moon was the space in which divinely-empowered heroes functioned. Augustus was one such hero of whom Philo says '[t]his is the Caesar who calmed the torrential storms on every side' (Philo, *Embassy to Gaius* 144-45). Cotter goes on to draw the conclusion that in the first century CE '[b]oth Jesus and Augustus are credited with the type of salvific activity which Psalm 107.28-33 reserves for God... (who) made the storm be still, and the waves of the sea...hushed' (126).

Returning to the inner texture of the Matthean text, we note that Jesus' bodily posture constructs him as being without fear, as if he knows more than the experience of a *seismos megas* would indicate. Like the rest or sleep of the divine one, whose spirit has descended on Jesus at his baptism, Jesus' sleeping manifests his sharing in the imaging of that divinity (prerogative and power) that is 'with' the Earth community (1.23), in right relationships (the *dikaiosynē* of Mt. 3.15; 5.6, 10, 20; 6.1, 23).[23] In Jesus, asleep

---

23. Carter (2000: 211) provides examples from classical literature that point to empire/emperor being 'master of sea and land' (Apollonius 7.3), the one who has control or power over Earth and all its constituents.

in a boat being swamped by the waves, G*d is 'with' the community constructed in the narrative—disciples, boat, *seismos megas* and the waves.

The disciples, like the people of Israel before them (Isa. 51.9-11; Ps. 44.24-25, 27) and those of us after them, are afraid, crying out to Jesus with the title with which readers have become familiar, *Kyrie*, with all its indicators of power. It can be claimed as power within the Matthean context only after it has been critiqued as power-over. The invocation of the disciples—*sōson*/'save'—reminds readers for the first time of the name and the commission given to Jesus in 1.22, the one who will save because he is, as 1.23 indicates, the one in whom divinity enters into a unique relationship 'with' us/the Earth community.

Jesus, however, rebukes the disciples as being cowardly or afraid (*deiloi*) and of little faith (*oligopistoi*). This seems a strange rebuke to contemporary readers who are rightly afraid in the face of today's powerful ecological disasters. It sends us back to look again at the *seismos megas* and its eschatological imagery in Mt. 24.7: nation will rise against nation, and kingdom against kingdom, and there will be famines and earthquakes in various places. The Matthean response to such seismic challenges is an exhortation to endurance in the preaching of the *basileia*. The disciples have either not yet learnt or have lost sight of their being caught up into and implicated in this preaching and making present of the *basileia* that is of the heavens/of G*d. This is the response that Jesus, asleep in the boat, would ask of his disciples. It is the recognition that in the face of disaster, the proclaiming and doing of the ethic of the *basileia* is what is required because G*d is 'with' the Earth community. This is the faith/*pistis* that will unfold with the gospel. It is a faith that requires a broadening of our anthropocentric perspectives, enabling us to enter deeply into a new way of seeing our belonging within the Earth community.

The next verse, however, seems to move into a different mode as Jesus does indeed rise up and rebuke (*epitimēsen*) the wind and the sea resulting in a great calm. Jesus seems to accede to the disciples' faithless request with a bodily gesture of speaking with authority, in a way that constructs that authority. It has an effect—it is as if Jesus has woken up as did G*d of the Isaian text cited earlier and has acted in response to the cry of distress, linking his power with that of the divine. Problematically, however, the language of rebuke is that used in relation to the demonic (12.16; 17.18) and so can function to construct the *seismos megas* as demonic or as participating in demonic power.

Such a world view as discussed earlier constructed the threatening and the demonic as inheriting the sublunar realm between the earth and moon (Martin 1987: 4-15). For contemporary readers this hint of the evil or the demonic may evoke the unethical attitudes and behaviors among Earth's human constituents that may need to be driven out if Earth's seismic activity is not to be compounded by behaviours that are destructive of the delicate interrelationships within the universe. This must be a nuanced reading as I do not wish to equate Earth's seismic processes with the demonic. Indeed, I have sought to demonstrate earlier that such Earth processes are caught up with and in the Divine.

The challenge of Jesus to the disciples, 'you of little faith' is already familiar to the ecological reader. In Mt. 6.30, the ones of little faith were challenged to believe that they would be cared for by G*d who likewise cares for the 'grass of the fields'. Jesus' rebuking of the winds and the sea, bringing about a *galēnē megalē* or great calm, is in contrast to the earlier *seismos megas* or great movement of Earth. Narratively, it invites the readers to recognize that G*d acts, as Denis Edwards' title suggests (2010), and that the human community is invited to recognize that action in the calm as in the storm. It is action that is subtly caught up with and in the very movements of Earth's unfolding and is not interventionist or 'interruptionist' on behalf of selected Earth constituents.

The exclamation of the disciples—'what sort of human person is this'—recognizes Jesus as Emmanuel, the one in whom divine power is 'with' the Earth community. For this recognition to be named *pistis* in gospel terms, it must be attentive to this presence in dramatic seismic activity. It is this that will lead to wonder (*ethaumasan*), expanding the horizons of our thinking and our knowing of G*d and the ways of G*d. Earth is speaking, are we listening?

5. *Matthew 8.28–9.1: Of Demons and Pigs*

Earth continues to function as actant in the unfolding 'good news' of the Matthean narrative. Jesus and the disciples safely cross the Sea to the countryside of the Gadarenes. Because of textual variations, there are differences among scholars as to the location or habitat woven into the text inter-con/textually. Luz and Metzger both conclude that Gadara is the more likely reading and I would concur (Luz 2001: 23 and Metzger 1975: 23-24). It was a built environment on an acropolis east of the Jordan, just north of the Yarmuk River and overlooking the south-east corner of the Sea of Galilee where the harbour of Gadara was situated, some seven to nine kilometres from the acropolis. This may well be what is called the 'countryside' of the Gadarenes (8.28) because the significance of the waterway and the harbour would have rendered the region between harbour and city a vital area (Dvorjetski 1994: 100-101, 103; Nun 1989: 17-18).

Woven into the ecological texture of the Matthean narrative are traces of the socio-political context of Gadara. It was a Hellenistic city founded by the Ptolemies and was one of the cities of the Decapolis, the league of ten cities of the Roman period. Religious and political differences existed between these cities and the Galilean towns and countryside, especially since Gadara and its 'fertile lands' had been granted to Herod by Octavian and since the Gadarenes had sided with Rome during the Jewish war of the late sixties (Weber 2007: 454, 457). Matthew's gospel, however, has already claimed in 4.25 that 'great crowds' have followed Jesus from 'Galilee' and the 'Decapolis' along with 'Jerusalem, Judea, and from beyond the Jordan'. This is in keeping perhaps with Weber's conclusion that '[t]here is some evidence in the material culture of Gadara that the local Jewish diaspora maintained economical relations with the neighboring Galilee during the 1st and subsequent c. CE.' (460). He is right to conclude that relationships between Galilee and Gadara both at the time of Jesus (first decades of the first century) and of the development of the Matthean traditions into a gospel narrative (the latter decades of that century) were both 'antagonistic' as well as reflecting 'peaceful symbiosis' (476-77). This region as it is encoded in the Matthean text functions at the level of First- or geographic space and tensively at the socio-cultural or symbolic 'Second-space' level. The tension in the narrative opens up a Third- or borderland space in which there is potential for an alternative. For the reader, both ancient and contemporary, the question might be, is healing possible in this complex space or location that constitutes the ecological texture of this Matthean text?

In this space, according to the narrative, Jesus encounters two demon-possessed (*daimonizomenoi*) coming out of the tombs. Previously the reader has only heard passing reference to the *daimonizomenoi* as a group in summary passages (4.24 and 8.16; 7.22 alludes to demons/*daimonia* being cast out with a word). In a previous study in which I explored the intertextuality informing this word or word-group, I concluded that a cosmology developed in the Hellenistic period which is reflected in classical Greek and gospel texts in which other-worldly beings or spirits, named as both good (angels) and evil (demons), inhabited a world between divinity and humanity (Wainwright 2010b; see also Martin 1987). Miquel says of these spirits that they were believed to be 'capable of possessing persons' while she also acknowledges 'the power of certain individuals to exorcise them' (2010: 195).

The language of the encounter (*hypēntēsan*) between Jesus and the two named as demon possessed in v. 28b does not tell the reader initially if it will be friendly or hostile but the remainder of the verse describes these demon-possessed as violent and dangerous, making it impossible for others to pass that way. Initially, therefore, the interpreter recognizes an ancient cosmology that characterizes the two named as demon-possessed. Michael Newheart has offered other explanations of such socio-cultural naming written onto these two human bodies. He uses the theories of Girard and Fanon (Newheart 2004: 70-85). First, a community under oppressive rule may scapegoat an individual from the community as 'possessed' in some way (in this instance 'fierce' or violent and dangerous). The scapegoated one can be isolated ('no one could pass that way') and their strange behaviour may draw the attention of the oppressor toward them and away from the community. On the other hand, a member of an oppressed community may take into or carry in her or his body the oppression suffered by the community. This may manifest in illness (as suggested for the *pais* in 8.6) or in behaviour that separates the person from the community. The association of the demon-possessed ones with the tombs in Mt. 8.28 evokes the first century recognition of the death-dealing aspects of oppression that we recognize as extending beyond the sociality of the human community and the materiality of bodies into the entire more-than-human sociality.[24]

The language or rhetoric in this narrative is strong and violent. The possessed ones cry out a challenge, addressing Jesus as son of G*d as did the *diabolos* in 4.3 and 6. They recognize his power to harass them or to 'subject (them) to severe distress' as they can do to others (*basanizō*—BDAG 168). The reader does not know if the demon-possessed ones are Jewish or not, but the struggle can be seen as symbolic of the oppression enacted on the Galilean population by their Roman masters both at the time of Jesus and moreso during the Roman war of the late 60s as well as the resistance to the Roman oppression in both instances. Both the inter-con/textuality of the Gadarean location and the exchange between Jesus and the demon-possessed through whom the demons speak, construct the tensive power struggle in this text (see Carter 2000: 212-13 for more extensive imperial intertextuality).

Verses 30-31 draw readers into the manner in which the other-than-human is likewise caught up into the struggle on the power grid operative in this text. What seems like a simple statement in v. 30—a large herd of swine was feeding at some distance from the encounter between Jesus and the two demon-possessed—encodes significant cultural inter-con/textuality. First, the statement draws readers into the ecological cycle, 'the way that plants, animals, and humans live together and affect each other'.[25] The pigs are grazing or feeding, but Firmage (n/d: 1119) says that:

> [t]he precise make-up of their diet in the wild will therefore depend on what is available in the environment. Common food items, however, include acorns, …but also small invertebrates, snakes, and carrion. However, pigs are not well adapted to a grass (cellulose) diet since they are not ruminants.

They tend, therefore, to be scavangers but the presence of the herdsmen indicates that this group of pigs has been brought out from the neighbouring

---

24. For an excellent study of some of the processes of colonization and the ascribing of 'demon possession', see Dube (1999: 33-59).
25. http://www.onelook.com/?w=ecology&ls=a (accessed 17 January 2011).

village or city to forage in woodland or fields such as olive groves perhaps lying fallow. Columella, *On Agriculture* 7.9.6 notes that 'pigs can make shift in any sort of country wherever situated' and he goes on to say that they are also able to 'use water freely' tearing up 'the sweet-flavoured rootlets of under-water growths' (7.9.7). It may not, therefore, be surprising to find a herd of pigs in the area between the Gadara harbour and the city, where there could have been at certain times water or at least muddy ground that they could wallow in (7.10.6; Varro, *On Agriculture* 2.4.8). In the ecological cycle, these pigs may, in turn, have provided food for the human community of the herdsmen (note the gift-exchange already cited earlier and its relation to the food cycle).[26]

Reference to the large herd of pigs who are participants in the habitat of this narrative also encodes in the ecological texture of the text the Jewish purity system which mapped the material world of bodies and of the other-than-human as clean and unclean (Lev. 11.7-8; Deut. 14.8). The pig is named unclean and hence its flesh must not be eaten nor should a pig carcass be touched within the Jewish Levitical system. This animal then carries a stigmatization like that of the leper which participates in the dualistic mapping of the universe that we have recognized as contributing to the social imaginary of anthropocentrism and mastery. Within this world, the swineherds are constructed as non-Jewish and within their religious ideology, the pig may well have been associated with religious ritual seeking the abundance of the harvest (Cato, *On Agriculture* 134.1). Socio-politically, 'the boar', according to Dvorjetski (1994. 105), was a symbol of the Tenth Legion *Fretensis* and the Roman presence, especially at the time of the Roman war of 66-70. It was a symbol that would have been appropriated positively by those of the Gadarean region who sided with Rome during that war.

The story then seems to take readers into a mythic world in which the demons, who have been identified obliquely in the naming of two possessed men, now directly confront Jesus. The narrator describes them as throwing down a challenge to Jesus (*parekaloun*) as did the centurion in Mt. 8.5 (BDAG 764-65). Their demand has a conditional clause, 'if you cast us out', which precedes the imperative, as if they are losing power in their direct encounter with Jesus. Their demand is to send them into the herd of pigs.

Verse 32a forms the core of this narrative—Jesus said to them: 'Go!' This command certainly highlights the authority of Jesus, as many commentators note, an authority that has been developing in the narratives of healing. On the other hand, that command and its aftermath create problems for the ecological reader. This may also have been the case for some first century hearers/readers, even while they would have recognized that 'experts in spirits'

---

26. See also Varro, *On Agriculture* 2.4.3.

who had the power to drive out 'a possessing spirit' also had 'the power to make it enter another person' (Miquel 2010: 193). Why would Jesus accede to the request of the demons? Would not a denial of their request have demonstrated more power?

As a first response to these questions, I place the account of Jesus' action within the first century world of demonology and exorcisms. For Josephus, exorcisms were of the kind performed by Solomon. He recounts the spectacular actions performed by Eleazar in his freeing of 'men possessed by demons', drawing the conclusion that through such manifestations of power: 'all men [*sic*] may know the greatness of his [Solomon's] nature and how God favoured him and that no one under the sun may be ignorant of the king's surpassing virtue of every kind' (J. *Ant* 8.46-49). Wendy Cotter notes in relation to what is described in this passage and Philostratus' description of Apollonius' performance of a spectacular exorcism (Philostratus, *Life of Apollonius* 4.20) that '[b]oth Philostratus and Josephus show that a listening audience appreciates some proof that demons are indeed present, and are subject to the hero' (Cotter 1999: 105). Matthew 8.32b and its description of the demons entering the swine and the whole herd rushing down a steep bank into the sea certainly fits that criterion of proof. Such a show of power, however, has not characterised Jesus' exercise of healing as it has been developing in Mt. 8 although it could be said that there is a hint of it in Jesus commanding a *seismos megas* and its becoming a great calm.

An ecological reader will critique this seemingly wanton destruction of a whole herd of pigs onto whom is transferred the demonic power that earlier possessed two human bodies. First, it is uncharacteristic of Jesus' healing and thus earlier healing accounts can stand as a critique. Second, there is a question as to whether Jesus' facilitating through his word the destruction of an entire herd of pigs constitutes a valid symbol of the *basileia* of the heavens/sky functioning as an alternative to the *basileia* of Rome, symbolized in the pigs. Such symbolism may be intended apocalyptically or eschatologically to point, as Carter concludes, 'to God's sovereignty over Rome' (Carter 2000: 213). It is, however, dangerous imagery, as it sanctions violent destruction of Earth beings. It likewise undermines the unfolding gospel narrative in which G*d is 'with' the Earth community in and through Jesus and the healing power he has been exercising. An ecological reader would indeed mourn for and with the herd of pigs, those Earth beings who have been made to bear what is not of G*d, not of G*d 'with' the Earth community.

In the Matthean narrative, the swineherd and all the townspeople recognize the destructive power unleashed upon the pigs as well as what happened to the two said to be demon possessed. The community may still need to insulate themselves from the threat of Roman oppression. Even though the people of the region collaborated with Rome, the power and wrath of the empire was not far from consciousness in its colonies. The people beg Jesus to leave their region, to take away from them his ambivalent power that can destroy their livelihood as well as unmask their scapegoating.[27]

Carter is right to conclude that conflict functions on many levels in this narrative: economic, political, social, ethnic and religious (213-14). It is a complex story which must be engaged critically so as not to sanction aspects of violence as a resolution of these various sites of conflict. At times, Jesus stands ambivalently in relation to some aspects of these conflicts. The narrator's response is to have Jesus return across the Sea to his own city. This foray of Jesus and his disciples across the Sea points to the challenges to the preaching of the *basileia* of the heavens/sky as it encounters new contexts. It points as well to the ways in which the cultural carrier of that message can be mistaken for the message itself or can shape the message in a way that needs to be critiqued. The ecological reader will need to identify with the herd of pigs that seem to be wantonly destroyed in this narrative and, from this position, to critique aspects of the story and its encoding of power. It is important to recognize, name and struggle with and against the destructive forces that can take over the lives of all more-than-human beings, destroying eco-systems, species, and habitats.

6. Conclusion

The more detailed ecological reading of five of the ten healing narratives in Matthew 8–9 undertaken above has provided readers with some tools and insights to bring to the remaining five narratives. Movement between word and touch that characterized the first three healing narratives continues. The critical reader will bring a hermeneutics of suspicion to a perspective on bodily impairment that associates it causally with sin while recognizing that ecologically the impairment done to habitats and ecosystems may well be associated with human sin (Mt. 9.1-8).

Bodies touch for healing in the two intercalated stories of women being healed in 9.18-26). There is language of touching not just of bodies but the fringe of a cloak (Wainwright 2006: 146-53). This can speak of the tactile engagement particularly between the more-than-human other and the human materiality of the body if ecological healing is to take place. Hands ought to be sunk into earth, water felt and known so that it might be conserved—these and many other touchings need to take place for Earth relationships to be healed.

---

27. Miquel (2010: 193) says that the power of 'experts in the spirit' as Jesus has been shown to be 'can also make them objects of suspicion…particularly vulnerable to any possible suspicion of manipulating the spiritual world for perverse ends.'

Seeing and speaking have also woven their way through earlier healing narratives as they do in Mt. 9.27-31 and 32-34. Eyes are touched so that they are opened (v. 30) and speech is restored to one possessed. Restoration of right relationships, the *dikaiosynē* of Jesus's *basileia* proclamation happens in and through the materiality of human bodies that touch, speak, and hear the cry for healing (the significance of the senses that will be further explored in the following chapter). Encountering stories of such restoration in the materiality of human bodies 'in place' enables all the materiality and corporeality of the more-than-human to be heard in the text's many textures, engaging the ecological reader and extending the invitation to and challenge of healing beyond the human to all Earth. In this way compassion, the moving of one's entire being in and through the materiality of one's iinner parts (9.36) can and will function within the entire community of Earth constituents (see Elvey 2011: 82-83). Matthew 9.35 frames the teaching and healing of Matthew 5–9 and opens the way for the commissioning of disciples who will be engaged in the same mission as Jesus: proclaiming the gospel of the *basileia* and healing.

Chapter 6

MATTHEW 10–12:
DOES CO-MISSIONING OBSCURE EARTH
AND WALKING REVEAL EARTH?

In the unfolding of the Gospel of Matthew, the co-missioning of disciples by (and with) Jesus to carry out the mission of preaching, (teaching) and healing which he has begun brings the gospel story to a key point. Readers have been given a glimpse into the heart of the Matthean mission of Jesus in Matthew 5–9 and it is this mission to which he co-missions the disciples in Matthew 10. It will not be possible to undertake an ecological reading of subsequent chapters of the gospel in the same depth as has characterized the commentary to this point. I continue with summary reflections on the narrative, an element that has already characterized some sections, together with indepth discussions of fewer selected pericopes. As I have already indicated, however, my hope is that these initial ecological readings will invite you, the readers, to undertake your own ecological reading of those segments of the narrative that I have been able only to summarize and that you will expand as you read. This invitation can function as a co-missioning parallel to that encountered in the Matthean gospel.

1. Matthew 10: Does Co-missioning obscure Earth?

On a first reading, Matthew 10 appears to be an anthropocentric and adrocentric text, requiring a *hermeneutics of suspicion* as well as of *retrieval*. If the reader begins reading the co-missioning of disciples at 10.1, which is characteristic of most scholarly commentary (Carter 2000: 232-33 and Luz 2001: 66 contra Davies and Allison 1991: 143), then the text is lacking the con-text that the reader has come to expect—this provides a challenge to an inter-con/textual reading such as I am undertaking. It has already been manifestly demonstrated in Chapter 2 that wilderness and waterfront contextualized the mission and ministry of both John and Jesus and that the preaching, teaching and healings of Jesus take place in con-text: on a mountain in Galilee and en route as Jesus undertakes his itinerant ministry of proclaiming the *basileia* of the heavens (4.17, 23-24; 5.1-2; 8.1; 9.35-36). Earth is habitat for this proclamation. It is surprising, therefore, that the co-missioning of disciples to a ministry parallel to that of Jesus lacks such a con-text.

The reader can certainly return to 9.35 to be reminded of the itinerant ministry of Jesus and its groundedness in city and village linked by countryside. Jesus walked Earth and learnt from Earth's others—sheep without a shepherd evoking for him the needs of the crowds for whom he was moved with compassion (9.36)—human and habitat are intimately interconnected. Those of the human community named as 'disciples' who are clearly with Jesus on his itinerant journeying, are engaged by Jesus in relation to the imagery of a harvest that is in need of labourers. Earth's elements—sheep and harvest—function metaphorically to point toward Jesus' recognition that the people of Galilee are in need of his *basileia* ministry and that he is in need of assistants in that ministry. These verses, especially, 9.36-38, can function, therefore, as the con-text for 10.1, linked as it is with the previous verses by the simple connective *kai*/and.

The focus of the text of Matthew 10 is the human community and in particular the new fictive kinship group that Jesus is establishing together with those to whom they are sent. While such groups function within the narrative to create the socio-cultural texture of the text, an ecological reading can place them within the sociality of the more-than-human community, thereby engaging the text's ecological texture. Jesus gives the explicitly named twelve disciples (vv. 2-4) authority/*exousia* over unclean spirits and the power to heal diseases and sicknesses as he has just done (Matthew 8–9). Indeed, the phrase used to describe the object of the healing ministry of the disciples is 'every disease and every infirmity', the phrase previously used in the framing verses around Jesus' healing ministry (4.23 and 9.35). It draws attention to the corporeality of healing that has characterized Jesus' ministry, a ministry located in different con-texts and engaging those contexts: outside and inside houses, in boats on the sea, coming to land, encountering demonic spirits.

On reading 10.2-3, the reader becomes aware that the twelve disciples named as authorized to cast out demons and to heal are in fact all male. This is surprising given that it was shown earlier that not only Peter and Andrew, James and John, and Matthew were explicitly called by Jesus (4.18-22; 9.9) but Peter's mother-in-law was also called to discipleship as the form of Mt. 8.14-15 indicates. She responded to this call by engaging in ongoing *diakonia*, the word used to describe Jesus' ministry in 20.28. A hermeneutics of suspicion queries the gendering of the co-missioning of the twelve and a hermeneutics of retrieval includes not only Peter's mother-in-law but also the other named and unnamed women of Galilee (27.55-56) in the co-missioning. My own earlier research on women healing in the Graeco-Roman world of the first century renders it plausible that women would have been engaged in healing not just in the privacy of the house but in the public arena (Wainwright 2006) and hence their *diakonia* (27.55) could have involved healing. They are not commissioned with the male disciples, however, and it is only when they are faithful to the foot of the cross that the reader is made aware of their extended *diakonia* ministry. An ecological reading seeking a new social imaginary will include the Galilean women, one of whom is Peter's mother-in-law as already noted in the text, among the co-missioned disciples.

The co-mission of vv. 5-6, 'Go nowhere among the Gentiles and enter no town of the Samaritans, but go rather to the lost sheep of the house of Israel' causes 9.36 to echo more strongly through this chapter, strengthening the links already highlighted above. The metaphor of the 'lost sheep' in 10.6 resonates with that of the 'sheep without a shepherd 'of 9.36. There are in these two verses echoes of significant intertexts. In Jer. 50.6, the metaphor of 'lost sheep' is used explicitly to highlight the failure of the shepherds or leaders of Israel, shepherds who have led their sheep astray, 'turning them away on the mountains; from mountain to hill they have gone, they have forgotten their fold'. Similarly in Ezek. 34.6, 8, 10 and 11, while the phrase 'lost sheep' is not used explicitly, the sheep have been scattered because of the failure of the shepherds/leaders, and so the prophet pronounces that G*d will seek out and rescue the scattered ones who in each of the four intertextual verses are called 'my sheep' by the divine voice. The co-mission to the disciples is, as has been the mission of Jesus, to the 'lost sheep' of Israel.

Before I look more closely at this co-mission that has troubled interpreters at times because it seems to be at odds with the final co-missioning (28.18-20), I want to turn to a consideration of the drawing of animals into the metaphoric texture of the text and the implications of this for an ecological reading. The particular metaphor to which I have already drawn attention is that of 'sheep' (9.36; 10.6, 16). One approach, as I have already hinted in terms of its functioning, would be to consider the animal references/sheep as metaphor operative in the inner and inter- textures of the text. As an ecological reader, however, I want to suggest that the sheep referent can also function in the ecological texture of the text drawing attention not only to the metaphorical function but to human/animal experiences and interrelationships or what Behnke calls 'inter-species sociality' (1999: 100).

> **Ecological Intertexts.** In reading ecologically toward a new social imaginary, the theory of 'inter-species sociality' provides a significant intertext. To engage this theory, I dialogue with Behnke together with Birki and Parisi (1999). Behnke lays out an agenda: 'we must learn to speak from within this Nature that surrounds and includes us, this Nature with which we are intermingled…this natural being that we are' (95). She concludes by recognizing that this intermingling, especially that of humans and animal is 'not to be observed, analysed, and discussed from the outside, but is to be embodied from within in an ongoing carnal intertwining that surrounds and

> supports us even as it moves through us and among us' (111). Birki and Parisi draw on Deleuze's and Guattari's idea of *becoming* highlighting that it is 'multiple in the sense that it shifts the emphasis from the individual organism to organisms-in-relation—not only to each other, other kinds, and environments, but also to themselves' (65). They draw attention to the shift in terms of 'insisting on connections and flows… on transformation and change rather than essence…an infinity of connections' (67). This will shift our imagination beyond the dualisms with which we are familiar to an awareness of the materiality of becoming that humans and animals share.

On close analysis, ecological readers attentive to the 'organisms-in-relation', can share with Jesus in being moved with compassion in the depths of their beings, their entrails, as one considers the crowds that Jesus encounters and the sheep who are without a shepherd. Echoes of Ezekiel 34 set up the 'connections and flows' as the reader moves between the harassed, prostrate and scattered crowd (Mt. 9.36; see BDAG 906) and the sheep 'scattered … with no one to seek or search for them' (Ezek. 34.6), their becoming 'food for wild animals' (34.8).[1]

The named disciples are then sent by Jesus to the 'lost sheep of the house of Israel' (10.6), continuing the 'connections and flows' between human and animal. Engaging Jer. 50.6 as intertext ('My people have been lost sheep; their shepherds have led them astray, turning them away on the mountains; from mountain to hill they have gone, they have forgotten their fold'), the reader can be attentive to the breakdown in the 'inter-species sociality' encoded in the ecological texture of the text. The reader is also invited to feel the embodied 'carnal intertwining' of sheep and people engaging with 'lostness'.

Scholars have struggled with what seems to be a very restricted mission given to the disciples. Levine has provided a very thorough analysis of 10.5, arguing convincingly that it functions on both a temporal and a social axis, axes which we have already seen are significant in an ecological reading. She demonstrates that along the temporal axis, 'the second discourse is crafted to indicate that during Jesus' ministry the mission of both master and disciples was restricted to Israel' (1988: 46). She goes on to argue that this mission continues beyond 28.18-20—it is not revoked in any way (47). She suggests that the repetition of 'sheep' in 9.36 and 10.5 and 16 indicates 'Jewish ethnic continuity among the crowds, the twelve and the future members of the church' (47). Along the social axis, Levine argues that the Jewish community will be split, 'some following Jesus and others

---

1. The reader is invited here to extend the 'connections and flows' not only through the human/animal dichotomy but also through the domestic/domesticated and 'wild' animal dichotomy.

persecuting his representatives'. The discourse seems to indicate that this split is along lines of power and authority. If we examine this power on the horizontal grid proposed by Sandoval (72.4), this 'globalized, flattened but mobile, gridlike terrain', we can map social shifts woven into the ecological texture of the text.

The co-mission given to the disciples is truly co-mission—they are to preach the *basileia* of the heavens/sky as did John (3.2) and as Jesus is doing (4.17 and passim); and they are to heal, to bring about the restoration of right order in accord with the *basileia* vision, including its material, its ecological aspects. Levine draws attention to the fact that they are not explicitly co-missioned to *teach* (cf., 4.23//9.35, see 1988: 40-41). That is reserved for Jesus until the risen one co-missions the eleven to *teach* all that he has commanded during his ministry (28.20). Dorothy Jean Weaver (1990: 84) summarizes the co-missioning in this way: where they are to go (10.5b-6); what they are to do (10.7-10); and how they are to deal with responses (10.11-15). We turn attention now to the encoding of materiality into what the co-missioned ones are to do and how they are to deal with responses.

Just as we sought to be attentive to the 'connections and flows' between human and animal in this discourse, so too we turn attention here to the material agency of the other-than-human and how these 'not only constitute the contexts of life but they also frequently re-constitute the fabrics of day-to-day life and the places and spaces in which it is lived' (Jones and Cloke 2008: 79). An ecological reading grounded in inter-con/textuality will be attentive therefore to the agency of the other-than-human as well as the human and the 'connections and flows' between and among these as constituting mission.

The co-missioned ones seem to be invited to separate themselves from the other-than-human (10.9-10): no gold, no additional tunic, sandals or staff. This is, however, a limited separation, one which enables them to be unencumbered for mission and invites contemporary readers to consider their own relationship with the 'other-than-human' and the danger of 'acquisition' of such material or Earth resources which can hinder the right ordering of the 'connections and flows' between the human and other-than-human. As this part of the discourse continues the co-missioned ones are instructed to engage with town and house, the 'it' of v. 12, alerting the ecological reader to the 'connections and flows' between the materiality of town and house as well as its sociality. The final verses of 10.7-15 remind readers that just as the proclamation of the *basileia* of the heavens, the alternative to the *basileia* of Rome, would be rejected by some in the first century, so too those seeking to proclaim a new 'right-ordering' in relation to Earth/Cosmos in the twenty-first century can also expect rejection.

I will turn now to the social axis of Matthew 10 to which Levine has drawn attention and which emerges in Mt. 10.16ff. In the opening verse (v. 16) and in vv. 29-31, the reader is once again invited to engage the ecological texture of the text in which the 'connections and flows' turn again to the human and animal interconnection. The reader encounters the tensive relationship between wolf and sheep, a 'connection' with which many first-century readers/hearers would have been familiar through what Birke and Parisi call an 'infinity of connections'. Likewise readers can draw into the text their connections with serpents and doves that are characterized one-dimensionally in the text in terms of wisdom and innocence. Verse 29 places the sparrow in the web of connectivity embracing the divine, human and other-than-human. Unfortunately, however, v. 30 privileges the human over the sparrow, awareness of which invites the ecological reader to read against the grain of the text or with suspicion while subsequently retrieving the web of connectivity.

The tension along the social axis of Matthew 10 is not only evoked metaphorically (see v. 16) but also socially. The opponents of the co-missioned ones are in collusion with councils of synagogues (v. 17) and with governors and kings (v. 18). These are the elite who will be seen to oppose Jesus more and more as the gospel story unfolds, hints of which have already been seen in Mt. 2.1-12 and 9.34. The marginality of Jesus and his followers which scholars like Duling (2012) have highlighted can be mapped on the horizontal grid of power noted earlier, rendering the tensive relationship between elite and marginal more tangible. Verses 21-22 and 35-37 map another group onto this grid, namely the family into which the proclamation of the *basileia* of the heavens or sky will bring division and rejection, even a handing over of a family member into the hands of elite power (v. 21). Indeed, the human social configuring that emerges in relation to co-missioning is that of marginalization. Carter says of such marginalization that it is:

> [a] difficult way of life in which one participates in prevailing societal values and power structures but challenges them in the pursuit of an alternative existence which manifests the presence of 'the reign of the heavens'... The audience's experience of its societal status as a marginal minority is a fundamental aspect of the difficult situation assumed and addressed by Matthew in his gospel (1997: 74-75).

He concludes that 'the audience is alerted to this difficult ambivalent and marginal identity and lifestyle early in the narrative' (viz. in 4.18-22; see also Moxnes 2003: 57-58). We can add here that this is further confirmed by a reading of Matthew 10. Matthew 11.1 concludes Jesus' co-missioning with the words 'when he had finished instructing his twelve disciples'. We see him taking up his itinerancy, he went on from there to teach and proclaim his message in their cities (11.1b). The question addressed in the subsequent section is: does walking reveal Earth?

2. Matthew 11–12: Does Walking Reveal Earth?

The connective verse (11.1) holds together two key aspects of an ecological reading, namely *time* and *space/place*, echoing through the 'when'/*hote* and the 'going on from there'/*metebē*. The human is always in interrelationship with the other-than-human creating a more-than-human imaginary and world which needs to be engaged in ecological thinking, ecological reading and ecological living. The summary statement at the end of this verse, namely that Jesus is teaching and preaching (see 4.23 and 9.35) in their cities evokes for readers not only the complex materiality of the built environment that constitutes 'their cities' but also the traversing, the walking of the land in-between with all its complex ecosystems and habitats.

In this section, therefore, careful attention will be given to place/space and where appropriate to time and their interrelationship. The opening verse of the first scene clearly orients readers in this way: John (the Immerser) is in prison and there/at that time he hears of the deeds of the Christ/the *erga tou Christou*. Jesus' reply to John's question through his disciples—are you the Coming One/*ho erchomenos* or shall we look for another?—also guides the reading of this section. Jesus does not respond to John's question in his terms that focus on titles (*christos* or *erchomenos*).[2] Rather, he sends John's disciples back to tell him what they have heard and seen of the ministry of Jesus. The senses bring the human person into intimate relationship with the other-than-human and, through these, the ministry. Indeed the identity of Jesus (the proclamation of the *basileia* of the sky/heavens) shall be encountered and known through the senses. Hearing and seeing and their opening into the dynamic materiality of the more-than-human provide a focus in this section, together with TimeSpace.

As already noted, Jesus does not respond precisely to John's question regarding a correct title. Rather he co-missions John's disciples to go and to tell or proclaim what they have heard and seen. It is through the senses of hearing and seeing that the identity of Jesus will be known and this will be conveyed to others by way of voice. I note in this regard that Elvey (2011b) subtitles her chapter on hearing as 'hearing and voice' (116). As we have already seen, Jesus teaches and preaches that the *basileia* of the sky/heavens is near (4.17, 23; 9.35) and commissions his disciples to preach. Hearing is, therefore, intimately connected with speaking or with voice. Indeed, Mt. 5.2 makes this very explicit by way of the phrase 'he opened his mouth and taught them saying…'.

In light of the above, it is surprising that the sense of hearing characterizes the Matthean narrative much less than that of seeing (10.27; 11.4;

---

2. For a much more extensive exploration of this section in relation to the Jesus of Matthew's Gospel, see Wainwright (1998: 67-83).

12.19; 13.16, 18; 21.16; 24.6 and 27.13). Matthew seems to differ, therefore, from other biblical narratives if Elvey is correct in her assertion that '[t]he command Hear! Listen! saturates the Bible...[in] its relation to oral tradition and its being read aloud' (116). Certainly the disciples have already been co-missioned by Jesus to proclaim from the housetops what they hear whispered, a response to the rejection that the co-missioned ones will experience along the social axis of the co-mission (10.27). Also, Jesus proclaims 'blessed' both the eyes of those who see and the ears of those who hear the proclamation of the *basileia* that occurs through parables (13.16) and then invites the hearers (both disciples and crowds) to attend to/hear the parable of the sower (13.18).

An ecological reading of the call in Mt. 11.4 to tell what one hears invites readers to explore beyond human words and texts and to listen for the 'heterogeneous assemblage' with its 'animal-vegetable-mineral sonority' of which Bennett (2010) speaks. Bernie Krause in his TED video recording, 'The Voice of the Natural World' provides further insight into such hearing. He draws attention not only to human noise ('anthrophony' - which has been our sole focus in reading the gospel text) and the sound of non-biological elements such as wind and waves ('geophony') but in particular to 'biophony', the sound of organisms in a given habitat or what he calls the 'signature voices of the natural world' (Krause 2013). It is his study of this biophony which has brought him to an awareness of the healing that needs to take place in our world so that human, abiotic and biotic Earth constituents might all be heard. In his words, 'careful listening gives tools to guage the health of a habitat.' As Jesus invites the disciples of John to a new hearing of the deeds of the *Christos*, so too the Jesus of Matthew's gospel calls today's disciples to a new hearing that includes biophony and geophony, a 'heterogeneous assemblage' whose call is to the right ordering/*dikaiosynē* which characterizes the *basileia* of the sky/heavens for today.

There is also an invitation to a new seeing in Mt. 11.4. At least three different verbs describe this sense in the gospel and each occurs multiple times. Elvey says of this sense that '[t]he visible has a voice to which the gaze responds' (2011b: 151). In continuity with this analysis of the 'hearing' through which disciples will know who Jesus is, so too a new 'seeing' is required, a new attentiveness to the voice to which the gaze responds. This attentiveness will lead to a 'seeing' not only of human healing—the lame walking, lepers being cleansed and the dead raised—but of healing among the biotic and abiotic Earth others constituting the 'heterogeneous assemblage' in myriads of habitats today. To see such healing is to recognize Jesus and to participate in the gospel mission.

Matthew 11.19 which frames 11.2-19 with reference to the *erga*/works of the *Christos* and of *Sophia* (see Deutsch 2001: 99 and Wainwright 1998: 68-72) reminds readers that it was these *erga* or works/deeds that impelled

John to inquire of the identity of Jesus. As we have seen, Jesus turned John back to the deeds and away from titles and to the 'heterogeneous assemblage' within multiple habitats if read ecologically. Initially, a reader might suspect that Wisdom/Sophia is yet another title used to mark Jesus. Deutsch suggests that the Matthean gospel, and 11.19 in particular, presents Jesus 'as Wisdom's own self' (99). Attentiveness to the identification of the male Jesus of the Matthean narrative with Sophia, the female figure of the Wisdom literature, turns the ecological reader to the 'queering' of this text and of the Jesus of the narrative. Such queering undoes 'normal categories', in this instance those of gender (Haraway 2008b: xxiv). Giffney and Hird (2008: 1-12) extend this hermeneutic to include among other binaries the 'human/animal…organic/inorganic, animate/inanimate, nature/culture'.

The queering of Mt. 11.19 can evoke myriads of intertexts from the Wisdom corpus. One which seems most significant for an ecological reading is Prov. 8.22-31. Sophia speaks in the first person as she plays between the divine and the human world (v. 31). She sings of being the first *ergon/* work of the divine *Kyrios* (v. 22 with echoes of Mt. 11.2). But also she was found before the *aiōnos/*ages or eternity (v. 23). She plays between time and eternity, between created one and participant in the work of the cosmos coming to be. She is there through the fashioning of the universe like a unique crafter or fashioner (v. 30), rejoicing in the inhabited world, the Earth or *oikoumenē* (BDAG 699) and in the human community. Against the backdrop of this deconstruction of the gendering of the human community in Prov. 8.31b, Mt. 11.19 can resonate with the heterogeneous assemblage of biotic and abiotic, of human and animal, and of divine and human: indeed 'Sophia is justified by her deeds'. This is the *dikaiosynē* of the *basileia* of the skies. It re-turns the reader to Mt. 1.1, to genealogy which in its turn invited the reader back through the genealogy of Earth and the universe. In Jesus/Sophia justified by her deeds, G*d is 'with' the Earth community (1.23).

Two seemingly unrelated and independent texts (11.21-24 and 25-27) break into the Wisdom trajectory in Matthew 11. In the first, Jesus berates the cities that do not recognize his deeds of power and so do not repent (the word *dynamis* replacing *erga*). Language of the senses is conspicuously absent from this text but hearing/speaking is backgrounded in the opening verse. It is more explicitly foregrounded in the opening verse of the second text (11.25-27) as the narrator has Jesus 'answering' and 'saying' (but the reader does not know to whom or what). The reader is thus an eavesdropper, one listening in on Jesus' conversation with G*d. The imagery for the divine is that of the kyriocentric patriarchal household where the Pater/Father and Kyrios/Lord has power over both the people and all the other-than-human in the household. This imagery is extended in the second half of v. 25 so that the heavens and the earth become the household of G*d. The other-than-human is completely absent, calling for further critical engagement (Wainwright 1998: 79-81; see also Schüssler Fiorenza 2007: 195-221 and Deutsch 2001: 98-100).

Verses 28-30 return to the identification of Jesus with Sophia as seen most vividly in 11.19. Jesus/Sophia speaks to *all* who are burdened in any way thus evoking intertextually Sir. 24.19-22. Wisdom's use of the metaphors of 'fruit', 'honey', 'honeycomb' and 'drink' (vv. 19, 20, 21) gather all, not just the human, into the realm of Wisdom and her right-ordering. The burdens of ecological degradation and destruction are borne by the entire more-than-human community.

The imagery of these verses differs radically from that of vv. 25-27. Even drawing intertextually on the notion of Wisdom/Sophia's *yoke* (Sir. 6.25 and 51.26), Jesus Sophia calls all wearied and burdened, all in the more-than-human community who are not able to function optimally, to take on the yoke of restoration or of healing, the *erga* of Sophia (11.19), the *erga* of the Christos (11.2). The final verse suggests that this yoke is easy and the burden light but experience suggests, however, that the human community at this point in cosmic history will need not only to *hear* and *see* but to draw on all its senses to learn a new wisdom. This will entail engagement with both the human community as well as all in the 'animal-vegetable-mineral sonority cluster' (Bennett).

Matthew 11 has not yet invited the reader into walking although the chapter is shadowed by Jesus' walking in 11.1. It has revealed Jesus as Wisdom/Sophia who speaks and acts and in doing so has revealed something of Earth. As we turn to Matthew 12, the text invites the reader to join Jesus and the disciples walking through the grainfields on the Sabbath. Time/Place characterizes the opening of this story as it did in 11.1 and 2.

The text of the opening scenario of Matthew 12, namely vv. 1-8, takes the inter-con/textual reader into a symphony of the senses and heterogeneous assemblages. The reader encounters a small itinerant group (Jesus and his disciples) walking through grainfields—a rich and vibrant habitat where earth and all its many microbes and organisms support the growth and life of the grain, truly a heterogeneous assemblage. The time is the Sabbath, that unique day in the human calendar of the Jewish people when all the people including slaves and the outsider/resident alien are to rest, together with the animals (Exod. 20.10 and Deut. 5.14), in order to renew their relationship with the Holy One who likewise rested, and with the created order (Gen. 2.2-3).

The next statement, 'the disciples were hungry', stands in contrast with the resource rich environment of the grainfields. In this context, the disciples pluck heads of grain to eat. The text does not give attention to the sense of taste they experienced as the materiality of the grain satisfies their hunger. Rather, it turns the readers' attention to another sense, namely that of 'seeing' and here it is the Pharisees who 'see' what is taking place.

Already the Matthean reader is becoming aware of the construction of this group called 'Pharisees' within the socio-cultural layer of the text's ecological texture. They are named with the Sadducees as 'brood of vipers' in John's eschatological preaching (3.7) and with the scribes whose righteousness the disciple of Jesus is to exceed (5.20). They question his disciples about his eating with tax-collectors and sinners (9.11) and accuse Jesus himself of casting out demons by the power of the prince of demons (9.34). In these few short verses, they are constructed as opponents of Jesus. Ecological readers attentive to the postmodern shift in an understanding and mapping of power as proposed by Sandoval will recognize Jesus and the Pharisees as 'speaking…to and against each other in a lateral—not pyramidal—exchange, although from *spatially* different…locations' (72.4). As the story continues, exchanges between Jesus and the Pharisees will function to move them further and further apart, to the margin and centre respectively, on the horizontal grid of power. The exchange that follows contributes to such a movement.

The Pharisees call Jesus' attention to the action of the disciples with the Matthean focalizer *idou*/look. He is invited to *see*, to 'attend to the visual voice' of what his disciples are doing, activity that the Pharisees interpret as unlawful on the Sabbath. Aaron Gale (2011: 22) discusses what is 'lawful' on the Sabbath not only according to the biblical injunction of Exod. 34.21 with regard to agricultural work but also what was considered such work in the later rabbinic laws that may have been developing within the circles of first century Pharisees. He comes to the conclusion that there is no explicit prohibition in relation to the 'plucking' of grain to satisfy one's hunger on the Sabbath.

In contrast to the Pharisees' turn to the law, Jesus turns attention to the story of David's asking the priest for the 'holy bread' to satisfy his hunger and that of his companions, bread that was legally or at lest customarily forbidden to them. Then he re-turns attention to the law but to an exception involving the priests of the temple who perform their duties, their work, on the Sabbath. He has engaged with the Pharisees in an incisive verbal exchange on the horizontal grid of power. Such exchange has distracted attention from the original situation—'the disciples were hungry'. Jesus' re-turns attention to this situation with his citing of Hos. 6.6: I desire mercy/ steadfast love and not sacrifice.

For the ecological reader, the hunger of the disciples can function to focalize the hunger that exists in today's world and the ways in which it is bound up with legal and socio-economic structures that can often obfuscate rather than provide solutions to this hunger. Solutions will require a prophetic vision, a new and different seeing, one informed by the steadfast love that comes from a knowing of G*d (Hos. 6.6b). This intertext needs to pulsate, therefore, not only in the Matthean text but in those contexts today where readers/hearers of the gospel seek to respond to the interrelationship between Earth's resources and the hunger in our world and not only of the human but of the entire more-than-human community. Walking has begun to reveal Earth. It is associated with a wisdom that will be contested in the crucible of local and global eco-justice.

Jesus' walking and the time indicator, 'the Sabbath', link the story just considered with the following story (12.9-14). Jesus leaves the grainfields and enters a synagogue, a material structure in the built environment of a village or town and another context of heterogeneous assemblages, some of which are captured in the narrative. The first of these is that the synagogue, a context for Jesus' preaching and teaching (4.23; 9.35), is evoked here as place of contestation associated with the Pharisees.[3] In this narrative, *idou* focalizes a man with a withered hand, a man lacking wholeness in his physical body, his corporeality. In Matthew 8–9, such an encounter would lead to healing, but the Pharisees cut across that potentiality with a question about whether it is lawful to heal on the Sabbath. The reader is informed that they do not seek a genuine engagement with Jesus on this legal question but seek evidence with which to accuse him.

Jesus' response can be seen to take us, as ecological readers, into an 'inter-species sociality'. He speaks wisdom, as it were, from 'within ... [n]ature which surrounds and includes us' (Behnke 1999: 95). The listener to the Matthean text is taken into the experience of one who has only one sheep that falls into a pit on the Sabbath. Verse 12 raises a difficult issue, namely that of a human/animal hierarchy within the 'inter-species sociality'. We can engage tensively with v. 12 from the position provided by Birke and Parisi who seek to move beyond the dualism of human/animal that leads to our pervasive anthropocentrism and sees the human being as much more valuable than the sheep. They invite a consideration of the animal (including the human) as engaged in 'becoming rather than being, process rather than essence, alliances and multiplicities rather than unitary individuals, heterogeneous populations (such as ecosystems) rather than species' (Birke and Parisi 1999: 64). Verse 12b can indeed capture something of this in the claim that it is lawful to do good for any being, whoever the endangered one might be, on the Sabbath. This text invites readers toward a searching after new wisdom, a wisdom requiring us to think anew about the human/animal nexus (see Hoggard Creegan 2013; Deane-Drummond, Artinian-Kyser and Clough 2013; and Moore 2014).

The healing itself is passed over very cursorily (v. 13) in comparison with the narratives of Matthew 8–9. It happens in the corporeality of the

---

3. Note, however, that the phrase 'their synagogues' has already occurred in 4.23 and 9.35, but there it functioned to designate the place of Jesus' proclamation of the message of the *basileia*.

human body and simply as a result of Jesus' inviting the man to stretch out his hand. There is no touch, no healing word, only the lone voice of the narrator informing readers that the Pharisees are beginning to plot to destroy Jesus (v. 14).

A tension that appeared only sporadically in the early part of the narrative reaches a much more critical point here, so much so that the following verse (v. 15) records Jesus going away or escaping (*anechōrēsen*) from there (a walking that is very deliberate). Already this verb has been used four times previously to describe events in the story of Jesus. When he was but a newborn infant, the *magoi* from the East who come to honour him escape home by a different route as Herod is plotting against Jesus, and anyone associated with him (2.12, 13). Joseph escapes to Egypt with the child and his mother because of Herod's threats (2.14) and then to the region of Galilee when it is discovered on his return from Egypt that Herod Archelaus is on the throne in Judea in place of his father, a situation no better than that from which they had escaped (2.22). The very beginning of Jesus' ministry is characterized by his escaping from Judea to Galilee when John is imprisoned (4.12). The Galilean ministry that has already been under threat politically is now being challenged by religious leaders. Each of these experiences further marginalizes Jesus on the grid of power in relation to both political and religious power-brokers. As the second half of 12.15 together with vv. 22-32 indicate, far from subverting Jesus' healing ministry, these threats seem, in fact, to enhance it. Many crowds follow (they walk after Jesus, the one walking very deliberately and wisely away from what threatens) and into further itinerant ministry. He heals 'all' of them and engages the leaders in robust challenge and riposte.

What is at issue in this particular encounter between Jesus and the religious leaders is the nexus between the dis-abled body and the naming of this dis-abling in the language of demon possession. The narrator has already made this connection in introducing a man into the narrative as *daimonizomenos*/demon possessed. He goes on to indicate that he is both blind (not able to 'see') and mute (not able to speak in a voice that invites others to 'hear'). Within the world-view of the first century, demon possession is written onto this man's dis-abled body. The Matthean text says very simply that Jesus healed the man as he has healed many others (see 4.23, 24; 8.7, 16; 9.35; 12.10, 15), re-storing and re-storying the body—the material. There is no focus on the casting out of demons here.

The crowds and the religious leaders/the Pharisees interpret this healing action of Jesus very differently. The crowds are amazed at such healing and the narrator places on their lips the affirmation of Jesus as 'son of David', the messianic healing one (Novakovic 2003: 103-109 and Duling 1992; see also Mt. 9.27). His opponents accuse him of casting out demons by the power of the 'prince of demons'. This contestation echoes in the ecological texture of the text that encodes the socio-political and religious struggles surrounding bodies and power in first century Galilee. This power was located in Herod Antipas, who was backed by the power of Rome, and in the Pharisees (see Moxnes 2003: 136-40). Inability to contend with such power was written on the bodies of individuals and named as demon-possession.

Such contestation in relation to healing evokes for contemporary ecological readers claims and counter-claims in relation to the dis-abling of bodies/species, as a result of the chemicals poured into the Earth, water and atmosphere; of oil spills and of fracking. The words of Jesus in relation to the nation/the city/the house divided against itself can ring out for those seeking to enact ecological justice. They function as an invitation to engage those who are opposed to such a vision and praxis, to 'bind up' those strongly pitted against them, and to evoke the spirit of G*d to bring about the *basileia* vision of the Matthean gospel interpreted through our contemporary lens.

Other-than human material imagery of a tree and its fruits (v. 33), a brood of vipers (v. 34), a treasury (v. 35), and even the belly of a whale (v. 40) lie scattered through the remaining verses of Matthew 12 and each invites further exploration. Indeed the last image functions as a pointer to the material body of Jesus, like the bodies of all other living Earth beings, returning to the Earth (even if, in Jesus' case, only for a predicted three days—v. 40). This narrative section, in which the ecological reader has encountered the materiality at the heart of the ministry of Jesus, healer and Wisdom teacher, against whom opposition is mounting, closes with an encounter with his mother and 'brothers' (12.46-50). Jesus affirms in this context a new fictive kinship: his mother, sister, brother is whoever 'does' G*d's will.

In the final chapter of this segment of the gospel, walking reveals an Earth wisdom that is not cowered by political and religious threats, as the intertextuality in 12.16-21 indicates. If Earth and all its constituents in right relationship are to flourish in accord with a new vision that an ecological reader of the Matthean gospel might link to the *basileia* vision, then engagement with political and religious systems of power and destruction is essential as is the new fictive kinship in which such a dream can be nourished.

Chapter 7

MATTHEW 13:
HABITAT/HUMAN/HOLY IN-FORM PROCLAMATION IN PARABLES

> That same day Jesus went out of the house and sat beside the sea. Such great crowds gathered around him that he got into a boat and sat there, while the whole crowd stood on the beach. And he told them many things in parables (Mt. 13.1-3).[1]

These opening verses of Matthew 13 can easily be overlooked as readers turn attention to what is considered the important material in this chapter, namely Jesus' teaching in parables. The verses are rich in detail when reading ecologically and point both backwards and forwards. The reader is provided with temporal location ('on that same day'), with physical location ('out of the house', 'beside the sea' and 'into a boat'), and social location and interdependence (great crowds gather around Jesus on the beach). Lorraine Code emphasizes that 'temporal, physical, social location and interdependence are integral to the possibility of being, knowing and doing' (Code 2006: 69) and these have been woven into the Matthean text of Mt. 13.1-3.

The first aspect of this ecological texture that the reader of Mt. 13.1-9 encounters is the temporal: 'on that day' or 'on that same day'/*en tē hēmera ekeinē*. This day has been shaped by the sociality already connected with it, namely significant controversy with the Pharisees (12.14-15, 24-45) on the one hand, and Jesus' proclaiming a new fictive kinship or household on the other (12.48-50), presumably from within a house (see 13.1 with its reference to leaving the house). These aspects in their turn shape and are shaped by what follows in Matthew 13. Temporality functions interconnectedly with spatiality and social interaction. Each are woven into the opening verses of this narrative, creating TimeSpace which captures the multiple and heterogeneous experience of social time and the inseparability of time, space and sociality (May and Thrift 2001). The human actor, Jesus, moves from the constructed space of 'the house' to the edge of the sea and into a boat on the sea. A large crowd of people gathers around him on the seashore.

Jesus comes out of the house, the material and located space of human habitation and the space in which human kinship structures are conceived

---

1. This section of the narrative is developed much more fully in Wainwright 2012b.

and enacted. In the previous narrative (12.46-50), house is the place outside which Jesus own kin were located (see particularly 12.46), a place where kinship structures were challenged and redefined in the *basileia* of Jesus. As Matthew 13 opens, Jesus' taking his place 'outside' locates what will follow within the same context of alternative possibilities, outside *oikia*.[2] Jesus sits, a gesture that we have already seen in 5.1-2 designates authority to teach.

Human action is not separate from but intimately connected to location: 'by the sea'. The seashore links land and sea but can also be seen as a borderland between the two, a marginal space. Here it is associated with the new fictive kinship of 12.46-50 evoked by the reference to 'that same day'. Hence it functions as border or marginal space. This multidimensional space is peopled by a large crowd (13.2) from whom Jesus separates himself by getting into a boat. The boat, the sea and the seashore function to create meaning. They give relational authority and power to Jesus in that they separate him from and yet relate him to the crowd on the beach. New meaning is possible here in this 'Thirdspace'. The materiality or spatiality of houses, boats and sea/shores intertwine and interact with the social—Jesus and the crowds. This is the hybrid habitat in which and from which Jesus speaks to the crowds in parables in ways that break open the binaries associated with mastery. Habitat, in all its complexity, functions to authorize Jesus who in turn by his characterization authorizes the crowd within the dynamic of the new kinship and its characterizing of a *basileia* of the heavens/sky to follow.

1. *Matthew 13.3b-9: 'Parable' of the Sower*

A dynamic similar to that noted above, continues in the first 'parable' (Mt. 13.3b-8) that Jesus proclaims. As a narrative within a narrative, it introduces another level to the dynamism of meaning-making within an ecological reading. This parable is rich in inter-con/textuality, rich in the hybridity of habitat. The words given to Jesus by the Matthean redactor in 13.18— you then hear the parable of the 'sower'—have drawn attention to the sower in the parable of 13.3b-8. There is, however, much more to this text than a simple focus on the sower.

---

2. *Oikos* and *oikia* are both employed in the Matthaean narrative, almost interchangeably. *Oikia* seems to be the word used to designate specific houses rather than the more general household but 9.6-7 seems to contradict such a distinction. Many scholars draw attention to the possible links between this house by the seashore and the reference in Mt. 9.1 to Capernaum as Jesus' own town and his going into his house in 9.7. Note that the latter uses *oikos* and the former *oikia*. Both words function to locate Jesus in a house in Capernaum that is designated as his own.

Exploring the ecological texture of the text, we note first that the sower encoded in the text may be imagined as slave or tenant farmer on one of the large Herodian or Roman estates which were becoming more numerous in the growing entrepreneurial or latifundial processes in first century Galilee. She or he may have been a self-sufficient small farmer, member of a farming family (see Freyne 1994: 105-10 and Fiensy 1991: 75-117). Each farmer would have been connected with their social fabric in different ways but would have shared the understanding of the seasons, with their rhythms of time for planting and for harvesting.[3] The sower is engaged in a task of sowing seed, the seed not being specified but implied in the verb *speirein*. It is likely to be wheat or barley, the two most common agricultural products of Galilee in the first century, seen throughout the region in areas like the Bet Netofa Valley just north of Nazareth and Sepphoris or the Gennesareth plain on the north-west corner of the Sea of Galilee. These would have been well known to Jesus and his followers (Hanson and Oakman 1998: 104) or to Galilean/Syrian readers of the gospel and hence are encoded into the ecological texture of the Matthean text.

The clear patterning of the Greek draws readers into the process and its outcome:

> en tō speirein auton ha men epesen... (as he sowed, some seeds fell...)
>   kai...
> alla de epesen epi... (others fell upon...)
>   Kai... (three times, vv. 5, 7, 8).

The seed seems to be being cast rather than carefully planted in rows[4] but either way it appears to have been hand sowing, linking the sower intimately to the process of planting with the goal of growing grain to feed family and animals and to have seed for the next year's planting. The pressure on farmers or tenants to produce abundant harvests so as to develop exports for the Empire also lurks within the world that the parable creates.[5] The parable draws the reader into the ecosystem or ecocycle of sower and seed. Birds take up the seeds on the pathway so that they are fed. Weeds take up their groundspace so that there is insufficient space for the sower's seed in some places. The sun with the wind and the rain, elements that are

---

3. May and Thrift (2001: 3-4), recognize 'timetables and rhythms' and 'social discipline' as two of their features of TimeSpace in its multidimensionality.

4. Xenophon, *Oeconomicus* 17.7 suggests that 'seed must be scattered from the hand'. See also Varro, *On Agriculture* 1.29.2, who speaks of the seed having been broadcast after which a third ploughing 'cover(s) the broadcast seed in ridges'.

5. It is not clear whether Galilee of the first century was producing sufficient grain to export to the larger centres of the Empire. See Freyne (1994: 107-108) and Fiensy (1991: 55-60) who note that even Jesus' own parables are replete with allusions to large land holdings and tenant workers.

not named, perhaps constituting a 're-mark' in this text, enable the seed to grow but if the root is not deep enough, some plants will wither under the sun and others will be choked out by plants which are not useful in the agricultural cycle. The seed that falls on the soil prepared for it produces richly. All this functions metaphorically within the parable which captures indeed a network of actants in this hybrid habitat—from sower, to seed, to bird, sun, earth/soil, weeds and thorns.

Stephanie Nelson in the foreword to her study of Hesiod and Virgil's poems on farming says that 'because farming is inescapably a part of human life that it may provide a clue to what is most basically human, and so a clue to our place within the cosmos' (1998: v). Jesus the parabler and his audience would have known the agricultural system of their first century Galilee and the Matthean author and readers that of Galilee/Syria. Jesus in his first parable by the sea invites listeners/readers into the parabolic process in the same way that Xenophen can say in the *Oeconomicus* 16.3 that 'anyone who does not know what the soil is capable of producing…would not know what he ought to plant or to sow'. Listeners would have known, as did Cato (*On Agriculture* 6.1-4, 34.1-2 and 35.1-2) and Varro (*On Agriculture* 23.1-2; 24.1), the importance of the soil and its various types for particular crops. They too would have known the prolific nature of grain given the right conditions as well as the desired proliferation in the face of the Roman taxation on a small farmer's grain or soil. Varro notes the variety in yields: tenfold in one district, fifteen in another, even a hundred to one near Gadara in Syria (Varro, *On Agriculture* 1.44.2) while Pliny proclaims that nothing is more prolific than wheat giving yields of 150, 360 and 400 (*Nat.* 18.21.94-95). Given, however, that Pliny's figures are in the context of impressing the emperor, such figures may be exaggerated.[6] The three ears of grain springing from one stalk on the coins of Agrippa I (Madden 1967: 104-105), like the seeds of the parable, symbolize the fertility of the land. In the former, abundance is attributed to the reign of Agrippa.

This first parable is not introduced by the phrase the reader will come to expect as the story moves on: the *basileia* of the heavens/of G*d is like… Rather, Jesus simply presents the complexly woven world of the more-than-human in which multiple actants including the human are intertwined. Two different cosmologies are implicitly in tension within the parable and the network of associations it creates. First there is that of the emperor and his representatives, whether a Herodian king in Galilee or landowners supporting the imperial system, who are identified as the source of abundance. On the other hand, the parable evokes a more complex system of interwoven

---

6. Moldenke and Moldenke (2002: 233) suggest that a yield of about 20-fold can be expected of a crop of wheat in the Levant but that good soil and certain strains might produce '60 or even 100 grains each'.

elements that intersect in the process of sowing seed. The surprise is that there is an ecology that can produce abundance. It is hybrid ecology, consisting of multiple actants. Jesus simply invites reflection on or attentiveness to the richness of habitat and what such attentiveness will allow us to hear: 'let those who have ears, let them hear'.

Matthew 13.10-17 is a tantalizing text breaking into the rich imagery of Jesus' proclamation. First, it appears to be entirely anthropocentric and second, it constructs a hierarchical wedge between two human groups, the crowds and the disciples. The Matthean ecological reader will, therefore, read against the grain of this segment of the text and its dualisms that shape a social imaginary of mastery.

The rich Earth imagery and evocative tenor of the parable of the seed and the soil is tempered by the continuation of the anthropocentrism of the previous verses in the call to hear the parable of the sower (13.18-23). Elements of the parable are interpreted in a one-to-one correspondence with a human response to the 'word of the kingdom (13.19). The parable itself evokes the *mystēria* of the *basileia* through the world drawn into the ecological texture of the text. Its interpretation renders it exclusively in terms of human ethical behaviour but not behaviour grounded in habitat. The hearer is removed from the constituents of habitat evoked by the parable. An ecological reading will on the one hand, call attention to the hybridity of the imagery and its relationship to habitat and its implications for ecological ethics. On the other hand, such a reading notes the paucity of the interpretation ('what was sown...is...') with its sole focus on human behaviour. The imagery in the parable, however, evokes the multi-dimensionality of ecological ethics. The word of the *basileia* spoken in ecological imagery invites an ecological response that will in its turn be multidimensional. Attentiveness to habitat will be caught up in this response and enable ecological readers to hear the call of the *basileia* that is imaged not only in seed and sowing but in the constituents and their sociality in the world of the more-than-human.

2. *Matthew 13.24-50: Weeds and Wheat and... Parabled*

Matthew 13.24 introduces readers to phraseology that will become familiar: 'the kingdom of the heavens/sky may be compared to'. There are aspects of the *basileia* of the heavens or the sky that can only be understood by way of metaphor and image, like the finger pointing at the moon, to borrow a metaphor from a Zen sutra (Trible 1978: 16; Kapleau 1965: 167, 174). As with the initial parable, the ecological texture of this parable is constituted by habitat. It evokes TimeSpace where the human, human activity of sowing, seed in all its potential for life, and the production of many seeds in the cycle of sowing and harvesting, the soil which receives it as well as weeds and their impact within the agricultural cycle, all actively intersect in the materiality of the text of Mt. 13.24-30.

This parable draws readers once again into the world of seed, sower, soil and yield that characterizes this Parable Discourse (12 of the 16 verses in Matthew in which some form of *speirein*/to sow occurs are in Matthew 13: vv. 3, 4, 18, 19, 20, 22, 23, 23, 27, 31, 37, 39). Also *anthrōpos*, except when qualified as an *oikodespotēs* or 'householder' in 13.52, seems to function as the indicator of the human actor/s not only in this parable but in the Parable Discourse as a whole (13.24, 25, 28, 31, 44, 45) although the *anthrōpos* of v. 24 is named as *oikodespotēs* in v. 27. The parable which begins in generic terms of a sower sowing good seed in a field evoking the range of farming practices and structures already discussed above moves into imagery of the larger estate on which an *oikodespotēs* has *douloi* or slaves rather than workers. The narrative and metaphoric world created by this parable is quite complex and is often overlooked by biblical scholars who move immediately to the allegorical interpretation of the parable in vv. 37-43 and allow it to obscure the hearing of the parable itself and its wealth of imagery (McIvor 1995: 643-59).

While in the initial parable of Matthew 13, the various places of reception of the seed which determined the different yields could be seen as part of the natural ecosystem, in this parable, there is direct human intervention into the process of sowing, germination and growing to harvest, and it is a negative intervention. The human subject sows good seed (*kalon sperma*) in the field, evoking the agricultural process of the initial parable. The *basileia* of the heavens or sky is compared to the process of sowing good seed that is interrupted by the arrival of an enemy while all are sleeping, and the sowing of *zizania* among the grain (*siton*). There is ambivalence, however, around *echthros*/enemy at this point in the narrative. Listeners have been instructed to love their enemies (5.43-44) and even if that enemy is of one's own household (10.36). There is a relational link around the very point of tension in the parable. Time, space and sociality intersect in the ecological texture of the text to draw attention to the rupture in the ecological process. This very rupture is multidimensional inviting reflection on both process and rupture, especially for contemporary readers in the face of ecological disasters that rupture the ecosystems of Earth.

The word *zizania*/weeds, a *hapaxlegomenon* in both the LXX and the New Testament occurring only in this parable and its allegorical explanation (13.25, 26, 27, 29, 30, 36, 38, 40), is rare in ancient Greek.[7] Theophrastus, *Enquiry into Plants* 8.8.3 suggests that it 'comes from degenerate wheat

---

7. Moldenke and Moldenke (2002: 134), who say that it is not used by any of the ancient or classic Greek authors. The designation 'weed' from an ecological perspective is generally human centred as Håkansson (2003: 1-2), indicates: 'plants occurring in

and barley' linking it with a particular type of weed, namely *aira*. He goes on to say that it 'loves chiefly to appear among wheat' and in this same paragraph muses that 'in the case of nearly every crop there is a plant which grows up with it and mingles with it, whether this is due to the soil which is a reasonable explanation, or to some other cause.' While the grain and the *zizania*/weeds might grow naturally together, in the parable, however, there is a very explicit intervention of an enemy who has scattered the *zizania* among the good seed. Since they grow well together, it is not surprising that the presence of the weeds does not become visible until the grain appears. The rhythm of the season and human agricultural practices, two dimensions of time, intersect with the life-cycle of the grain. This evokes the *basileia* of the heavens/sky into which a counter movement is introduced whose processes are very similar, indeed hardly distinguishable until the final phrase of coming to fruition or seed.

At this point in the narrative the reader learns that the *anthrōpos* of the parable is an *oikodespotēs*/householder with slaves. It seems that the householder and not the slaves was responsible for the planting of the good seed[8] and the vigilence of the *douloi*/slaves on behalf of the householder suggests that they work together with him for the good of the whole *oikos*. What we see in this parable is the Roman practice of using slaves and masters as literary figures in *exempla* or example stories, a practice taken over by early Christians (Harrill 2006: 3), especially in the parables. This practice participates in the maintenance of the social imaginary of mastery that was 'widely diffuse in the ancient Mediterranean, which supported what the Romans called *auctoritas*' (Harrill: 2). The ecological reader will read against the grain of this aspect of the text and its encoding of power, noting the shared participation of householder and slaves in the desired outcome of the crop for the household, each exercising particular power.[9] These power relations can be mapped on Sandoval's horizontal grid of power in a way that allows for intersecting relationships as well as different placements in terms of authority. The complexity needs to allow for different configurations to be mapped, in a way that the horizontal grid makes possible.

The surprising or confronting aspect in the parable, especially to the gospel's first century hearers, would have been the instruction given by the

situations where they are unwanted...plants occurring on arable land without the grower's intention.'

8. Varro, *On Agriculture* 1.17.2, says that 'freemen...till the ground themselves (as many poor people do with the help of their families)'.

9. Sarah B. Pomeroy suggests this in relation to Xenophon's *Oeconomicus* (1994: 65-67). Varro, *On Agriculture* 1.17.5, also notes that 'foremen [who may themselves be slaves] are to be made more zealous by rewards, and care must be taken that they have a bit of property of their own.' There is a complex power grid encoded in the text inviting the critical engagement of the hearer/reader.

householder to the *douloi*, namely to leave both the grain and the *zizania* to grow to the harvest (v. 30). Xenophon says that 'if weeds spring up with the grain and choke it by robbing it of its nourishment', then it is 'reasonable … to send in men to hoe the soil' (*Oeconomicus* 17.15) while for Varro, *On Agriculture* 1.30, 'crops should be weeded, that is, the grass cleared from the crops'. He links this agricultural practice with time: 'between the vernal equinox and the rising of the Pleiades'.[10] The householder of the parable also interacts with time but the advice given to the slaves is to *aphete*/leave the weeds and the grain to grow to fruition together. This householder does not seem to be concerned about the weeds robbing the grain of nourishment, as was Xenophon. Rather the focus is on the *kairos*/the time of the harvest. This is to be the time of separation, the culminating point of the parable which images the *basileia* of the heavens/sky.[11]

Kairos has connotations of a period characterized as crisis time (BDAG 497). In the parable it seems to designate that particular moment in the agricultural process when both weed and grain come to fruition, signalling the time of the harvest. Echoes of the crisis time may function only faintly in the text, especially given that the only other reference to harvest is in 9.37-38 where the metaphoric aspect seems to be strong. Also the related imagery of the *siton*/grain being gathered into the barn while the weeds (or the chaff) are burnt has been used metaphorically to describe the role of John the Baptist (3.12). This parable invites attentiveness to TimeSpace and the sociality associated with it in ecological processes, if one is to understand the *basileia* of the sky/heavens. The parabolic turn ruptures hearers'/readers' expectations and invites them into a new TimeSpace/sociality nexus. It entails a waiting, a waiting on the *kairos* or the time of fruition and of separation. The challenge is to be able to distinguish what is grain and what is weed and to know the point at which such distinctions can be made. This is invitation into *mystērion*, that which is associated with the divine mystery whose presence in Earth's processes has been made visible in a particular way in Jesus (1.23). This *mystērion* reveals itself in and through Earth

---

10. Moldenke and Moldenke (2002: 134), suggest that 'poorer people do not clean it out of their grainfields, lest in so doing they accidentally pull up and thus lose a single grain plant' but they do not give any documentation to support this claim at least in antiquity. If this was so, the parable's imagery moves between the larger landowner and the poorer subsistence farmers and if the latter is evoked, then the parable's imagery draws on a justice motif characteristic of the Matthaean Gospel.

11. The imagery of this parable can evoke the contemporary ecological approaches to weed management which is often complex and attentive to ecosystems in which 'life form', 'growth form', and 'lifespan' and in which 'multiple ecological interactions' have their place. As examples of such approaches see Håkansson (2003) and Liebman, Mohler, and Staver (2001).

and its processes in which TimeSpace and the sociality of the more-than-human intertwine.

Matthew 13.31-34 continues the unfolding of the Parable Discourse, drawing on the materiality accessible to Jesus' listeners, both experientially as well as imaginatively or parabolically. Inter-con/textually, it is the processes of the material that are highlighted by Jesus as parabolic, thus constituting the ecological texture of the text of Mt. 13.31-32. The focus of the parable is the mustard seed that is sown in a field, continuing the agricultural imagery of previous parables. What Jesus highlights as parabolic, at least for first century Galilean or Syrian audiences, is that this tiniest of seeds known to them,[12] grown as a herb for its oil as well as being beneficial for health (Pliny, *Nat.* 19,54, 170), exceeds their expectations. It grows up to become a shrub or almost like a small tree, from between three to four feet up to ten to fifteen feet (Moldenke and Moldenke 2002: 59). It can become a home for birds that feast on its seeds. The parabolic imagery is extended to the birds making their dwelling place or their nests there. The surprising interconnectedness of the ecosystem becomes source for Jesus' challenge to the readers' imagination in relation to the *basileia* of the heavens/sky. Even the smallest in an ecosystem can image the *basileia*, can be the place where the G*d of Jesus, the parabler is 'with' the Earth community.[13]

This symbolism continues into the next parable, linked as it is by the phrase 'another parable'. Imagery shifts from the field or the household herbal garden, in which tiny mustards seeds were planted to the daily activity of the leavening of flour carried out by the women of a household or households around a shared courtyard. These women may have been householders themselves, wives or daughters of householders, or slaves. The activity of leavening would have been visible and known to all members of the household (and hence the audience), carried out in workrooms that may or may not have been gendered spaces (Meyers (2003: 44-69) and also in courtyards which may have been private or shared. Hybridity of habitat

12. Moldenke and Moldenke (2002: 61), note that the mustard seed is very small and may well have been the smallest seeds planted and cultivated in first century Palestine and Syria. Zohary (1982: 93) says that 'it is conspicuous in the vegetation around the Sea of Galilee and farther north'.

13. See Allan H. Cadwallader (2013: 141-44), especially p. 143, in which he demonstrates that the Matthaean redaction of the Markan parable of the mustard seed has the following effect: 'Rather than being a resistant movement of those dependent on the refusal of nature to be contained by imperial control, the church has become modeled upon an imperial template, laying the foundations for its eventual ideological endorsement of an integration into imperial (Byzantine) governance. Such governance inevitably carried a cost for the Earth.' An ecological reader is alerted to be attentive to and to read against the grain of such a tendency in the Matthaean redaction of the parable of the mustard seed.

constitutes the ecological texture of this text as readers imagine the leaven, the small amount of fermented dough that permeates what is approximately a bushel or thirty-four kilos of flour, enough to feed a hundred people (Carter 2000: 291). Again the contrast between small and large characterizes the parable but in this instance, it is the permeation of the leaven through such a large amount of flour that startles listeners' imagination, the parable ending with the statement: 'the whole was leavened'! Intertextually, this fermentation process contrasts with the starkness of unleavened bread that was a reminder of the people's slavery in Egypt (Exod. 13.3; cf. Exod. 12.15, 19; 13.7; Deut. 16.3). The *basileia* of the heavens/sky in which leaven is but one small element of habitat constitutes freedom from such slavery. An ecological reading will seek to understand what leaven is needed today to permeate human consciousness so that entire habitats might be set free from the burden of exploitation.

Matthew 13.34-35 provides a summary articulating what has taken place in the parable discourse to this point. Jesus has taught the crowds in parables. Jesus the parabler has drawn Earth and its ecological processes into the pithy narratives that are the parables imaging what is at the heart of his preaching, the *basileia* of the heavens/sky. John Haught has suggested that the evolution of the cosmos is the most 'fundamental mode of the unfolding of the divine mystery' (2004: 236). It is Earth and its processes as part of the cosmos which Jesus parables or stories, leaving traces of the divine mystery.

In the second half of the Parable Discourse, save for the two concluding verses (vv. 51-52), both location and audience shift, reminding readers of the complex interweaving of time, location and sociality at the beginning of the discourse. Jesus now leaves the crowd (v. 36) and goes into the house from which he came out in 13.1 and the disciples who separated themselves from the crowd in v. 10 come to Jesus in the house to ask for an explanation of the parable of the weeds in the grain. That explanation, like the previous one of the parable of the seed and its yield (13.18-23), is changed into an allegory with univocal equations given for just some of the rich imagery of the parable. Attentiveness to time, to waiting and to wisdom are lost to the singular focus on end-time judgment that requires no wisdom, no attentiveness, no respectful waiting, especially on the divine. Elements of the parable are equated with players in the end-time judgment all overseen by divinity imaged as king and father. Power in the allegorical explanation of the parable is not within Earth processes but is rather power that dominates and separates. One wonders whether the two explanations of Jesus' parables represent the voices of a Matthean household in which eschatological judgment was the dominant theological perspective. Rather than letting the allegories dominate as *the* meaning of the parable, they need to be critiqued within an ecological reading.

A very explicit collection of three parables (Mt. 13.44-50) concludes the parable discourse. Readers will recognize the intended interrelationship from the pattern that is established:

> Homoia estin hē *basileia* tōn ouranōn... (the *basileia* of the sky/heavens is like... (v. 44).

> Palin homoia estin hē *basileia* tōn ouranōn... (the *basileia* of the heavens/sky is like... (vv. 45, 47).

In the first two parables, Jesus invites listeners into complex habitats of interrelationship although the imagery has shifted from the ecological to the related area of the economic. The *agros*/field is no longer the rich soil that receives the seed but rather the place where some form of unidentified material treasure has been hidden making the field an economic prize in the dynamic imagery of the *basileia* (v. 44). The treasure has been found (v. 44) as has the expensive pearl of the second parable (v. 45). What the economic imagery backgrounds in relation to the pearl is the long process of its formation. A mollusk deposits multiple layers of calcium carbonate around an irritant that has penetrated its shell. The resulting pearl is the product of an ecological process in which a living creature converts an unwanted intrusion into something highly valued in Earth's sociality. There is a warning that needs to be sounded here, namely that in the pearl becoming something of great price in the human economy, there is a danger that hundreds of mollusks or shell fish might be destroyed before the one pearl is found. With the commercial production of pearls, this process is no longer necessary but nonetheless calls for critique.

In a house by the edge of the Sea of Galilee, the disciples listen to the final parable (vv. 47-50). They would have been very familiar with the process of catching a net of fish and sitting by the shore sorting the good from the bad (vv. 47-48). Mendel Nun identifies the 'net' of v. 47 as a 'seine net' (Nun 1993: 51-52). It is spread out in the sea and then dragged into shore by a group of fishers so that it catches up all kinds of fish. It is necessary, therefore to sort them on the shore, first to separate the 'clean' from the 'unclean' or those with scales and fins from those such as the catfish without fins (this practice identifying the fishers as Jewish according to Jerome Murphy-O'Connor [1999: 24-25]). Interestingly, in Matthean terminology, the two groups of fish are called 'good' and 'bad' rather than clean and unclean reflecting a division along ethical lines characteristic of the gospel (cf. Mt. 5.45). This parable invites readers into the reciprocity process within ecosystems. It also sounds a note of warning of human domination, especially for contemporary ecological readers who are aware of the extreme danger of overfishing Earth's waters and the problem of dragnets which indiscriminately pull in all fish in the pathway made for them, many of those fish being simply cast aside as are the 'bad' in the parable. The parable, therefore, invites critical reflection and, ecological readers aware of the complexity of processes into which Jesus' parable draws readers, will be slow to jump to the final eschatological interpretation that seems one-dimensional. It is fixed and rigid and obscures the way humans and other Earth-constituents within their habitat Earth will need to respond to the present ecological crisis and collaborate in not just waiting for but shaping the journey toward their shared future, however it may be imagined.

3. *Matthew 13.51-52: Have You Understood*

In the final verses of the parable discourse (vv. 51-52), Jesus addresses the disciples who are in the house (the literary habitat for these verses): 'Have you understood all these?' The phrase *tauta panta* is generally used in Matthew's gospel as a collective to gather up what is at issue in a context (4.9; 6.32-33; 19.20; 23.36; 24.2, 8, 33-34). It occurs twice in the parable discourse (13.34 and 13.51) where what is at issue is all that Jesus has taught, to the crowds and/or disciples, about the *basileia* in and through the parables in this discourse. The verb *suniēmi* can be translated as 'understand' but BDAG give another nuance, 'to have an intelligent grasp of something that challenges one's thinking or practice' (972). This seems to fit this context in which parables are by their very nature intended to challenge one's thinking and practice. It would seem more appropriate to understand Jesus' question as: 'are you thinking rightly' about all of these things or 'has your thinking and your practice been challenged' by all these parables in which habitat and human are never separated but function interconnectively, because such is the *basileia* of the skies, of the holy. It is this right thinking or this challenge to one's thinking and practice that leads into Jesus' final parable of the scribe being discipled for the *basileia*, the scribe whose thinking and practice is to be changed by understanding Jesus' parables.[14]

Matthew 13.52 is a significant verse. It is the final verse of the parable discourse that began in 13.1 and which concludes with the Matthean formula 'and when Jesus had finished...' (13.53; cf. 7.28; 11.1; 19.1; 26.1). It gathers into a climactic statement, both themes and language of the discourse. The disciples (13.10 and 36) and the material *oikos*/house shape the movement in the discourse (Crosby 1988: 69); the parabled *basileia* or *basileia* of the sky/heavens forms its content (13.11, 19, 24, 31, 33, 38, 41, 43, 44, 45, 47 and 52).

Within the ecological texture of v. 52, habitat (house with its treasure/ treasury and householder) functions interactively to create meaning, as it does within the whole discourse in which the *basileia* is imaged by the human/habitat nexus. There is no imagery of the *basileia* in this parable

---

14. This section of the narrative is developed much more fully in Wainwright (2011).

discourse in which habitat, the human and the holy, are not intimately interconnected and embedded in a way that invites readers into and enriches their interconnectivity.

The logion of 13.52 begins with the phrase 'every scribe discipled to the *basileia* of the heavens/sky)' bringing together images that have not yet appeared together in the Matthean narrative. The word 'scribe' has already occurred six times. Twice, it refers to the scribes as a designated group within the society (2.4 'scribes of the people' and 7.29 'their scribes'). In the second of these occurrences, it sets their authority over against that of Jesus. Twice they are linked with the Pharisees, first as insufficiently righteous for entering into the *basileia* of the heavens (5.20) and later as challenging Jesus to provide a sign to authenticate his teaching (12.38). They also evaluate his teaching as blasphemous (9.3). They are presented among the crowd, listening to Jesus' teaching, observing his healing and evaluating these according to a knowledge that characterizes their role.

Saldarini (1988) examines the intertextual traces of 'scribe' functioning in Mt. 13.52. The scribe was educated and could record the words of a prophet (Jer. 36.32) and read the Book of the Law (2 Kgs 22.10). Ben Sira contrasts the role of the scribe with that of those who work with their hands at manual labour as well as of those who have judicial and political power and authority. The scribe, on the other hand, is concerned with the study of the laws, with wisdom, with 'sayings', 'parables' and 'proverbs', indeed is the ideal wise one (Sir. 38.24–39.3; see Saldarini [254-59] and Orton [77-120]).[15]

Saldarini's sociological analysis enables us to hear the inter-cont/textuality functioning in Mt. 13.52. He has observed that scribes are in various ways associated with learning and interpretation of the tradition and therefore have a social role or function throughout Israel's history. Their particular role/s differed at different times, depending on whether they were associated with political or religious leadership groups (kings, prophets, or priests by way of example). They are not a group themselves, as are the Pharisees, the Sadducees or the 'chief priests' with whom they are variously associated in Matthew's gospel. Saldarini places them sociologically within the retainer not the ruling class in first-century Palestinian society and notes that any power or influence that they may have had came from the ruling class with whom they were associated. Traces of power and social relationships play, therefore, in the background of Mt. 13.52 as this *grammateus* is

---

15. From an ecological perspective, I would want to engage critically with Ben Sira's setting of those who work with material elements (the plow and oxen, iron and fire, clay and the wheel) over against the scribe who is concerned with wise thinking, subtleties of parables and hidden meanings of proverbs. Both have unique contributions to make in ecological communities.

not associated with the designated leadership groups but with Jesus through the participle *mathēteutheis*/being discipled.

The particularity of the scribe of Mt. 13.52 is that s/he is said to be discipled. I do not want to render the scribe exclusively male. Even though I have no direct evidence to hand that would indicate that first century Jewish women could function in the role of *grammateus*, I draw attention to the studies of Tal Ilan who addresses the question of women within Second Temple Judaism and its groups.[16] I also argue elsewhere that women functioned within the traditioning process of the Matthean community (1991: 339-52). I want, therefore, to leave open the potential for this inclusion historically but also in relation to the contemporary ideological functioning of the text.

The phrase 'the being discipled scribe' (*grammateus mathēteus*) is linked in 13.52 to the *basileia* of the heavens/sky (*basileia tōn ouranōn*) in a way that is unique not only to Matthew's gospel but in the entire New Testament. Significant attention has been given to the phrase as it has occurred in the unfolding Matthean text. Here it is important to note that the greatest concentration of the phrase has been in Matthew 13 as explored above. The *basileia* is accessible through images and imagination. It is of the heavens as realm of the divine in ancient Jewish cosmology, of the sky evoking the materiality of the universe. It encompasses the more-than-human in its very name just as it is imaged by the more-than-human, by human/habitat interconnections.

If the *basileia* Jesus preaches can only be fully understood through parables engaging human/habitat/holy, so too, it would seem can this new function of being scribe or interpreter discipled to or trained for this *basileia*. This scribe is likened to or parabled as a householder who brings out or throws out what is new and what is old.

The *oikodespotēs* evokes considerable wealth—the householder of 13.27 has slaves,[17] and the one of 13.52 has a storehouse or depository/treasury for excess. The activities associated with the *oikodespotēs* are agricultural, the planting of seed, the working of vineyards with their association with earth, with weather conditions, plants and their produce. These activities also draw into the text the network of landownership in Roman Galilee and Syria where Roman occupation was beginning to put pressure on the more

---

16. Ilan (1995: 190-204) draws from writings across a broad historical period and cannot be used to claim explicit scribal activity for women in the first century. See also idem (1999: 11-37), for the appeal of Pharisaism to wealthy Jewish women, and idem (2006: 73-110), in which she questions whether some women were, in fact, full-fledged Pharisees.

17. An aspect of the power relations within the Matthaean narrative that requires an ecological critique which cannot be undertaken here.

traditional subsistence farming on small holdings in favour of the production of excess leading to larger holdings, absentee landlords, tenancy and rising taxes (Freyne 1994: 106-107). The two forms seem to have existed side by side and to have impacted one another during the first century CE (Freyne 2004: 44-48) with the imagery in the parables capturing the potentiality of such a shift.

The particular *anthrōpos oikodespotēs* of the Matthean parable of 13.52 is one who has a *thēsauros*, a storehouse or a storeroom, drawing into the ecological texture of the text the first-century Galilean/Syrian house as the physical amalgam of brick and mortar, wood and stone that constitutes the dwelling place called 'house'. Yizhar Hirschfeld has undertaken the most extensive study of first-century Palestinian dwellings that, in an agricultural context, were generally of the style of what he called either the 'simple' or the 'complex' house (1995: 21-56). Storerooms of a range of sizes are characteristic of many houses excavated in Galilee (22, 50, 52, 71, 90). Such storerooms were often in the courtyard or in a separate wing of the house (289). While archaeology has not yielded significant information as to what was stored in these rooms or repositories, one can speculate that oil and wine would be preserved for later use as would dried produce or even seed. Particular rooms or storage boxes or repositories within such storerooms may have been reserved for valuable items such as coinage or precious stones/jewellery.[18] The contents were a wide range of material items that would have been significant for food, clothing, agricultural and economic activities—indeed, the very life of the family for the months ahead. Intertextually, the reader catches a glimpse of what was held in the royal storehouses—silver and gold, spices, precious oil (2 Kgs 20.13; Isa. 39.2); in temple storehouses—grain, wine, oil (Neh. 10.39); and in private storehouses—wheat, barley, oil and honey (Jer. 41.8; LXX 48.8). All these function within a socio-economic and cultural milieu.

The householder may be male or female as the generic *anthrōpos* suggests and as knowledge of the households of Roman Palestine and early Christianity demonstrate (Osiek and McDonald 2006). Predominantly, the social network of first-century Galilean or Syrian households consisted of the paterfamilias, his wife and children (perhaps with their families in extended households around courtyards), and perhaps with male and female servants and slaves and other members of such a unit depending on the household's level of wealth or poverty. Such a house in its first century context was the foundation of the Roman Empire (Schüssler Fiorenza 1992: 114-20). The designation *anthrōpos oikodespotēs* connotes power, possessions and

---

18. Meyers (2003: 63-64), says of 'a very large storage room P' that it 'had the greatest number of spindle whorls and items of personal adornment with extensive underground space for olives, olive oil, wine, etc.'

prestige. Power and prestige would have functioned and would have been performed differently depending on the gender of the holder of the position. Possessions as well as persons in all their multiplicity and diversity were under the control of the householder, especially those elements that were highly valued, that would have been designated *thēsauros* or placed within the treasury/*thēsauros*.

The image that shocks hearers and subverts their expectations in a way that is typical of parables is that of the householder casting out both new and old from the household's storehouse or depository if one takes up Peter Phillips' recent argument (2008: 3-24). He demonstrates convincingly that *exballō* in Mt. 13.52 should be translated as 'cast out' even though traditionally, from the time of the early church, scholars have translated the verb in this verse as 'bring out'. First, he argues that 'cast out' is the meaning that predominates not only in Matthew's gospel but elsewhere in Greek literature (6-16). Second, he claims that this traditional meaning, namely 'to cast out', is more appropriate to Mt. 13.52 than the meaning that has developed in the history of Christian interpretation, to bring out selectively what is new and old.[19] This final Matthean parable of the scribal interpreter of the *basileia* is, therefore, more radical than previously envisaged. The scribe is imaged as householder casting out both new and old from the treasury, the new first as it would be nearest the opening of the storehouse, and then the old, what had been stored up for the family's use into the future, both immediate and more long-term.[20] As Phillips says most clearly, '[t]his is a radical clearing out of the treasure to make way for something else, for something new, for the kingdom of heaven' (20). No wonder interpreters from as early as Origen wished to shift the meaning of *ekballō* so that Mt. 13.52 was much less parabolic.

The scribe discipled for the *basileia* of the heavens/sky, is imaged in human and material terms as a householder who casts aside what has been carefully stored up to sustain both him/her-self and the family for the time ahead: next year's seed would be lying on the ground to be destroyed by the weather rather than be enhanced by it as in 13.3-8; food stores cast aside so that the household might be left hungry; or precious resources in the form of money or jewellery that could ensure that a small landholder retained land or a larger landholder could extend holdings. This is a radical reversal of the power and prestige of the *anthrōpos oikodespotēs* as

---

19. In this regard, Philips (16-21), points out that Mt. 13.52 must be interpreted in the context of Matthew 13 not in relation to 12.35, the other occurrence of *ekballō* in Matthew which is generally translated as 'bring out'.

20. Phillips (18) summarizes his position thus: a householder…who has placed his valued possessions within a treasure…and is now expected…presumably as proof of his training…to expel…from that treasure that which is both new and old…

constructed in the Matthean gospel and of the householder's interrelationships within habitat.

One way of understanding this would be within the hierarchical and dualistic framework of spirit/matter or human/material: unencumbered by the material, such a scribe is able to claim the 'right thinking' of 13.51, to have understood the mysteries of the *basileia* as proclaimed in parables. We have already seen, however, that these parables always evoke the *basileia* by way of material images that draw together in the ecological texture of this text, habitat and human. To claim that the ideal scribe discipled to the *basileia* of Jesus' proclamation casts aside the material seems to negate the very role of the scribe to work with parables, images, and mysteries that draw on materiality or the interconnectivity of human/habitat. Such a dualistic interpretation runs contrary to the Matthean text and an ecological reading of it. Placing mind over matter is characteristic of a social imaginary of mastery.

On the other hand, it could be argued that rather than seeing attention to the material and to the metaphoric or parabolic aspect of the task of the discipled scribe as set over against one another, within a perspective of ecological thinking the material and metaphoric function interactively. The scribe must know and understand well human/habitat interrelationships, must know and understand, in its materiality, the radical image of a householder casting out the precious items from the household's storehouse while critiquing or backgrounding the violence that severs interrelationships within the more-than-human context.[21] Only in knowing and understanding this, can the gospel reader understand the radical role of the scribe discipled to the *basileia* who must be *like* such a householder and likewise cast out what is stored and treasured.

As already noted, a scribe would normally preserve and pass on the law and the wisdom tradition [Eccles. 12.9-12] as well as teach them anew [Sir. 51.23-30], would bring out the new with the old—and hence the long history of interpretation of this verse. Matthew 13.52 is parabolic—it up-turns or over-turns the social imaginary. As one being discipled for the *basileia* of the sky/heavens, this scribe who relies on the tradition of the past and its new interpretations is challenged to discern what of the new and old must be cast aside in order to hear a new message, the radical message of the *basileia* proclaimed in parables. This is the new thinking, the right thinking, that attention to the parables of Jesus entails (13.51). From an ecological perspective, one could add that what constitutes an imaginary of mastery, a paradigm of patriarchy, of imperialism and of anthropocentric domination

---

21. It has been drawn to my attention and rightly so that the text does not say that 'all' the new and the old are cast out. This, however, does not undermine the radical nature of the parable. New and old are still to be cast out—an extraordinary challenge to the householder.

and dualism—their new and old manifestations in the reading or interpretations of biblical traditions—must be cast out in order that the discipled scribe can say yes to Jesus' immediately previous question in 13.51: Have you understood/are you thinking rightly about all these things that I have proclaimed in parable? To say 'yes' is to commit to new thinking, to strain toward ecological thinking, to understand all Earth's beings, including the human and the sacred, in new and different relationships.

This has been a detailed reading of Matthew 13 but an important one given its positioning in the gospel at the turning point of a chiasmic structure as well as the abundant play of materiality in its ecological texture. The reading has also highlighted the webs of interconnection in the parable discourse of which 13.52 provides the final verse. It was claimed that the 'right thinking' of 13.51 was an affirmation of that interconnectedness which functioned to uncover the mysteries of the *basileia*. The parable of 13.52 draws in such interconnectedness to highlight the radical reversal that constitutes the role of the scribe discipled to this *basileia*. An ecological reading sounded a warning that the *casting out* of the material items in the store room be seen parabolically as well as materially and that it not be used to underpin material/spiritual dualistic interpretations. That being undertaken, an ecological reading could then suggest the type of thinking that needs to be cast out by the scribe discipled to the *basileia*. Such a reading demonstrates how this text of Mt. 13,52 with its rich inter-texts and inter-con/texts can facilitate a reading of the text ecologically in the twenty-first century.

Chapter 8

MATTHEW 14–17:
BREAD AND BOATS, MOUNTAINS AND
MISSION ENGAGED AND OPPOSED

The Parable proclamation of Jesus concluded in 13.52 followed by the narrator's formula: 'when Jesus had finished all these parables, he left that place' (13.53). The place, as we saw in 13.1, was the edge of the lake where there was a house that he came out of (13.1) and went back into (13.36) in the course of his parable discourse. Now he goes away from the edge of the lake and comes to his *patris/patrida*, his homeland. It is unclear to readers whether this is Capernaum where he made his home (4.13) or Nazareth where he was taken as a child (2.2) and to which he returned following the arrest of John (4.13) but which he then left for Capernaum. The very opening of this transition segment focusses on place/space even in its ambiguity and invites the ecological reader into a particularly focussed reading process for this section of the gospel. The encoding of place/space and the other-than-human in the ecological texture of the text invites readers to engage with these aspects of the text in the continuing story of the one in whom G*d is 'with' the Earth community, with its concomitant themes of recognition and rejection.

In order to undertake such a reading, I dialogue with several theorists as intertexts. Place/space and materiality are foregrounded in keeping with Morton's notion of the re-mark (2007). Kate Rigby warns of 'the inevitable failure of the written word to restore to presence that to which it refers' (2004: 437). At the same time Buell acknowledges the possibility of our reading being 'bent toward' the other-than-human (2005: 33). There are two new theorists whose work I want also to draw into the reading to assist this bending toward the other-than-human: E.S. Casey's *Getting Back into Place* (1993) and Donna Haraway's *When Species Meet* (2008a).

> **Ecological Intertexts.** Casey and Haraway together with others who are already intertextual dialogue partners will impact reading in a variety of ways. Here I call attention very briefly to a key aspect of each. Casey (1993: 275-311) explores the way in which pilgrimage can enable the participants to re-place themselves along the journeys of Jesus. I suggest that an ecological reading can function in a similar way to re-create the ecological self who 'inhabits (or will re-inhabit) the place in question' as it functions inter-con/textually.

> Haraway (2008a) extends the notion of hybridity of species' interconnectivity. She speaks in terms of 'figures' that 'have always been where the biological and literary or artistic come together with all of the force of lived reality' (4).
>
> She recognizes an '"intersectionality"…or patterns of relationality and… intra-actions at many scales of space-time that need rethinking…' (17-18). In this intersectionality, one encounters a 'motley crowd of differentially situated species, including landscapes, animals, plants, microorganisms, people and technologies' (41). Later she will speak of such intersections as 'co shapings all the way down, in all sorts of temporalities and corporealities' (164).
>
> For ecological readers, her insight that 'syntactically and materially, worldly embodiment is always a verb, or at least a gerund' (164) is important. She adds that 'embodiment is ongoing, dynamic, situated, and historical'.

The narrative of Matthew 14–17 is significant in the unfolding story. It is replete with language of 'seeing' which will enrich our attention to space/place and to 'patterns of relationality' or 'intersectionality' in the more-than-human realm of the story.[1] A particular focus will be on the *dynamis* or deeds of power wrought by Jesus that will be read ecologically in relation to sociality and power.

1. *13.53–14.12: Rejection and Death*

Matthew 13.54 takes the ecological reader to a place that is undefined in ecological terms but categorized in relation to the journeying Jesus—it is his *patrida*: 'familial connections and personal life, *fatherland, homeland*' or 'locale of one's immediate family and ancestry, *home town, one's own part of the country*' (BDAG 788, italics theirs). Note that this reference is both material and relational, replete with Haraway's notion of 'co-shapings…in all sorts of temporalities and corporalities' (2008a: 164 as above). Jesus engages his familial group, his townspeople, in their synagogue, recognizing the intersection of materiality and sociality that have characterized his mission.

The response of Jesus' townspeople is unexpectedly strong. The Greek verb is *skandalizein* that BDAG (926) translate in relation to this verse as being 'repelled' by Jesus because he is seen to draw on a source of power beyond that associated with the family of Jesus whom they think they know. Power functions significantly in this narrative and if we examine it on the horizontal grid suggested by Sandoval, we see Jesus making a choice not to do many of his deeds of power/*dynamis* there (his preaching, teaching and healing which earlier summarized his ministry (4.23-24; 9.35). These deeds

---

1. Jerome Murphy-O'Connor wrote an article on the structure of Matthew 14–17 in 1975 which is still valuable in its uncovering of literary patterns which guide the reading of this section of the Gospel. See Murphy-O'Connor (1975: 360-84).

of power are characterized by bodies in place touching and being touched for healing and ears open to hearing and understanding parables and proclamation. They depend on material and social interrelationships: bodies, eyes, ears must be open to touch, to seeing and to hearing. They cannot be forced. It is this 'dynamic, situated and historical' embodiment of healing and transformative deeds of power that the people of Jesus' *patrida* reject and into which contemporary ecological readers are invited.

The theme of 'the prophet' and the prophet's rejection because of deeds of power that offend continues into the next section (14.1-11, noting v. 2), linked by the designator 'at that time'. The narrator relates retrospectively or in 'flashback' (Kraemer 2006: 323) how the body of the prophet, John the Immerser, had been dealt with violently by Herod resulting in his death and his burial by his disciples. Power plays within this narrative, a power over life and death that has already been associated with Herod in 2.1-11. Gender intersects with this power as it is intricately woven into the sociality playing within the ecological texture of this Matthean text. Momentarily, Herodias and her daughter grasp power from a weak Herod who is afraid to execute John because of his fear of the people (v. 5). However, complying with the request for the head of John the Baptist on a platter enables Herod to reclaim something of his masculinity and to do what he already wanted to do, namely put John to death.

The stark materiality of death confronts the ecological reader in the final verses of this narrative. The beheading of John takes place off-site, as it were, simply narrated as '(Herod) sent and had John beheaded in prison'. The reader and the viewer of the myriads of representations of this scene on canvas over millennia are confronted with the stark image: the head was bought on a platter to the girl who gave it to her mother (v. 11). In contrast v. 12 narrates an alternative dealing with the body of the prophet: his disciples came and took the body and buried it. The prophet of the *basileia* of the sky/heavens (3.2), the one who lived in *dikaiosynē* or right relationship with all Earth's constituents (3.4), is returned to that earth. A similar pathway will be trodden by the prophet Jesus who will continue to work his *dynameis* (14.2).

Time and place/space in their biological and artistic manifestations and representations together with what Haraway calls 'a motley crowd of differently situated species' come together in this section of the narrative around 'bodies and boats, mountains and mission'. They move through a range of dynamic interrelationships of engagement with and opposition to the *dynameis* which constitute the *basileia* of the skies or heavens. In this section, I propose to read Mt. 14.13–17.20 in dialogue with those ecological intertexts noted above, giving more substantial attention to some segments than others, aware also that this section continues the mission of preaching, teaching and healing seen earlier in 4.23–9.35.

2. *Matthew 14.13-36: Bread and Life*

Twice in this next section, the verb *anachōreein* (to go away or to escape) occurs, suggesting a heightening of tension among political and religious leaders in response to the *dynameis* of Jesus (see 2.12, 13, 22; 4.12; 12.15 for previous withdrawals or escapes). The first occurrence is in 14.13—a response to Herod Antipas' beheading of John whose mission to proclaim the *basileia* of the skies paralleled that of Jesus. Later Jesus will 'withdraw' in response to controversy with the Pharisees and scribes (15.21). These acts of 'going away'/withdrawing, however, simply take Jesus to another place, reminding readers that the *Emmanu-el* of the gospel cannot escape the materiality of body and of place/space and that this is so also for the readers of the gospel.

The place encoded in the ecological texture of the Matthean text is an *erēmos*, a lonely/place, a desert, and Jesus goes there alone only to find a great crowd awaiting him. The use of the verb *splagchnizōmein*/'to have compassion' evokes a strong corporeal element reminiscent of the touching and being touched associated with healing as already noted. It is to be moved in the depths of one's being, one's entrails, one's gut. Here it is generally understood to characterize Jesus' healing response to the crowd whom he *sees* (see also 9.36). Sallie McFague raises the question as to whether that compassion might also be extended to place (in this instance, the *erēmos*), to the material world, seeing place and people with the loving rather than the arrogant eye, the eye of the ecological self (1997: 67-117).

One might ask if the response of the 'disciples' (v. 15) to the *erēmos* and its being peopled by a great crowd is informed by an arrogant rather than an ecological eye, an eye for commodity exchange in an imperial economy as a way of feeding hungry communities. They propose to send the people into the villages to 'buy food for themselves'. Jesus proposes a different scenario, that of hospitality and gift giving: you give them something to eat (14.16). Anne Primavesi describes such a 'gift giving' as 'a conscious acceptance of and commitment to the fact that our lives depend on indivisible benefits, on our being given what we need to sustain life whether or not we can or do pay for it' (2000: 159). It also entails our giving in return for the benefit of others in the more-than-human community.

Jesus enacts such a gift event when he garners the five loaves and two fish which are able to feed the more than five thousand women, children and men (14.21) with twelve baskets of broken pieces left over. His 'looking up to heaven (the skies)' reminds gospel reader of his prayer in 6.11 for the bread of daily sustenance. He then 'blessed, and broke and gave the loaves to the disciples and the disciples gave them to the crowds'. It was in the giving of the loaves to be blessed, broken and then in their being given to disciples and crowds that hunger was satisfied (v. 20). Wendell Berry (2009:

231-32) extends this interconnectivity further when he says that '[e]aters… must understand that eating takes place inescapably in the world, that it is inescapably an agricultural act, and how we eat determines, to a considerable extent, how the world is used… To eat responsibly is to understand and enact…this complex relationship.' Such insights can then inform the gathering up of twelve baskets of *klasmata* or broken pieces so that in the words of Michael Trainor, '[n]othing is to be wasted' (Trainor 2012: 161 in relation to the Lukan story). It is such reflections that might inform an ethical theology of food/eating as well as an ecological theologizing of eucharist which is so often associated with this narrative as well as its parallel account of the feeding of more than four thousand in Mt. 15.32-38 (see Elvey, Hogan, Power and Renkin 2013, especially Dowling and Lawson: 78-90, and Elvey: 186-206).

Bread and place functioned as key material actants in Mt. 14.13-21. In the next section (14.22-32), water is encoded in the ecological texture of the text and in particular the Sea of Galilee with its wind and waves. It is water, in its materiality and its more-than-human sociality, which will be given attention in the interpretation to follow since it has so often been overlooked by interpreters. Overman (1996: 201) sees the story as a 'parable about the church's life following Jesus' death'. Carter (2004b: 146) suggests that it discloses 'Jesus' identity' while Nolland (2005: 597) notes that '[t]o be able to pass over water is a divine quality, which when found in humans identifies them as having some kind of kinship with the gods or as gaining access by magic to the power of the gods.' His emphasis is on human and divine. Talbert (2010: 185) focuses on the symbolism in and for the human community of instances both from the Hebrew Bible and Graeco-Roman literature where God/s walk on water as well as transfer such power to their son/s. Agency in these narratives tends to be attributed to the divine figure alone, not to the materiality of the water itself.

In order to assist my turn to the agency of the material element, the water in 14.22-32, I draw into the ecological intertexture Lambros Malafouris who argues that 'if human agency *is* then material agency *is*, there is no way that human and material agency can be disentangled' (2008: 22). In the same collection of articles, Owen Jones and Paul Cloke reaffirm this claim when they demonstrate that '[n]on-human agencies not only co-constitute the contexts of life, but they also frequently reconstitute the fabrics of day-to-day life and the places and spaces in which it is lived' (Jones and Cloke 2008: 79). All of this is encoded into the ecological texture of the Matthean text.

Such processes of human and material constituting and reconstituting are being played out in the opening verses of Mt. 14.22-32. First, Jesus compels or forces the disciples to get into the boat and go before him to the other side of the sea. It is unclear why the human agency attributed to Jesus in this opening verse is so strong. The material agency evoked is that of the boat that will transport the disciples and the other side of the lake that will receive them and their boat. These 'co-constitute the contexts of life' (Jones and Cloke) that are being narrated in this opening verse. As a result of Jesus' impelling the disciples to go to the other side, the agency of Jesus continues, in that he dismisses the crowds who have gathered and been fed and then goes up the mountain by himself to pray. As in Mt. 5.1-2 when Jesus goes up the mountain and sits to teach, the agency of the mountain as the place of authorization is clear. In this instance (14.23), it also functions in its material agency as providing the place for divine encounter. As v. 23 draws to a close, temporality and material and human agency are intimately entangled: when evening came, he was there (on the mountain top) alone.

In the remainder of this inter-con/textual reading of 14.22-33, I examine the way in which the agency of the material 'reconstitute[s] the fabrics of day-to-day life and the places and spaces in which it is lived' (Jones and Cloke 79). The connective '*de*'/but which opens v. 24 (as well as functioning in the final phrase of v. 23) alerts readers to this reconstitution. Interestingly for our analysis, each subsequent verse except the last (i.e. v. 32) contains this same connective in second place in the sentence, highlighting further the multiplicity of agents in this text.[2]

As v. 24 opens, it is the agency of the boat to which the connective draws attention (*to de ploion*) and the verb *apeichen* indicates its activity in having travelled 'many furlongs distant from the land'. The entanglement of agents in their interrelationship becomes clear in the second half of v. 24 when the reader learns that the boat is being 'severely beaten' (*basanizomenon*) by the waves as it travels into the wind. Entanglements of agents will often be fraught with tension as they seem to collide. As Jones and Cloke indicate, 'to appreciate the agencies of nature and materiality, not only do we need to appreciate the very differing forms of beings and processes in which they are articulated, but also the very differing velocities and rhythms they might be operating in' (88). The material/Earth and its forces are not merely servant of the human but have their own rhythms and power.

The 'de' of v. 25 can turn the reader's attention from the tensive relationality of material (and human) agencies to their ideal interrelationships. Narratively, the sea functions fully to support Jesus who walks across it, just as it supports the boat. One might speculate that Jesus is presented narratively in such right relationship with the sea in its material agency that he

---

2. Of the use of this connective, BDAG 213, says it is used 'either to express contrast or simple continuation. When it is felt that there is some contrast between clauses—though the contrast is often scarcely discernible—the most common translation is "but". When a simple connective is desired, without contrast being clearly implied, "and" will suffice, and in certain occurrences the marker may be left untranslated.'

is supported by it and hence able to walk toward the boat on the sea. The verse speaks of right relationships: here the 'velocities and rhythms' are in harmony rather than in tensive relationship as in the previous verse. Is it this that is storied in the ancient biblical and cultural narratives such as Job 9.8 in which the divine agent/G*d is said to walk on the waves of the sea in right relationship? This, in turn, is contrary to the notion of the waters being afraid of God in Ps. 77.16 and it differs from a similarly cited intertext Ps. 77.19 in which God's way is said to be 'through the sea', 'through the mighty water', hence different imagery and a different understanding of material agency. Another frequently cited intertext, Hab. 3.15, has G*d trampling the sea. Such images of power and power over do not, however, resonate through v. 25 in the Matthean narrative we are examining. Rather velocities and rhythms are 'in creative right relationship.

The *oi de mathētai*/but the disciples' of v. 26 contrasts the relationship of the disciples to the velocities and rhythms with that of Jesus' relationship in the previous verse. They cannot imagine the right relationship between human and material agency manifest in Jesus' walking toward them on the water and so they are afraid, even terrified, thrown into confusion (BDAG 990 suggests). They name the experience *phantasma*, something without materiality. Perhaps we can see in the disciples' confusion and fear something of our own as we seek to shift our consciousness of and our relationship with the agency of materiality and to read the biblical narrative in light of this.

The response of Jesus to the fear and confusion of the disciples in the face of the extraordinary interrelationship between human and material agency is immediate and he speaks saying: take heart; it is I; do not be afraid. The verb *tarassein*/'take heart' has a range of meanings according to BDAG 990: *to be firm or resolute in the face of danger or adverse circumstances, be enheartened, be courageous*. We can understand Jesus' words as challenging the disciples to a new understanding: be resolute, stay in this context of a new relationship between human and material agency that is being manifest. The *egō eimi* of Jesus is often interpreted as his sharing the divine name, the 'I am' of the G*d of Moses (Exod. 3.14). It can also be heard as the simple 'it is I' of the human Jesus. Jesus is the Emmanuel of Mt. 1.23, the human and the material one in whom the divine is 'with' the Earth community in all its materiality and sociality. The invitation is not to be afraid of the right relationship between human, material and divine agency manifest in Jesus' walking *on* the water, the partnering of such agencies.

The next four verses (vv. 28-31) recount the response of Peter to Jesus' partnering of his human agency with that of the material water and its agency manifest not only in the waves but its carrying of Jesus 'on' the sea. The initial *apokritheis de* (answered) of v. 28 alerts readers to the challenge that Peter will throw down to Jesus. Peter takes Jesus' simple *egō eimi* of

v. 27 and turns it into a challenge: if it is you! This is augmented by his words, command me to come to you *on* the water.

It is in response to Jesus' command 'to come' that Peter leaves the 'safe' materiality of the boat and trusts himself to the material agency of the water, walking toward Jesus as Jesus walked toward the disciples in the boat (v. 25). Given the challenge that Peter threw out to Jesus, it is reasonable to suggest that Peter's agency in walking on the water is not as a result of a relationship with the water and its power and agency but rather with the power of Jesus whom he challenged. This is borne out further in v. 30 when Peter sees the wind and becomes afraid and hence begins to sink. He does not recognize the agency of the sea as Jesus did and its potential to carry him as it did Jesus. Rather the materiality of the wind and its power frightens Peter and he begins to sink. And yet he still does not adjust his perspective, or his relationship, but cries out to Jesus: save me. The cry of Peter is reminiscent of the cry of the disciples in 8.25. Peter, like the disciples does not have faith in a partnering with the waters and/or the wind (see Elvey 2011c for this terminology of 'partnering') which characterizes Jesus' relationship and so cries out to Jesus to save him when, indeed, he could have learnt from Jesus the right relationship with the wind and the water that could have enabled him to reach Jesus across the waves. In contrast, the agency of the material has to be bypassed and Jesus reaches out and catches Peter's hand (v. 31). He rebukes Peter's lack of recognition of the material agency of the water and its sociality that includes Jesus and Peter who walk on the water: you of little faith; why did you doubt?

The final two verses of this scene return the reader to restored material and social relationships. The wind ceases to threaten the small human community in the protection of the boat and such security enables them to recognize the extraordinary right relationships between the material and the social/materiality and sociality that they have just witnessed in Jesus. BDAG (882) say of the verb *proskuneein* (often translated as 'worship') when used in relation to human beings, it can function in recognition of the person's 'belonging to a superhuman realm' or demonstrating right relationship with the holy. Verse 33 constitutes a pivotal point of right relationship between habitat, the human and the holy, a manifestation of *Emmanu-el*, G*d 'with' the entire more-than-human community. For the ecological reader the naming of Jesus as *uios* or son/child of the Holy One can point to him as the embodiment of such right relationships. This has unfolded in and with bread and boats, mountains and mission engaged and opposed.

The short summary verses of 14.34-36 capture this well. The verb 'crossed over' draws attention to the two sides of the sea that functioned as key actants in the previous narrative. The place of landing is made very explicit, Gennesaret, which is both town and region (Carter 2000: 313). The human actants in this scene are identified not as the crowd of 14.15,

19, 22 (the account of the feeding of the five thousand) but as the men/ *andres* of that place (14.35). Participants in the two scenes differ. Matthew 14.21 makes it very explicit that the 5,000 who are numbered as having eaten of the five loaves are men only, but that women and children also participated rendering the number much greater. Matthew 14.35, on the other hand, has only the men recognizing Jesus as he comes ashore. The sick who are brought to Jesus are, however, not gendered: rather they bring 'all that were sick'. All are included in the restoration of right bodily relationships. The restoration here is not by way of human touch/being touched that the reader has come to expect. Rather it is through touching the 'fringe of his garment'. The Greek verb used here is *diasōzein* which carries connotations of rescuing or delivering 'from a hazard or danger' (BDAG 237) rather than *therapeuein* that has characterized earlier descriptions and summaries of healing/s (4.23, 24; 8.7, 16; 9.35; 12.15, 22; 14.14). It links healing with the broader mission/ministry of Jesus Emmanu-el first encountered in 1.22, namely saving, delivering or restoring. For the ecological reader, that restoration is of all more-than-human sociality or right relationships.

3. *Matthew 15.21-28: Borders and Bread Negotiated*

Readers are invited to undertake their own ecological reading of Mt. 15.1-20 as we turn our attention here to 15.21-28.[3] Place is the first narrative element that engages the reader of the Greek text of these verses. The phrase *echelthōn ekeithen*/'going away from there' turns attention to the place/ space from which Jesus comes/goes namely Gennesareth (14.34) where he carried out his ministry of healing (35-36). There are no textual indicators of movement from there until 15.21. For the ecological reader, the *ekeithen* of v. 21 encodes, therefore, a place characterized by the corporeality associated with healing and also a place that was, in its own materiality rich in agriculture, the bread basket of the lakeside region of Galilee.[4] The uniqueness of the material agency of this region is entangled, in the first century, with the political and socio-cultural dynamics that characterize it. Attention to habitat will, therefore, facilitate awareness of the multidimensionality of the ecological interrelationships that are shaping and being shaped by interpretation and which can be mapped on a horizontal grid. The complex dynamics that constitute the Galilean habitat from which Jesus has moved contribute to the dynamic of power functioning in this text.

---

3. Much of the material in this next section has already appeared in Wainwright (2013b: 114-26), as well as a number of other interpretations of this text which I have undertaken over several years.

4. BDAG (194) say of this region that it was 'the fertile and (in 1 AD) thickly populated plain south of Capernaum'.

Entanglement in habitat continues in v. 21 where the verb *anachōreein* occurs again, this time with Jesus withdrawing from an encounter with the Pharisees and scribes. His previous encounter with them concluded with their going out and taking counsel against him 'how to destroy him' (see 12.14 and 15) and so readers are not surprised at this withdrawal. Jesus' destination is explicit and even surprising for readers, the region of Tyre and Sidon.

Jesus moves to/towards/into[5] the region of Tyre and Sidon. Theissen (1992: 61-80) has explored the ethnic, cultural, economic, political, and social/psychological encodings in the text's reference to the region of Tyre as has Pablo Alonso (2011: 124-29), albeit both in relation to the Markan text which refers only to Tyre. Both Tyre and Sidon are ancient Phoenician cities or built environments, Sidon being a royal city historically. The built environment of the city of Tyre, which leads the pair of cities in the Matthean text, was beautiful as indicated by Josephus (*J.W.* 2.504). The Matthean text, however, has Jesus going into or toward the region or the hinterland only not into the city.

This hinterland is a borderland or boundary space where ethnicities and access to material resources were in complex interrelationship and negotiation. It was a space in which the flows and forces of the material intersected dynamically with the political, economic and the socio-cultural, a rich habitat evoked in the complex ecological texture of this text. Historically, Israel had shared a tensive relationship with Tyre. It was wealthy, the production of purple dye being one of its staple and wealth-producing industries. As an island city it needed not only its own hinterland to supply its inhabitants with food/bread but also that of its most immediate neighbor Galilee. Acts 12.20 provides evidence of this dependence and the conflict it generated. The physical boundary between these two regions was likewise porous or complex as Josephus suggests that there were Jewish villages in the Tyrian hinterland steeped in Jewish culture (*J.W.* 2.588). Bread and borders and the economic power that functions in relation to them are, therefore, evoked by this opening verse and encoded within the ecological texture of the text. As Jones and Cloke (2008: 79) indicate and as cited earlier, '[n]on-human agencies not only co-constitute the contexts of life, but they also frequently reconstitute the fabrics of day-to-day life and the places and spaces in which it is lived.' This dynamic space of the region of Tyre and Sidon participates with the human characters in the reconstituting of the fabric of life woven into this story and will be considered on Sandoval's horizontal grid of power.

The focalizer, *kai idou* (v. 22) turns attention to the second human character in this scene, the Canaanite woman who is said to be from that region/

---

5. See BDAG 288 for a range of meanings.

orion. This locates her in relation to her habitat as was Jesus. BDAG give as the dominant meaning of *orion*, the 'marker of division between two areas' while translating the phrase in Mt. 15.22 as 'from that region'.[6] The woman is constructed, therefore as either on the border or as inhabiting that hinterland area where Tyrians, Sidonians and Jews lived in tensive interrelationship with the Tyrians possessing wealth but the Jews the grain [bread] that Tyre needed and which its wealth enabled it to obtain to the detriment of the poorer Jewish Galilean farmers (Carter 2000: 321). Even before taking any account of gender, complex power relationship between not only the two key human characters introduced into this story but also the materiality of city and region in all its multidimensionality can be mapped on Sandoval's horizontal grid. Each constituent, whether human or other-than-human, brings the uniqueness of his/her/its contribution to the web of relationships existing in the region and evoked in the text.

The name 'Canaanite' has puzzled scholars as it seems more symbolic than descriptive especially when one is aware of the Markan designator 'Greek, Syro-Phoenician by birth' (Mk 7.6). Recently, Mark Nanos has drawn attention to echoes in the text and its intertexture as well as its politico-ecological texture of tensive relationships between Northern Israelite tribes and the southern Judahites (especially given the woman's use of the title 'son of David' and Jesus' use of 'house of Israel'). He suggests that the woman might be 'a descendent of those from the Northern tribes who suffered deportation, or descended from intermarriage with those the Assyrians sent to repopulate the area some 700 + years earlier' (Nanos 2009: 470). She could, therefore, be considered hybrid, a truly borderline inhabitant, neither fully Greek, Syro-Phoenician nor Israelite/Jewish, associated with shifting political boundaries mapped onto land/earth. If Nanos is correct, this tension is being woven into the characterization of the woman in the text's inner texture and into the ecological texture of the Matthean text where land, possession of land and the power associated with this is encoded in the ecological texture of the text. The agencies of land, power, memory, bread and borders intertwine in this complex text. The above discussion has mapped some of their interrelationships on the proposed horizontal grid of power as borders are crossed by different human characters as well as by bread and grain.

What the woman seeks from Jesus in this borderline space is healing for her daughter who is severely possessed with a demon (v. 22b). Here we find echoes of an ancient worldview encoded in the Matthean text, namely that of the Hellenistic era and one which we have already encountered in this commentary. It was a world view that functioned interactively with healthcare systems; with political, socio-economic and cultural factors; and with

---

6. BDAG 723.

apocalyptic and other worldviews and perspectives within the varied contexts of the first century from which the gospels arose. In Matthew's gospel it functions to give a contextual frame of meaning to a socio-cultural and corporeal or material disruption borne on the bodies of human characters: the woman's daughter is said to be demon-possessed (we might add 'in her body'). We learn nothing further of the disruption in the lives of the Canaanite woman and her daughter by what was called demon possession but we can imagine the dislocation or disruption in the body of the daughter and the socio-cultural lives of both mother and daughter.

In the hybrid location of the porous border of Tyre and Sidon, the male Jew, Jesus, who has been constructed as preacher, teacher and healer (4.23; 9.35) and confirmed by G*d in that activity (3.17), is confronted by a woman called 'Canaanite' with all that term's connotations of outsider or foreigner and boundary walker (Wainwright 1998: 86-92). Gender and power characterize the grid mapping this encounter and extensive studies have been undertaken in relation to the socio-cultural encoding of these first century cultural characteristics (see Koperski 2011: 524-36 for an overview of scholarship). Such mapping has, however, generally been done according to what Sandoval (2000) recognizes as 'a vertical, up-and-down, and pyramidal' construction with 'white, male, heterosexual, capitalist realities on hierarchically top levels' (72). I do not wish to rehearse such vertical modeling in this study. Nor do I want to minimize the hermeneutic of suspicion that has informed and that needs to inform readings of power attributed to Jesus and the male disciples over against the woman and her daughter. Rather, taking up Sandoval's horizontal mapping leads to an exploration of ways in which each character in this pericope, Jesus, the woman, her daughter and the disciples, have access to their own 'racial-, sexual-, national-, or gender-unique forms of social power'. Sandoval goes on to say that '[s]uch constituencies are then perceived as speaking "democratically" to and against each other in a lateral, horizontal—not pyramidal—exchange, although from *spatially* differing geographical, class, age, sex, race, or gender locations' (73). Within an ecological reading, other than human characters, in particular the borderline space, can be likewise mapped on the horizontal grid of material agency as already indicated earlier.

Gendered human agency characterizes the encounter, in the borderland region of Tyre and Sidon, between Jesus and a woman who is identified as Canaanite in vv. 22-23. The woman initiates the encounter, voicing a request to Jesus to have mercy on her because her daughter is severely demon-possessed. She claims her voice and crosses the socio-cultural constructs of gender and public voice engaging Jesus in a challenge and riposte that genders the text quite radically. Jesus enacts his male identity, remaining silent in the face of the woman's confronting encounter in the borderland space with all its complexities. He is confronted again by the group of disciples who beg him to send the woman away, presuming that he has the power to do so. This group is gendered male in the language of the text. If they are all male, then ethnicity and gender link Jesus and the disciples and it would seem, as the story unfolds, that they are united in their desire to be rid of the woman who is crying after them (v. 23).

When Jesus does speak (v. 24), he is characterized as mapping his own power to respond to the woman's cry for mercy for her daughter in what seems to be a formulaic understanding of his ministry: I was sent only to the lost sheep of the house of Israel (cf. 10.6 in which Jesus characterizes the sending out of the named 'twelve' as 'to the lost sheep of the house of Israel'). This is in contrast to the woman's mapping of his power when she addressed him as 'son of David' reminding Jesus that he had already healed supplicants under that title (9.27; 12.23). Nanos (469-70) may well have recognized two different understandings of the ministry of Jesus in the words of the Cannanite woman and those of Jesus. He suggests that the words of the woman may be recognition of the tradition of 'Judahide dynastic aspirations' while the response of Jesus may be a recognition that 'she is a descendent of those from the Northern tribes...' Nanos (470) suggests that Jesus' words in v. 24 may be 'an opening for her approach rather than rejection'. Power and gender are being constructed in this borderland habitat as Jesus and the woman engage in this challenge/riposte with the body of the woman's daughter always in the background but pushing to the foreground for those seeking to read the multi-dimensionality of gender, power, ethnicity and the materiality of bodies.

Jesus' reply in v. 24 also evokes the materiality of the other-than-human element in the text. He uses the referent 'lost sheep' metaphorically. The intertextuality in relation to this phrase is meager. Only twice does this phrase occur as such in the scriptures, namely at Ps. 119.176 and Jer. 50.6 evoking one of the most common other-than-human creatures in the agricultural life of the Jewish nation. It is the materiality, the corporeality of the straying sheep that Jesus calls upon to contrast his mission to the lost with the dynastic implications of the title 'son of David' given him by the Canaanite woman. I would suggest that for the ecological reader, the sheep are not just literary ciphers. Rather they function in the words of Haraway cited above as the site/creatures where 'the biological and literary or artistic come together with all of the force of lived reality' (Haraway 2008a: 4).

The Canaanite woman continues her agency (v. 25) as she re-addresses her plea to Jesus. This time, she uses no title for Jesus. The reader might imagine that she has understood well, from her hybrid position in the Tyrian hinterland with all its history of tensive interrelationship with Israel, the implication of Jesus words in v. 24. They seem to challenge her use of the 'son of David' appellation in her first plea. She is clearly and cleverly negotiating her power relationship with Jesus, refusing to interpret his silence as rejection and nuancing her approach according to his words in v. 24. She appeals simply: help me. She uses her body to strengthen her appeal. She kneels before Jesus or to use Jennifer Glancy's terminology she is 'corporally lowering herself' (2010a: 350). BDAG (882) say of the verb, *proskyneein* used by the Matthean author, that it means 'to express in attitude or gesture one's complete dependence on or submission to a high authority figure', noting that it is often accompanied by a kissing of the person's feet. It is used elsewhere in Matthew's gospel to accompany a plea for healing (8.2 and 9.18) and as a recognition of Jesus' power (14.23). It is significant to note that, in the case of the leper and the leader who seeks healing for his daughter, both supplicants are male. The body is used and functions within a socio-cultural context to strengthen the plea. The body speaks and pleas for healing are embodied. The Canaanite woman uses corporeal language, the language of her body, to speak her desperate plea. One might ask in the remapping of power according to Sandoval's horizontal grid whether her corporeal plea throws out a challenge to Jesus in a new way.

The response of Jesus continues the verbal interchange that predominantly characterizes the mode of negotiation between the woman and Jesus in this short narrative. His language seems strange to the reader in the face of a request for healing: it is not good (*kalon*) or right to take the children's bread and throw it to the dogs. The reader has encountered Jesus performing many healings (Mt. 8–9; 12.9-14; 14.34-36) and his ministry has been characterized by healing in two key summary statements (4.23 and 9.35). What is it that is not good or right, not 'morally good or pleasing to God' (BDAG 504)?

Jesus follows his moral judgment with highly metaphoric language: it is not *kalon*/good or right to take the children's bread and throw it to the dogs. He draws two other-than-human constituents, namely 'bread' and 'dogs', into his conversation and he uses them both metaphorically. As an ecological reader, I want to pay attention to how these elements and their agency are encoded in the text. To do this, I hold in tension Rigby's claiming that 'the inevitable failure of the written word to restore to presence that to which it refers us' (Rigby 2004: 437) and Buell's 'leaning toward' such restoration (2005: 33). As we have already seen in relation to the Tyrian hinterland, bread is a highly charged commodity that needs to be mapped onto our grid of power. Without the bread from the Jewish communities of its hinterland, Tyre could not survive. Does the woman's persistent challenging of Jesus confront him with the powerful function of bread that at least had the potential to join the peoples of this hinterland region? Jesus' response represents the way it divides them. Bread in its materiality significantly impacts the sociality of the entire more-than-human community in this region. It is this that the words of Jesus encode within the narrative.

In the second half of Jesus' answer to the woman's plea in v. 26, he metaphorically evokes a second other-than-human constituent encoded in the ecological texture of the text. In this instance, however, it is the animals, 'the dog/s' which share the bread. Laura Hobgood-Oster addresses the implication of this evocation for an ecological reader:

> [w]hen humans represent animals and, therefore, tell ourselves what and who they (the animals) are in relationship to us, animal subjectivity or objectivity and human subjectivity form simultaneously. We humans understand ourselves differently because of the way animals are used as symbols, and humans understand animals differently. But what of the real animals? Because of the assumed and often enacted power of humans over animals, such representation impacts animals as much as humans, though in different ways (2008: 8).

A recent study by J.R. Harrison (2012: 110-17) demonstrates the range of literary representations of the 'dog' in Hellenistic and early Roman times that need not be rehearsed here. Suffice it to recognize that the evocation of 'the dogs' in v. 26 encodes into the ecological texture of text ancient ethology whereby connections are made regarding the character of the human from that of an animal. Such an approach is problematic in that its focus is on the human character and the animal is simply a vehicle for exploring human characteristics (see Cadwalader 2008). Here, however, an ecological reader can recognize the potential agency of 'the dog' encoded in the metaphoric referent.

The encounter between Jesus and the Canaanite woman draws into the ecological texture of this text a particular aspect/s of those 'dogs' to whom reference is made. It is the woman's words in particular which situate them within the house, indeed under the table of the householder, the kyrios. Her linking of the dogs and bread (or at least the 'crumbs' of the 'bread of the children') gives life to these two material elements causing them to 'lean towards' an encoding of their materiality in the text (for a more detailed exploration of this, see Wainwright 2013b: 126-27). It also draws all the actants onto the Sandoval grid of power. Here, both Jesus and the woman have voice, bread links Tyrian and Jew and comes to represent the power to heal and dogs, in their leaning toward their own materiality, can enable Jesus to negotiate his own internal struggle to determine what is 'word of God' and what is 'human tradition' (15.6-9) in his encounter. He recognizes the great faith of the woman (v. 28) as not only what she desires (*theleis*) but what G*d desires (see 6.10; 7.21; 26.42 and passim). Power, which has been skillfully negotiated between Jesus and the woman in their verbal encounter, extends now to the woman's daughter. She is healed from that hour, not as a result of touch or flesh on flesh, but by desire negotiated in human encounter around the materiality of bread and dogs.

This story of healing of the daughter of a woman called 'Canaanite' and its encoding in the narrative of both bread and dogs stands at the centre of a chiastic structure (see Wainwright 1991: 100):

A   The Feeding of 5,000 (14.13-21)
        + a disciple's little faith (14.28-33)
   B   Jesus heals many (14.34-35)
           The Tradition of the Elders (15.1-20)
      C
           The Canaanite Woman (15.21-38)
   B¹   Jesus heals many (15.29-31)
A¹   The Feeding of 4,000 (15.32-39)
        + the disciples' little faith (16.5-12)

It will not be necessary, therefore to give further attention to sections B¹ and A¹ as these can be read in light of the earlier readings of sections A and B. Our attention can turn, therefore, to the text of Mt. 16.13-20 which I have read earlier in parallel with 15.21-28 (1998: 84-100).

4. *Matthew 16.13–17.23: Turning between Life and Death and Transformation*

As the ecological reader of the Matthean story of Jesus has come to expect, aspects of habitat are continually encoded into the ecological texture of the narrative. Matthew 16.13 is no different. Here, Jesus comes into the region/the *merē* of Caesarea Philippi just as he came into the *merē* of Tyre and Sidon (15.21), not it seems into those cities themselves (see Freyne 2000: passim). Narratively, he does not go into the built environment of the city, in this instance with its temples, statues, coinage and many other aspects symbolic of the Roman Empire (Chancey 2002). It is as a counter to such a *basileia* that he preaches his core message of a transformative vision of a *basileia* of the skies or the heavens (4.17). Not only does Jesus preach this message but enacts it in his healing and his feeding of multitudes and plays it out in his teaching (see 4.23 to the current verses). With the contrast between these two different *basileiai* playing in the narrative through the opening verse, the focus shifts to a dialogue between Jesus and 'his disciples' around his identity, an issue that he has sidestepped earlier in order to focus attention on/validate his ministry that has been of word and deed (see 11.2-6). The narrative does not give reasons for such emphases.

This text (16.13-20) interrogates the ecological reader in relation to how we answer the question of Jesus to the disciples, 'who do you say that I am?' in a new age, one which Thomas Berry called an *ecozoic* era.[7] The question of Jesus: how does the human community describe the one who is called *huios tou anthrōpou*/the child of humanity[8] evokes the contemporary question. The designation associated with the crowds, namely 'prophet' is certainly correct. We have already seen that McVann has demonstrated how the narratives of Matthew 3 and 4 can be read as John the Baptizer handing on the prophetic mantle to Jesus (1993: 14-20). Peter's reply that Jesus is the *Christos* opens up a range of prophetic and political possibilities (see Neusner, Green and Frerichs 1987 and Horsley and Hanson 1985 for many first century understandings of this term). It is, however, the phrase *huios tou theou*/son or child of G*d or in 16.16, 'son/child of the living God' which will be the focus of my exploration.

Earlier in relation to 14.33, I read that title as recognition of Jesus' living of the right relationship between habitat, the human and the holy and I linked this to the *Emmanu-el* title given to Jesus in 1.23. In Jesus, divinity named as 'the living God' is with the entire more-than-human community. At a particular point in the unfolding of the universe, divinity, as far as we can know it, has entered into the history of one planet, namely Earth with all its more-than-human interrelationships, in a human person, Jesus. To name Jesus as 'child of divinity' and divinity among us/*Emmanu-el* is to seek in limited human terms to capture the extraordinary divine/more-than-human nexus ignited in Jesus. It is this that theologians such as Denis Edwards (2006: 48-64) and Elizabeth A. Johnson (2014: 192-201) seek to explore and articulate in the language, imagery and in light of the knowledge that characterizes this ecozoic era.

Jesus does not allow himself or his disciples to bask in his titles but he does turn to Peter with a blessing and a change of name together with a commission (16.17-19). This is a complex passage over which much ink has been spilled (for a summary of much of this see Davies and Allison 1991: 621-41). Its concern seems to be what authorizes Peter as 'rock' on which the *ekklēsia* of Jesus is to be founded just as Jesus sought to ensure in the earlier verses that 'his disciples' of v. 13 knew who he was or indeed who/what authorized him. These conversations involving Jesus and the disciples take on a very particular meaning in the habitat in which they are

---

7. See n/a 'What does Ecozoic Mean?', in *Ecozoic Times*, for an explanation of the word in relation to Berry's coining of it. http://ecozoictimes.com/what-is-the-ecozoic/what-does-ecozoic-mean/ (accessed 28 January 2015).

8. BDAG 1024, give the first meaning of *uios* as male-gendered son but then give more generic meanings such as a 'person related or closely associated as if by ties of sonship'. It is such an association which seems most appropriate to the Matthaean text.

located, namely the 'region' of Caesarea Philippi, the focus of significant political and religious authority in the first century. The ecological reader may choose to read against the grain of the reference to Peter's coming to his understanding of Jesus identity as having only a divine or holy source not a human one. Rather, one could argue that it is in the very interaction of the human community around Jesus (disciples) in the habitat in and through which they have journeyed that Peter has come to his recognition of Jesus' unique and intimate relationship with divinity.

Into this segment of the narrative characterized predominantly by the human or the human and the holy, one element of habitat is encoded, namely the 'rock'. It functions multivalently in the Matthean text, at times in its solidity (7.24-25), at times preventing the taking hold of seeds (13.20-21) (see Wainwright 1998: 98-99). Generally, it has been interpreted in 16.18 in relation to solidity but perhaps the ecological reader can hold the two possibilities in tensive relationship just as the materiality of 'the keys' can evoke both binding and loosing. The wise leader and the ecological reader will be attentive to both.

A new element enters the Matthean narrative at this point (16.21-28). The narrator alerts readers to the time referent: 'from that time'. It indicates a beginning point but no end. That will be contained in what Jesus shows his disciples he must/*dei* do, namely go to Jerusalem, a new place/space that has not yet featured in the narrative of his ministry. He indicates that here he will encounter an escalation of the plotting against him among his co-religionists (with the elders, chief priests and scribes being identified). The ecological reader will be attentive to Jesus' reading of his future, the recognition that death is integrally related to the life cycle—life and death and life and… The one who is *Emmanu-el* has truly entered into this life cycle shared by all in the more-than-human Earth community. Peter, on the other hand, wants to deny Jesus' embeddedness in that cycle, a denial that Jesus calls a *skandalon*, a challenge thrown out to many in today's human community who also act in the more-than-human community as though they had power over death. As the unfolding gospel turns to death as well as life and their intricate connectedness, the reader is challenged to enter into this interconnectedness in the call to pattern one's life on that of Jesus (16.24-28).

A very explicit time designator opens the next scene in this section of the narrative, namely 17.1-8. The reader does not know the *terminus a quo*, the point from which the six days of v. 1 are measured and so while grounding the story in explicit time in the inner texture of the text, the reference may also function intertextually. Indeed, many scholars turn to the six days evoked in Exod. 24.15-18, although there the phrase indicates the length of time that the glory of G*d settled on Mount Sinai (v. 16). In both texts, the place encoded in the text is a high mountain (see Mt. 5.1). Time and place ground this narrative in the material.

The senses function powerfully in this scene as Elvey has already drawn to our attention (2011b: 22-23, 93, 147-50), especially that of seeing. The translation of the verb *metamorphoein* as 'transfigured' can tend to obscure this and hence a turn to BDAG (639) and their longer explanation, 'to change in a manner *visible* (italics mine) to others', evokes the bodily sense of seeing. Jesus is changed in a manner visible to the three disciples and yet this change is one that is beyond the human: his face shone like the sun and his garments became white as light (17.2). Language grapples to articulate this change that the disciples 'see'. The human and the holy intersect in the materiality of the body of Jesus transfigured and this is 'seen' by attentive disciples.

The verb *horaein*/'to perceive by the eye' in v. 3 continues to focus the reader's attention on seeing or perceiving (BDAG 719). The verb is in the passive and carries the sense of 'appeared' or 'ma(d)e their appearance in a transcendent manner'. Two 'holy ones' from Israel's history are speaking with the transfigured Jesus, Moses and Elijah. They too experienced transformative encounters with the holy (Exod. 24.15-18 as noted above and Elijah on Horeb, 1 Kgs 19.11-15). All this takes place in an earthly place—on a mountain. Indeed, Peter seeks to capture this extraordinary experience, to 'earth' it in 'three booths', rather than to let it function at that point of radical intersection between the human/Earth and the holy. The voice from out the cloud confirms this radical intersection, a voice which engages another of the senses, that of hearing. The beloved of the holy one in whom that holy one is 'with' the 'us' of the Earth community is confirmed in this encounter, in the divine voice that the human ones 'hear' (v. 6). And they are charged to 'listen' (v. 5).

The response of the three to this divine/human encounter earthed on the mountain and in the visible body of Jesus is one of awe and prostration (v. 6), but this is not the goal of such encounters. Rather Jesus draws into the encounter another of the bodily senses, that of 'touch' as he invites the disciples to stand up and to have no fear. Their eyes that have seen the human and the holy meet in transfiguration, now see 'only Jesus', the human one. The encounter has further confirmed the nexus of the human and the holy that is Jesus. As the narrative continues, it will focus on the human one who continues to heal, casting out those forces that mar human lives (17.14-20). It will also turn again to the death threats that Jesus now knows hang over him (17.22-23).

Chapter 9

MATTHEW 18:
A COMMUNITY OF RECONCILIATION—CAN IT INCLUDE EARTH?

We have come to a significant turning point in the unfolding of the Matthean story of Jesus. In the previous section (14–17), readers found themselves in many different locations: either side of the Sea of Galilee and its hinterlands, on the borderland between Tyre and Sidon and Galilee, and in the region of Caesarea Philippi. As Matthew 19 opens, readers are caught up in a shift in geographic context: he went away from Galilee and entered the region of Judea beyond the Jordan (19.1). This is not surprising given the shift in sociality that is emerging in the text. On three occasions, beginning in the region of Caesarea Philippi, Jesus turns his and his disciples' attention to his suffering and death that will take place in Jerusalem (16.21; 17.12b, 22-23). The body of Jesus will be dealt with violently. Matthew 18 seems to be a narrative interlude before this relentless journey will unfold. It is also categorized as the fourth of the discourses in the Matthean construction of the gospel narrative (see Mt. 5–7; 10; and 13 and their concluding phrase: when Jesus had finished: 7.28; 11.1; 13.53 cf. 19.1).

Given the transitional nature of Matthew 18, it seemed appropriate to make this short chapter of the commentary transitional also. Matthew 18 has traditionally been seen as the 'Community Discourse', this named in different ways by different scholars: Carter, 'A Community of Sustaining Relationships and Practices' (2000: ix) and Hagner—'Life in the Community of the Kingdom' (1995: x) by way of example. At the heart of the discourse seems to be restoration of right relationships, reconciliation, and forgiveness. These play within the narrative with their dominant focus being on how these function or ought to function within the human community. The senses (vv. 6-9) and the parabolic encoding of the other-than-human (sheep in vv. 10-14) alert readers to the materiality and sociality that characterize the ecological texture of the text highlighted in this commentary. These could be taken up in a reading of Matthew 18 and I invite the reader to do so. Here, however, at this transitional point, I want to engage in another mode or aspect of ecological interpretation.

One of the key features of the Earth Bible Project's approach as this has been developed over the last fifteen years has been that of *Retrieval of the*

Voice of Earth (see Habel 2000: 24, 46-48; 2008: 7-8; and Introduction to this series). The approach has been that of creative retrieval of the voice of Earth, similar to the creative articulation phase of earlier feminist biblical interpretation (see Schüssler Fiorenza 1995: 15-22). I propose to undertake such a creative reading at this transition point in the commentary. My goal, in light of the approach undertaken in this commentary, is to give voice to the interrelationship of materiality and sociality of the more-than-human as this has been engaged in the Matthean text. Just as my reading of that text throughout has been in creative dialogue with contemporary intertexts, the same will apply to this creative engagement with the other-than-human.

> **Ecological Intertexts.** The strong Matthean thematic of 'reconciliation' within community by way of the seeking out of the lost, the restoration of community relationships, and the forgiveness of debts no matter how great in the human community turned my attention to the broader arena of the other-than-human or even the more-than-human. Here I discovered that ecologists have been exploring a concept and a practice called 'reconciliation ecology' which '(r)ather than insist(ing) on protecting habitat from human use, reconciliation ecology works in and with the human dominated habitats that cover most of the terrestrial surface of the Earth… [and] gives us the realistic hope that we can prevent most losses of species' (Rosenzweig 2003: 194). Rosenzweig goes on to say that '[r]econciliation [e]cology discovers how to modify and diversify anthropogenic habitats so that they harbour a wide variety of wild species…it seeks techniques to give many species back their geographical ranges without taking away ours' (201).

As the Matthean author/s heard the human cry from the fractures in their community and addressed these in their telling of the Jesus story, so too today we hear heart-wrenching cries rising up from the Earth, from other-than-human communites, as species are made extinct, soil is polluted, land is scarred by fracking and our sea is polluted by deep sea oil drilling and its spillages. 'Reconciliation ecology' is seeking new ways to bring together and preserve both the diversity of species and life-forms and the societal aspects of the human community. As Francis and Lorrimer say, '[t]he concept of reconciliation ecology, by which the anthropogenic environment may be modified to encourage non-human use and biodiversity preservation without compromising societal utilization, potentially represents an appropriate paradigm for urban conservation given the generally poor opportunities that exist for reserve establishment and ecological restoration in urban areas' (Francis and Lorimer 2011: 1429). Some ways in which this movement is taking root is by way of walls and roofs and other structures being developed as habitats for a range of biodiverse species in urban areas. In this creative articulation of Matthew 18, I propose to allow 'reconciliation ecology' and imaginative extensions of that to inform the undertaking.

9. *Matthew 18*

In the present era of ecological crisis, the disciples of the reconciliation ecologist ask her: 'Who is the least threatened in the renewing/reconciling Earth Community?'

The reconciliation ecologist called one of the most endangered species of planet Earth into the midst of the seekers of a renewed Earth and said: Truly I tell you unless you change and become attentive to survival for all, as is this endangered one, then you cannot participate in the dream of an Earth Community in right relationships. Whoever works collaboratively for this dream will participate most fully in its realization. Whoever welcomes the one/s most endangered welcomes me, the dreamer of a renewed Earth.

If anyone should threaten the most endangered ones, any biotic or abiotic members of the Earth community, it would be better that their power, their social capital and even their material resources be taken away from them. Threats to members of the Earth community will come but woe to those through whom they come.

If a member of the Earth community is causing threat or harm to another species, another Earth element, whatever resources are being used to fuel such threat will be taken away from them. They are better to be without those resources than that the whole planet and all its constituents should suffer.

Do not despise the threatened ones, the weakest of Earth's beings, whoever or whatever they may be. Each makes a unique contribution to the right relationships within a reconciling ecology. Each will flourish in the movement toward a renewed Earth. And so, I want you to imagine your planet Earth, one among myriads of those discreet bodies that make up the Universe. It has gone astray—its human community has broken down right relationships with the other-than-human community members, species are being lost, toxins released into the atmosphere destroy human and other lives, and the planet itself is threatened. Will not the reconciliation ecologist go and seek to restore right relationships, rejoicing in such restoration more than in the stability of all the other universal bodies. It is not the dream of the Holy One that one Earth being, let alone Earth itself be lost.

If it does happen that a member of the Earth-community sins against another or others causing harm in any way, then a member of that community, any member ought to go and demonstrate the fault in order to win back that one to a reconciled community. If that community member does not listen, then a delegation of humans and other-than-humans might witness to the sin. If this does not turn the member's heart, then tell it to the whole assembly and if the assembly is not able to re-incorporate the straying one, then that one will remain an outsider until she/he should seek to return to the Earth community. Whatever life forms and life forces you bind up in the Earth community, they will remain bound up in the entire Cosmos; and whatever you set free in the Earth-community, will be set free in the entire Cosmos.

Wherever two or three members of the Earth community gather in the name of Habitat, the Human and the Holy, then I, the Holy One am 'with' that Earth-community.

One of the Earth-community asks: If another member of the Earth-community wrongs me or wrongs the community, how many times ought we to forgive that wrong and reconcile with that member? Should it be a finite number of times? The reconciliation ecologist replies: Not finite but infinite if true reconciliation is to flourish in the Earth-community. And for this reason the transformative dream for a renewed Earth may be compared to a reconciliation ecologist who had engaged a small number of plant, animal and human species to live and flourish together in a selected bioregion. When it came time to review the project, many goals had been met, though not all. The reconciliation ecologist forgave the community the unmet goals as time was necessary for the new to flourish. But some of the human community dealt harshly with the plant and animal species in their region as they were not flourishing sufficiently. When the reconciliation ecologist heard this, the immediate reaction was distress: I forgave you the goals you had not met as I know that time, care and ongoing nurture are necessary for a flourishing bio-region. Why did you not forgive? Why did you not stay in right relationship with your plant and animal co-species. Return and re-new those relationships, as it is only in right relationships, continually restored and renewed following forgiveness that the dream of transformed/right relationships between Habitat, the Human and the Holy will be truly realized.

Chapter 10

MATTHEW 19–23:
HUMAN CONFLICT IMPACTING EARTH

Jesus' teaching, preaching and healing continues in this section of the narrative but sounds a more subdued note in the background of the text. What is foregrounded is the growing conflict between the religious leaders in Jerusalem and Jesus as he enters into the space/place where their power is concentrated.

This conflict, which heightens as the gospel narrative unfolds to the end (Mt. 19–28), is grounded in place by means of the words of the narrator. As noted in the previous chapter, Jesus and his disciples shift location in 19.1 to the 'region of Judea beyond the Jordan'. It is here that the Pharisees confront Jesus. By 20.17, the reader finds Jesus is 'going up to Jerusalem' and in 20.19, he and his disciples are 'leaving Jericho'. As Matthew 21 opens (21.1), the group has 'come near Jerusalem and has reached Bethphage, at the Mount of Olives'. In 21.10, they enter the city. But that is not all. In 21.12 the text encodes Jesus' entry into the temple that is located within the city (see also 21.14-15, 23). As the story continues, Jesus moves between Bethany, Jerusalem and the temple (21.17, 18, 23), all material places/spaces whose very materiality echoes through the text. Given that 24.1 opens with the phrase '[a]s Jesus came out of the temple', the text of 21.23–23.39 encodes all the encounters within these verses as taking place in the temple, with the different groups of opponents of Jesus coming and going. The text is characterized by bodies in place, even though little attention seems to be given to the materiality of such bodies or the spaces in which they are located. In this ecological reading, attention will be given to space/place not as a 'mere backdrop' as Casey warns (1993: 274) but as 'indispensable material medium…furnishing way stations as well as origins and destinations'.

In this reading, therefore, attention will be directed to the places/spaces along the journey narrated in these five chapters. Place/space, as we have already seen, is not just 'First-space'/material space or 'Second-space'/ space functioning symbolically. These are layered into the text and integrally serve an ecological reading. The ecological reader will be attentive to these but will also turn very explicit attention to Third/Lived Space drawing in additional intertexts (Soja 1999).

> **Ecological Intertexts.** Complementary to Soja's notion of 'Third Space' as lived space in which new meaning is possible beyond the material and symbolic aspect of space, Isabel Hoving provides a further perspective, namely that 'Third Space' is 'shaped by the discourses and practices of the people and institutions that inhabit it' (2013: 113). Also, in literary contexts, Third/Lived space can be conceived as that 'experienced and valued by the narrator or (one of the) characters in an ideological, emotional, experiential relation to society and power' (Heirman and Klooster 2013: 5). Third Space is, therefore often infused with conflict. It is into the materiality and sociality that characterizes space/place in Matthew 19–23 that an ecological reading draws its reader/s.

In this reading of Matthew 19–23, place or space will be read in its materiality and sociality. Such sociality includes the interrelationships not only among human but all the more-than-human characters encoded in the ecological texture of the narrative. The reader of this text becomes quickly aware that it is predominantly human bodies and their materiality and sociality that are not only encoded in the text but inform the conflict building in the narrative.

As Jesus reaches Jerusalem, the groups who confront him, who enter into conflict with him, change. On his arrival in Jerusalem, the reader finds the 'chief priests and scribes' questioning Jesus' actions (21.15). In 21.23, it is the chief priests and elders of the people who question Jesus' authority. In 21.45, chief priests and Pharisees combine and their goal is to arrest Jesus (21.46). The Pharisees (22.15) trade places with the Sadducees (22.23) in plotting to entrap Jesus by questioning him and it is a lawyer from among the Pharisees (22.41) who challenges Jesus as to which commandment is the greatest. Jesus' riposte to this escalating conflict occurs in Matthew 23. The group/s whose names are repeated in Jesus' scathing rebuke are 'scribes and Pharisees' (23.2, 13, 15, 23, 25, 27). Additional names are added but these are emotive rather than descriptive: 'hypocrites' in vv. 13, 15 and 29; 'blind Pharisees' v. 26; with 'snakes, brood of vipers' in v. 33 as the final escalation of the diatribe. The dominant group characterized as opposing Jesus and his teaching is the 'scribes and Pharisees'.

1. *Matthew 19.1–20.34: En Route to Jerusalem*

The opening verse of Matthew 19–23 has Jesus *in place*. Indeed he is traversing space: leaving Galilee and going into the region of Judea beyond the Jordan, or Perea as it was called at that time. From the outset the materiality of place and conflict within the socio-cultural context are encoded in the opening verse of this extended narrative. Jesus leaves Galilee where most of the unfolding narrative up to this point has been located. The reference to 'the region of Judea beyond the Jordan' encodes in the text the area known as Perea on the east side of the river through which Jews from Galilee would have walked on pilgrimage to Jerusalem (human bodies on other-than-human earth and in relationship to all the materiality and sociality of the region). A note of conflict echoes through this opening verse when it is realized that Galilean pilgrims to Jerusalem generally went through Perea because of the danger inherent in Samaria. Sean Freyne (2000: 130) draws attention to Josephus' account of the murder of a Galilean who was going up to Jerusalem through Samaria (*J.W.* 2.232). Place and power collide from the opening verse of this section all but overshadowing the reference to Jesus' healing there (19.2), a reference which evokes the materiality of bodies in their brokenness.

This initial focus on place and power is in contrast to the remainder of Matthew 19 whose inner texture turns readers' attention to socio-cultural/human encodings in the ecological texture of this text. Listeners first hear Jesus' teaching on divorce and marriage (vv. 3-12), the focus being human ethics. They then encounter textually the bodies of children who are brought to Jesus and he lays hands on them, he touches them, just as he touched those in need of healing (vv. 13-15). The encounter is material, flesh on flesh, but it leads to a moment of teaching by Jesus: it is to such as these (little children) that the *basileia* of the skies belongs. This further extends the inclusive vision that Jesus names as *basileia of the skies/heavens*. It is not constrained by the socio-cultural lower status of children in first-century society (see Carter 2000: 384-85) but is extended to include them by right—it is to them that the proclamation of Jesus belongs. Attentiveness to bodies in place alerts readers to the complex materiality and sociality that is encoded in this unfolding narrative. Narrative focus is predominantly on the human community as is the ethical question from an unknown character as to what is necessary to enter into life (vv. 16-22).

If we listen attentively to Jesus' reply, we note that the commandments cited by Jesus are characterized by right relationships lived out in the materiality of bodies (no murder, no adultery but honouring of parents and love of neighbour vv. 18-19). Each commandment can also be heard in relation to the other-than-human elements encoded in the text: instruments of murder, gifts and property that pass between parents and children as well as among neighbours. The human and other-than-human are always inextricably bound up with one another and must be attended to in the inner and the ecological texture of the text. It is the commandment not to steal which draws the other-than-human most explicitly into the text.[1] It remains there in the final challenge Jesus offers the young man who has kept all the

---

1. See Phillips (1970: 132, 145-46) who argues that the originating meaning of this commandment was in relation to the stealing of human persons and only later with the Deuteronomic reform did it come to refer to property.

commandments, living in right relation with human and other-than-human. It is to go and to sell all his *hypachonta* or 'property, possessions, means' (BDAG 1029), the meaning with which we are most familiar. But this present active participle also carries a foundational meaning, namely, 'to really be there, exist, be present' (BDAG 1029). The invitation to the young man to give over property and possessions (all that is material), to be in right relationships in the more-than-human *basileia* of the skies/heavens is an invitation to all readers. The enactment of such relationships will involve the human community in intimate and right relationship with the sociality of all that is other-than-human.

Before leaving Matthew 19, the ecological reader might note the material items as well as the human persons which must be left behind if one is to 'enter into life'—houses and fields together with family members. This is indicative of how profoundly connected are materiality and sociality. Habitat, human and holy are intimately interrelated in this chapter and the ecological reader is invited into their play within the text. The brief passing reference to the *paliggenesis* in v. 28 further re-iterates this given that BDAG (752) translate *paliggenesis* as rebirth or renewal on a cosmic level. This links the reader back across the entire narrative to 1.1.

The intimate interplay of materiality and sociality continues to characterize Jesus' ongoing teaching in Perea as narrated in Matthew 20. We have already seen in relation to the parable chapter of Matthew 13 that parables are rich in inter-con/textuality, and in the hybridity of habitat that they encode (earth and seed and weeds and fish by way of example). Matthew 20.1 opens with the formula with which the reader is familiar: the *basileia* of the skies/heavens is like… (see by way of example: Mt. 13.24, 31, 33, 44, 45, 47). In this instance, it is like a householder who went out early in the morning to hire labourers for his vineyard. The complex web of the material and the socio-cultural is woven in the ecological texture of this parable and is evoked in its proclamation. Listeners/readers can imagine the soil, the vines heavy with grapes, the hired day-labourers working under the heat of the sun, together with time as the hours of the day go by. Conflict enters the scene when the owner of the vineyard has his manager pay those who have worked all day the same wage as those who worked only the last hour of the day. The owner responds to the complaint of those who worked a full day with the enigmatic statement: is your eye evil because I am *agathos/*good (NRSV translation is 'generous'). This question seems to take readers to the heart of this parable.[2]

---

2. Contemporary readers, informed by employment laws and contracts and often engaged in movements for workers' rights, critique what seem to be layers of injustice in this parable. I have chosen here to read it with a focus on v. 15 and the enigmatic statement about the evil eye and its first century context as this is encoded in the text.

The English translation can obscure the encoding of the cultural feature of the 'evil eye' in the text. In an agonistic society where male honour and status were constantly being negotiated and constantly under threat,[3] there was a level of fear because the eyes of others were always upon an individual male seeking to dishonour him, to bring him down so that the gazers themselves might gain more status. In the face of this, there were certain items including amulets bearing the image of an eye that were believed to be imbued with power to resist the 'evil eye' of the gazers (see Elliott 1992: 52-65). The vineyard owner in this parable confronts the workers of the full day with their envy, with the evil eye they have cast on him—is their eye evil because the owner is generous to those who were without labour for most of the day? The vineyard owner challenges the injustices of the social system in which land is being acquired and held by the powerful thus forcing many small farmers off their land so that they had to become day labourers who were not guaranteed work or wage. Relationships between the human community and land were being disrupted, habitat and human interconnections were broken. Readers' attention has also been drawn to the cultural system or the honour/shame system that pits one against another in the human community for honour and status. Both faces of injustice are uncovered in this parable of the *basileia* providing yet another indicator of the *dikaiosynē* or right ordering which this gospel proclaims as characteristic of that *basileia* (see Mt. 5.6). Such *dikaiosynē* concerns the right relationships between and among the other-than-human and the human.

In Mt. 20.17, a shift in spatiality occurs in the text—Jesus is going up to Jerusalem (leaving Perea). This phrase 'going up to Jerusalem' is first on the lips of the narrator and then on the lips of Jesus within two verses. The words of Jesus make very explicit that Jerusalem will be the place of profound human conflict that will be played out on his own body (20.18-19). This is not the first time the reader has encountered the material and politico-religious aspects of Jerusalem encoded in the text. These have already been, in the words of Heirman and Klooster, 'experienced and valued by the narrator or (one of the) characters in an ideological, emotional, experiential relation to society and power' (2013: 5). Readers have encountered Jerusalem as the political centre of Herodian rule in 2.1, 3, a place of power and of danger for the new-born child and the wise ones from the East attracted there by his birth. But also great crowds of its people came out from the city to receive John's baptism (3.5) or to follow Jesus the preacher, teacher and healer (4.23-25). Pharisees and scribes came to Jesus from Jerusalem to question him (15.1) and Jesus himself predicts that he must go to Jerusalem

---

3. For a brief summary of this socio-cultural characteristic, see Rohrbaugh (2007: 31-34).

and there he will be put to death by religio-political forces, 'elders, chief priests and scribes' (16.21). Jerusalem is a place/space of ambivalence, of religio-political alliances against Jesus and of popular acceptance. It is in such an ambivalent lived space that the final chapters of the Matthean narrative unfold but this lived space cannot be separated from material and symbolic space. In relation to Jerusalem, these have been treated earlier and shall not be repeated here.

Power and struggle for power do not characterize just the opponents of Jesus and his teachings, preaching, and healing, whether encountered in Galilee (15.1) or to be encountered on arrival in Jerusalem. These features also permeate the community of followers en route with him to Jerusalem. For the ecological reader, power and its gendering and the way these are encoded in the sociality of Mt. 20.20-28 require attention. In the Matthean gospel (in contrast to Mk 10.35-45), it is the mother of the sons of Zebedee who requests of Jesus that her two sons sit at his right and left in his kingdom (*basileia*) imagined and evoked materially by this mother and her sons but functioning metaphorically in the Matthean unfolding narrative. She, together with her sons and the other ten disciples (vv. 24-28), misunderstands Jesus' teaching in relation to an alternative *basileia*. The woman requests places of hierarchical power not having recognized that the *basileia* Jesus has been preaching and teaching is characterized much more by power mapped on a horizontal grid as already discussed. Jesus draws both the mother and sons (v. 22) into this horizontal framework by asking whether they can 'drink the cup that he is to drink'. All reply 'we are able' (v. 22). As the story unfolds, the mother will indeed 'drink the cup' as she stands with the many women at the foot of Jesus' cross of execution (27.55-56). Her two sons, on the other hand, are numbered among 'all the disciples who forsook him and fled' (26.56). It is gendered power that is being remapped in the places or the spaces that the narrative constructs contributing to the ecological texture of this text.

The narrative of the journey to Jerusalem pauses in a very explicit place, namely Jericho (20.29). Materially it was an ancient city that, in the first century, was rich in agriculture in its surrounding oasis. It was also a Herodian city with palaces, baths and, Carter notes (2000: 408), 'royal estates'—a significant socio-political site. It lay on the west side of the Jordan and at the foot of the ancient road up to Jerusalem. Narratively, the reference to their leaving the city keeps alive the readers'/listeners' awareness that the journey to Jerusalem is continuing. Place is 'experienced and valued by the narrator' (Heirman and Klooster 2013: 5) on a number of levels and the reader notes that the two blind men are 'sitting by the roadside', the materiality of Earth itself providing them with a place/space. It is from this place that they cry out to Jesus words with which a reader/listener is already familiar: have mercy on us, Son of David (9.27; 15.22).

Twice the two blind men seated on the roadside have called out to Jesus for mercy/*eleēson* (vv. 30 and 31). After the second cry, Jesus is moved with compassion (*splagchnistheis*—v. 34), moved in the depth of his material body, his entrails, as was discussed earlier. The bodies of each blind man and Jesus meet in a corporeal exchange as he *touches* their eyes. As noted earlier, Jesus' embodied touch is at the same time an allowing of himself to be touched. The Jericho roadside is the place that witnesses this profound tactile encounter that brings healing and in/sight. A relationship is established in this place: the healed ones follow Jesus, they become part of the group going up to Jerusalem. At the same time, their healing turns readers' minds back to the healing that characterized Jesus' entire ministry in Galilee, one particular account being the healing of two blind men (9.27-31). And it is also only with newly opened eyes that we can read the gospel text ecologically, thus shaping a vision that can, in our day, characterize Jesus' *basileia* vision or new dream. And it is the ethic of this *basileia* vision that disciples today are called to live in their lives. This is to read ecologically.

Readers learn nothing of the journey of the Jesus-group as they make their way up along the ancient road connecting Jericho to Jerusalem characterized by an elevation of 1060 metres and 25 km of winding road traversing the Judaean Desert with all its flora and fauna and the physical challenge of the ascent (Salla n/d). The text is silent about this material space but for the ecological reader it is an element of the inner texture of the text. The narrator, on the other hand, next locates readers 'near to Jerusalem, (coming) to Bethphage, to the Mount of Olives' (21.1).

Little is known of the village of Bethphage: it does not appear at all in the Jewish scriptures. It is believed to be on the eastern side of the Mount of Olives and approximately a Sabbath's journey from the city.[4] Its name means "house of un-ripe figs" and hence may evoke not only material but also symbolic elements in the unfolding story. While the narrator does not linger on this village, it is the place within and from which the next stage of this dramatic narrative is played out. Attention to it shapes and develops the reader's capacities for ecological awareness of the materiality of those spaces/places in which life is enacted.

2. *Matthew 21.1–22.46: Towards and Into the City*

Ched Myers says of the Markan parallel to Mt. 21.1-11 that it resembles 'carefully choreographed street theatre' (Myers 2008: 204). Such an assessment would seem to apply even more so to the Matthean narrative in which Jesus is said to ride on two animals (v. 7). This, together with the growing narrative tension evoked by Jesus' warnings of what will befall him in

---

4. See http://dictionary.reference.com/browse/beth-phage (accessed 15.4.15).

Jerusalem at the hands of the religious elite, suggests a carnivalesque reading of this entry narrative with particular attention given to the animals and the world/s that are turned upside down in the narrative.[5]

Bethphage, a village rich in materiality as well as sociality, including all its biotic and abiotic inhabitants, re-emerges in the narrative as the village in front of the Jesus-contingent to which Jesus sends two disciples to collect a donkey and a colt that is with her (v. 2). The carnivalesque atmosphere is evoked already with Jesus assuming the right to the use of the donkey and colt of which he is not the owner and this under the title of *kyrios*.[6] The two disciples go and do exactly what Jesus had asked. An ecological reader will be attentive to the donkey and colt inscribed into the narrative with all the biological and literary layering this entails (note Haraway's notion of 'figures' where the 'biological and the literary or artistic come together with all the force of lived reality' (2008a: 164). There is an ambivalence created by this double inscription. The donkey/*onos* is a constant character in Israel's sacred story and in the lives of the people of first century Judea. It was, on the one hand, a most common animal for agricultural and transport purposes (Job 1.3; Tob. 10.11; Judg. 2.17) and on the other hand highly valued, even included in the Sabbath rest (Deut. 5.14).

In the first century Graeco-Roman world and its centres of power, it was not the donkey but the war horse that carried a victorious king/emperor or general triumphantly into a city to claim it as his prize (Duff 1992), hence another carnivalesque element in the narrative. Augmenting this is the word used to describe the second animal. Linked with the initial reference to 'donkey' the word *polos* means 'colt' or 'foal' (BDAG 900) but should it have stood alone it would mean 'horse', the animal of a triumphant entry. The very language of the text together with what is enacted in the narrative contributes to the carnivalesque and this is even further underlined by the intertextuality of v. 5 that echoes through the prior and subsequent elements of the narrative. The narrator encodes in the Matthean verse a composite text from the Jewish scriptures, namely emended Zech. 9.9 and an opening phrase echoing Isa. 62.11 as well as removing the stanza referring to triumph from Zech. 9.9. This, indeed, adds to the carnivalesque. We do not, however, want to allow the enactment of carnival to obscure the materiality of the animals. Both function together in this text read ecologically and invite readers to reflect on the human-animal interrelationship.

---

5. Rozi (2014: 140) says that '[c]arnival fulfills a cathartic function' in that it momentarily up-turns the power structures of the participant's context. He goes on to say that another feature of this genre is 'parodic treatment of ritual'.

6. 'Kyrios' is generally translated as 'lord' (BDAG 577) with connotations of 'one who is in charge by virtue of possession, owner' or 'one who is in a position of authority, lord, master'. It also designates the male head of the kyriarchal household in antiquity.

Verses 6-8 see the enactment of carnival reach its climax and this is made possible through the extraordinary agency, one might say, of the material elements. The disciples bring the donkey and the colt to Jesus and put their garments on them mirroring the splendid blankets on the horse of the triumphant Roman general or king as he enters his city. Then, the text says, Jesus sat on 'them', an extraordinarily carnivalesque act—the riding of two animals simultaneously. Not only are the donkey and colt out-of-place as they carry the one rider but the other material elements are also out of place. The crowds spread cloaks or clothing on the road and take branches from trees and lay them on the road. The world is being turned upside down. This continues as the crowds that go before and follow Jesus cry out with 'hymns and acclamations' in a way that mimics what would accompany a triumphant entry (Duff: 66). They participate in this drama which functions to parody the religious and political powers residing in Jerusalem who will be aligned against Jesus as the narrative fast unfolds. The final irony in this segment of the carnivalesque narrative is that the Jerusalem crowds who could have participated in the pageantry fail to do so. They simply say of Jesus that he is 'the prophet from Nazareth of Galilee'. Of interest is the absence of the leaders from this entire scene and hence, accompanying this, the absence of conflict.

Elements of the carnivalesque also characterize the subsequent narratives as Jesus continues to enact the upturning of the prevailing world. In 21.12-14, readers see him entering onto the temple mount and creating mayhem, undertaking actions that he was not authorized to carry out in the prevailing order of the religio-cultural society. This text is characterized by bodies in-place/out-of-place, by the corporeality and the materiality of context and inter-con/textuality. It opens into a network of time, space, the human and habitat that are woven together in hybrid ways in the text. At the level of the inner text, the character Jesus enters the temple, his corporeality being very evident as the text unfolds. The temple can be read simply as setting within the inner texture of the text. Given, however, the three-fold repetition of *hieros* within the entire pericope (vv. 12-17) and twice within vv. 12-14, an ecological reader, like others, must give further attention to it. The temple is, therefore, in the words of Heirman and Klooster who are functioning in this chapter as significant intertext, 'experienced and valued by the narrator or (one of the) characters in an ideological, emotional, experiential relation to society and power (2013: 5).

Returning to Soja's theory of space (1999: 260-78), we can identify readily the First-space or physical level evoked by the reference to temple in the text. It is that of the material building of massive Jerusalem stones constructed as part of Herod's grandiose building programme in Jerusalem, the memory and traces of which are encoded in the text. It reminds readers of the built environment within which the Herodian dynasty functioned and which constituted a threat to the infant Jesus as the Matthean narrative opened. It was the domain of ritual or cultic practices presided over by Jerusalem's priestly aristocracy, predominantly the high priest, chief priests and Sadducees. These formed the Jewish elite who not only controlled the temple but also occupied the wealthy houses that archaeologists have uncovered on the western slope opposite the temple. At a Second-space or symbolic level, the physical and constructed space points beyond the material to the presence of the divine with Israel evoked in the explicit intertexuality with Isa. 56.1-8 in v. 13 of the Matthean text:

> …these I will bring to my holy mountain,
> and make them joyful in my house of prayer;
> their burnt offerings and their sacrifices
> will be accepted on my altar;
> for my house shall be called a house of prayer
> for all peoples (Isa. 56.7).

Jeremiah 7.11 with its reference to a 'den of robbers' contributes further intertextuality to this same verse (v. 13). This evokes the social and cultural legacy of Israel's failure to care for the alien, the orphan and the widow that was covered up by empty proclamations of 'the temple of God, the temple of God' (Jer. 7.6 and 4). A Third-space perspective opens up the potential that 'temple' might be functioning within the ecological texture of the text as marginal space in or from which alternative readings or meaning-making might emerge, a potential that only further reading can actualize.

If we re-examine v. 12, particularly its ecological texture through the lens of habitat i.e. the social-political, cultural, and psychological elements together with the physical and material, we find ourselves in the midst of bodies and birds, tables and stools. Jesus casts out bodily those named as 'buying and selling' in the temple as he has cast out demons (8.16, 31; 9.33; 10.1, 8; 12.24, 28), *exballein* being used in all cases. Human bodies are caught up in this melee that Jesus is creating as are the material tables of the money-changers and the stools or seats of those selling doves (the fate of the doves themselves is a lacuna in the text).[7] This is indeed carnival. Given that the encoded temple of first century Palestine functioned as 'the center of cultic life and of the Jewish political, economic and social leadership under Rome' as Warren Carter indicates (2000: 418), the ecological texture of this scene is rich indeed. Jesus is, through his actions,

---

7. Indeed the reference to the 'doves' as one group of animals being sold opens up further areas of exploration as to what was being traded, what constituted the materiality of this reference—was it other animals also that were being bought and sold? There is scope for extending this ecological reading to both the past and present trade in animals and what cruelty might be rended to them in those processes.

re-ordering the economic, socio-political, religious and material relationships embodied in the Temple. This is the hope of those who enter into the carnivalesque.

We have already seen that v. 13 is richly intertextual. Through its explicit recitation of phrases from Isa. 56.7 and Jer. 7.11, it contrasts the 'ideal' temple that Jesus' actions are symbolically enacting and the temple evoked in pious words that are accompanied by profound injustices in the lives of the people and their leaders. Jesus' challenge in this verse is not to the leaders but to those trading in the temple, those using this space inappropriately. This invites the ecological reader into the world opening up in front of the text, a world in which contemporary readers can likewise be challenged to ask about space and its relationship to economic, socio-cultural and religious activities—where they might intersect and where they must diverge. This is not to suggest a retreat into a dualism of sacred and secular space but rather a much richer exploration of material space (habitat) and its relation to the human and the holy that this text evokes.

The temple can also function as a Third-space where new meaning is possible. In the temple, Jesus makes a claim for it as space where G*d is 'with' G*d's people in relationship (prayer in this instance), a claim that challenges the way the temple officials were administering the temple. This claim has, however, already been enacted in and through the body of Jesus as he cleared out the space of the temple. It will also be enacted in a second way in the subsequent verse of this narrative, namely v. 14.

At the level of inner texture, the temple is named very explicitly as the space in which the blind and the lame come to Jesus. This space has just been cleared by Jesus of economic activities and it can, therefore, function in a new way/s that would be in keeping with its being called a 'house of prayer'. The language of the gospel is sparse in its representation of the 'blind' and the 'lame' who enter this new space. They are merely named. Glancy has already reminded us that it is 'through bodies and embodied exchanges that cultural complexity takes place' (2010a: 342-43). This is not Jesus' first encounter with those who are blind or lame. Jesus has been approached twice by a pair of blind men whose eyes he has touched and opened (9.27-28 and 20.30). The blind are also included with the lame among those to whom Jesus restores sight and ability to walk (11.5) and whom he is said to heal (15.30-31). Bodies have touched and healing has happened.

In v. 14 the focus is not on touch but on place with all its cultural complexity as we have seen in the previous verses. Intertextually, this verse confronts 2 Sam. 5.8 drawing it into the text: …the blind and the lame shall not come into the house. The ecological reader will note that in v. 13 'house' has already occurred twice with reference to the temple and so this intertexture.

The material and the socio-cultural are intimately intertwined in the ecological texture of this text. The Third-space function of the *hieros*/temple is revealed in Jesus' words. It is the place/space where bodies can be restored contrary to the tradition of religio-cultural exclusion founded in 2 Sam. 5.8. This is confirmed by the reaction of the chief priests and scribes in v. 15. Space is being contentiously negotiated as is the power relationship between Jesus and the religious officials. It can be read/understood as being negotiated on a horizontal grid. In this short narrative rich in inner, inter- and ecological textures Jesus enacts, by way of carnival reversal, sacred space and sacred symbol. He does this over against the chief priests and scribes as representative here of the leadership of the Jewish people and in particular of their temple. This is carried out through bodily encounters and bodily representations.

As vv. 18-22 open, Jesus is on the move again heading back to the city after an overnight sojourn in Bethany (v. 17), another village on the eastern slope of the Mount of Olives near to Bethphage. The text is laden, therefore, with all the textures encountered in the previous scene as well as those of his initial entry into the city prior to his actions in the temple in 21.1-11. The new element introduced in the opening verse (v. 18) is that Jesus is hungry (*epeinasen*). The starkness of this statement draws attention to Jesus' embodiment in a way that the same statement did in 4.2. There Jesus had been fasting forty days and nights. Here the cause of Jesus' hunger is less accessible. The reader may recall intratextually that those hungering (*peinōntes*) for *dikaiosynē*/righteousness or justice were called *makarioi* or honoured/blessed (5.6). Jesus had, the previous day, been engaged in a work of right ordering or of re-establishing justice in relation to the temple, its leaders, and the blind and the lame. As a new day begins, he carries in his body a hunger for justice or right ordering as well as his hunger for the materiality of food.

The material focus in this narrative is, as v. 18 indicates, a fig tree by the wayside, an initial layer in the ecological texture of this text or an encoding of a material element of life in first century Palestine. The material, namely the fig tree, can also function intertextually as metaphor for the good land with which Israel had been gifted (Deut. 8.7-10). When it has no figs on it as in Jer. 8.13, it likewise functions metaphorically but now as an indictment against Israel's leaders as well as against the people of Jerusalem who have turned away from G*d as in Jer. 8.1-3 (Carter 2000: 422). In this same vein, but intratextually, a tree and its fruits function symbolically in Matthew's gospel for doing what is good or what is evil (7.16-20; 12.33). Jesus' powerful word against the fig tree that causes it never to bear fruit again have traditionally been seen as a prophetic indictment against the Jewish leaders and/or the people. The fig tree's withering and dying in response to a human command continues the carnivalesque that turns the world of first century Jerusalem upside down.

The ecological reader may wish to engage critically with what seems to be wanton destruction of the fig tree by Jesus. It is necessary to read against the grain of the text and the power over the material that it encodes. That having been undertaken, the reader can turn to the symbolic layer of the text. The fig tree withers at Jesus' word, opening up the potential for new understanding, namely that it is not Israel envisaged here as withering but Rome. This returns us then to the earlier bodily experience of Jesus, namely that he was 'hungry'. The empire rich in material resources will fail to satisfy both physical hunger and also the hunger for *dikaiosynē/righteousness or justice* that characterizes the *basileia* that Jesus preaches—not a *basileia* in the sky but rather 'of the skies', pointing to its materiality worked out in the multi-dimensional lives and contexts of those who hear the gospel message.

As noted earlier in this chapter, Jesus re-enters the temple or presumably one of the courts of the temple rather than the holy of holies and there a number of different groups among the Jerusalem religious leaders contend with Jesus on a range of issues. The effect of this is a growing tension among the human characters in the unfolding narrative. The materiality encoded in the ecological texture of this unfolding text is minimal. The reader encounters vineyards (21.28, 33) within parable discourse; a reference to 'stone' and 'corner stone' (21.42, 44); the materiality and sociality of a wedding banquet with the slaughter of oxen and calves to serve human celebration (an issue which calls forth ecological engagement not possible here) together with a wedding hall and wedding robe (22.2-12). In 22.18, a coin/denarius appears in the text, evoking the politico-cultural issue of taxation. These material elements function as backdrop to the negotiation of power between Jesus and the leaders that is foregrounded in the narrative. An ecological reader will give them attention, bringing them to the foreground.

3. *Matthew 23: Devastating Diatribe*

One of the most difficult and challenging sections of the Matthean gospel for the contemporary interpreter, including the ecological reader, is Mt. 23.1-36, a devastating diatribe against the 'scribes and Pharisees' (or the Pharisees and their scribes as another way of naming them). It is particular to the religio- and socio-cultural context of the first century Matthean community in an agonistic honour and shame culture. It has, outside of this very explicit context, functioned to fuel anti-Jewish and anti-Semitic hatred. I do not propose to read this chapter in detail as it would require much more space than is available here and could become an independent study. I do wish to draw attention to some broad interpretative brush strokes because of the intimate weaving of power and conflict into the materiality and sociality encoded in the ecological texture of this text as well as to bring to the fore aspects of this text demanding a strong hermeneutics of suspicion.

Anders Runesson has argued very persuasively (2008: 95-132) that the Matthean gospel reflects serious tensions and divisions within a Pharisaic community in post-70 CE Galilee. He sees that all members of this community shared a common foundation in Pharisaism and that the Christ-believers in the group were distinguishing themselves from others in relation to leadership, sources of authority and issues of belief within Pharisaism. He suggests that '[t]he post-70 changes, both social and theological, resulted in the fierce polemic in Matthew's gospel against the Pharisees' (132), finding expression in Matthew 23.

The fierce nature of this diatribe is not only religio-historical but also influenced by the all-pervasive honor/shame culture which dominated the first century Mediterranean region. Rohrbaugh (2007: 31) says of honour that it was 'the fundamental value, the core, the heart, the soul' of 'public life in the Mediterranean world'. One manifestation of the constant challenge to honour in the male public arena relevant to Matthew 23 is the process called 'labelling'. Malina and Neyrey (1988) state that this process might be described as the 'successful identification of a person and his/her personhood with some trait or behavior' (35). They go on to say that '[t]o label a person or group negatively is a social act of retaliation for some alleged deviance' and if Runesson is correct about the context of the Matthean community, alleged deviances between the different sectors identified above were growing almost to breaking point (37). This sociality is encoded in the ecological texture of this text.

The explicit audience for Jesus' discourse is 'the crowds and his disciples' (23.1) but just prior to this narrative identification in 22.44, the Pharisees are said to be gathered in conversation with Jesus and this encounter concludes with the statement that no-one 'dared ask him any more questions' (22.46). The reader is not told of the exit of the Pharisees from the scene: Jesus' direct address to them (vv. 13-36) underlines their continuing presence.

The opening words of Jesus recognize the teaching authority of the Pharisees. Indeed, if Runesson is correct, the members of the Matthean community have been firmly grounded in Pharisaism. Jesus himself is acclaimed as fulfilling the law and the prophets (5.17). Hence the Pharisaic teaching of the law is affirmed (do whatever they teach you and follow it—23.2). It is the actions which follow from this that Jesus rails against here. Woven into the socio-cultural labelling that unfolds is the materiality not only of bodies in the crowd and their location on the platform rock on which the temple was constructed but of the material referents in the words of Jesus.

The first material element encoded in this text is 'Moses' seat' (23.2), a referent which has puzzled scholars even as to whether it is an actual seat or has merely a symbolic function (Carter 2000: 452). It may have referred to a particular seat of authority in the Matthean community's synagogue. If this is so, the material functions to authorize although the words of Jesus indicate that more is needed than such authorization. Right teachings and right actions must flow from the place or the symbol of authorization. Materiality continues to be woven into the socio-cultural labelling process unfolding in this narrative through the references to broad phylacteries and long fringes on the garments of the scribes and Pharisees (23.5) as well as seats of honour in synagogues and banquets. The material is very easily co-opted into the socio-cultural. It is necessary for the ecological reader to foreground these material elements that are backgrounded in the narrative and to recognize that ethics is always engaged with both the material as well as the socio-cultural/socio-political. Attention needs to be given to both and to the effects of their inter-relationship.

The labelling process continues more strongly when Jesus addresses the scribes and Pharisees very explicilty seven times (23.13, 15, 16, 23, 25, 27, 29) and with the exclamatory indictment: Woe! Its use in Isaiah in particular suggests that it is a prophetic denouncement (see Isa. 3.9, 11; 5.8, 11,18, 20, 21, 22 by way of example) in keeping with the socio-cultural contextuality of Matthew 23 identified above. Materiality is encoded in the denouncement, not as the object of such but in its interrelationship with those being condemned: they traverse sea and land; swear by the temple and its gold, they tithe mint and dill and cummin, and cleanse cups and plates but Jesus hurls at them the accusation that this is all hypocricy (23.28). The 'hypocrite' label is a strong one meaning 'pretender or dissembler' (BDAG 1038), and it draws on language and practice related to the ancient theatre in which actors wore a mask in order to play a character other than their own. So the scribes and Pharisees are accused of playing a role that is not in keeping with their key task of interpreting the law in relation to the daily lives of their constituents in the Matthean community. They neglect the 'weighter matters of the law: justice, mercy and faith' (23.23) that has characterized the preaching of Jesus (see in particular the beatitudes—5.3-11) for minutiae. Jesus challenges them to a valuing of the justice or right-ordering that concerns all aspects of life (a perspective that is important for contemporary ecological reading).

As the labelling gains momentum (vv. 27-36), the ecological reader will critique the use of the material such as beautiful tombs (vv. 27-29), the serpent and the viper (v. 31) as negative ciphers in that process (both here and throughout this chapter). In the same vein that readers will critique the very labelling process itself, questioning how it may have impacted members of the first century Matthean community. These included those '(non–Christ-believing) Pharisees', in the terminology of Runesson (132), whom the separatists (Christ-believing Pharisees) 'hoped would join their community now when the end of time was nearer than it was when they had first embraced a faith in Jesus of Nazareth as the risen Messiah'. We have learned more of how this segment of the Matthean gospel has impacted the Jewish people and Jewish-Christian relations down through the centuries when it has been taken out of its narrative and socio-historical contexts and interpreted as universal. An ecological reading concerned not only with the materiality but also with the sociality of the more-than-human community will critique this text of Matthew 23 profoundly and raise the question as to whether it should be named as a 'text of terror'.[8]

Before Matthew 23 concludes, there is a most extraordinary turn in the text—from the pronouncement of woes to a cry of lament—'Jerusalem, Jerusalem…how often would I have gathered your children together as a hen gathers her brood under her wings' (23.37). The image of the hen protectively gathering her young under her wings echoes with intertextuality— Ruth 2.12 and Isa. 31.5 by way of example. This earth creature provides the image of protective care and love that Jesus knows for Jerusalem, symbol here of his own people. Despite two subsequent verses, this segment of the narrative ends on a plaintive note: *kai ouk ēthelēsate*—and you did not will or desire it. The encoding of the protective hen into the ecological texture of this text exacerbates the pain of lament. Indeed, Catherine Keller says of this 'mother-hen apocalypse' that it 'does not boldly stride toward new worlds but rather laments the self-destructiveness of this world' (1994: 332-33) and in this she supplies us with an important lens through which to read the Matthean apocalyptic eschatology (Mt. 24–25).

---

8. This is the language used by Phyllis Trible (1984).

Chapter 11

MATTHEW 24–25:
PARABLE, PROCLAMATION AND END
TIME IMAGERY—AND WHAT OF EARTH?

The ecological reader of the Matthean gospel does not have to progress very far into the next section of the narrative, indeed just three short verses, to begin to encounter language of massive destruction (of the temple in v. 2) and the close of the age/the end time (v. 3). There have been brief hints of both of these thematics throughout the gospel but in Matthew 24–25 we find a concentration of language of the end (time/the universe or cosmos) and that within a genre characterized by catalysmic destruction. And hence these two chapters are identified as eschatological and/or apocalyptic discourse and that across a range of nomenclatures by scholars.[1] Keller (1994: 327) provides a clear explanation of the language of 'eschatology' and 'apocalypticism'. She says of 'eschatology' that it is 'talk about end things' and that 'apocalypse' means 'disclosure' or 'revelation'. Apocalyptic eschatology is, therefore, a particular type of discourse about the 'temporal or spatial end, edge, or horizon'.

We may well ask whether such perspectives and discourses are able to be read ecologically at a time of almost apocalyptic destruction of Earth; and if so, then how? These were the questions that troubled me as I began this reading of Matthew 24–25. In the midst of my being troubled, however, I saw the documentary film, *Salt of the Earth*, which tracks the career of the Brazilian photographer, Sebastião Soldago. Through his project of reforestation and conservation of the land of his childhood, he demonstrated that it is possible to reverse apocalyptic doom, in this instance not just the image/language but the reality of a charred and barren earth. Reading eschatology and apocalypse or apocalyptic eschatology ecologically may, indeed, make

1. Davies and Allison (1997) use the titles 'The End of the Age' (326); 'Eschatological Vigilance' (374) and 'The Judgement of the Son of Man' (416) for the three segments into which they divide Matthew 24–25. Donald Hagner (1995) names the Fifth Discourse: The Destruction of the Temple and End of the World (682). For Nolland (2005: 954), it is named 'The Shape of the Future'. And finally, for Warren Carter (2000: 466): The Final Establishment of God's Empire.

some contribution to the reversal of apocalyptic doom which faces Earth and all its constituents at this point in the unfolding of the cosmos. This can be amplified by certain readings of biblical and Matthean apocalyptic eschatology. Recognizing the strong ethical component present in Matthew 24–25 can only enhance the critical engagement with the text.

Such a reading once again calls for the twofold modes of suspicion and reconfiguration that constitute my ecological hermeneutic. I am aware that the hermeneutic of suspicion may need to characterize the initial reading of this text and its imagery more extensively than has been the case up to this point in the commentary, especially given the anthropocentric dualism that is a strong characteristic of the apocalyptic genre. Also, such a hermeneutic needs to be brought to bear on the way that theologians and biblical scholars have understood and interpreted the very genre itself as well as texts that utilize that genre. It is important, therefore, before beginning an ecological reading of the Matthean text, to give more explicit attention to an ecological way of reading apocalyptic eschatology. In the Ecological Intertextures below, I introduce the work of two key scholars who most explicitly inform this reading of Matthew 24–25 and follow that with a more extensive discussion of how their scholarship can be read intertextually in the interpretation of the Matthean text.

> **Ecological Intertexts.** The previous chapter concluded with these words of Catherine Keller in relation to the 'mother hen' imagery of 23.37: it 'does not boldly stride toward new worlds but rather laments the self-destructiveness of this world' (1994: 332-33). She shifts the focus of apocalyptic eschatology from a temporal end in some distant future to a 'now' that faces catastrophic consequences for the very materiality of Earth itself and all its more-than-human constituents. This shift of both temporal and material perspectives resonates well with Bruce Malina's 1989 'Christ and Time: Swiss or Mediterranean?' article which constructs a first century CE Mediterranean modelling of time and hence a lens for reading the Matthean eschatology. It too focuses on the present, albeit an extended or protracted present. Before turning to Matthew 24–25, however, it is necessary to expand a little how these chosen intertexts will inform this ecological reading.

Catherine Keller puts out a challenge to contemporary readers/interpreters of eschatological texts when she says that 'a responsible Christian eschatology is an ecological eschatology [which] motivates work—preaching, teaching, modelling, organizing, politics, prayer—to save our planet' (1994: 328). She goes on to say that '[t]his is not a matter of competition but of profound cooperation with the other issues of social justice—racial, economic, sexual...' (328-29). The ethics of Matthew 24–25 will, therefore, be shown to be for the *now* of the first-century Matthean community, as is the ethic that has unfolded in and through the gospel narrative, especially that of *dikaiosynē*/righteousness or justice—for the entire more-than-human Earth community (5.6, 20; 6.1). Keller extends our eschatological gaze beyond the temporal to the spatial (two aspects which have danced and played through the entire Matthean gospel and this interpretation). She points out that *eschaton*/end is not only temporal but also has a spatial reference, namely, the 'edge' (328). Eschatological discourse is that which 'takes place and takes time at the edge of wherever we as a people are' (328), or to state it in another way that can inform our interpretation of the text: '[e]schatology is discourse about the collective encounter at the edge of space and time, where and when the life of the creation has its chance at renewal—that is, it is about the present' (328). Given the distant future orientation that has generally characterized eschatology and the reading of eschatological texts along a linear time trajectory, a hermeneutics of suspicion of such futurism needs to be brought to bear initially on my own lens as interpreter but also on many prevailing interpretations (a task beyond the scope of this work).

The interpretative tool that can assist an ecological reading of the Matthean apocalyptic eschatology as focussed on the present is Bruce Malina's modelling of first-century Mediterranean time (1989). He demonstrates that it is a present-oriented model in stark contrast to our contemporary Western linear/future-oriented view. At the centre of such a present-oriented perspective is experience, although this is not the momentary experience of future-oriented linear perspectives but a present in which potentials from the past (such as becoming pregnant) are 'operationalized' in the present birth of the child. That present, that birth, is not confined to a moment in time but carries all the forthcoming potential of whatever that child shall become and do. The forthcoming potential is realized in the cyclical or processual working out of the present. Outside of such an 'extended' present is an imaginary past and future which belong to G*d and are outside human experience (see 1989 passim and diagram p. 31). They are imaged and described, however, by the prophets, both of old and in the present of the close of the first century. The Matthean story-teller/s were such prophets and Matthew 24–25 is an example of such prophetic imagining. As the time of Jesus' expected return moved to the edge of 'forthcoming potential' grounded in and linked to the present of his life and death and expected imminent return and began to spill over into the 'imaginary' of G*d's future time, the language and imagery of the end times evoked and described possibilities which circled back on the extended present. This future imaginary was not understood as a description of a future as it would unfold but rather a vision that informed the ethics to which the prophetic community was being called by the life, death and resurrection of Jesus, the awaited one. Malina's model may be better understood by the diagram below—an abbreviated form of the model that he gives at the conclusion of his article (31).

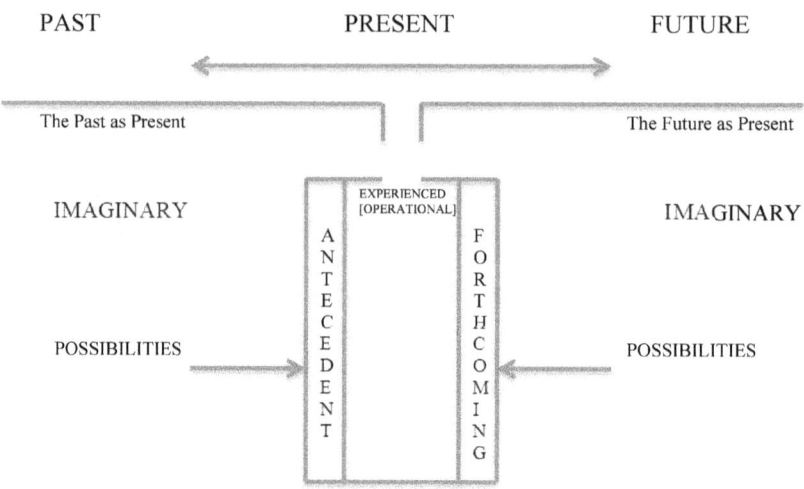

Revision of Malina (1989), 31.

The Matthean narrative continues in Matthew 24–25, grounded in the material and the temporal. Jesus and the disciples leave the temple, the context for much of what was narrated in the previous section. As they do so, they draw Jesus' attention to the built environment they have just left—the buildings constituting the temple. The Matthean community living in conflict with their Pharisaic neighbours in post-70 CE Galilee (see Runesson) write their present experience after the Roman War and its attendant destruction of the temple into the life of Jesus. The narrative takes on the dimension of apocalyptic eschatology or a 'future as present' and leads readers into the discourse to follow. It also invites the ecological reader to recognize the present destruction—of species and habitats in contemporary contexts—as symbolic of or evoking a future cataclysm environmentally and cosmologically. It too folds back onto the present with an ethical challenge to today's global population.

The ecological reader caught up into apocalyptic imagery will also be attentive to the simplicity of Jesus sitting on the Mount of Olives, sitting presumably on the ground just as he sat on the mountain in Galilee (5.1). In each instance, the ground can be seen to authorize the discourse that follows. The intimacy of this relationship of earth creature to earth is powerfully captured in the words of Keller (1994: 342): '…there is no creature [no more-than-human] that is not home to many other creatures. Inhabitant is habitat. Being at home means being a home.' Here, the ground, home to multiple creatures, authorizes the human creature Jesus and his theologizing in relation to time and place, both grounded in the extended present or that which is forthcoming out of the present (see the diagram above). The disciples' questions—'when will this be, and what will be the sign of your coming and of the end of the age?'—address the present of the Matthean community experiencing the destruction of the temple, the imminent return of Jesus, and the 'end of the age' which belongs to the imaginary future. That future is in the hands of G*d but folds back onto the now in prophetic expectation (Malina 1989: 28-31).[2]

Jesus' initial reply to the disciples' eschatological questions about *when* and *what* is highly significant—*beware that no one leads you astray* (v. 4). In this enigmatic statement, the imaginary future circles back into the present shaping contemporary *ethical* demands, demands as to the way one lives in the now. This brief statement could be seen to infuse the entire discourse: the end times are in the hands of G*d, in imaginary time, but you, the listeners/readers, are in the now, the now of ethical integrity. It is the present, the 'edge' of time and place of which Keller speaks, that is to be characterized by ethical integrity, a profound challenge in the face of ecological apocalyptic.

1. *Matthew 24.1-44: Proclaiming End Time Imagery*

As this section (24.4-8) unfolds, we hear described what has been and continues to be the fate of the entire Earth community—wars and famines and earthquakes. These eschatological images are drawn from the prophets who constitute the past imaginary enfolded into the present as well as from the actual experiences of the Matthean audience for whom war and rumours of war, famine and earthquakes were a very present reality (see Carter 2000: 470-71 for extensive examples of such intertexts). In this reading, I want to draw attention to the image that closes this section, namely the phrase 'the beginning of the birth pangs'. First, it draws powerful female imagery (see as intertexts: Isa. 13.8; 26.17-18; 66.7-8) into the foreground of this segment of the unfolding gospel narrative reminding readers of the materiality, the corporeality that infuses all the imagery. This alerts readers to the dominant maleness that characterizes the text as well as the mapping of power, both human and other-than-human. Anne Elvey (2005) has explored in depth both the experience of the pregnant woman and its symbolic resonances from an ecological perspective. Relevant to this text (Mt. 24.8), Elvey says that '[s]he (the pregnant woman) inhabits a space and time of *active waiting*, in which common distinctions between passivity and activity are called into question... [and that] discloses the analytical and ethical complexities of an inter-relational corporeality... This space of extended

---

2. Note that Mark P. Theophilos (2012: 229) makes similar connections when he says that 'the parousia of the Son of Man was seen to refer to the city's destruction through Roman intervention'.

waiting figures an expectation of an end of pregnancy in birth, characterised by certainty that pregnancy will end and uncertainty concerning precisely when it will end' (112). Such experience is not confined to the human community but extends to the world of other creatures as well.

Apart from this final image, 24.4-8 uses cataclysmic events from the more-than-human world to image the future potential and future imaginary for the Matthean community. These categories blur in the Matthean community for whom the shift from one stage (future potential) to the other (future imaginary) was still in process (1989: 28-29). This stands as a challenge to contemporary ecological readers of this text whose concept of time is linear rather than cyclical. It invites us to see the impact of present actions not on a future which we envisage as distant and separate from ourselves in the now but rather as circling back on our now—fracked earth, polluted waters and air, destruction of species and environmentally-induced human illnesses by way of example of what constitutes an ecological apocalyptic eschatology.

The next segment of the narrative (vv. 9-14) focuses on the break down of human relationships which, like the destruction of the temple, the Matthean community may well be experiencing (Runesson) and which are cast as future potential or future imaginary in this eschatological discourse. The material and the social are woven into the language of the text that echoes the warnings of human opposition. Jesus predicted such opposition for those he sent out (see 10.16-23), again linking the present with its future potential. Already in the earlier commissioning, we find parallel language to that of 24.13: 'anyone who endures to the end will be saved' (10.22). To be saved can be understood as participating in the work of Jesus and the gospel as a 'freeing [of] something into "its own presencing"', not only a freeing of humans but a freeing of Earth and all its constituents into their own presencing, their own fullness of being in the now (Rigby 2004: 431). Verse 14 suggests that such freeing/saving is constituent of the gospel of the *basileia* named almost exclusively throughout this narrative as the '*basileia* of the heavens or the skies', a new ordering, a new cosmology, a new ecology in which relationships will be rightly ordered (Pennington 2008: 28-44). This *basileia* is characterised as/by an ethic, a right ordering of relationships in the now. The end/the *telos* points toward the time when the ethic of the 'gospel of the *basileia*' has been proclaimed and lived within the *oikoumenē*—the entire inhabited earth, the world (BDAG 561). This first century text can function to draw its readers into a future imaginary that supports their ethical life but it can also circle back from its future potentiality to inform a profound ecological ethic for their now.[3]

---

3. There are other aspects of this segment of the text that could be explored ecologically but that will need to be part of a future project.

It is becoming clear and will become more so as our analysis progresses that these two chapters of the Matthean gospel share characteristics of what David Sim calls 'an apocalyptic-eschatological perspective' (1996: 28). These seem to intensify as we move into the next section of the discourse (24.15-28) although the Matthean eschatology still remains profoundly grounded in the material and the social rather than esoteric language of the future and hence can be read critically and ecologically. As we have already seen earlier, the Matthean story-tellers weave into the future imaginary of the return of the Human One (24.27) what has just been experienced in and through the Roman War and what can be expected in their occupied land. It has been and will be experienced 'on the ground' so to speak, in and through the materiality of social and Earth-bound bodies. It echoes into the now of contemporary readers.

The 'desolating sacrilege standing in the holy place' draws the Danielic references (8.9-14; 9.27; 11.31 and 12.11) into the text's socio-cultural intertextuality (a past imaginary now and in the first century CE). These texts encode allusions to the altar to Olympian Zeus that Antiochus IV set up in the Jerusalem temple in 168–167 BCE (see Carter 2000: 473). Similarly they encode Titus' desecration of the Jerusalem temple in 70 CE and his soldiers' sacrificing before their standards that bore the eagle, symbol of the Empire. Political power as power over is inscribed into this brief reference. Profoundly linked with this is the desecration of what is holy, what is religious, among the conquered peoples. It cannot but call to mind the devastation of lands, of species, of peoples, of Earth itself in the name of or for the protection of religious beliefs, religious practices in today's world, the now of these eschatological texts. The reference to the 'suffering of those days' (v. 29) indicates that v. 28 has closed off this section.

As one reads on in 24.15-28, the immediacy of the Matthean community's experience of the Roman war projected into the future imaginary is almost palpable. In the flight into the mountains with no time to turn back even for a coat, the suffering of pregnant and nursing women, the winter when flight is most difficult find echoes in Sean Freyne's account of 'Galilee under the Romans' in the latter years of the 60s CE (1980: 78-89). We also find in this text a mirror for what is happening in contemporary Syria and Iraq. While the suffering evoked is predominantly that of the human community, the ecological reader will be attentive to the impact of military campaigns upon the land itself, its animal and plant species, its waterways. The 'great suffering such as has not been from the beginning of the world until now' (v. 21) evokes countless situations on planet Earth today of the suffering of the entire more-than-human community. The apocalyptic vision of the days of suffering needing to be cut short (vv. 21-22) impacts our now when the immediacy of the threat of climate change and an ethical response to it cries out to the entire Earth-community. This challenges the human community for an urgent response, a cutting short of the days of inaction so that not just the 'elect' but the entire planet and all its constituents might be saved.

Messianic claims abounded in pre- and post-70 Galilee (see Horsley and Hanson 1985: 118-23) with many seeing their engagement in the war against Rome as 'ultimately part of God's eschatological holy war against oppression' (123). So too in the current struggle for the health and future of Earth itself, there must be careful discernment as to where wisdom is to be found. Indeed the materiality woven into the image in v. 28, namely that where there are vultures there is death, suggests that an attentive reading of Earth's own wisdom will show the way forward to what is life-giving as well as what is death-dealing.

It is not only Earth but the cosmos which is drawn into the Matthean apocalyptic eschatology (vv. 29-31). This was so not only in the first century but also in earlier Jewish prophetic imagining of the future (Carter 2000: 477). In the future imaginary of v. 29, the cosmos itself will be undone: the sun darkened, the moon not giving its light and stars falling from the heavens. For the ecological reader this is not futuristic, but a recognition that the reach of the human with emissions pollution, debris from space probes together with data tracking sattelites and many more phenomena is impacting almost apocalyptically on the cosmos. On the other hand, contemporary scientific cosmology has provided inhabitants of the twenty-first century with a much more complex understanding of the universe. Scientists propose an initiating 'big bang' fourteen billion years ago, the emergence of an infinite number of galaxies of stars and later planets, a long history of the emergence of planet Earth within the Milky Way galaxy around 4.6 billion years ago with life on that planet developing 3.5 billion years ago, *homo erectus* appearing about 2 million years ago, and modern humans only 200,000 years ago.[4] The Matthean apocalyptic cosmology turned readers back to their extended present. Likewise, the new cosmology together with an urgent attentiveness to the danger the human community poses to our emerging planet Earth, can turn contemporary readers to Earth and to ethical ways of living on this fragile planet. Its future is unknown ('no one knows'—Mt. 24.36). This is in the realm of a future imaginary.

It is the turning of the future imaginary back into the present that prepares for what readers find in 24.32. They are invited to learn from a most significant earth element, the fig tree, the 'last of the fruit trees to produce leaves' (Musselman 2012: 57). Its leaves are a sign of summer being near, as the texts suggests (v. 32). Earth will provide the signs of the seasons to those

---

4. Edwards (2010: 2-4) summarizes data which has been compiled by scientists over more than a century. See also Primack and Abrams (2006) and Abrams and Primack (2011) for accessible insight into this new cosmology for the non-specialist.

who are attentive. There are, however, times in the future imaginary that are known only to G*d (both in the 'then' of the first century and the 'now' of the twenty-first). This Matthean imaginary that has been developing in the apocalyptic/eschatological discourse turns the listener back into the present with a strong ethical call that will characterize the remainder of the discourse. It is the call: 'keep awake', keep awake in the now, in the present. The ecological readers faced with the profound challenges of Earth's future can be assured that we have to live a radical ecological ethic for the sake of the planet now. The Matthean community did not know the time of the end. Neither do we know the time, even though we, like them, live in a moment of apocalyptic exigency profoundly material and profoundly social.

2. *Matthew 24.45–25.46: Parabling End Time Imagery*

As this Matthean discourse continues, there is a range of images from the social world encoded in the text to emphasize the key message: 'stay awake', not just physically but ethically. Staying awake is the ethical response to the apocalyptic eschatology—it has all the 'now' features that Keller has already emphasized. Another element of the remaining discourse is its focus on time, not a future potential time or future imaginary time but the now of socio-cultural human relationships and interactions, indeed an ethic for the now, for the contemporary 'edge' we occupy in this present moment.

The first image is that of a house being burgled and of the householder claiming that he would have stayed awake had he known the hour intended for the crime (24.43-44). The image offers a challenge into the ethical lives of the listeners: you also must be ready, must be living the ethic of the *basileia*. This is followed by a question about the identity of the 'faithful and wise slave?' (24.45) and a parabolic playing out of two different scenarios. As noted in the analysis of Matthew 13, it is important to critique the social system embedded in this ethical exhortation. It affirms the structure of master/slave, simply using this structure as well as slave performance within such a structure to teach an ethic of staying awake, of living ethically within the time that remains. The power differential in this text is significant. For the ecological critic, the excessive punishment of the second slave is evident: cutting him in pieces, putting him with the hypocrites (reminding readers/listeners of the diatribe against the scribes and Pharisees in the previous chapter), where there is weeping and gnashing of teeth. This last phrase—weeping and gnashing of teeth—is used repeatedly throughout Matthew's gospel to categorize the fate of those who do not comply with the ethic of the *basileia*. In this instance, it is specifically directed to those not living the ethic informed by the community's eschatology. This dualism needs more extensive critique, but this too belongs to a future undertaking.

Together with a reading against the grain of the hierarchical slave system encoded in the ecological texture of this text, the ecological reader will be attentive to the material and social relationships woven into this imaginative text: food and work in particular. It is the right ordering of these and the critique of any unjust material and social inter-relationships that point to the ecological ethic in the face of end-time potentialities: be attentive to, be ethical in the 'now'.

It is such an ethic that is played out in the three parabolic narratives that conclude this apocalyptic eschatological discourse (Matthew 24–25). We find the materiality and sociality of the more-than-human community encoded in the ecological texture of these texts. These include bridesmaids and bridegroom, a master and his slaves and the hungry, thirsty, naked and imprisoned ones who are intimately connected to lamps and oil, coins and places of human suffering. All of these are being storied to speak to the Matthean and contemporary readers about time/the now and about ethics or conduct in this time.

There is a tendency in interpretations of parables generally to seek a 'meaning' for all the details. Carter (2000: 486), for instance, asks what the lamp oil represents and concludes that it seems to be 'a generic reference to faithful and obedient discipleship as defined by the whole gospel'. The ecological reader would do well to avoid such allegorizing of the parable, however subtly it is done, and to let the materiality and sociality play in the text as it creates a scenario. Readers are drawn into and invited to be attentive to the sociality of a wedding with all its expectations, its future potential that links the now to the future. The lamps, and oil for lamps should the waiting be delayed embed readers/listeners into the intimate relationships between the social and the material and the exigencies of time that are woven into this imagined or parabled scenario. The final imperative captures the impact of the parable: stay awake, be watchful, be in constant readiness, be on the alert (BDAG 208). It calls the Matthean listeners to be attentive to their narrative and to their now with all its ethical demands. It turns the ecological reader to the urgency of living an ecological ethic in this now because it is from this moment that the future potential is seeded.

The next story begins 'for it is just like …' (BDAG 1106), continuing to parable the 'present' of Matthean eschatology, the ethical now. At the outset, the contemporary ecological reader would bring a hermeneutics of suspicion to the social structure of master and slave encoded in this text. The master has sole authority over his possessions named as *tous idious/ that which belongs to an individual* such as house, land, animals (BDAG 466) and also *his* human workers. He is able to dispose of all these as he chooses. This was a prevailing social structure in the first century and is rarely critiqued in the gospel text. Rather, it tends to be seen by scholars as functioning parabolically without their taking account of the effects of the social hierarchy in shaping readers' perspectives. I draw into this reading Richard Rohrbaugh's engagement with this text under the title 'A Peasant Reading of the Parable of the Talents/Pounds: A Text of Terror?' (2007: 109-23), addressing the fact that this parable seems to run contrary to the tenor of the unfolding discourse.

Rohrbaugh has, through his analysis of prevailing first century cultural codes of 'limited good' and 'use value and exchange value' demonstrated the materiality and sociality encoded in this text. Briefly (see 110-16), first century Mediterranean culture was informed by a belief that all elements in the social, economic and natural universes were limited. Should one person gain more then there was less for another. At the same time, one's 'goods' were for use and not for exchange, not for active accumulation to the disadvantage of another. The scenario of a wealthy slave owner encodes into the fabric of the parable the socio-economic and political structures within which most first-century peasants lived. It also evokes the hierarchy not only of power but also of 'goods' that functioned in such a society. The challenge confronting the reader is that the parable approves such structures.

The key character is a man, indicative of the patriarchal society, who is about to journey from his home and who wants 'what he possesses'/ *hypachonta* to be in safe hands. His slaves to whom he entrusts his 'possessions' also belong in that category of possessions in a socio-political structure that needs to be critiqued rather than parabled. As the parable unfolds, however, the man distributes coinage or 'talents'. The value of talents 'differed considerably in various times and places, but was always comparatively high; it varied also with the metal involved, which might be gold, silver, or copper' (BDAG 988). What is distributed, therefore, is of significant value. The first two recipients, on receiving their portions, enter into exchange mode, trading the money they have received for more, regardless of the limited goods culture. The slave owner rewards them, thus undermining the strong cultural norm of use rather than exchange. One wonders if this norm was under threat or negotiation in the Galilee of the end of the first century characterized by wealthy and often absentee landholders.

The slave who received one talent seeks to protect the master's money. Rohrbaugh says this is 'exactly what, in the peasant view, an honorable person should do' (117). He also cites Josephus reporting that 'if a depositary loses any portion of a deposit, he must face a tribunal of seven judges, swearing that he has neither used a portion of it nor has lost it through malice or intent' (117 see *Ant.* 4.285-87). The actions of the third slave are informed by what is, no doubt, an accurate assessment of his master and by the socio-political structure of mastery encoded in this text. He knows him to be *sklēros* which translates as 'hard, strict, harsh, cruel, merciless' (BDAG 930). The slave has ensured that the talent is safe and can now return it to his master. He does not use and abuse to accumulate as does the master (v. 24) but is attentive to the socio-cultural web that considers the needs of all.

The behaviour of the third slave is not behaviour that the parable approves. The householder takes the talent from the one with the least (one talent) and gives it to the one with the most (ten). Such action cries out to the ecological reader of further injustice, amplified by reference to the casting out of this slave into outer darkness 'where there is weeping and gnashing of teeth' (see Reid 2004 for a critical analysis of this violent language). Surprisingly, it is this which the Matthean text says is the 'as if' (v. 14) of the *basileia* of the heavens. How can this be? This text cries out for a hermeneutic of suspicion that unmasks the violence that is affirmed and refuses an identification of the slave master with the *basileia*. The appropriate response to such a 'text of terror' is—never again![5]

The Matthean apocalyptic eschatological discourse concludes with a very well known parabolic image of the 'end', namely the identification and separation of the ethical and the unethical or righteous and unrighteous (vv. 45-46), imaged as sheep and goats (25.32). This time of final separation is projected as 'the end' when the Human One/Jesus comes 'in his glory'. Of all the future imaginings contained in eschatological discourse, this one demonstrates most strongly that those imaginings are intended to circle back into the ethical now. Those who address the most material of needs of others, seemingly others in the human community are called blessed.[6] They are those who give food to the hungry, who give something to drink to the thirsty, who welcome the stranger, give clothing to the naked, care for the sick and visit the imprisoned. They re-order or order in right relationship (*dikaiosynē* or righteousness/justice) not just the human but the other-than-human and the interrelationship of the two. This is the most explicit, the most material of Jesus' ethical teaching—as you do this re-ordering of relationships both material and social, among 'the least'/ lowest in status (BDAG 315), you are doing it to me/*emoi*. When you do not do this re-ordering of relationships among the least, you are not doing it to me/*emoi*.

This is an ethic for the *now* of the Matthean community and for the *now* of communities today. It is an ethic that can catch up the human and

---

5. It is on this note that Phyllis Trible in her book entitled *Texts of Terror* ends her analysis of the extravagant violence against the woman of Bethlehem in Judges 19 and its importance for contemporary biblical interpretation. Never again can unjust patriarchal socio-political and economic structures and practices be used as images for the divine or for Jesus the awaited one in the now.

6. This is not the *makarios* of the beatitudes but just as that text (5.1-12) opens Jesus' teaching, this text closes it.

other-than-human in a re-ordering of right relationships. If such an ethic, such a right ordering, were to be undertaken by today's human communities in their relationships with all in the other-than-human communities around planet Earth, this would truly manifest the *basileia* of the heavens.

Chapter 12

Matthew 26–28:
Life and Death and Life Intertwined—An Earth Process

The opening words of Matthew 26, 'when Jesus had finished *all* of these sayings', refer not just to the previous discourse but to all the teachings in the five discourses of the Matthean gospel which conclude with a similar phrase (7.28, 11.1, 13.53; 19.1 and 26.1). Here, however, there is a re-turn to narrative, a narrative that differs somewhat from other narrative sections in the unfolding plot of the gospel. In the final three chapters of the Gospel of Matthew, *time* seems to be constantly in the foreground of the narrative as in 26.2 with its reference to the Passover occurring 'after two days'. On the other hand, time seems to slow down across the events of Jesus' final days. *Place* is also made very explicit. *Bodies* in their materiality, and one human body in particular, negotiate the time and the space/s woven into the text.

Such a description of Matthew 26–28 might suggest to the ecological reader that the gospel closes on a profoundly anthropocentric note or even trumpet blast. The reader has seen, however, as this commentary has unfolded, the potential for a reading beyond anthropocentrism. This has been achieved through attention to the materiality of human and other-than-human bodies as well as to their intimate interrelationship and functioning in the sociality of the broad more-than-human matrix of relationships. It may also be significant for this reading that *cosmos* (26.13) and a cosmic temporal marker (the *end of the age*—28.20) frame the entire concluding narrative of this gospel text. As has characterized the ecological reading of previous sections, engagement with significant contemporary intertexts will enable such a reading.

> **Ecological Intertexts.** There are three scholars or groups of scholars with whom I engage explicitly in this reading of the death/resurrection of Jesus ecologically, while the voices of others will be heard in the background as the chapter unfolds.
>
> The emphasis in the Matthean narrative on the *materiality of the body of Jesus* in these three concluding chapters and its intimate interweaving within a complex sociality turned my attention again to the work of Owain Jones and Paul Cloke who explore 'relational materiality'. While their focus is on materiality, they recognize that it has a 'social aspect

> [which] is thoroughly dependent on the life–making capacities of a whole range of natural processes which are articulated through various forms, flows and exchanges of energy and matter/materiality' (2008: 79). They use the phrase 'entanglements of flows, forces and materials' (86) to characterise agency within materiality associating it with 'temporal processes where all manner of trajectories—of people, non-humans, economies, technologies, ideas and more—come, are brought or are thrown together to assemble enduring, but also changing, formations which settle out into distinctive patterns of places, yet which are still fully networked into the wider world' (86-87).
>
> Earlier in the commentary, we encountered Jennifer Glancy's recognition that 'through bodies and embodied exchanges...cultural complexity takes place' (2010: 362), a cultural complexity that can be seen to encode a sociality that is attentive to 'entanglements of flows, forces and materials' as recognized by Jones and Cloke.
>
> The third intertext informing this reading of Mt. 26–28 will be Manuel Villalobos Mendoza's *Abject Bodies in the Gospel of Mark*. Mendoza turns our attention to 'the abject body' of Jesus. Drawing on the work of Julia Kristeva, he recognizes the abject as that which 'disturbs identity, system, order ... [and] does not respect borders, positions, rules'. The Jesus of Matthew's gospel is the one who has not only preached and taught but who also healed (4.23; 9.35), who dealt with human bodies bringing them from the margins to the centre of a new community (Matthew 8–9). Bodies healed, flesh in its materiality restored, bread broken and shared (Mt. 14.13-21; 15.32-39), crowds gathering around the agency of the human/of the material—all these point to the abject, to the disturbing of the system, the crossing of boundaries that ought not be crossed. This reaches a climax, Mendoza suggests, 'when Jesus identifies his own body with the broken bread' (Mendoza 2012: 96).

As in other sections of this commentary, it will not be possible to engage with the entire narrative of Matthew 26–28 in detail. Appropriate sections will be chosen while others can be taken up by readers beyond this work.

1. *Matthew 26.6-13: She Pours out Healing Ointment*

As the final narrative opens, readers encounter the materiality of the body of Jesus (and of others), a body embroiled in an 'entanglement of flows, forces and materials' as the narrator refers to the projected handing over of Jesus to be crucified (26.2)—a grotesque dealing with the human body of those considered deviant by Rome's political system. The reader also encounters the first of many locations in time: two days before the Passover. Such entanglement continues into vv. 3-4 in which the 'chief priests and elders' gather in the courtyard or the building complex of Caiphas from which or within which he conducted his public religious and political affairs (BDAG 150). This is a material space which is entangled in sociality as the gathered 'chief priests and elders of the people' conspire to arrest Jesus and to kill him—to annihilate him, to deal with his body violently.

Matthew 26.6-13 provides an alternative dealing with the body of Jesus: a woman pours *myron*, a costly ointment, over the head of Jesus (v. 7) and Jesus interprets this pouring of *myron* over his body as a preparing of him/ of his body for burial (v. 12). The woman is unnamed (simply *hē gynē*) but she enters the story with what Sandoval (2000: 73.4) calls her own 'racial-, sexual-, national-, or gender unique forms of social power', as do Jesus, Simon and the disciples (v. 8). She enters what is a liminal space, a time-space in which Jesus' body, his very life, hangs in the balance. And she comes with and in relation to a material element that in some ways dominates the narrative, an alabaster jar of very expensive perfume/*myron* (v. 7). Furthermore, she does not simply come. She also acts, pouring ointment from the alabaster jar over the head of the reclining Jesus.

In the inner texture of the text, the woman, the *myron* and the reclining Jesus are woven into a dynamic movement at the centre of which is the alabaster jar of *myron*. It is an entanglement of materiality and sociality, of 'flows, forces and materials': the *myron* with all its dynamics for soothing and healing, the bodies of the unnamed woman and of Jesus with their powers to give and receive, and the sociality that they and the *myron* are caught up in and for which the house provides a place or space.[1]

The most significant source of intertextuality functioning in this narrative is the *Deipnosophistae* of Athenaeus. Chapter 15 of that text is devoted entirely to *myron*, the perfumed ointment similar to what the woman brings into the house of Simon the Leper where Jesus is reclining. According to Athenaeus, at the beginning of the symposium (learned conversation) that follows the *deipnon* or supper, slaves 'passed round perfumes/*myra* in alabaster bottles/*alabastois*' (xv. 686). Elsewhere, I have explored the materiality of the *alabastros*, drawing into the text the 'stalagmitic deposits from which this transluscent marble called *alabastros* was obtained and going on to point out that '(i)t was often used for decorative vases to hold perfumes or perfumed oils because it was believed to preserve them' (Wainwright 2008: 134). The intertextuality associated with *myron* is vast and cannot be explored in detail here. Suffice it to note that the pouring of ointment over the head does not appear extensively in the *Deipnosophistae* but in xv.687, Athenaeus cites classical texts to provide meaning: '[t]o these words of Cynulcus, Masurius replied: Good heavens, man, you don't know that the sensations of our brain are soothed by sweet odours and cured (*therapeuontai*) besides, even as Alexis says in *Love-lorn Lass*: A highly important element of health is to put good odours to the brain' (or *head* we might add).

This intertextuality engages the sociality surrounding the very material element, *myron*, and the entanglement of material substance and the

---

1. I acknowledge here my article (Wainwright 2015a) which has significantly informed this interpretation.

corporeality of human bodies. *Myron* refers to a range of perfumes and oils, as the *Deipnosophistae* makes evident. Its varieties are listed in xv.688 under the heading that '[c]ertain places produce the best perfumes' but the entanglements of materiality and sociality become more evident when Athenaeus says that 'the excellence of the perfume is due in each case to those who furnish the materials, the material itself, and the manufacturers, rather than the localities' (xv.688).

An ecological reading of this text can be extended if we bring Jones and Cloke and their 'entanglements of flows, forces and materials' to v. 7. The exploration of the inner and inter-texuality of the text has demonstrated that it evokes 'temporal processes' in and through which *alabastron* and *myron* are processed from Earth elements into gifts given to the human community. They are intimately connected to Jesus who faces death and to an unknown woman who brings the gift of *perfumed ointment* to pour over his head. Both the materiality, which has been made more visible in the discussion above, as well as the sociality of the more-than-human constitute the ecological texture of this Matthean text. The *myron* is rich in history and potentiality and its being poured over the head of Jesus is an act of healing and comforting drawing Jesus, the *myron* and the woman into the rich sociality that the text constructs at this crucial moment in the unfolding story beyond numerous confines, including that of gender. Of such an intimate interrelationship Malafouris (2008: 22) says, as cited earlier:

> [i]f human agency *is* then material agency *is*, there is no way that human and material agency can be disentangled. Or else, *while agency and intentionality may not be properties of things, they are not properties of humans either: they are the properties of material engagement, that is, of the grey zone where brain, body and culture conflate* (emphasis is that of the author).

The next verses (8-9) break onto what we have learnt from Sandoval (2000: 76) as the 'flat grid-like terrain' of inter-relationships. It is this that has characterized v. 7. Those named 'disciples' indignantly refer to the outpouring of *myron* as *apōleia*—waste or destruction. They have failed to recognize the poignancy of this time despite Jesus having alerted them to it just prior to his entry into the house of Simon: the Human One will be delivered up to be crucified (26.2). It is as if they have not heard the words nor understood the actions of the woman nor recognized the healing effect of the *myron*. They have not allowed themselves to be drawn into the web of relationships, the sociality that links human bodies and other-than-human healing ointment. Rather, they interpret the action of the woman as a waste, placing themselves outside the gift event which has taken place. The *myron* is interpreted as a commodity and they question why it was not used in a commodity exchange process—sold for a large sum which in turn could be given to the 'poor'/*ptōchois*. There is no specificity of persons in this group called 'the poor' nor is there any indication of human relationship with them on the part of the disciples that could make this exchange a gift event such as that described in v. 7. This is made abundantly clear in light of Anne Primavesi's discussion of what she calls 'gift event':

> [t]hese interactive relationships between giver and receiver, between giver and gift and between gift and receiver link them openly, materially, sensually, with the link made tangible (usually) in some object passed by one to the other, chosen by one for the other and received by one from the other. They are also (usually) linked privately and/or publicly in and across individual boundaries, through bodily, familial, political, emotional, sexual or economic relationships or contractual bonds (Primavesi 2000: 154-61, in particular 156).

It is important to nuance this indignant objection of the disciples so as not to lock their response into a dualistic meaning-making process. In a previous interpretation of their question, I noted that it could function repetitively and radically in the contemporary ecological crisis. They [the disciples] draw attention to the potential for excess in a gift event, to what may seem to be the squandering of Earth's resources by some so that others are rendered poor, so that they become the scapegoats whose lives are given up for the many who live beyond their means (Wainwright 2008: 138). As indicated above, however, this is not the foregrounded emphasis in this interpretation which seeks to honour Earth's more-than-human ones in an intimate exchange.[2] The ecological reader will, however, not allow the disciples' radical question to be backgrounded as it needs to echo, as a warning, through all gift exchanges in our current context.

Verse 12 re-turns the reader to the impending death of Jesus and the violent dealing with his body. The words of Jesus re-emphasize the materiality and corporeality of the gift exchange of v. 7, claiming that the pouring out of healing ointment/*myron* upon his body/his *sōma* is a preparation for his burial, with *sōma* here evoking the dead body or corpse (BDAG 983).[3] The *myron* again evokes the 'entanglements of flows, forces and materials' continuing to be encoded in the text in its materiality. This is linked to and links inextricably the woman and Jesus in the house of Simon with the disciples present and challenged by Jesus' interpretative words. An ecological reading of this text demonstrates the diverse agencies that constitute this scene.

---

2. I have previously drawn attention to the phrase *eis eme*/to me which Jesus uses to describe the woman's actions in v. 10 echoing his last great parable: what is done to the least, to those hungering, thirsting, a stranger, naked and in prison, is done *emoi*/to me. See Wainwright (2015: 216) and the final paragraphs of the previous chapter.

3. See the article of McDuffie (2012) who explores understandings of birth, death and burial from an ecological perspective—our giving back to the Earth in the cycle of nurturing.

Verse 13 concludes this short but highly significant narrative (26.6-13). It continues to foreground the woman and her action focussing readers/listeners on the entanglement of flows, forces and materials (including human bodies) with and in which she has engaged. This is placed at the heart of the 'good news' that is to be proclaimed *en holō tō kosmō* (in the whole cosmos), the entire planetary realm for contemporary readers.

The Matthean story-teller does not place Jesus at the centre of this story and its remembering. Rather he affirms the extraordinary interconnectedness within the story's interaction that collectively constitutes 'good news'. It far transcends a single human action or person. It echoes in and through the person of the woman, the materiality of her *myron*, her extraordinary action and in the body of Jesus. The ecological reader remembers the woman precisely in relation to the complex materiality and sociality present and enacted in the house of Simon. Thus, to remember the woman (and the poured out *myron*) in this way is to read ecologically. It is to *proclaim the good news* 'in'/across planet Earth. BDAG (56) gives one meaning of *kosmos* as 'planet earth...place of inhabitation, the world'). Jesus proclaims, however, that it will have a powerful ethical effect 'in' the *kosmos* (the 'sum total of everything...the universe' [BDAG 561]). While the first century Matthean readers/listeners would not have understood the word *kosmos* and the meanings given to it as we do today, both meanings can echo through the text and through our contemporary reading of it.

2. *Matthew 26.17-30: The Second Supper*

The text shifts focus or foregrounding from materiality to sociality as it turns from the action of a woman pouring out healing ointment on the body of Jesus to Judas Iscariot, one of the twelve, negotiating with the chief priests how he might betray Jesus to them (26.14-16). The opening words of Mt. 26.14, 'one of the twelve', and the unfolding of Judas' negotiations with the chief priests who are already plotting to kill Jesus, to annihilate his body (26.3-4), alert readers to the *abject* nature of what the narrative calls 'betrayal' (vv. 15 and 16). As cited above, Mendoza draws on the words of Julia Kristeva to grasp the abject, that which '"does not respect borders, positions, rules"' (Mendoza 2012: 94). Indeed, this entire narrative of the betrayal, the death and burial of Jesus can be characterized as abject.[4] This is conveyed in the repeated use of the verb *paradidōmi*/hand over or betray: indeed, fifteen times between 26.2, when Jesus foreshadows his body being

---

4. Brown (1994: 211), says that '… because Jesus was given over (nay, betrayed) to his judges by his trusted friend and because Jesus was innocent, there is a stigma of guilt in the human chain of those who gave Jesus over: Judas…; the chief priests…(and) Pilate.'

'delivered up to be crucified', and 27.36 when Pilate hands him/his body over to be crucified (26.2, 15, 16, 21, 23, 24, 25, 45, 46, 48; 27.2, 3, 4, 18, 26). The materiality and sociality associated in the narrative with the abject body of Jesus can evoke for the ecological reader all that *disturbs* among all that is more-than-human.

The narrative turns in v. 17 to the beginning of the feast of Unleavened Bread and to the second 'last supper' where once again the body but now that body together with the bodily fluid, blood, command the reader's attention (26.26-28).[5] The Matthean second supper is grounded in time ('when it was evening'–26.20) and in the sociality encoded in the text, ('[w]hile they were eating' 26.26). The words of this verse unfold slowly. Jesus' action of taking a loaf of bread, blessing, breaking and giving it echo back into his ministry when, on two occasions, he took loaves, blessed, broke and gave (14.19; 15.36). Bread is material that is shared in community, bread shapes community: this community on the margins, this abject community. The disciples gathered around Jesus for this meal have been implicated in the sharing of bread on these two previous occasions just as Jesus' life has been implicated in the lives of others: the blind receive their sight, the lame walk, lepers are cleansed and the deaf hear, the dead are raised up and the poor have good new preached to them (Mt. 11.5). Jesus has in the words of Kristeva as noted above: '"disturb[ed]... order..."'.

This culminates in Jesus' taking of bread (simply *arton* in the Greek) the most foundational of material elements linking the other-than-human and human communities and identifying it with his body—take, eat, this is my body. This body is going to be made most abject, dealt with violently by a state system established on violence. Carlos Bravo imagines Jesus saying:

> What is happening to the bread [as it is eaten] is going to happen to me. I will be both broken and given in order to give life ... Like this bread, I have never sought anything for myself. I have only sought to give life... I am this: bread that is broken and shared. I am this bread.[6]

The lines, the boundaries that we establish between the human and the other-than human are broken down. As Jesus suffers violence and abjection in his body so too the bread suffers violence, the other-than-human and the human are intimately related so that they are one—I am this bread.

Poured out wine that Jesus identifies with his blood reiterates the shaping of an abject community—I am this blood. As noted above, however, this

---

5. For some time now I have drawn attention to the two last suppers that Jesus attends. I note here that Mendoza (96) also makes reference to 'his last two meals, at Bethany and Jerusalem'.

6. Carlos Bravo, *Jesús, hombre en conflict: El relato de Marcos en América Latina* (Mexico: Centro de Reflexion Teológica, 1986), cited and translated in Mendoza, *Abject Bodies* (100).

community is not only constituted by humans on the margins as a result of war and displacement, hunger, and sickness of all kinds. Bread broken and wine poured out, materials symbolizing the 'radically inclusive companionship' that Jesus' ministry sought to establish, must include the entire materiality and sociality of the more-than-human community and cosmos. Earth is being raped by logging, by fracking, by deep sea drilling and myriads of processes too numerous to mention. So many species are sharing the same fate as Jesus, their bodies annihilated by a rapacious human empire like that of Rome. And the cosmos is being polluted by human interventions and inventions. Judith Butler asserts that: 'it is through the body that notions of gender, sexuality, race and ethnicity become exposed to others, implicated in the social process' (cited in Mendoza: 105). If Butler is right, the ecological reader can extend this, recognizing that it is through the body of all more-than-humans that we are also engaged in the material processes, the 'flows, forces and materials' that constitute the planet Earth and the cosmos of which it is a part.

Woven into the narrative of the supper (and what follows immediately) is the thread of betrayal or handing over, as noted above. Closely associated with this is the denial and abandonment of Jesus by his closest companions. Such a shattering of identity, a crossing of borders emphasizes the abject nature of this final narrative. It evokes for the ecological reader the shattering of identities and betrayal of boundaries in today's more-than-human world where not only human bodies but so many other-than-human bodies are rendered abject.

It is not possible to follow this thread in detail but attention to some key words and phrases convey the pathos woven into these betrayals and abandonments. In 26.24, the betrayer dips his hand into the same bowl of water with Jesus. The intimacy and the irony of this action collide in the water, the most foundational element of human and animal bodies and of the universe itself. The betrayer tears at the very fabric of human and other-than-human relationships just as the betrayal tears at the body of Jesus. This is evident in his poignant words at the end of the second supper: you will all become deserters…you will deny me (26.31 and 31-35).

3. *Matthew 26.31–27.5: Betraying, Denying/Deserting and Denying*

Jesus is not deserted by the other-than-human as he courageously faces his own death. A place (a piece of land or a field—BDAG 1095) called Gethsemane on the Mount of Olives (v. 30) receives Jesus and his disciples. This mount, on the eastern side of the Temple 'is composed of cretaceous limestone with a chalklike top layer and was named "Olives" because of its extensive olive groves. The olive tree, one of the hardier trees, was able to thrive in this terrain' (Heard 1992: V, 13). It is this earth, weather-worn and hardy which receives the body of Jesus (v. 39) as he casts himself down to pray. Indeed, in v. 39, habitat, human, and holy meet as they do in vv. 43 and 44 as Jesus prays the prayer he had taught others to pray—Father, your will/*thelēma* be done (6.10)—from a heart/spirit that is 'deeply grieved and agitated'. Through this poignant moment, the disciples sleep nearby on the same ground contributing further to the abjection of Jesus and of the discipleship community he has established. Both material and social fabric are being rent as the narrative unfolds.

The poignancy continues into the next scene in Gethsemane. Further tension is created in the social texture or sociality woven into this text as Judas is named once again as 'one of the twelv' but arrives with a large crowd from the chief priests and elders to hand Jesus over (26.47). He reaches toward Jesus and kisses him, flesh meeting flesh, body meeting body but in the ultimate act of betrayal, a betrayal that is profoundly material and profoundly social. The whirl of 'flows, forces and materials' is strong here continuing to tear, it would seem, at the fabric of the text and evoking further the abject. All this is captured perhaps in its closing verse that carries threads of the inseparable materiality and sociality: 'then all the disciples deserted him and fled' (v. 56).

Jesus is now left completely alone in a hostile environment. Materiality and sociality continue to be woven together in the fabric of the text and are written on the body of Jesus. The writers are a conglomerate group: Caiaphas the high priest, scribes and elders, chief priests and council, and false witnesses, with Peter following at a distance (vv. 57-60). Jesus remains silent before their false witness. He cannot, however, remain silent before the truth of the claim that he is the *Christos*, the 'child of divinity'. It is for this that he is pronounced deserving of death (v. 67). Before turning to the narrative unfolding of this sentence written on the body of Jesus, we pause to consider the final unravelling of two threads of betrayal of Jesus by his own disciples.

While Jesus has been alone in the mock trial before a diverse group of accusers, Peter has been in the courtyard of the high priest among the guards, not in solidarity with Jesus, but 'to see how this would end' (26.58). In vv. 69-75, two young women recognize him as having been with Jesus and this is picked up by some by-standers. To each he replies with growing vehemence—*ouk oida*/I do not know… (26.70, 72, 74). The cock crowing, the voice of the Earth creature, reminds Peter of Jesus' earlier prediction that he would deny three times. The words of human participants in designated space and the voice of the other-than-human cock shatter Peter's awareness—he goes out and weeps bitterly, responding in his body (26.71). Just three verses further in the story, Judas comes to a similar realization of the depth of his betrayal of Jesus. In the Matthean narrative, he cannot forgive himself nor believe himself forgiven—he goes out and hangs himself (27.5).

4. *Matthew 26.57-68; 27.6–66: Abjecting the Body of Jesus*

The narrative of the abjection of the body of Jesus begins to crescendo following the proclamation by the conglomerate group in the house of Caiaphas that Jesus deserves death (26.66). Betrayal, denial and false accusations are replaced by physical violence and mockery, beginning in 26.67. The face of Jesus is exposed to spittle and striking. Mendoza says of this text that it 'exposes Jesus' face as the most vulnerable part of his body that is mercilessly exposed to the gaze of others'. He later adds that 'Jesus' vulnerable, precarious and naked face receives the worst aggressive violence when he is spat upon by the mob' (111-12). Given that BDAG (888) suggest that one possible meaning of *prosōpon/face* is 'the entire bodily presence (or) person', readers will recognize in this act of abjection of the body of Jesus the entire narrative theme that is unfolding. As the ecological reader follows this narrative, it can evoke not just the abjection of Jesus but of all Earth's other-than-human as well as human constituents who suffer and endure such abjection today at the hands of others, most predominantly from human others and powerful coalitions among them.

Action against the body of Jesus continues as the chief priests and elders confer to bring about his death (27.1-2), handing him over to the Roman 'governor', Pilate. After a mock trial, Pilate then hands Jesus over for flogging and crucifixion. Before we follow the body of Jesus along that path, I want to pause to consider two significant material elements that are encoded in 27.24-25. When Pilate is unable to secure Jesus' release, he takes water and washes his hands before the crowd, proclaiming his innocence. Water is a powerful material as we know from floods and tsunamis as well as being a necessity in maintaining and preserving life in most of the more-than-human constituents of Earth. Pilate, however, asks more of it than it can yield, that water, clean pure water poured over his hands, render him innocent of the shedding of Jesus' blood despite the fact that as representative of the empire he holds the life and death of all under its power in his hands. This is evident in the concluding words of the trial—after flogging Jesus, he handed him over to be crucified (27.26).

Readers/listeners may easily miss the very brief reference 'after flogging Jesus'. Encoded into this reference is profound materiality and sociality. Jennifer Glancy and others have drawn attention to the fact that '[i]n Roman habitus, whipping was the archetypal mark of dishonor'—it spoke 'degradation and dishonourable dismissiveness' (Glancy 2010: 30). It was not only a social process. Josephus gives an account of his whipping of city delegates 'until their innards were laid bare' (J.W. 2.612) and his displaying of their 'flesh drenched in blood' to intimidate the citizenry (Glancy: 30). It was power enacted on the material flesh of the human body. The ecological reader who pauses over these three short words of the Matthean text could find her or himself encountering, in the ecological texture of this text, the degrading violence wrought by human powers over the body of the earth today. The flogged body of Jesus, the Earth mired by power and pollutant, these cry out from the text. They are, in the language of Glancy 'truth incarnate', 'spelled out, mark by mark in Jesus' carnal history', a history that continues into our day in the history of all that is material.

Between Pilate's handing over of Jesus and the crucifixion ritual of the carrying of the crossbar, there is a further degrading ritual carried out on the body/person of Jesus, one rendering him abject among the abject, further dishonouring his material flesh, his socio-cultural person (27.27-31). In response to Pilate's handing over of Jesus, the soldiers take him before the whole cohort. They strip him naked twice (vv. 28 and 31), exposing him, exposing his flagellated body to their gaze, a more profound dishonouring than the whipping (Mendoza: 126-37). Whatever violence, physical and sexual, that may have been perpetrated on the naked body of Jesus as it was twice stripped is passed over by the Matthean narrator. This, together with his being clothed in mockery, must have been such that Jesus was unable to carry the crossbar (*patibulum*) to the place of execution. These are the life-destroying processes in the ecological texture of the Matthean text. They invite contemporary readers to be attentive not only to the state violence operative in the Roman Empire but to imperial violence done to Earth and all its more-than-human constituents by nations, multi-national giants and all manner of coalitions.

The mocking of Jesus does not stop with the cohort–it continues on the road to the place of crucifixion and beyond. Even while Jesus is suspended naked on the cross awaiting death, his exposure to the penetrating gaze of all bystanders is not sufficient for the chief priests, scribes and elders. They continue to degrade Jesus using his own teachings against him (27.42-43). Even two bandits crucified with him join in the taunts (27.44). The final abjecting of the body of Jesus in its sociality and materiality is reached at Golgotha, the Place of the Skull, and goes beyond even Jesus' last breath in 27.50.

Indeed, the very name Golgotha (Place of the Skull) evokes death. Archaeology has demonstrated that in the first century CE, the place was an abandoned quarry, a place that had known violence to the Earth itself. It had been filled in with rubble and topsoil to make it garden-like. It was a place outside the city where tombs were located and hence it carried the marks not only of violence but of death (Corbo 1992: 1071-72). The Matthean narrative demonstrates that such forces continue in this place. There is an irony in v. 34 in that the 'soldiers of the governor' (v. 27) who have lead Jesus to the place of crucifixion (v. 31) give him *wine* to drink but it is wine mixed with 'bitters' which may be a type of poison (BDAG 1086). Verse 21 of Psalm 69 that the NRSV calls a 'prayer for deliverance from persecution' echoes intertextually through Mt. 27.34: 'they gave me poison for food and for my thirst they gave me vinegar to drink'. The abject one who had given bread and wine as body handed over and blood poured out for others is himself given wine laced with bitterness or some poisonous substance reminding the ecological reader of the poisons poured into the earth, the soil of planet Earth, this Earth being crucified by human political and economic powers.

Clothing is also woven into the play of materiality and sociality in this poignant narrative (v. 36). As we noted earlier in relation to John the Baptist, clothing is caught up in the gift exchange, the life/death process in which all Earth beings participate in the evolution of the universe. Chapman and Schnabel (2015: 674) note its social import in that it was one of the most important possessions of the poor in antiquity (in 25.36 Jesus parables the clothing of the naked). Mendoza considers that clothing is 'inextricably linked' with the person's very self, a 'second skin' (136). He goes on to say that 'in antiquity, clothing could raise or reduce someone's personality or status'. For the soldiers to barter with this 'second skin' of Jesus, with this symbol of human status, indeed human *being*, continues and deepens the process of abjection that has unfolded in this section of the Matthean narrative where materiality and sociality are intricately interwoven in a process that is death-dealing.

The very cosmos itself is caught up in Jesus' final moments as darkness covers *pasan tēn gēn*/all the earth/Earth from noon until three (27.45). It is as if Earth mourns the profound and absolute abjection of Jesus and carries this across time. The cry of Jesus concludes the relentless process of degradation/abjection—my God, my God why have *you* (the Holy One) abandoned me.[7] This can be the cry of all who suffer today, all the more-than-human constituents of Earth, all in-habitants of every habitat that is being degraded, abjected at this time, as was the body of Jesus.

> Why have you abandoned me? Why leave me/leave us to those who strip bare the Earth, penetrate its core and all its corners, ravaging its clothes dividing them as spoils, abjecting it in myriads of ways until finally bringing it to the moment of death?

Such a cry is powerful and it is repeated: Jesus *again* cries out in a loud voice and gives over/gives up his last breath, his spirit (*pneuma*) (v. 50). The *Emmanuel*, the one in whom G*d was/is with the Earth community (Mt. 1.23) enters not only into life in human flesh (1.18-23) but also into another material process of the life-cycle: death. Donna Haraway's reflection on the death of her father may provide us with a short but significant intertext

---

7. As is well known, these words on the lips of Jesus evoke the cry of the innocent suffering one of Psalm 22 and hence can also evoke the cry of innocent and suffering Earth.

here. She distinguishes between 'body' and 'corpse' and says that at death, the body is no longer there—'that body which is always in-the-making; it is always a vital entanglement of heterogeneous scales, times, and kinds of being webbed into fleshly presence, always a becoming, always constituted in relating' (Haraway 2008a: 163). Only the corpse remains. She goes on to say that '[m]y father is undone and that is why I must remember him. I and all those who lived entangled with him become his flesh; we are kin to the dead because their bodies have touched us'. At this point in the unfolding Matthean narrative of the death of Jesus, it seems that it is only the corpse that remains. Elizabeth Johnson adds to the import of this saying: 'No exception to perhaps the only ironclad rule in all of nature, Jesus died, his life ending in a spasm of state-sponsored violence.'[8] But Haraway's words will not allow us to separate body and text.

The Matthean narrator, however, does not focus on the corpse of Jesus but continues to evoke a different power, a power which rends the curtain of the temple, that which symbolically divides the human and the holy. The ecological reader can extend the rending to include all that divides habitat, human and holy. G*d has not abandoned, G*d/Emmanuel is with the Earth community. Readers need to be attentive because at this moment the material body of Jesus/his corpse is silent though Earth itself speaks. Earth speaks in seismic language disturbing the corpses of holy ones who have died, who have gone back into the Earth, who have 'give[n] back to their ecosystem by providing nutrients and food for the beings that once provided the same for them' (McDuffie 2012).

Habitat, human, and holy remain profoundly entangled as the final stages of the narrative unfold around the abjecting of the dead body of Jesus on the wooden beams of state torture, the torture of flesh/of materiality. Time almost stands still around this profound entanglement. A Roman centurion (27.54) *sees* the earthquake and all that accompanies the movement of Earth and *recognizes* that the holy is caught up in all that is happening here— this human one, savagely crucified in a place of scarred Earth, is intimately linked to the Holy One.[9]

Readers also learn that there are many women *looking on from afar*, their bodies straining toward the body of their companion (27.55-56) who has died before their eyes. The narrator's description of them is that they have *followed* Jesus from Galilee, *doing diakonia*, the tasks of disciples of Jesus (16.24; 20.28). This retrospective recognition of the faithful discipleship of

---

8. See Johnson, 'An Earthy Christology', *America* (2009), http://americamagazine.org/issue/693/article/earthy-christology (accessed 30 May 2015).

9. See Mendoza (154-62) for a more extensive analysis of the physical and symbolic import of the presence and participation of the 'centurion' in the final moments of Jesus's life and beyond.

women in all its materiality and sociality across the ministry of Jesus invites us to draw into our text the body of another woman whose engagement in the final unfolding of Jesus' life we passed over earlier, namely Pilate's wife. She warns against participation in the violence being done to an innocent one that she has learnt in and through her body, in a dream (27.19). Pilate, however, has ignored this source of wisdom just as contemporary readers can miss not only the faithful discipleship of women generally in this scene but also the specific fidelity of the 'mother of the sons of Zebedee' who is named among the women (27.55) and who has indeed faithfully drunk the cup as she promised (20.20-22).[10] Two of the faithful women remain even beyond the burial of Jesus (27.61), sitting opposite the tomb. The ecological reader might imagine them sitting on Earth itself, drawing the life transforming power of Earth into their watching and waiting.

It is not only the women disciples who keep watch over the body of their crucified leader and friend. *When it is evening*, a new time in this unfolding, another disciple, Joseph of Arimathea requests the body of Jesus. This body, that has been dealt with abjectly and could have been left on the cross as food for carrion birds and animals[11] or simple decomposition, is returned to Earth in another manner—it is laid in Joseph of Arimathea's own tomb hewn from rock. While the ecological reader recognizes the processes of gift exchange that enable certain birds and animals to feed on flesh, there is a sociality around bodies that returns them, human and often other-than-human also, to Earth and Earth's processes. The actions of Joseph of Arimathea remind readers of these processes and invite an honouring of them in the right ordering of habitat, human and holy. They are, however, dishonoured by 'the chief priests and Pharisees' (27.62-66) who plot against the corpse of Jesus by setting a guard at the tomb. The right ordering of habitat, human and holy cannot be so controlled. It will break open such bonds of control as the final unfolding of the narrative will indicate.

5. *Matthew 28: Life overcoming Abjection*

The unfolding of time continues to mark this narrative: 'after the Sabbath' (a human marking of time) and 'as the first day of the week was dawning' evoking Earth's own marking of time. The two women who have kept watch after the placing of Jesus' body in the rock-hewn tomb, Mary Magdalene and the other Mary, return after the Sabbath to 'see' the tomb (28.1). Elsewhere, I have shown that the Matthean narrative presents these women as witnesses (1991: 103 and 302). Their bodily senses are alert as they sit

---

10. For more extensive explorations of women disciples in this final narrative, see Wainwright (1991: 118-50; 288-318; 1998: 101-118).

11. See Cook (2014: 85-387, 429); and Chapman and Schnabel (2015: 678-81).

opposite the tomb, the only two occasions in the gospel in which *theōreein* is used to indicate 'seeing'. BDAG (454) translate this verb strongly as 'to observe something with sustained attention...look at, observe, perceive, see' or 'to come to an understanding of something'. Using the language of Anne Elvey, we can say that they 'rely on 'their' eyes...to assist 'them' in listening for the traces of materiality' in what they encounter (2011: 150).

As the text unfolds, such encounter is powerful. The 'great stone' which Joseph of Arimathea had rolled across the door of the tomb (27.60) and which the guards of the chief priests and Pharisees made secure by sealing it (27.66) is suddenly rolled back. This is attributed to the appearance and action of an angel of G*d and is accompanied by a movement of Earth, a great earthquake, *seismos megas* (28.2-3). Power is present in this scene, the power of Earth and the power of the heavenly, of the cosmos. Materiality is drawn into the narrative to characterize the angel: appearance like lightening and clothing white as snow (28.4). There is, in this scene, entanglements of 'flows, forces and materials' of which Jones and Cloke have made us aware and which an ecological reading foregrounds.

Verse 4 moves the reader from materiality to sociality with the ironic statement that the guards keeping watch over the dead body of Jesus and the secured tomb themselves become like dead ones through fear. In contrast, the angel engages the women with the announcement that continues the irony: Jesus who had been crucified and whose corpse had been sealed in the tomb has been raised (vv. 5-6). Elizabeth Johnson (2009) explores this brief and enigmatic statement, noting that what 'this means in the concrete is not seriously imaginable to us who still live within the space-time grid of our known universe'. She also affirms the materiality of the claim when she says: 'the proclamation that Jesus is risen from the dead has always connoted corporeality as an essential element. It is not his soul alone that is saved from death but his whole body-person-self'. Her claim echoes back to Donna Haraway's reflection on the body of her father: we are kin to the dead because their bodies have touched ours. The angel affirms this corporeality by the invitation: come see the place where he (his corpse) lay (28.6). It was 'in place', the place of death as corpse. The corpse is no longer there.

This does not mean that the narrative focus shifts to some ethereal realm. Indeed, materiality and sociality continue to characterize its final unfolding as they have across its entire course. The reader continues to encounter bodies in place, in time, in interrelationship. This is evident in v. 7. The two women, Mary Magdalene and the other Mary, witnesses to the empty tomb, to the material space, are commissioned by the announcing angel to go away from this place, and to go to Jesus' disciples to tell them that he has been raised. They are the first witnesses of Jesus' resurrection and the first commissioned to proclaim it in all its materiality. There is also a sociality in this narrative which would have challenged the first century Matthean communities of reception and which continues to challenge communities of interpretation today (see Wainwright 1998: 112-18 for a more comprehensive exploration of this aspect of the narrative). The faithful women disciples are the first commissioned to proclaim that Jesus has been raised and what this means: he is going ahead of them to Galilee and there they will see him with their eyes, with their bodily senses. The materiality of the raised one and the materiality of place and space characterize this resurrection narrative.

This continues to be evident as the women go away from the tomb, the place of death, go away with fear and joy and run to tell the disciples. Elisabeth Schüssler Fiorenza recognizes in the Matthean resurrection account the proclamation that 'Jesus, the Living One, goes ahead of us' on the 'open road' pointing ahead to Galilee (1994: 123-28). It is here on the 'open road', that Jesus meets and greets the women. They take hold of him, of his feet, the text says, thus continuing to narrate materiality. Their accompanying action indicated by the verb 'to worship' catches up the human, even the more-than-human, into divinity. It gives recognition to the holy one who has been with Jesus as the Emmanu-el/'with us G*d' from his taking on flesh in the womb of Mary (1.23) and who is still with us in Jesus crucified and raised.

Jesus reiterates the commission of the angel, namely that the reconciling women invite the male disciples onto the 'open road' to Galilee where they will see Jesus as the women have. This is assurance that the materiality of the raised one continues present and visible to the disciples' eyes and that encounter with the raised one can take place in the same locale as his bodily ministry—in Galilee. Such an experience is not available to those responsible for the death of Jesus. Rather they create a false narrative to negate rather than to proclaim resurrection. They may remind contemporary ecological readers of those who deny the contribution and potential of alternative energy sources and their impact and import in attempts to combat death-dealing climate change. Even beyond the death and resurrection of the body of Jesus, the leaders continue to plot, to create a false narrative.

There is a carefully woven tapestry of text and meaning in this final chapter of the Matthean gospel. Around the false narrative of those responsible for Jesus' death, encounter and commission are woven, first of the female disciples and then, through their reconciling activity of the males, the eleven called and named ones (10.1-4). In a critical ecological reading of the gospel, these two moments with all their accompanying sociality can be mapped on what we have already encountered as Sandoval's 'flattened but mobile grid-like terrain'. Each is neither first nor last, more or less important, one to the other, but each can and must function uniquely in the ecological texture of the Matthean text.

The disciples' re-turn to Galilee evokes all that has been encoded into the entire text in relation to the materiality and sociality of this place/region that readers have already encountered. They are reminded that Galilee is rich in agriculture, providing bread not only for themselves but for their Tyrian neighbours; that it is under threat from the wealthy and entrepreneurial Romans who likewise sought its grain. It was also a place of suffering and pain for many—the blind, the lame, the deaf and many more. It is the place where Jesus' ministry of compassion (9.36) took place through his preaching, teaching and healing (4.23; 9.35). It may well have been the region in which the Matthean community producing these gospel traditions was located (see Runesson 2008). The reader thus re-turns to all that the reference to 'Galilee' evokes.

The identification of a specific mountain 'to which Jesus had directed them' as the place of encounter is extra-textual—there is no reference to such direction in the Matthean text. Readers will, however, not only be attentive to the materiality of the place of encounter but also that there were two significant mountain-top experiences narrated in the Galilean ministry—the mountain of Jesus' first discourse (5.1) and the mountain of transfiguration (17.1-2). The disciples both see and hear Jesus raised (28.17-18). He is accessible to their human senses but they are left free and independent in their response—some doubted (v. 17). Some, however, like the women (v. 9) worship. As with the women, this verb connotes the catching up of the disciples into the re-iterating, the re-manifestation of Emmanuel/the 'with us G*d' of 1.23. In the raised Jesus encountered by faithful women and men, G*d is with the Earth community (and remains with this community).

The risen Jesus converses with the eleven, commissioning them as the women were commissioned earlier. This is woven into the sociality encoded in the text, into its ecological texture. The words of Jesus open with a claim to authorization, indeed a universal claim: all authority/*exousia* in heaven and on earth has been given to me. BDAG (352-353) give a range of meanings for *exousia*: control, command, power, authority, and in relation to Mt. 28.18's use of *exousia*, 'absolute power'. The ecological reader who has engaged Sandoval's horizontal grid of power and who is aware of the use of this final text of Matthew's gospel as an underpinning for the colonization of entire continents (Dube 2000b) will attend here to the voice of the crucified raised one encountered in the final chapters of the Matthean narrative rather than the voice of exalted ruler and king. The authorization, the *exousia*, is to proclaim the *basileia* of the heavens/skies as Jesus proclaimed it (4.17), the vision of the *dikaiosynē* or right ordering of all (5.10), human and other-than-human. It is a right ordering that encompasses the heavens and Earth, indeed the universe for the contemporary ecological reader. All that is material, all that is social is to be ordered according to Jesus' proclaimed vision of what is just and right. This will be worked out in both local and global strivings toward an ecological ethic.

Indeed, as the contemporary ecological reader continues to engage these final four verses of Matthew 28, a hermeneutic of suspicion becomes more urgent, especially in light of the scholarship of Musa Dube who brings a feminist and postcolonial lens to her reading of this text and, indeed, to its translation (2000b, 2011). We have already critiqued a hierarchical reading of the authority of Jesus. The command, 'make disciples of all nations' (28.19) has been read as giving authorization to Christian missionaries to 'convert' those whose lands they conquered as they came with the imperialists. Indeed, as Musa Dube has claimed, there is a profound connection between the biblical text and Western imperialism (2000b: 20). She also points out the intimate link between imperialism and patriarchy, arguing that it takes on a different hue in the contexts of the colonizer from that of the colonized (34-39). The ecological reader is attentive to these radical critiques of the closing verses of the Matthean gospel and to their import across the centuries up to this day so that they will no long be used to underpin human and ecological imperialism.

In this same mode, attention must be drawn to the divine naming into which disciples, beyond the ministry of Jesus, are to be baptised: Father, Son and Holy Spirit (v. 19). First, it will be noted that the command to baptize is unique to this verse. The Matthean Jesus did not baptize nor did he commission disciples to do so (prior to this point) even though John characterized Jesus' mission as baptizing with the [h]oly [s]pirit and fire (3.11). Jesus' own baptism did, however, commission him for his *basileia* ministry of preaching, teaching and healing (3.17; 4.23-24; 9.35). The baptism of followers of Jesus can likewise authorize them for living out all that Jesus commanded, living out the gospel vision we have been exploring in this commentary (v. 20) and that has been addressed above. It is a vision that seeks right ordering in relation to the gendering of the divine, and the interconnectedness of habitat, human and holy.

The triadic naming into which followers of Jesus are to be baptized is not a static naming to be confessed. The resurrection commissions are not confessional; they are not characterized by stasis. They point beyond the present to a new future if one follows the invitation 'go' given to both female and male disciples (28.7, 19): go and tell, go and disciple—offer the invitation to a new way of hearing a right ordering for the entire universal community. In the opening of the gospel, in the baptism of Jesus, and in the unfolding narrative, readers have encountered this G*d in a spirit that is holy. They have encountered G*d in Jesus named 'son' in relation to the heavenly one under a variety of rubrics and titles as the community narrates and theologizes Jesus. The interrelationship of divine and human power is named in relation to Jesus in the unfolding story. It is into this named interrelationship of G*d—imaged as father but also more than father, of Jesus named as son/beloved in myriads of ways, and of a spirit that is holy—that those who hear and receive this gospel proclamation are to be baptized. As the gospel unfolding of this naming has been manifold, so too have been the ways in which it has been received. An ecological reading informed by feminist and postcolonial as well as ecological perspectives will craft the naming of the G*d who is with the Earth community as they live out the gospel that Jesus preached and that we have interpreted through the new lens of an ecological hermeneutic in this commentary.

The second half of the final verse—*kai idou*/and behold I am with you all days until the close of the present age—leaves the reader with a promise of the ongoing presence of the crucified and raised Jesus. The gospel opened with the naming of Jesus as *Emmanu-el*, as the one in whom divinity is with the Earth community. His preaching, teaching and healing as well as his abject suffering and death, read through an ecological lens, have shown us as readers just what the gospel appellation of *Emmanu-el* might mean, not in first-century Palestine, but rather in and through a twenty-first century ecological and cosmic consciousness in the age of the Anthroposcene. The promised ongoing presence of the raised Jesus with those baptised into his gospel message might enable not just a reading of the intimate play of habitat, human and holy through this gospel but an enactment of their right relationships in our lives today so that we, as human community, may not hasten the 'close of the present age'.

BIBLIOGRAPHY

The Scriptural quotations in this publication are from the New Revised Standard Version of the Bible copyrighted 1989 by the Division of the Churches of Christ in the United States of America and are used by permission. Version 4.9. Accordance 11.0.6bl; OakTree Software, 2015.

The Greek text of the New Testament is from *Novum Testament Graece* (ed. Barbara and Kurt Aland; Stuttgart: Deutsche Bibelgeselschaft, 27th edn), version 4.3.

Abrams, Nancy E., and Joel R. Primack
    2011   *The New Universe and the Human Future: How a Shared Cosmology Could Transform the World* (New Haven: Yale University Press).
Allison, Dale C.
    1993   *The New Moses: A Matthean Typology* (Minneapolis: Fortress Press).
Alonso, Pablo
    2011   *The Woman Who Changed Jesus: Crossing Boundaries in Mk 7,24-30* (Biblical Tools and Studies, 11; Leuven: Peeters).
Anzaldúa, Gloria
    1999   *Borderlands/La Fontera: The New Mestiza* (San Francisco: Aunt Lute Books, 2nd edn).
Athenaeus
    1927–41   *The Deipnosophists* (trans. Charles Burton Gulick; LCL; London: Heinemann).
Avalos, Hector
    1999   *Health Care and the Rise of Christianity* (Peabody, MA: Hendrickson).
Batto, Bernard F.
    1987a   'The Sleeping God: An Ancient near Eastern Motif of Divine Sovereignty', *Biblica* 68.2: 153-77.
    1987b   'When God Sleeps', *Bible Review* 111.4: 16-23.
Bauckham, Richard
    2009   'Reading the Sermon on the Mount in an Age of Ecological Catastrophe', *Studies in Christian Ethics* 22.1: 76-88.
Behnke, Elizabeth A.
    1999   'From Merleau-Ponty's Concept of Nature to an Interspecies Practice of Peace', in *Animal Others: On Ethics, Ontology and Animal Life* (ed. H. Peter Steeves; Albany, NY: State University of New York Press), pp. 93-116.
Bennett, Jane
    2010   *Vibrant Matter: A Political Ecology of Things* (Durham, NC: Duke University Press).

Bergant, Dianne
    1997   *Israel's Wisdom Literature: A Liberation-Critical Reading* (A Liberation-Critical Reading of the Old Testament; Minneapolis: Fortress Press).

Berry, Thomas
    1988   *The Dream of the Earth* (San Francisco: Sierra Club).
    1999   *The Great Work: Our Way into the Future* (New York: Three Rivers Press).

Berry, Wendell
    2009   *Bringing It to the Table: On Farming and Food* (Berkeley: Counterpoint).

Betz, Hans Dieter
    1995   *The Sermon on the Mount* (Hermeneia; Minneapolis: Fortress Press).

Birch, Charles
    1990   *On Purpose* (Sydney: University of New South Wales Press).

Bird, Phyllis A.
    1994   '"Male and Female He Created Them": Genesis 1:27b in the Context of the Priestly Account of Creation', in *"I Studied Inscriptions from before the Flood": Ancient near Eastern, Literary and Linguistic Approaches to Genesis 1–11* (ed. Richard S. Hess and David Toshio Tsumura; Sources for Biblical and Theological Study; Winona Lake, IN: Eisenbrauns), pp. 329-61.

Birke, Lynda, and Luciana Parisi
    1999   'Animals, Becoming', in *Animal Others: On Ethics, Ontology, and Animal Life* (ed. H. Peter Steeves; Albany, NY: State University of New York Press), pp. 55-73.

Borowski, Oded
    2002   *Agriculture in Iron Age Israel* (Boston: American Schools of Oriental Research).

Brindal, Emma
    2008   'Climate Change Refugees the Forgotten People', *The Age*, 18 March, 2008. http://www.theage.com.au/opinion/climate-change-refugees-the-forgotten-people-20080617-2s5b.ht?page=-1 (accessed 7 March 2009).

Brown, Raymond E.
    1993   *The Birth of the Messiah: A Commentary on the Infancy Narratives in the Gospels of Matthew and Luke* (ABRL; London: Geoffrey Chapman).
    1994   *The Death of the Messiah: From Gethsemane to the Grave: A Commentary on the Passion Narratives in the Four Gospels* (Vol. 1; New York: Doubleday).

Brueggemann, Walter
    1978   *The Land* (Overtures to Biblical Theology; London: SPCK).
    1987   *Hope within History* (Atlanta: John Knox Press).
    1988   *Israel's Praise: Doxology against Idolatry and Ideology* (Philadelphia: Fortress Press).

Buell, Lawrence
    2005   *The Future of Environmental Criticis* (Environmental Crisis and the Literary Imagination; Oxford: Blackwell).

Butkus, Russell A., and Steven A. Kolmes
    2011   *Environmental Science and Theology in Dialogue* (Theology in Dialogue; Maryknoll, NY: Orbis Books).

Cadwallader, Alan H.
    2008   *Beyond the Word of a Woman: Recovering the Bodies of the Syrophoenician Women* (Adelaide: ATF Press).

2013 'The Peasant, the Farmer and the Gardener: Approaches to the Environment of the Mustard Seed', in *Where the Wild Ox Roams: Biblical Essays in Honour of Norman C. Habel* (ed. Alan H. Cadwallader with Peter L. Trudinger; Sheffield: Sheffield Phoenix), pp. 128-44.

Carter, Warren
 1997a 'Narrative/Literary Approaches to Matthean Theology: The "Reign of the Heavens" as an Example (Mt 4.17–5.12)', *JSNT* 67: 3-27.
 1997b 'Matthew 4:18-22 and Matthean Discipleship: An Audience-Oriented Perspective', *CBQ* 59.1: 58-75.
 2000 *Matthew and the Margins: A Socio-Political and Religious Reading* (JSNTSup, 204; Sheffield: Sheffield Academic Press).
 2001 *Matthew and Empire: Initial Explorations* (Harrisburgh, PA: Trinity Press International).
 2004a 'Matthew and the Gentiles: Individual Conversion and/or Systemic Transformation?', *JSNT* 26.3: 259-82.
 2004b *Matthew: Storyteller, Interpreter, Evangelist*, Revised Edition (Peabody, MA: Hendrickson).
 2005 'Matthean Christology in Roman Imperial Key: Matthew 1:1', in *The Gospel of Matthew in Its Roman Imperial Key* (ed. John Riches and David C. Sim; JSNTSup, 276; London: T. & T. Clark), pp. 143-65.
 2011 'God as "Father" in Matthew: Imperial Intersections', in *Finding a Woman's Place: Essays in Honor of Carolyn Osiek* (ed. David L. Balch and Jason T. Lamoreaux; Princeton Theological Monograph Series; Eugene: Pickwick), pp. 81-102.

Casey, Edward S.
 1993 *Getting Back into Place: Toward a Renewed Understanding of the Place-World* (Bloomington: Indiana University Press).

Cato, Marcus Porcius
 1936 *On Agriculture* (trans. William Davis Hooper; Cambridge: Harvard University Press).

Chancey, Mark A.
 2002 *The Myth of a Gentile Galilee* (SNTSMS, 118; Cambridge: Cambridge University Press).
 2005 *Greco-Roman Culture and the Galilee of Jesus* (SNTSMS, 134; Cambridge: Cambridge University Press).

Chapman, David W., and Eckhard J. Schnabel
 2015 *The Trial and Crucifixion of Jesus* (WUNT, 344; Tübingen: Mohr Siebeck).

Cicero
 2006 *On Divination* (trans with introduction and commentary; Clarendon Ancient History Series; Oxford: Clarendon Press).

Code, Lorraine
 2006 *Ecological Thinking: The Politics of Epistemic Location* (Studies in Feminist Philosophy; Oxford: Oxford University Press).

Collins, John N.
 1990 *Diakonia: Re-Interpreting the Ancient Sources* (New York: Oxford University Press).

Columella
 1954 *On Agriculture, Volume II: Books 5-9* (trans. E.S. Forster; LCL, 407; London: Heinemann).

Cook, J.G.
    2014   *Curcifixion in the Mediterranean World* (WUNT, 327; Tübingen: Mohr Siebeck).

Corbo, V.C.
    1992   'Golgotha', in *Anchor Bible Dictionary* (Yale University/Oak Tree Software), II, pp. 1071-1072.

Cotter, Wendy
    1997   'Cosmology and the Jesus Miracles', in *Whose Historical Jesus?* (ed. William E. Arnal and Michel Desjardins; Studies in Christianity and Judaism; Ontario: Wilfrid Laurier University Press), pp. 118-31.
    1999   *Miracles in Greco-Roman Antiquity: A Sourcebook* (London: Routledge).

Cox, Brian
    1996   *Wonders of the Solar System.* DVD Video.

Crosby, Michael H.
    1988   *House of Disciples: Church, Economics, and Justice in Matthew* (Maryknoll, NY: Orbis Books).

Curtin, Deane
    2005   *Environmental Ethics for a Postcolonial World* (Lanham, MD: Rowman & Littlefield).

D'Angelo, Mary Rose
    1992   'Abba and "Father": Imperial Theology and the Jesus Traditions', *JBL* 111.4: 611-30.

Davies, W.D., and Dale C. Allison
    1988   *The Gospel according to Saint Matthew: A Critical and Exegetical Commentary.* I. *Introduction and Commentary on Matthew I–VII* (ICC; 3 vols; Edinburgh: T. & T. Clark).
    1991   *The Gospel According to Saint Matthew: A Critical and Exegetical Commentary.* II. *Commentary on Matthew VIII–XVIII* (ICC; 3 vols.; Edinburgh: T. & T. Clark).
    1997   *The Gospel According to Saint Matthew: A Critical and Exegetical Commentary.* III. *Commentary on Matthew XIX–XXVIII* (ICC; 3 vols.; Edinburgh: T. & T. Clark).

Deane-Drummond, Celia
    2006   *Wonder and Wisdom: Conversations in Science, Spirituality and Theology* (London: Darton, Longman and Todd).

Deane-Drummond, Celia, Rebecca Artinian-Kaiser and David L Clough (eds.)
    2013   *Animals as Religious Subjects: Transdisciplinary Perspectives* (London: Bloomsbury).

Deutsch, Celia M.
    1996   *Lady Wisdom, Jesus, and the Sages: Metaphor and Social Context in Matthew's Gospel* (Valley Forge, PA: Trinity Press International).
    2001   'Jesus as Wisdom: A Feminist Reading of Matthew's Wisdom Christology', in *A Feminist Companion to Matthew* (ed. Amy-Jill Levine with Marianne Blickenstaff; Sheffield: Sheffield Academic Press), pp. 88-113.

Donaldson, Laura E.
    2006   'The Sign of Orpah: Reading Ruth through Native Eyes', in *The Postcolonial Biblical Reader* (ed. R.S. Sugirtharajah; Oxford: Blackwell), pp. 159-70.

Dowling, Elizabeth, and Veronica Lawson
    2013   'Women, Eucharist, and Good News to All Creation in Mark', in *Reinterpreting the Eucharist: Explorations in Feminist Theology and Ethics* (ed. Anne Elvey, Carol Hogan, Kim Power and Claire Renkin; Sheffield: Equinox), pp. 78-90.

Dube, Musa W.
    1999   'Consuming a Colonial Cultural Bomb: Translating *Badimo* into "Demons" in the Setswana Bible', *JSNT* 73: 33-59.
    2000a   'To Pray the Lord's Prayer in the Global Economic Era (Matt 6:9-13', in *The Bible in Africa: Transactions, Trajectories and Trends* (ed. Gerald O. West and Musa W. Dube; Leiden: Brill), pp. 611-30.
    2000b   *Postcolonial Feminist Interpretation of the Bible* (St. Louis: Chalice).
    2005   'Rahab Is Hanging out a Red Ribbon: One African Woman's Perspective on the Future of Feminist New Testament Scholarship', in *Feminist New Testament Studies: Global and Future Perspectives* (ed. Kathleen O'Brien Wicker, Althea Spencer Miller and Musa W. Dube; New York: Palgrave Macmillan), pp. 177-202.
    2011   'Towards Postcolonial Feminist Translations of the Bible', in *Reading Ideologies: Essays on the Bible and Interpretation in Honor of Mary Ann Tolbert* (ed. Tat-Siong Benny Liew; Sheffield: Sheffield Phoenix Press), pp. 215-39.

Duff, P.B.
    1992   'The March of the Divine Warrior and the Advent of the Greco-Roman King: Mark's Account of Jesus' Entry into Jerusalem', *JBL* 111: 55-71.

Duling, Dennis C.
    1992   'Matthew's Plurisignificant "Son of David" in Social Science Perspective : Kinship, Kingship, Magic, and Miracle', *BTB* 22.3: 99-116.
    2012   *A Marginal Scribe: Studies of the Gospel of Matthew in Social-Scientific Perspective* (Matrix: The Bible in Mediterranean Context; Eugene: Cascade Books).

Dvorjetski, Esti
    1994   'Testimonia: Nautical Symbols on the Gadara Coins and Their Link to the Thermae of the Three Graces at Hammat-Gader', *Mediterranean Historical Review* 9.1: 100-115.

Eaton, Heather
    2005   *Introducing Ecofeminist Theologies* (Introductions in Feminist Theology, 12; London: T. & T. Clark International).

Edwards, Denis
    2004   *Breath of Life: A Theology of the Creator Spirit* (Maryknoll, NY: Orbis Books).
    2006   *Ecology at the Heart of Faith: The Change of Heart That Leads to a New Way of Living on Earth* (Maryknoll, NY: Orbis Books).
    2010   *How God Acts: Creation, Redemption and Special Divine Action* (Minneapolis: Fortress Press).

Edwards, Douglas R.
    2007   'Identity and Social Location in Roman Galilean Villages', in *Religion, Ethnicity, and Identity in Ancient Galilee* (ed. Jürgen Zangenberg, Harold W. Attridge and Dale B. Martin; WUNT, 210; Tübingen: Mohr Siebeck), pp. 357-74.

Ehrlich, Paul R., Anne H. Ehrlich, and Gretchen C. Daily
    1995   *The Stork and the Plow: The Equity Answer to the Human Dilemma* (New Haven: Yale University Press).

Elliott, John H.
    1992   'Matthew 20:1-15: A Parable of Invidious Comparison and Evil Eye Accusation', *BTB* 22: 52-65.

Elvey, Anne F.
    2005   *An Ecological Feminist Reading of the Gospel of Luke: A Gestational Paradigm* (Studies in Women and Religion; Lewiston, NY: Edwin Mellen Press).
    2009   'Ashes and Dust: On (Not) Speaking About God Ecologically', in *Eco-Theology* (ed. E.M. Wainwright, L.C. Susin and F. Wilfred; Concilium 2009/3; London: SCM Press), pp. 33-42.
    2010   'Earthing the Text? On the Status of the Biblical Text in Ecological Perspective', *Australian Biblical Review* 52: 64-79.
    2011a   'The Matter of Texts: A Material Intertextuality and Ecocritical Engagements with the Bible', in *Ecocritical Theory: New European Approaches* (ed. Axel Goodbody and Kate Rigby; Charlottesville: University of Virginia Press), pp.181-93.
    2011b   *The Matter of the Text: Material Engagements between Luke and the Five Senses* (Bible in the Modern World, 37; Sheffield: Sheffield Phoenix Press).
    2011c   'Partnering the Waters in Luke 8:22-25', in *Water: A Matter of Life and Death* (ed. Norman C. Habel and Peter Trudinger; Interface, 14.1; Hindmarsh: ATF), pp. 81-94.
    2013   'Living One for the Other: Eucharistic Hospitality as Ecological Hospitality', in *Reinterpreting the Eucharist: Explorations in Feminist Theology and Ethics* (ed. Anne Elvey, Carol Hogan, Kim Power and Claire Renkin; Sheffield: Equinox), pp. 186-205.

Elvey, Anne, Carol Hogan, Kim Power and Claire Renkin
    2013   *Reinterpreting the Eucharist: Explorations in Feminist Theology and Ethics* (Sheffield: Equinox).

Fiensy, David A.
    1991   *The Social History of Palestine in the Herodian Period: The Land Is Mine* (Studies in the Bible and Early Christianity, 20; Lewiston, NY: Edwin Mellen Press).

Firmage, E.
    n/d   'Zoology', in *ABD* 6 (ed. David Noel Freedman; Accessed in Accordance), pp. 1109-67.

Foucault, Michel
    1977   *Language, Counter-Memory, Practice: Selected Essays and Interviews* (trans. Donald F. Bouchard and Sherry Simon; Oxford: Blackwell).

Francis, R.A., and J. Lorimer
    2011   'Urban Reconciliation Ecology: The Potential of Living Roofs and Walls', *Journal of Environmental Management* 92: 1429-37.

Freyne, Seán
    1980   *Galilee from Alexander the Great to Hadrian—323 BCE to 135 CE: A Study in Second Temple Judaism* (Edinburgh: T. & T. Clark).
    1988   *Galilee, Jesus and the Gospels: Literary Approaches and Historical Investigations* (Dublin: Gill and Macmillan).
    1994   'The Geography, Politics, and Economics of Galilee and the Quest for the

Historical Jesus', in *Studying the Historical Jesus: Evaluations of the State of Current Research* (ed. Bruce Chilton and Craig A. Evans; Leiden: E.J. Brill), pp. 75-121.
2000   *Galilee and Gospel* (WUNT, 125; Tübingen: Mohr Siebeck).
2002   'Galilee and Judea in the first Century—The Social World of Jesus and His Ministry', in *Texts, Contexts and Cultures: Essays on Biblical Topics* (Dublin: Veritas).
2004   *Jesus, a Jewish Galilean: A New Reading of the Jesus-Story* (London: T. & T. Clark International).
Gale, Aaron M.
2005   *Redefining Ancient Borders: The Jewish Scribal Framework of Matthew's Gospel* (New York: T. & T. Clark International).
Gerber, Lisa
2002   'Standing Humbly Before Nature', *Ethics and the Environment* 7.1: 39-53.
Giffney, Noreen, and Myra J. Hird
2008   'Introduction: Queering the Non/Human', in *Queering the Non/Human* (ed. Noreen Giffney and Myra J. Hird; Queer Interventions; Aldershot: Ashgate), pp. 1-16.
Glancy, Jennifer A.
2010a   'Jesus, the Syrophoenician Woman and Other First Century Bodies', *Biblical Interpretation* 18.4-5: 342-63.
2010b   *Corporal Knowledge: Early Christian Bodies* (Oxford: Oxford University Press).
Goodenough, Ursula
1998   *The Sacred Depths of Nature* (Oxford: Oxford University Press).
Goodman, Martin
2000   *State and Society in Roman Galilee, A.D. 132–212* (London: Valentine Mitchell, 2nd edn).
n/a
2008   *The Green Bible* (San Francisco: Harper Collins).
Guardiola-Saenz, Leticia
1988   'Borderless Women and Borderless Texts: A Cultural Reading of Matthew 15:21-28', *Semeia* 78: 69-81.
Habel, Norman C.
1995   *The Land Is Mine: Six Biblical Land Ideologies* (Overtures to Biblical Theology; Minneapolis: Fortress Press, 1995).
2000a   'The Challenge of Ecojustice Readings for Christian Theology', *Pacifica* 13: 125-41.
2000b   'Geophany: The Earth Story in Genesis 1', in *The Earth Story in Genesis* (ed. Norman C. Habel and Shirley Wurst; The Earth Bible, 2; Sheffield: Sheffield Academic Press), pp. 34-48.
2000c   'Guiding Ecojustice Principles', in *Readings from the Perspective of Earth* (ed. Norman C. Habel; The Earth Bible, 1; Sheffield: Sheffield), pp. 38-53.
2003   'The Implications of God Discovering Wisdom in Earth', in *Job 28: Cognition in Context* (ed. Ellen van Wolde; Leiden: Brill), pp. 281-98.
2008   'Introducing Ecological Hermeneutics', in *Exploring Ecological Hermeneutics* (ed. Norman C. Habel and Peter Trudinger; SBL Symposium Series, 46; Atlanta: SBL), pp. 1-8.

> 2009   *An Inconvenient Text: Is a Green Reading of the Bible Possible?* (Adelaide: ATF Press).
>
> 2011   *The Birth and Curse of Earth: An Ecological Reading of Genesis 1–11* (The Earth Bible Commentary Series; Sheffield: Sheffield Phoenix Press).

Habel, Norman C., and Peter Trudinger (eds.)
> 2008   *Exploring Ecological Hermeneutics* (SBL Symposium Series, 46; Atlanta: SBL).
>
> 2011   *Water; a Matter of Life and Death* (Interface, 14.1; Hindmarsh: ATF).

Hagner, Donald A.
> 1993   *Matthew 1–13* (Word Bible Commentary, 33a; Dallas: Word Books).
>
> 1995   *Matthew 14–28* (Word Bible Commentary, 33b; Dallas: Word Books).

Håkansson, Sigurd
> 2003   *Weeds and Weed Management on Arable Land: An Ecological Approach* (Oxon: CABI Publishing).

Hanson, K.C.
> 1997   'The Galilean Fishing Economy and the Jesus Tradition', *BTB* 27.3: 99-111.

Hanson, K.C., and Douglas E. Oakman
> 1988   *Palestine in the Time of Jesus: Social Structures and Social Conflicts* (Minneapolis: Fortress Press).

Haraway, Donna J.
> 2008a   *When Species Meet* (Posthumanities, 3; Minneapolis: University of Minnesota).
>
> 2008b   'Companion Species, Mis-Recognition, and Queer Worlding', in *Queering the Non/Human* (ed. Noreen Giffney and Myra J. Hird; Queer Interventions; Aldershot: Ashgate), pp. xxiii-xxvi.

Harrill, J.A.
> 2006   *Slaves in the New Testament: Literary, Social and Moral Dimensions* (Minneapolis: Fortress Press).

Harrison, J.R.
> 2012   'Every Dog has its Day', in *New Documents Illustrating Early Christianity*, Volume 10 (ed. S.R. Llewelyn and J.R. Harrison; Grand Rapids: Eerdmans), pp. 110-17.

Hauck, F., and S. Schulz
> 1968   'Πραυς, Πραυτης', in *TDNT* 6 (ed. Gerhard Kittel and Gerhard Friedrich; trans.Geoffrey W. Bromiley; Grand Rapids: Eerdmans), pp. 645-51.

Haught, John F.
> 2004   'Christianity and Ecology', in *This Sacred Earth: Religion, Nature, Environment* (ed. Roger S. Gottlieb; New York: Routledge), pp. 232-47.
>
> 2006   *Is Nature Enough? Meaning and Truth in the Age of Science* (Cambridge: Cambridge University Press).

Heard, W.J.
> 1992   'Olives, Mount of', in *Anchor Bible Dictionary* (Yale University/Oak Tree Software), V, pp. 13-14.

Heirman, Jo, and Jacqueline Klooster
> 2013   'Introduction: The Ideologies of "Lived Space", Ancient and Modern', in *The Ideologies of Lived Space in Literary Texts, Ancient and Modern* (ed. Jo Heirman and Jacqueline Klooster; Gent: Academia Press), pp. 3-11.

Hillel, Daniel
    2006   *The Natural History of the Bible: An Environmental Exploration of the Hebrew Scriptures* (New York: Columbia University Press).

Hippocrates
    1923a   *Airs Waters Places* (trans. W.H.S. Jones; LCL; London: Heinemann).
    1923b   *Epidemics I and III* (trans. W.H.S. Jones; LCL; London: Heinemann).

Hirschfeld, Yizhar
    1990   'Edible Wild Plants: The Secret Diet of Monks in the Judean Desert', *Israel Land and Nature* 16.1: 25-28.
    1995   *The Palestinian Dwelling in the Roman-Byzantine Period* (Studium Biblicum Franciscanum Collection Minor, 34; Jerusalem: Franciscan Printing Press/Israel Exploration Society).

Hobbs, T.R.
    2001   'Soldiers in the Gospels: A Neglected Agent', in *Social Scientific Models for Interpreting the Bible: Essays by the Context Group in Honor of Bruce J. Malina* (ed. John J. Pilch; Biblical Interpretation Series, 53; Atlanta: Society of Biblical Literature), pp. 328-48.

Hobgood-Oster, Laura
    2008   *Holy Dogs and Asses: Animals in the Christian Tradition* (Urbana, IL: University of Illinois Press).

Hoggard Creegan, Nicola
    2013   *Animal Suffering and the Problem of Evil* (Oxford: Oxford University Press).

Hoppe, L.
    2005   'Peter's House in Capernaum', *Bible Today* 43.4: 244-49.

Horsley, Richard A.
    1995   *Galilee: History, Politics, People* (Valley Forge, PA: Trinity Press International).
    1996   *Archaeology, History and Society in Galilee: The Social Context of Jesus and the Rabbis* (Valley Forge, PA: Trinity Press International).

Horsley, Richard A., and John S. Hanson
    1985   *Bandits, Prophets, and Messiahs: Popular Movements at the Time of Jesus* (New York: HarperSanFrancisco).

Hoving, Isabel
    2013   'Testing Three Oppositions to Find out What (Lived) Space Means', in *The Ideologies of Lived Space in Literary Texts, Ancient and Modern* (ed. Jo Heirman and Jacqueline Klooster; Gent: Academia Press), pp. 111-24.

Hughes, J. Donald
    1994   *Pan's Travail: Environmental Problems of the Ancient Greeks and Romans* (Baltimore: The Johns Hopkins University Press).

Ilan, Tal
    1995   *Jewish Women in Greco-Roman Palestine: An Inquiry into Image and Status* (Texte Und Studien Zum Antiken Judentum, 44; Tübingen: Mohr Siebeck).
    1999   *Integrating Women into Second Temple History* (Texts and Studies in Ancient Judaism, 76; Tübingen: Mohr Siebeck).
    2006   *Silencing the Queen: The Literary History of Shelemzion and Other Jewish Women* (Texts and Studies in Ancient Judaism, 115; Tübingen: Mohr Siebeck).

Jennings, Theodore W., and Tat-Siong Benny Liew
    2004   'Mistaken Identities but Model Faith: Rereading the Centurion, the Chap, and the Christ in Matthew 8:5-13', *JBL* 123.3: 467-94.

Jensen, Morten Hørning
    2006   *Herod Antipas in Galilee* (WUNT, 2.215; Tübingen: Mohr Siebeck).
Jenson, R.
    2006   *The Rough Guide to Climate Change* (London: Roughguides).
Jones, Owain, and Paul Cloke
    2008   'Non-Human Agencies: Trees in Place and Time', in *Material Agency: Toward a Non-Anthropocentric Approach* (ed. Carl Knappett and Lambros Malafouris; New York: Springer), pp. 79-96.
Johnson, Elizabeth A.
    1992   *She Who Is: The Mystery of God in Feminist Theological Discourse* (New York: Crossroad).
    2009   'An Earthy Christology', *America* April 13. http://americamagazine.org/issue/693/article/earthy-christology (accessed 1 June 2015).
    2014   *Ask the Beasts: Darwin and the God of Love* (London: Bloomsbury).
Johnson, Marshall D.
    1988   *The Purpose of the Biblical Genealogies with Special Reference to the Setting of the Genealogies of Jesus* (SNTSMS, 8; Cambridge: Cambridge University Press).
Josephus, Flavius
    1927   *The Jewish War, Volume 1: Books 1-2* (trans. H. St. J. Thackeray; LCL, 203; London: Heinemann).
    1928   *The Jewish War, Volume III: Books 5-7* (trans. H. St. J. Thackeray; LCL, 210; London: Heinemann).
    1930   *Jewish Antiquities, Volume VI: Books 4-6* (trans. H. St. J. Thackeray; LCL, 490; London: Heinemann).
    1937   *Jewish Antiquities, Volume IV: Books 9-11* (trans. Ralph Marcus; LCL, 326; London: Heinemann).
Kapleau, Philip
    1966   *The Three Pillars of Zen: Teaching, Practice, and Enlightenment* (New York: Harper & Row).
Kee, Howard Clark
    1986   *Medicine, Miracle and Magic in New Testament Times* (SNTSMS, 55; Cambridge: Cambridge University Press).
Keller, Catherine
    1994   'Eschatology, Ecology, and a Green Ecumenacy', in *Reconstructing Christian Theology* (ed. R.S. Chopp and M.L. Taylor; Minneapolis: Fortress Press), pp. 326-44.
    2003   *Face of the Deep: A Theology of Becoming* (London: Routledge).
Kidger, Mark
    1999   *The Star of Bethlehem: An Astronomer's View* (Princeton, NJ: Princeton University Press).
Klein, L.R.
    2000   'Bathsheba Revealed', in *Samuel and Kings: A Feminist Companion to the Bible* (ed. A. Brenner; Sheffield: Sheffield Academic Press), pp. 47-64.
Knappett, Carl, and Lambros Malafouris
    2008   *Material Agency: Toward a Non-Anthropocentric Approach* (New York: Springer).
Koperski, Veronica
    2011   'The Many Faces of the Canaanite Woman in Matthew 15,21-28', in *The*

Gospel of Matthew at the Crossroads of Early Christianity (ed. Donald Senior; Leuven: Peeters), pp. 524-36.

Kraemer, Ross S.
2006 'Implicating Herodias and Her Daughter in the Death of John the Baptizer: A (Christian) Theological Strategy?', *JBL* 125.2: 321-49.

Krause, Bernie
2013 *The Voice of the Natural World*. TEDGlobal. See http://www.ted.com/talks/bernie_krause_the_voice_of_the_natural_world?utm_source=email&source =email&utm_medium=social&utm_campaign=ios-share.

Laughlin, John C.H.
1993 'Capernaum from Jesus' Time and After', *BAR* 19.5: 54-61.

Leal, Robert Barry
2004 *Wilderness in the Bible: Toward a Theology of Wilderness* (Studies in Biblical Literature, 72; New York: Peter Lang).
2005 'Negativity Towards Wilderness in the Biblical Record', *Ecotheology* 10.3: 364-81.

Levine, Amy-Jill
1988 *The Social and Ethnic Dimensions of Matthean Salvation History: "Go Nowhere among the Gentiles…" (Matt. 10:5b)* (Lewiston, NY: Edwin Mellen Press).

Liebman, M., C.L. Mohler, and C.P. Staver, (eds)
2001 *Ecological Management of Agricultural Weeds* (Cambridge: Cambridge University Press).

Lovelock, James
2006 *The Revenge of Gai* (London: Allen Lane).

Lucas, Gavin
2005 *The Archaeology of Time* (Themes in Archaeology; London: Routledge).

Luz, Ulrich
2001 *Matthew 8–20* (trans. James E. Crouch; Hermeneia; Minneapolis: Fortress Press).

McAfee, Gene
2000 'Chosen People in a Chosen Land: Theology and Ecology in the Story of Israel's Origins', in *The Earth Story in Genesis* (ed. Norman C. Habel and Shirley Wurst; The Earth Bible; Sheffield: Sheffield Academic Press), pp. 158-74.

McCasland, S. Vernon
1939 'The Asklepios Cult in Palestine', *JBL* 58.3: 223-24.

McDuffie, E.
2012 'Theology and Ecology in Dialogue on Death and Resurrection', in AAR Upper-Midwest Regional Conference, 2012. Academia:edu: Luther Seminary. https://www.academia.edu/2446172/Theology_and_Ecology_in_Dialogue_ on_Death_and_Resurrection?login=em.wainwright@auckland.ac.nz& email_was_taken=true (accessed 23 March 2015).

McFague, Sallie
1993 *The Body of God: An Ecological Theology* (Minneapolis: Fortress Press).
1997 *Super, Natural Christians: How We Should Love Nature* (Minneapolis: Fortress Press).

McIvor, Robert K.
1995 'The Parable of the Weeds among the Wheat (Matt 13:24-30, 36-43) and

the Relationship between the Kingdom and the Church as Portrayed in the Gospel of Matthew', *JBL* 114.4: 643-59.

McVann, Mark
- 1993 'One of the Prophets: Matthew's Testing Narrative as a Rite of Passage', *BTB* 23: 14-20.

Macy, Joanna, and John Seed
- 1996 'Gaia Meditations', in *This Sacred Earth: Religion, Nature and Environment* (ed. R.S. Gottlieb; Routledge: New York), pp. 501-502.

Madden, Frederic W.
- 1967 *History of Jewish Coinage and of Money in the Old and New Testament* (Library of Biblical Studies; New York: KTAV).

Malafouris, Lambros
- 2008 'At the Potter's Wheel: An Argument *for* Material Agency', in *Material Agency: Toward a Non-Anthropocentric Approach* (ed. Carl Knappett and Lambros Malafouris; New York: Springer), pp. 19-36.

Malina Bruce J.
- 1989 'Christ and Time: Swiss or Mediterranean?', *CBQ* 51.1: 1-31.
- 1993 *The New Testament World: Insights from Cultural Anthropology* (Louisville, KY: Westminster/John Knox Press, rev. edn).

Malina Bruce J., and Jerome Neyrey
- 1988 *Calling Jesus Names: The Social Value of Labels in Matthew* (Sonoma: Polebridge Press).

Malina, Bruce J., and Richard L. Rohrbaugh
- 1992 *Social-Science Commentary on the Synoptic Gospels* (Minneapolis: Fortress Press).

Manolopoulos, Mark
- 2009 *If Creation Is a Gift* (Suny Series in Theology and Continental Thought; Albany, NY: State University of New York Press).

Manor, Dale W.
- 1997 'Bethlehem', in *The Oxford Encyclopedia of Archaeology in the Near East* (ed. Eric M. Meyers; New York: Oxford University Press), p. 302.

Marlow, Hilary
- 2008 'The Other Prophet! The Voice of Earth in the Book of Amos', in *Exploring Ecological Hermeneutics* (ed. Norman C. Habel and PeterTrudinger; SBL Symposium, 20; Atlanta: SBL), pp. 75-84.

Martin, Luther H.
- 1987 *Hellenistic Religions: An Introduction* (New York: Oxford University Press).

Massey, Doreen, John Allen and Philip Sarre (eds.)
- 1999 *Human Geography Today* (Cambridge: Polity Press).

May, Jon, and Nigel Thrift
- 2001 'Introduction', in *Timespace: Geographies of Temporality* (ed. Jon May and Nigel Thrift; London: Routledge), pp. 1-46.

Meadowcroft, Tim
- 2006 *Haggai* (Readings: A New Biblical Commentary; Sheffield: Sheffield Phoenix Press).

Mendoza, Manuel Villalobos
- 2012 *Abject Bodies in the Gospel of Mark* (The Bible in the Modern World, 45; Sheffield: Sheffield Phoenix Press).

Metzger, Bruce M.
  1975 *A Textual Commentary on the Greek New Testament* (London: United Bible Societies).
Meyers, Eric M.
  2003 'The Problems of Gendered Space in Syro-Palestinian Domestic Architecture: The Case of Roman-Period Galilee', in *Early Christian Families in Context: An Interdisciplinary Dialogue* (eds David L. Balch and Carolyn Osiek; Grand Rapids: Eerdmans), pp. 44-69.
Milton, Kay
  2002 *Loving Nature: Towards an Ecology of Emotion* (London: Routledge).
Miquel, Esther
  2010 'How to Discredit an Inconvenient Exorcist', *BTB* 40.4: 187-206.
Moldenke, Harold N., and Alma L. Moldenke
  2002 *Plants of the Bible* (The Kegan Paul Library of Religion and Mysicisim; London: Kegan Paul).
Moore, Stephen D. (ed.)
  2014 *Divinanimality: Animal Theory, Creaturely Theology* (New York: Fordham University Press).
Morton, Timothy
  2007 *Ecology Without Nature: Rethinking Environmental Aesthetics* (Cambridge: Harvard University Press).
  2010 *The Ecological Thought* (Cambridge: Harvard University Press).
Moxnes, Halvor
  2003 *Putting Jesus in His Place: A Radical Vision of Household and Kingdom* (Louisville, KY: Westminster/John Knox Press).
  2010 'Identity in Jesus' Galilee—from Ethnicity to Locative Intersectionality', *Biblical Interpretation* 19.4-5: 390-416.
Murphy-O'Connor, Jerome
  1975 'The Structure of Matthew XIV-XVII', *RB* 82: 360-84.
  1999 'Fishers of Fish, Fishers of Men: What We Know of the First Disciples from Their Profession', *BRev* 15.3: 22-27, 48.
Musselman, L.J.
  2012 *A Dictionary of Bible Plants* (Cambridge: Cambridge University Press).
Myers, Ched
  2008 *Binding the Strong Man: A Political Reading of Mark's Story of Jesus* (Maryknoll, NY: Orbis Books).
n/a
  2011. *Our Planet: The Past, Present and Future of Earth* (Magna).
  n/d 'What does Ecozoic Mean? In *Ecozoic Times*, http://ecozoictimes.com/what-is-the-ecozoic/what-does-ecozoic-mean/ for an explanation of the word in relation to Berry's coining of it (accessed 28 January 2015).
Nanos, Mark D.
  2009 'Paul's Reversal of Jews Calling Gentiles "Dogs" (Philippians 3:2): 1600 Years of an Ideological Tale Wagging an Exegetical Dog?', *Biblical Interpretation* 17: 448-82.
Nash, James A.
  1991 *Loving Nature: Ecological Integrity and Christian Responsibility* (Nashville: Abingdon Press).

1996 'Toward the Ecological Reformation of *Christianity*', *Interpretation* 50.1: 5-15.
2009 'The Bible Vs. Biodiversity: The Case against Moral Argument from Scripture', *JSRNC* 3.2: 213-37.

Nelson, Stephanie A.
1988 *God and the Land: The Metaphysics of Farming in Hesiod and Vergil* (New York: Oxford University Press).

Neusner, Jacob, William S. Green and Ernest Frerichs (eds.)
1987 *Judaisms and Their Messiahs at the Turn of the Christian Era* (Cambridge: Cambridge University Press).

Newheart, Michael Willett
2004 *'My Name Is Legion': The Story and Soul of the Gerasene Demoniac* (Interfaces; Collegeville, MN: Liturgical Press).

Neyrey, Jerome H.
1991 'The Symbolic Universe of Luke–Acts: "They Turn the World Upside Down"', in *The Social World of Luke–Acts* (ed. Jerome H. Neyrey; Peabody, MA: Hendrickson), pp. 271-304.
1998 *Honor and Shame in the Gospel of Matthew* (Louisville, KY: Westminster/John Knox Press).

Nolland, John
2005 *The Gospel of Matthew: A Commentary on the Greek Text* (NIGTC; Grand Rapids: Eerdmans).

Novakovic, Lidija
2003 *Messiah, the Healer of the Sick* (WUNT, 2.170; Tübingen: Mohr Siebeck).

Nun, Mendel
1989 *Newly Discovered Harbour from New Testament Days around the Sea of Galilee* (Kibbutz Ein Gev).
1993 'Cast Your Net Upon the Waters: Fish and Fishermen in Jesus' Time', *BAR* 19.6 (1993): 46-56, 70.

Nunn, Patrick D.
1997 *Keimami Sa Vakila Na Liga Ni Kalou (Feeling the Hand of God): Human and Nonhuman Impacts on Pacific Island Environments* (Suva: University of the South Pacific, 3rd edn).

Oakman, Douglas E.
2008 *Jesus and the Peasants* (Matrix: The Bible in Mediterranean Context; Eugene: Cascade Books).

Ortner, Sherry B.
1974 'Is Female to Male as Nature Is to Culture?', in *Women, Culture and Society* (ed. Michelle Zimbalist Rosaldo and Louise Lamphere; Stanford, CA: Stanford University Press), pp. 67-87.

Orton, David E.
1989 *The Understanding Scribe: Matthew and the Apocalyptic Ideal* (New York: T. & T. Clark International).

Osiek, Carolyn, Margaret Y. Macdonald, with Janet H. Tulloch
2006 *A Woman's Place: House Churches in Earliest Christianity* (Minneapolis: Fortress Press).

Overman, J. Andrew
1996 *Church and Community in Crisis: The Gospel According to Matthew* (The New Testament in Context; Valley Forge, PA: Trinity Press International).

Pardes, I.
   1992   *Countertraditions in the Bible: A Feminist Approach* (Cambridge, MA: Harvard University Press).

Pennington, Jonathan T.
   2007   *Heaven and Earth in the Gospel of Matthew* (Grand Rapids: Baker Academic).
   2008   'Heaven, Earth, and a New Genesis: Theological Cosmology in Matthew', in *Cosmology and New Testament Theology* (ed. Jonathan T. Pennington and Sean M. McDonough; Library of New Testament Studies, 355; New York: T. & T. Clark), pp. 28-44.

Phillips, Anthony
   1970   *Ancient Israel's Criminal Law: A New Approach to the Decalogue* (New York: Schocken Books).

Phillips, Peter
   2008   'Casting out the Treasure: A New Reading of Matthew 13.52', *JSNT* 31.1: 3-24.

Philostratus
   2005   *Life of Apollonius of Tyana, Volume 1: Books 1-4* (ed. and trans. Christopher P. Jones; LCL, 16; Cambridge: Harvard University Press).
   2005   *Life of Apollonius of Tyana, Volume 2: Books 5-8* (ed. and trans. Christopher P. Jones; LCL, 16; Cambridge: Harvard University Press).

Pilch, John J.
   2000   *Healing in the New Testament: Insights from Medical and Mediterranean Anthropology* (Minneapolis: Fortress Press).

Pliny
   1951   *Natural History: with an English Translation in Ten Volumes I* (trans. W.H.S. Jones; Cambridge: Harvard University Press).

Plumwood, Val
   1993   *Feminism and the Mastery of Nature* (Feminism for Today; London: Routledge).

Pomeroy, Sarah B.
   1994   *Xenophon, Oeconomicus: A Social and Historical Commentary, with a New English Translation* (Oxford: Clarendon Press).

Ponting, C.
   1991   *A Green History of the World: The Environment and the Collapse of Great Civilizations* (London: Penguin).

Powell, Mark Allan
   2000a   'The Magi as Kings: An Adventure in Reader-Response Criticism', *CBQ* 62.3: 459-80.
   2000b 'The Magi as Wise Men: Reexamining a Basic Supposition', *NTS* 46.1: 1-20.

Primack, Joel R., and Nancy Ellen Abrams
   2006   *The View from the Center of the Universe: Discovering Our Extraordinary Place in the Cosmos* (New York: Riverhead Books).

Primavesi, Anne
   2000   *Sacred Gaia: Holistic Theology and Earth System Science* (London: Routledge).
   2003   *Gaia's Gift* (London: Routledge).
   2011   *Cultivating Unity within the Biodiversity of God* (Salem: Polebridge).

Rasmussen, Larry L.
    1996   *Earth Community, Earth Ethics* (Geneva: WCC Publications).
Reddish, Mitchell G.
    1992   'Heaven', in *The Anchor Yale Bible Dictionary* (ed. David Noel Freedman; New York: Doubleday), p. 253.
Reid, Barbara
    2004   'Violent Endings in Matthew's Parables and Christian Nonviolence', *CBQ* 66.2: 237-65.
Resseguie, James L.
    2005   *Narrative Criticism of the New Testament: An Introduction* (Grand Rapids: Baker Academic).
Rich, Adrienne
    1972   'When We Dead Awaken: Writing as Revision', *College English* 34: 18-30.
Richardson, Peter
    1996   *Herod: King of the Jews and Friend of the Romans* (Columbia: University of South Carolina Press).
Rigby, Kate
    2004   'Earth, World, Text: On the (Im)Possibility of Ecopoiesis', *New Literary History* 35.3: 427-42.
Robbins, Vernon K.
    1996a   *The Tapestry of Early Christian Discourse: Rhetoric, Society and Ideology* (London: Routledge).
    1996b   *Exploring the Texture of Texts: A Guide to Socio-Rhetorical Interpretation* (Valley Forge, PA: Trinity Press International).
    2009   *The Invention of Christian Discourse* (Rhetoric of Religious Antiquity Series, 1; Blanford Forum: Deo).
Rohrbaugh, Richard L.
    2007   *The New Testament in Cross-Cultural Perspective* (Matrix: The Bible in Mediterranean Context; Eugene: Cascade Books).
Rose, Deborah Bird
    2004   *Reports from a Wild Country: Ethics for Decolonisation* (Sydney: University of New South Wales Press).
Rosenfeld, Anne Wertheim, with Robert T. Paine
    2002   *The Intertidal Wilderness: A Photographic Journey through Pacific Coast Tidepools* (Berkeley: University of California Press, rev. edn).
Rosenzweig, Michael
    2003   'Reconciliation Ecology and the Future of Species Diversity', *Oryx* 37.2: 194-205.
Rozi, E.
    2014   *Jewish Drama and Theatre: From Rabbinical Intolerance to Secular Liberalism* (Eastborne: Sussex Academic e-Library).
Ruether, Rosemary Radford
    1992   *Gaia and God: An Ecofeminist Theology of Earth Healing* (New York: HarperSanFrancisco).
Runesson, Anders
    2008   'Rethinking Early Jewish-Christian Relations: Matthean Community History as Pharisaic Intragroup Conflict', *JBL* 127.1: 95-132.
Russell, Robert John
    2008   *Cosmology: From Alpha to Omega* (Theology and the Sciences; Minneapolis: Fortress Press).

Saddington, D.B.
    2006   'The Centurion in Matthew 8:5-13: Consideration of the Proposal of Theodore W. Jennings, Jr., and Tat-Siong Benny Liew', *JBL* 125.1: 140-42.

Saldarini, Anthony J.
    1988   *Pharisees, Scribes and Sadducees in Palestinian Society* (Edinburgh: T. & T. Clark).

Sandoval, Chela
    2000   *Methodology of the Oppressed* (Minneapolis: University of Minnesota Press).

Schroer, Silvia
    2000   *Wisdom Has Built Her House: Studies on the Figure of Sophia in the Bible* (trans. Linda M. Maloney and William McDonough; Collegeville, MN: Liturgical Press).

Schüssler Fiorenza, Elisabeth
    1985   'The Will to Choose or to Reject: Continuing our Critical Work', in *Feminist Interpretation of the Bible* (ed. Letty Russell; Philadelphia: Westminister Press), pp. 125-36.
    1992   *But She Said: Feminist Practices of Biblical Interpretation* (Boston: Beacon).
    1994   *Jesus, Miriam's Child, Sophia's Prophet: Critical Issues in Feminist Christology* (New York: Continuum).
    1995   *Bread not Stone: The Challenge of Feminist Biblical Interpretation* (10th Anniversary Edition; Boston: Beacon).
    2007   *The Power of the Word: Scripture and the Rhetoric of Empire* (Minneapolis: Fortress Press).

Segal, Allan F.
    1991   'Matthew's Jewish Voice', in *Social History of the Matthean Community* (ed. David L. Balch; Louisville, KY: Westminster/John Knox Press), pp. 3-37.

Sim, David C.
    1996   *Apocalyptic Eschatology in the Gospel of Matthew* (SNTSMS, 88; Cambridge: Cambridge University Press).

Soja, Edward W.
    1996   *Thirdspace: Journeys to Los Angeles and Other Real-and-Imagined Places* (Oxford: Blackwell).
    1999   'Thirdspace: Expanding the Scope of the Geographical Imagination', in *Human Geography Today* (ed. Doreen Massey, John Allen and Philip Sarre; Cambridge: Polity Press), pp. 260-78.

Spivak, Gayatri Chakravorty
    1993   *Outside in the Teaching Machine* (New York: Routledge).

Stegner, William Richard
    1967   'Wilderness and Testing in the Scrolls and in Matthew 4:1-11', *Biblical Research* 12: 18-27.

Stewart, Eric C.
    2009   *Gathered around Jesus: An Alternative Spatial Practice in the Gospel of Mark* (Matrix: The Bible in Mediterranean Context; Eugene: Cascade Books).

Strabo
    1930   *Geography, Volume 7, Books 15-16* (ed. and trans. Horace Leonard Jones; LCL, 241; London: Heinemann).

Strange, James F., and Hershel Shanks
    1982   "Has the House Where Jesus Stayed in Capernaum Been Found?', *BAR* 8. 6: 26-37.

Talbert, Charles
    2010   *Matthew* (Paideia Commentaries on the New Testament; Grand Rapids: Baker Academic).

Taylor, Apirana
    1996   'Whakapapa', in *Soft Leaf Falls of the Moon* (ed. Apirana Taylor; Wellington: The Pohutukawa Press), pp. 10-11.

Taylor, Joan E.
    1997   *The Immerser: John the Baptist within Second Temple Judaism* (Grand Rapids: Eerdmans).

Theissen, Gerd
    1992   *The Gospels in Context: Social and Political History in the Synoptic Tradition* (trans. Linda M. Maloney; Edinburgh: T. & T. Clark).

Theophilos, Mark P.
    2012   *The Abomination of Desolation in Matthew 24:15* (Library of New Testament Studies; London: T. & T. Clark).

Theophrastus
    1916   *Enquiry into Plants* (ed. Arthur Hort; Loeb Classical Library, 70; Cambridge: Harvard University Press).

Thrift, Nigel
    1999   'Steps to an Ecology of Place', in *Human Geography Today* (ed. Doreen Massey, John Allen and Philip Sarre; Cambridge: Polity Press), pp. 295-322.

Trainor, Michael
    2012   *About Earth's Child: An Ecological Listening to the Gospel of Luke* (The Earth Bible Commentary Series, 2. Sheffield: Sheffield Phoenix).

Trible, Phyllis
    1978   *God and the Rhetoric of Sexuality* (Philadelphia: Fortress Press).
    1984   *Texts of Terror: Literary-Feminist Readings of Biblical Narratives* (Philadelphia: Fortress Press).

Tsumura, David Toshio
    1994   'The Earth in Genesis 1', in *"I Studied Inscriptions from before the Flood": Ancient near Eastern, Literary and Linguistic Approaches to Genesis 1–11* (ed. Richard S. Hess and David Toshio Tsumura; Sources for Biblical and Theological Study; Winona Lake: Eisenbraun), pp. 310-28.

Tzaferis, Vassilios (ed.)
    1989   *Excavations at Capernaum: Volume 1 1978–1982* (Winona Lake, IN: Eisenbrauns).

Varro
    1934   *On Agriculture* (ed. Harrison Boyd Ash; trans. W.D. Hooper; LCL, 283; London: Heinemann, 1934).

Volohonsky, H., A. Kaplanovsky and S. Serruya
    1983   'Storms on Lake Kinneret: Observations and Mathematical Model', *Ecological Modelling* 18: 141-53.

Wachsmann, Shelley
    1988   'The Galilee Boat: 2,000-Year-Old Hull Recovered Intact', *BAR* 14.5: 18-33.

Wainwright, Elaine M.
    1991   *Toward a Feminist Critical Reading of the Gospel According to Matthew* (BZNW, 60; Berlin: W. de Gruyter).
    1998   *Shall We Look for Another? A Feminist Rereading of the Matthean Jesus* (Maryknoll, NY: Orbis Books).

2006	*Women Healing/Healing Women: The Genderization of Healing in Early Christianity* (London: Equinox).
2008	'Healing Ointment/Healing Bodies: Gift and Identification in an Ecofeminist Reading of Mark 14:3-9', in *Exploring Ecological Hermeneutics* (ed. Norman C. Habel and Peter Trudinger; Atlanta: Society of Biblical Literature), pp. 131-40.
2009a	'The Book of the Genealogy: How Shall We Read It?', *Eco-Theology* (ed. L.C. Susin, E.M. Wainwright, and F. Wilfred; *Concilium* 2009/3; London: SCM Press), pp. 13-23.
2009b	'Land of the Kauri and the Long White Cloud: Beginning to Read Matthew 1–2 Ecologically', in *Postcolonial Interventions: Essays in Honor of R.S. Sugirtharajah* (ed. Tat-Siong B. Liew; Sheffield Sheffield Phoenix), pp. 332-36.
2010a	'Place, Power and Potentiality: Reading Matthew 2:1-12 Ecologically', *ExpTim* 121.4: 159-67.
2010b	'"Clothed and in His Right Mind": An Exploration of Spirit Possession in Early Christianity', in *Spirit Possession, Theology and Identity: A Pacific Exploration* (ed. Elaine M. Wainwright, Philip Culbertson and Susan Smith; Hindmarsh: ATF Press), pp. 155-81.
2011	'Beyond the Crossroads: Reading Matthew 13,52 Ecologically into the Twenty-First Century', in *The Gospel of Matthew at the Crossroads of Early Christianity* (ed. Donald Senior; BETL, 243; Leuven: Peeters), pp. 375-88.
2012a	'Images, Words, Stories: Exploring Their Transformative Power in Reading Biblical Texts Ecologically', *BibInt* 20: 280-304.
2012b	'"Hear then the Parable of the Seed": Reading the Agrarian Parables of Matthew 13 Ecologically', in *The One Who Reads May Run: Essays in Honour of Edgar W. Conrad* (ed. Roland Boer, Michael Carden and Julie Kelso; New York: T. & T. Clark), pp. 125-41.
2013a.	'Reading the Gospel of Matthew Ecologically in Oceania: Matthew 4:1-11 as Focal Text', in *Matthew* (ed. Nicole Wilkinson Duran and James P. Grimshaw; Minneapolis: Fortress Press), pp. 255-70.
2013b	'Of Borders, Bread, Dogs and Demons: Reading Matthew 15:21-28 Ecologically', in *Where the Wild Ox Roams: Biblical Essays in Honour of Norman C. Habel* (ed. Alan H. Cadwallader and with Peter L. Trudinger; Sheffield: Sheffield Phoenix), pp. 114-26.
2014	'"Save Us! We Are Perishing!" Reading Matthew 8:23-27 in the Face of Devastating Floods', in *Bible, Borders, Belonging(s): Engaging Readings from Oceania* (ed. Jione Havea, David J. Neville and Elaine M. Wainwright; SBL SemeiaSt, 75; Atlanta: SBL), pp. 21-37.
2015a	'"In Memory of Her"! Exploring the Political Power of Readings—Feminist and Ecological', *Feminist Theology* 23.2: 205-220.
2015b	'Queer[y]ing the Sermon on the Mount', in *Sexuality, Ideology, and the Bible: Queer Readings from the Antipodes* (ed. Robert J. Myles and Caroline Blyth; Sheffield: Sheffield Phoenix), pp. 115-31.

Wainwright, E.M., Robert J. Myles and Carlos Olivares
  2014   *The Gospel According to Matthew: The Basileia Is near at Hand* (Phoenix Guides to the New Testament; Sheffield: Sheffield Phoenix Press).

Weaver, Dorothy Jean
  1990   *Matthew's Missionary Discourse: A Literary Critical Analysis* (JSNTSup, 38; Sheffield: Sheffield Academic Press).

Weber, Thomas M.
    2007   'Gadara and the Galilee', in *Religion, Ethnicity, and Identity in Ancient Galilee* (ed. Jürgen Zangenberg, Harold W. Attridge and Dale B. Martin; WUNT, 210; Tübingen: Mohr Siebeck), pp. 449-77.

Weissenrieder, Annette
    2003   *Images of Illness in the Gospel of Luke* (WUNT, 2.164; Tübingen: Mohr Siebeck).

Whatmore, Sarah
    1999   'Hybrid Geographies: Rethinking the "Human" in Human Geography', in *Human Geography Today* (ed. Doreen Massey, John Allen and Philip Sarre; Cambridge: Polity Press), pp. 22-45.

Windle, Phyllis
    1992   'The Ecology of Grief', *BioScience* 42.5: 363-66.

Xenophon
    2013   *Memorabilia, Oeconomicus, Symposium, Apology* (ed. O.J. Todd; trans. E.C. Marchant: LCL, 168; London: Heinemann).

Yamasaki, Gary
    1998   *John the Baptist in Life and Death: Audience-Oriented Criticism of Matthew's Narrative* (JSNTS, 167; Sheffield: Sheffield Academic Press).

Zohary, Michael
    1952   'Ecological Studies in the Vegetation of the Near Eastern Deserts: 1—Environment and vegetation Classes', *Israel Exploration Journal* 2.4: 201-215.
    1982   *Plants of the Bible: A Complete Handbook to All the Plants with 200 Full-Color Plates Taken in the Natural Habitat* (Cambridge: Cambridge University Press).

Indexes

Index of References

Old Testament/Hebrew Bible

Genesis		23.2	77	34.21	126
1.1–2.4	26	26.17	35	34.27-28	65
1.6-8	61	26.19	35	34.28	65
1.11-12	60	37.34	77		
1.26-28	14, 15	37.35	78	*Leviticus*	
1.26	14, 79	38.13	35	11.7-8	112
1.27	30, 31	38.14	35	25 LXX	87
1.28	30	38.18	36	25.10 LXX	87
2.2-3	125	38.26	36	25.11 LXX	87
2.4	26, 29, 31	41.57–46.7	52	25.12 LXX	87
2.8	46	50.3	77	25.13 LXX	87
2.15	79			25.28 LXX	87
2.23-24	46	*Exodus*		25.30 LXX	87
3.1	59	1.1–3.15	56	25.31 LXX	87
3.16	31	3.8	60	25.33 LXX	87
5.1-32	33	3.14	154	25.40 LXX	87
5.1-2	29-31	3.17	60	25.41 LXX	87
5.1	14, 29	9.22-35	61	25.50 LXX	87
5.2	31	12.15	139	25.52 LXX	87
9.1-6	14	12.19	139	25.54 LXX	87
10.18	34	13.3	139		
11.2	46	13.5	60	*Numbers*	
12–50	33, 34	13.7	139	12.3	78
12.6	34	13.17–20.26	56	22–24	45
13.7	34	14	105	24.17-19	45
13.10	34	16	86	26.53	79
14.3	35	17.1-7	67		
14.6	34	17.2 LXX	67	*Deuteronomy*	
14.8	35	19.1-6	74	5.14	125, 178
14.10	35	19.17-20	74	6.13	68
14.17	35	20.10	125	6.16	67
15.21	34	24.12-18	74	8.1-10	56
16.7	34, 56	24.15-18	165, 166	8.3	67
16.14	34	24.16	165	8.7-10	182
16.20	34	32.15-19	74	12.2	67
16.21	34	33.19	81	14.8	112
21.14-19	56	34	67	15	87
22.2-19	74	34.1-9	74	15.1	87

Deuteronomy (cont.)		1 Chronicles		72.16	32, 83
15.2	87	7.22	78	77.16	154
15.3	87			77.19	154
15.9	87	Job		84.4-5	75
16.3	139	1.3	178	84.12	75
27.3	60	9.8	154	85.10-13	80, 81
30	56	28	11	89.15	75
		38–39	11	91.11	67
Joshua				91.12	67
2.1-21	36	Psalms		94.12	75
2.1	37	1.1	75	105.11	79
2.6	37	2.7	63	106.3	75
2.15	37	22	211	107.28-33	107
6.16-17	36	24.1	79	119.1	75
6.20-22	36	25.9	78	119.2	75
6.21	37	32.1-2	75	119.176	160
10.11	61	34.2	78	128.1	75
		34.8	75	146.5	75
Judges		35.22-23	107	148.4	61
2.17	178	37	79, 80	149.4	78
		37.9	80		
Ruth		37.11	79, 80	Proverbs	
1.8	38	37.12	80	3.13	75
1.16-17	38	37.16	80	8.22-31	124
2.12	186	37.17	80	8.22	124
4.17	38	37.21	80	8.23	124
4.18-22	38	37.22	80	8.29	4
		37.25	79, 80	8.30	124
1 Samuel		37.28-29	79	8.31	124
15.35	77	37.29	80	8.34	75
		37.30	80	9.1-6	91
2 Samuel		37.32	80	10.10	83
5.2	48	37.39	80	14.1	91
5.8	181, 182	40.4	75	24.3	91
11–12	39	41.1	75	31.8	75
11	39	44.24-25	108	31.9	75
11.5	39	44.27	108		
12.7	39	65.4	75	Ecclesiastes	
12.24	39	69.21	210	12.9-12	146
		72	32, 83		
1 Kings		72.1-7	32	Isaiah	
19	67	72.1	32, 83	3.9	185
19.8-18	74	72.2	83	3.11	185
19.8	65	72.3	83	5.8	185
19.11-15	166	72.6	83	7–9	42
19.19-21	70	72.7	83	7.9	42
		72.8-11	83	7.14	69
2 Kings		72.8	83	8.23–9.1 LXX	69
1.8	59	72.11	50	9.1-7	69
20.13	144	72.12-14	32	9.1-2	69
22.10	142			9.7	80

Index of References

11.5	80	*Jeremiah*		2.10 LXX	45	
11.18	185	4.28	12, 77	2.27 LXX	45	
11.20	185	7.4	180	4.7 LXX	45	
11.21	185	7.6	180	5.7 LXX	45	
11.22	185	7.11	180, 181	5.11 LXX	45	
13.8	191	8.1-3	182	5.15 LXX	45	
26.17-18	191	8.13	182			
31.5	186	12.4	77	*Hosea*		
33.9	77	12.11	12	4.3	77	
39.2	144	36.32	142	6.6	126	
40.6-8	76	41.8	144			
41.2	46	48.8 LXX	144	*Jonah*		
42.1	63	50.6	118, 119,	1.4-5	106	
49.13	81		160			
51.9-11	106-108			*Micah*		
51.9	106	*Ezekiel*		5.1 LXX	48	
51.10	106	20.40	67	5.2	48	
52.7	58	25.4	46			
54.10	81, 82	25.10	46	*Habakkuk*		
55.10	61	34	119	3.15	154	
56.1-8	180	34.6	118, 119			
56.7	180, 181	34.8	118, 119	*Zephaniah*		
60.6	50	34.10	118	3.12	78	
61.2-3	77, 78	34.11	118			
61.2	78			*Zechariah*		
61.3	78	*Daniel*		9.9	78, 178	
62.11	178	1.20 LXX	45			
66.7-8	191	2.2 LXX	45			

NEW TESTAMENT

Matthew				62, 65	2.1	43-46, 50,
1–2	28, 29	1.20		40, 51, 62,		51, 59,
1	43			65		101, 175
1.1	29, 31, 32,	1.21		41, 42, 70	2.2	45, 49, 59,
	39, 57, 68,	1.22-23		41		148
	124, 174	1.22		108, 156	2.3	59, 175
1.2-17	33	1.23		42, 53, 58,	2.4	142
1.2	33-35			62, 63, 65,	2.5-6	48, 49
1.3	35, 40			68, 69, 75,	2.5	43, 59
1.5	35, 36, 40			82, 84, 91,	2.6	43, 48
1.6-16	39			108, 124,	2.7	49
1.6	35, 39, 40			137, 154,	2.8	43, 50
1.16-25	40			164, 211,	2.9	50
1.16	32, 40			215, 216	2.11	44, 50, 53
1.17	32	2		43, 50, 51	2.12	50, 51, 151
1.18-25	40	2.1-12		43, 48, 51,	2.13-25	68
1.18-23	211			66, 97, 121	2.13-23	51
1.18	32, 40, 41,	2.1-11		150	2.13-15	53

Matthew (cont.)		4.8	74	5.6	32, 66, 78,
2.13-14	51	4.9	94, 141		80, 86,
2.13	50-53, 151	4.10	68, 94		107, 175,
2.14	51, 53, 69	4.12-25	68		182, 189
2.16-18	51, 52	4.12-13	63	5.7-10	81
2.16	43	4.12	128, 151	5.9	82, 83
2.19-20	51	4.13	69, 148	5.10-12	83
2.19	44, 51	4.15-16	69	5.10	32, 66, 78,
2.20	51, 53	4.17	58, 70, 73,		80, 83, 86,
2.21	51, 53, 55		75, 77, 86,		107, 216
2.22-23	52, 55		103, 116,	5.12	83
2.22	69, 128,		120, 122,	5.13-16	83
	151		163, 216	5.14	74
3–4	28, 54, 67	4.18-22	70, 94,	5.17-42	83
3	59, 63, 64,		104, 117	5.17	184
	164	4.18	70, 103	5.20	66, 78, 80,
3.1-12	55	4.20	70, 72		84, 107,
3.1	54, 55, 57,	4.21-22	105		126, 142,
	59, 60	4.21	70, 103		189
3.2	58, 59, 63,	4.22	70, 72	5.21-48	84
	67, 69, 73,	4.23–9.35	150	5.21	32
	77, 86,	4.23-25	71, 175	5.43-48	84
	120, 150	4.23-24	92, 116,	5.43-44	135
3.4	58, 64, 150		149, 217	5.45	84, 140
3.5-6	59	4.23	72, 73, 77,	5.48	84
3.5	175		117, 120,	6.1-4	84
3.7-12	59		122, 127,	6.1	32, 66, 78,
3.7	59, 126		128, 156,		80, 84,
3.8	60		159, 161,		107, 189
3.10	60		163, 201,	6.5-15	84
3.11-12	61, 67		216	6.9-15	74
3.11	62, 65, 217	4.24	72, 110,	6.9-13	84
3.12	60, 137		128, 156	6.9	85
3.13-17	60, 61, 63	4.25	74, 110	6.10	86, 162,
3.13	60	5–9	115, 116		208
3.15	32, 66, 80,	5–7	28, 72, 73,	6.11	151
	107		91, 93, 167	6.12	87
3.16-17	68, 73	5.1-12	74, 198	6.13	88
3.16	61, 62, 65,	5.1-2	75, 116,	6.14-15	88
	103		131, 153	6.19-24	89
3.17	65, 70, 217	5.1	74, 103,	6.19-21	84, 88
4	63, 64, 164		165, 190	6.22-23	88
4.1-12	67	5.2	74, 122	6.23	107
4.1-11	63, 64	5.3-12	75	6.24	88
4.1	63, 64	5.3-11	185	6.25-34	74, 88, 89
4.2	65, 182	5.3-10	91	6.25	89, 90
4.3-10	65	5.3	76, 77, 80,	6.26	89, 90
4.3	68, 111		86	6.27	89
4.4	66	5.4	77, 78	6.28	89
4.6	111	5.5	79, 80	6.30	89

6.31	89	8.23-27	104, 105	10.6			118, 119, 160
6.33	32, 66, 78, 80	8.25	155				
		8.28–9.1	109	10.7-15	120		
6.34	89	8.28	109-11	10.7-10	120		
7.1-5	90	8.30-31	111	10.8	180		
7.6	90	8.30	111	10.9-10	120		
7.7-12	90	8.32	112, 113	10.11-15	120		
7.9	90	9.1-8	114	10.12	120		
7.10	90	9.1	131	10.16-23	192		
7.13-14	90	9.3	142	10.16	118, 119, 121		
7.13	90	9.5	161				
7.15-20	90	9.6-7	131	10.17	121		
7.15	90	9.7	131	10.18	121		
7.16-20	60, 182	9.9	70, 104, 117	10.19	89		
7.21-29	74			10.21-22	121		
7.21	86, 90, 162	9.11	126	10.21	121		
7.22	110	9.13	82	10.22	192		
7.24-29	90	9.18-26	114	10.27	122, 123		
7.24-25	165	9.18	161	10.29-31	121		
7.24	90	9.27-31	115, 177	10.29	121		
7.28-29	74	9.27-28	181	10.30	121		
7.28	91, 141, 167, 200	9.27	128, 160, 176, 193	10.35-37	121		
				10.36	135		
7.29	76, 142	9.32-34	115	11–12	28, 122		
8–9	28, 71, 72, 92, 93, 96, 102, 117, 127, 161, 201	9.33	180	11	125		
		9.34	121, 126	11.1	91, 121, 122, 125, 141, 167, 200		
		9.35-36	116				
		9.35	71-73, 115, 117, 120, 122, 127, 128, 149, 156, 159, 201, 216, 217				
				11.2-19	123		
8.1-4	94			11.2-6	163		
8.1	74, 93, 116			11.2	124, 125		
8.2	95, 161			11.4	122, 123		
8.3	95, 96			11.5	181, 206		
8.4	96	9.36-38	117	11.19	123-25		
8.5-13	96, 102	9.36	115, 117-19, 151, 216	11.21-24	124		
8.5	98, 112			11.25-27	124, 125		
8.6	98, 100, 103, 111			11.25	124		
		9.37-38	137	11.28-30	125		
8.7	128, 156	10	28, 116, 117, 121, 167	11.31	193		
8.9-14	193			12	125, 129		
8.9	98			12.1-8	125		
8.10-12	101	10.1-4	215	12.7	82		
8.14-15	70, 102, 117	10.1	116, 117, 180	12.9-14	127, 161		
				12.10	128		
8.15	104	10.2-4	117	12.11	193		
8.16-22	104	10.2-3	117	12.12	127, 128		
8.16	110, 128, 156, 180	10.5-9	118	12.13	127, 128		
		10.5-6	120	12.14-15	130		
8.18-22	121	10.5	119	12.14	128, 157		

Matthew (cont.)		13.22	135	14.3	69
12.15	128, 151, 156, 157	13.23	135	14.5	150
		13.24-50	134	14.11	150
12.16-21	129	13.24-30	135	14.12	150
12.16	108	13.24	134, 135, 141, 174	14.13–17.20	150
12.19	123			14.13-36	151
12.22-32	128	13.25	135	14.13-21	152, 163, 201
12.22	156	13.26	135		
12.23	160	13.27	135, 143	14.13	151
12.24-45	130	13.28	135	14.14	156
12.24	180	13.29	135	14.15	151, 155
12.28	180	13.30	135, 137	14.16	151
12.33	60, 129, 182	13.31-34	138	14.19	156, 206
		13.31-32	138	14.20	151
12.34	129	13.31	135, 141, 174	14.21	151, 156
12.35	129, 145			14.22-32	152
12.38	142	13.33	44, 141, 174	14.22-23	153
12.40	129			14.22	156
12.46-50	71, 129, 131	13.34-35	139	14.23	74, 153, 161
		13.35	74		
12.46	131	13.36	135, 139, 141, 148	14.24	153
12.48-50	130			14.25	153, 155
12.50	86	13.37-43	135	14.26	154
13	130, 131, 135, 143, 145, 167, 174, 195	13.37	135	14.27	155
		13.38	135, 141	14.28-33	163
		13.39	135	14.28-31	154
		13.40	135	14.28	154
13.1-9	130	13.41	141	14.31	155
13.1-3	130	13.43	141	14.32	153
13.1	55, 130, 139, 148	13.44-50	140	14.33	94, 164
		13.44	135, 140, 141, 174	14.34-36	155, 161
13.2	131			14.34-35	163
13.3-9	44, 131	13.45	135, 140, 141, 174	14.34	156
13.3-8	131, 145			14.35-36	156
13.3	135	13.47-50	140	14.35	156
13.4	135	13.47-48	140	15.1-20	156, 163
13.5	132	13.47	140, 141, 174	15.1	175, 176
13.7	132			15.6-9	162
13.8	132	13.51-52	139, 141	15.21-38	163
13.10-17	134	13.51	146, 147	15.21-28	156, 163
13.10	139, 141	13.52	141-48, 167	15.21	151, 156, 157, 163
13.11	141				
13.16	123	13.53–14.12	149	15.22-23	159
13.18-23	134, 139	13.53	91, 141, 148, 200	15.22	157, 158, 176
13.18	123, 131, 135				
		13.54	149	15.23	160
13.19	134, 135, 141	14–17	28, 148, 149, 167	15.24	160, 161
				15.25	160
13.20-21	165	14.1-11	150	15.26	162
13.20	135	14.2	150	15.28	162

15.29-31	163	19.20	141	21.45	172		
15.29	74	19.28	174	21.46	172		
15.30-31	181	20	174	22.2-12	183		
15.32-39	163, 201	20.1	174	22.15	172		
15.36	206	20.15	174	22.18	183		
16.5-12	163	20.17	171, 175	22.23	55, 172		
16.13–17.23	163	20.18-19	175	22.37-39	84		
16.13-20	163, 164	20.20-28	176	22.41	172		
16.13	163, 164	20.20-22	213	22.44	184		
16.16	164	20.22	176	22.46	184		
16.17-19	164	20.24-28	176	23	172, 183-86		
16.18	165	20.28	44, 104, 117, 212	23.1-36	183		
16.21-28	165			23.1	184		
16.21	167, 176	20.29	176	23.2	74, 172, 184		
16.24-28	165	20.30-31	177				
16.24	212	20.30	181				
17.1-8	165	20.34	177	23.5	185		
17.1-2	216	21	171	23.13-36	184		
17.1	55, 74, 165	21.1–22.46	177	23.13	172, 185		
17.2	166	21.1-11	177, 182	23.15	172, 185		
17.3	166	21.1	74, 171, 177	23.16	185		
17.5	166			23.23	172, 185		
17.6	166	21.2	178	23.25	172, 185		
17.9	74	21.5	178	23.26	172		
17.12	167	21.6-8	179	23.27-36	185		
17.14-20	166	21.7	177	23.27-29	185		
17.18	108	21.12-17	179	23.27	172, 185		
17.20	74	21.12-14	179	23.28	185		
17.22-23	166, 167	21.12	171, 180	23.29	172, 185		
18	28, 167, 168	21.13	180, 181	23.31	185		
		21.14-15	171	23.32	101		
18.6-9	167	21.14	181	23.33	172		
18.10-14	167	21.15	172, 182	23.36	141		
18.12	74	21.16	123	23.37	186		
18.14	86	21.17	171, 182	24–25	28, 186-90, 196		
19–28	171	21.18-22	182				
19–23	28, 171, 172	21.18	171, 182	24.1-44	191		
		21.19	60	24.1	171		
19	167, 173, 174	21.21	74	24.2	141, 187		
		21.23–23.39	171	24.3	74		
19.1–20.34	172	21.23	171, 172	24.4-8	191, 192		
19.1	91, 141, 167, 171, 200	21.28	183	24.4	191		
		21.31	86	24.6	123		
		21.32	32, 80	24.7	105, 106, 108		
19.2	173	21.33	183				
19.3-12	173	21.34	60	24.8	141, 191		
19.13-15	173	21.41	60	24.9-14	192		
19.16-22	173	21.42	183	24.13-14	106		
19.18-19	173	21.43	60	24.13	192		
19.19	84	21.44	183	24.14	192		

Matthew (cont.)		26.17	206	27.28	210
24.15-28	193	26.20	206	27.29	46
24.16	74	26.21	206	27.31	210
24.21-22	193	26.23	206	27.34	210, 211
24.21	193	26.24	206, 207	27.36	211
24.27	193	26.25	206	27.37	46
24.28	193, 194	26.26-28	206	27.42-43	210
24.29-31	194	26.26	206	27.44	210
24.29	193, 194	26.30	74, 207	27.45	211
24.32	194	26.31–27.5	207	27.50	210, 211
24.33-34	141	26.31-35	207	27.54	212
24.36	194	26.31	207	27.55-58	117
24.43-44	195	26.39	208	27.55-56	176, 212
24.45–25.46	195	26.42	86, 162	27.55	118, 213
24.45	195	26.43	208	27.60	214
24.54	105, 106	26.44	208	27.61	213
25.14	198	26.45	206	27.62-66	213
25.32	198	26.46	206	27.66	214
25.36	211	26.47	208	28	213, 217
25.45-46	198	26.48	206	28.1	213
26–67	209	26.56	208	28.2-3	214
26–28	28, 200, 201	26.57-68	209	28.2	105, 106
		26.57-60	208	28.4	214
26	200	26.58	208	28.5-6	214
26.1	91, 141, 200	26.67	208	28.6	104, 214
		26.69-75	208	28.7	104, 214, 217
26.2	200, 201, 203, 205, 206	26.70	208		
		26.72	208	28.16	74
		26.74	208	28.17	94
26.3-4	201, 205	27.1-2	209	28.18-20	118, 119
26.6-13	201, 202, 205	27.2	206	28.18	26, 30, 216
		27.3	206	28.19	217
26.7	202-204	27.4	206	6.32-3	141
26.8-9	203	27.5	208		
26.8	202	27.6-66	209	*Mark*	
26.10	204	27.11	46	7.6	158
26.12	202	27.13	123	10.35-45	176
26.13	200, 205	27.18	206		
26.14-16	205	27.19	213	*Acts*	
26.14	205	27.24-25	209	12.20	157
26.15	205, 206	27.26	206, 209		
26.16	205, 206	27.27-31	210	*Revelation*	
26.17-30	205	27.27	210	11.19	61

OTHER ANCIENT REFERENCES

Septuagint		*Wisdom of Solomon*		*Ecclesiasticus*	
Tobit		2.12-20	83	6.25	125
10.11	178	10.10	58	14.1	75

Index of References

14.2	75	Philo		14.158-17.191	45
14.20	75	*Embassy to Gaius*		14.381-389	45
24.19-22	125	144-45	107	15.409	46
24.19	125			16.291	46
24.20	125	*On the Life of Moses*		16.311	46
24.21	125	1.90-95	45		
31.8	75	1.276-277	45	*Jewish War*	
34.17	75			2.21.6	99
38.24–39.3	142	Josephus		2.232	173
40.1-11	76	*Jewish Antiquities*		2.504	157
48.24	78	4.285-87	197	2.588	157
50.28	75	8.46-49	113	2.612	209
51.19	77	10.195-218	45	7.71	99
51.23-30	146	10.195-203	46	7.216-217	69
51.26	125	14.9	46		

CLASSICAL AND ANCIENT CHRISTIAN WRITINGS

Apollonius		Philostratus		Varro	
7.3	107	*Life of Apollonius*		*On Agriculture*	
		1.5	47	1.17.2	136
Athenaeus		4.20	113	1.17.5	136
Deipnosophistae		7.3	32	1.29.2	132
15	202			1.30	137
15.686	202	Pliny		1.44.2	133
15.687	202	*Natural History*		2.4.3	112
15.688	203	2.24.95	47	2.4.8	112
		2.25.95-2.37.101	47	23.1-2	133
Cato		13.12	33	24.1	133
On Agriculture		13.71-72	33		
6.1-4	133	18.21.94-95	133	Virgil	
134.1	112	19.170	138	*Aeneid*	
34.1-2	133	19.54	138	1.282	31
35.1-2	133	30.6.16-17	45		
		30.6.17-8.21	45	Xenophon	
Cicero				*Oeconomicus*	
On Divination		Strabo		16.3	133
1.23.46	46	*Geography*		17.7	132
		15.315	45	17.15	137
Columella					
On Agriculture		Tacitus			
7.10.6	112	*Histories*			
7.9.6	112	3.33	99		
7.9.7	112				
		Theophrastus			
Dio Chrysostom		*Enquiry into Plants*			
Discourses		4.8.3	33		
49.7	45, 46	8.8.3	135		

INDEX OF AUTHORS

Abrams, N.E. 21, 30, 42, 194
Allison, D.C. 43, 45, 70, 74, 78, 79, 116, 187
Alonso, P. 157
Anzaldúa, G. 17
Artinian-Kaiser, R. 127
Aschbel 55
Avalos, H. 92-94, 96, 100

Batto, B.F. 106, 107
Bauckham, R. 89
Behnke, E.A. 117, 127
Bennett, J. 123, 125
Bergant, D. 88
Berry, T. 6, 7, 17, 47, 164
Berry, W. 151, 152
Betz, H.D. 75, 76, 78, 79, 81
Birch, C. 1
Bird, P.A. 31
Birke, L. 119, 127
Borowski, O. 38
Brindal, E. 38
Brown, R.E. 45, 47, 205
Brueggemann, W. 53, 79
Buell, L. 148, 161
Butkus, R.A. 20

Cadwallader, A.H. 138, 162
Carter, W. 30-32, 41, 42, 45, 58, 67, 69, 75, 77, 82, 85, 98, 101, 106, 107, 111, 113, 114, 116, 121, 139, 152, 155, 158, 167, 173, 176, 180, 182, 185, 187, 191, 193, 194, 196
Casey, E.S. 57, 148, 171
Chancey, M.A. 69, 72, 163
Chapman, D.W. 211, 213
Cloke, P. 120, 152, 153, 157, 200, 201
Clough, D.L. 127
Code, L. 6, 18, 21, 22, 31, 43, 73, 95, 130
Collins, J.N. 104
Cook, J.G. 213
Corbo, V.C. 210

Cotter, W. 107, 113
Cox, B. 61
Crosby, M.H. 50
Curtin, D. 73, 81

D'Angelo, M.R. 85
Daily, G.C. 31
Davies, W.D. 43, 45, 70, 78, 79, 116, 187
Deane-Drummond, C. 89, 127
Deutsch, C.M. 75, 89, 123-25
Donaldson, L.E. 36, 38
Dowling, E. 152
Dube, M.W. 37, 85, 88, 111, 216, 217
Duff, P.B. 178, 179
Duling, D.C. 97, 128
Dvorjetski, E. 109, 112

Eaton, H. 10, 30, 43, 73
Edwards, D. 5, 20, 40, 41, 82, 85, 107, 109, 164, 194
Edwards, D.R. 69
Ehrlich, A.H. 31
Ehrlich, P.R. 31
Elliott, J.H. 175
Elvey, A.F. 18, 21-23, 26, 33, 35, 40, 41, 53, 76, 93, 95, 115, 122, 123, 152, 155, 166, 191, 192, 214

Fiensy, D.A. 79, 132
Firmage, E. 111
Foucault, M. 40
Francis, R.A. 168
Frerichs, E. 164
Freyne, S. 72, 79, 97, 132, 144, 163, 173, 193

Gale, A.M. 27, 126
Gerber, L. 76
Giffney, N. 124
Glancy, J.A. 92, 93, 161, 181, 201, 209, 210

Index of Authors

Goodenough, U. 7
Goodman, M. 79
Green, W.S. 164
Guardiola-Saenz, L. 101

Habel, N.C. 1, 3, 8, 11, 26, 34, 61, 168
Hagner, D.A. 43, 101, 167, 187
Håkansson, S. 135, 137
Hanson, J.S. 194
Hanson, K.C. 70, 99, 103, 132
Haraway, D.J. 124, 148, 149, 178, 212
Harrill, J.A. 136
Harrison, J.P. 162
Hauck, F. 79
Haught, J.F. 19, 41, 52, 85, 139
Heard, W.J. 207
Heirman, J. 172, 176, 179
Hillel, D. 34
Hird, M.J. 124
Hirschfeld, Y. 44, 64, 144
Hobbs, T.R. 97
Hobgood-Oster, L. 162
Hogan, C. 152
Hoggard Creegan, N. 127
Hoppe, L. 69
Horsley, R.A. 72, 86, 194
Hoving, I. 172
Hughes, J.D. 24

Ilan, T. 143

Jennings, T.W. 98, 99, 101
Jensen, M.H. 96
Jenson, R. 4
Johnson, E.A. 85, 164, 212, 214
Johnson, M.D. 33
Jones, O. 120, 152, 153, 157, 200, 201

Kaplanovsky, A. 105
Kapleau, P. 134
Kee, H.C. 93
Keller, C. 70, 186-90
Kidger, M. 47
Klein, L.R. 39
Klooster, J. 172, 176, 179
Knappett, C. 21
Kolmes, S.A. 20
Koperski, V. 159
Kraemer, R.S. 150
Krause, B. 78, 123

Laughlin, J.C.H. 100
Lawson, V. 152
Leal, R.B. 56, 57, 64
Levine, A.-J. 119
Liebman, M. 137
Liew, T.-S.B. 98, 99, 101
Lorimer, J. 168
Lovelock, J. 4
Lucas, G. 45
Luz, U. 95, 109, 116

Macdonald, M.Y. 144
Macy, J. 7
Madden, F.W. 133
Malafouris, L. 21, 152, 203
Malina, B.J. 82, 86, 106, 184, 189-91
Manolopoulos, M. 33, 58
Manor, D.W. 44
Marlow, H. 12
Martin, L.H. 58, 108, 110
Massey, D. 21
May, J. 54, 130, 132
McAfee, G. 34
McCasland, S.V. 99
McDuffie, E. 204, 212
McFague, S. 151
McIvor, R.K. 135
McVann, M. 65-67, 164
Meadowcroft, T. 15
Mendoza, M.V. 201, 205-207, 209, 210, 212
Metzger, B.M. 109
Meyers, E.M. 96, 103, 138, 144
Milton, K. 78
Miquel, E. 113, 114
Mohler, C.L. 137
Moldenke, A.L. 133, 135, 137, 138
Moldenke, H.N. 133, 135, 137, 138
Moore, S.D. 127
Morton, T. 18, 52, 148
Moxnes, H. 70, 77, 121, 129
Murphy-O'Connor, J. 140, 149
Musselman, L.J. 194
Myers, C. 177
Myles, R.J. 72

Nanos, M.D. 158, 160
Nash, J.A. 43, 73, 75, 76, 78, 82, 84, 89
Nelson, S.A. 133
Neusner, J. 164
Newheart, M.W. 110

Neyrey, J. 70, 75, 94, 95, 184
Nolland, J. 94, 152, 187
Novakovic, L. 128
Nun, M. 70, 105, 106, 109, 140
Nunn, P.D. 64

Oakman, D.E. 87, 132
Olivares, C. 72
Ortner, S.B. 35, 73
Orton, D.E. 142
Osiek, C. 144
Overman, J.A. 152

Paine, R.T. 69
Pardes, I. 13
Parisi, L. 119, 127
Pennington, J.T. 29, 57, 84, 192
Phillips, A. 173
Phillips, P. 145
Pilch, J.J. 92-94
Plumwood, V. 9, 19, 31, 73, 77, 95
Pomeroy, S.B. 136
Ponting, C. 9
Powell, M.A. 45
Power, K. 152
Primack, J.R. 20, 21, 30, 42, 194
Primavesi, A. 50, 58, 76, 86, 87, 151, 204

Rasmussen, L.L. 22
Reddish, M.G. 61
Reid, B. 198
Renkin, C. 152
Resseguie, J.L. 23
Rich, A. 17
Richardson, P. 45, 46
Rigby, K. 22, 42, 148, 161, 192
Robbins, V.K. 22-25
Rohrbaugh, R. 86, 175, 184, 197
Rose, D.B. 56
Rosenfeld, A.W. 69
Rosenzweig, M. 168
Rozi, E. 178
Ruether, R.R. 37
Runesson, A. 184, 185, 216
Russell, R.J. 20

Saddington, D.B. 97
Saldarini, A.J. 142

Sandoval, C. 37, 101, 159, 202, 203
Schnabel, E.J. 211, 213
Schroer, S. 62, 63
Schultz, S. 79
Schüssler Fiorenza, E. 13, 17, 85, 100,
    125, 144, 168, 215
Seed, J. 7
Segal, A.F. 27
Serruya, S. 105
Shanks, H. 69, 96, 102
Sim, D.C. 193
Soja, E.W. 21, 54, 55, 65, 171, 179
Spivak, G.C. 44
Staver, C.P. 137
Stegner, W.R. 64
Stewart, E.C. 56
Strange, J.F. 69, 96, 102

Talbert, C. 152
Taylor, A. 31
Taylor, J.E. 55
Theissen, G. 157
Theophilos, M.P. 191
Thrift, N. 54, 130, 132
Trainor, M. 152
Trible, P. 81, 134, 198
Trudinger, P. 61
Tsumura, D.T. 30
Tzaferis, V. 69, 97

Volohonsky, H. 105

Wachsmann, S. 105
Wainwright, E.M. 18, 19, 21, 29, 35, 41,
    43, 44, 53, 54, 64, 70, 72, 74, 90, 94,
    102-104, 110, 114, 117, 122, 123, 125,
    130, 141, 143, 156, 159, 162, 163, 165,
    202, 204, 213, 215
Weaver, D.J. 120
Weber, T.M. 110
Weissenrieder, A. 95
Whatmore, S. 47, 90
Windle, P. 78

Yamasaki, G. 59

Zohary, M. 55, 138

www.ingramcontent.com/pod-product-compliance
Lightning Source LLC
Chambersburg PA
CBHW071329190426
43193CB00041B/1035